*The*

# Deplorable Gourmet

*The Horde*

Compiled from the contributions of the Morons and Moronettes of the Ace of Spades HQ: http://www.ace.mu.nu/

The Horde wishes to note that recipe results are not guaranteed due to various factors such as differences in ovens as well as the quality and source of ingredients, plus the obvious fact that these recipes are written by self-acknowledged Morons. Please practice safe food handling and storage, make these recipes at your own risk, and if you don't like the way a recipe turns out, feel free not to make it again. We are not actual real-life cookbook writers, nor do we play ones on television, nor did we stay at a Holiday Inn last night. But like you, we do enjoy good food!

Cover art by Michael (Bandersnatch) Powers
Layout by Penoaks Publishing, http://penoaks.com

*This book is dedicated to the Morons and Moronettes who congregate daily at the Ace of Spades HQ, for without them this book would not exist. It is truly a work of the Horde, by the Horde, and for the Horde. Because as we all know, every normal Moron must be tempted at times to wash his hands, hoist the apron, and begin slicing carrots.*

# Preface

The idea for this cookbook was born in the comments section of the Food Thread: Memorial Day Edition of 2017 at the Ace of Spades HQ, because of course it was. If you have been hanging out at the HQ for any length of time, you have learned to be wary of Memorial Day weekend threads. It turns out that 2017 was no exception.

It began as Weasel's brainchild, and quickly grew from there like a wildfire spreading through dry tinder, egged on by various 'rons and 'ettes. Bluebell eventually showed up, was informed that she had been volunteered to do this, overcame the urge to strangle Weasel, and said, sure. Shortly thereafter, we met for lunch and discussed the particulars. Weasel thought we would get about 50 recipes, while bluebell was confident we would get 100. Four weeks and 653 recipes later, we found ourselves back at the same table, blinking at each other in disbelief.

Then the real work began. And now, here we are, after only #twoweeks! (more or less).

We were and are blown away by the response we got. There is nothing like the Horde! Far and away the best thing was the little stories—some only a few words long—recalling the origins of the recipes, whether they were old and treasured family heirlooms, ones passed on by friends, or inventions of our own Morons. Some recipes even came with bragging rights! We made no attempt to verify the veracity of these claims, but trust that the Horde will give them the usual scrutiny, which is to say, none.

We wish to thank from the bottom of our hearts the Morons who assisted us in this effort. First off, to all who sent in their favorite recipes, THANK YOU! You all came through in spades. Our proofreaders JTB and Mrs. JTB, westminsterdogshow, moki, booknlass, Miley the Duchess, and cfo mom cleaned up after us and made us look good. The lovely artwork was done by Bandersnatch (prufrocksmermaid.blogspot.com). Our AoSHQ poet laureate Muldoon, of course, wrote the limericks for each chapter. RedMindBlueState gave us some valuable advice, for which we are very grateful. To these and to the many others who assisted us in ways both large and small—you have our eternal gratitude.

We thank the Cobloggers and Open Bloggers at ace.mu.nu, for not only letting us cajole, harass and otherwise beg commenters for recipes on their threads, but also for sending us recipes, too! Special thanks goes to CBD, on whose food threads this idea was conceived, nurtured, and seen through to completion. CBD sought and received permission from Ace for this project on our behalf, and helped us out in more ways than we can possibly list here. Cheers, CBD!

And last, but certainly not least, we wish to thank Ace, the Head Ewok, not only for letting us go forward with this project, but for giving us Morons a welcoming, fun, interesting and thought-provoking smart military blog at which to gather, day after day. There is no finer place on the internet.

~bluebell and Weasel
November 27, 2017

*The*

# Deplorable Gourmet

# Table of Contents

# driNks

*When it comes to libations, here's news*
*A patriot knows how to choose*
*Valu-Rite elixir*
*Doesn't need any mixer*
*Hooray for the reds, whites and booze!*

## Sunset Cheer

**1 *First!***
Sweet-fruity drink with rum. I'm sure this is modified from something I read on the web somewhere about a fruity drink with coconut rum. The homemade simple syrup with pineapple is definitely my twist to the concoction.

Posted by: adsila. Yield: 1 serving. Prep time: 5 minutes.

---

1 shot coconut rum
1 shot cranberry juice
1 shot lime juice
1 shot simple syrup with fresh pineapple
1 glass ice

Pour shots over ice. Stir and serve. Garnish as desired. To make simple syrup, combine 1 cup sugar, 1 cup water, and ¼ of a fresh pineapple. Heat until sugar is thoroughly dissolved, then cool and strain before using.

## The Dildo

2 A spicy take on a classic gin martini. The recipe is mine. All mine. Based of course on many, many different drinks made for me by one of my favorite bartenders, who wimped out and became—get this—an addiction counselor.

Posted by: CharlieBrown'sDildo. Yield: 1 serving. Prep time: 5 minutes.

---

3 ½ ounces London dry gin
½ ounce dry vermouth
1/2 teaspoon simple syrup
6 drops Thai bitters
1 Peppadew red pepper
1/4 teaspoon Peppadew brine

Shake everything but the pepper with ice. Serve in a martini glass with a Peppadew pepper garnish.

## Metropolitan

3 Designed to grow your 'ette bra collection. I learned of this drink while sitting in the bar at the American Embassy Club in Seoul. A very unlikely combination of ingredients that mix into a wonderful drink. VERY POTENT!!!

Posted by: Diogenes. Yield: servings for 1 'ron, 1 'ette. Prep time: 5 minutes.

---

bourbon
triple sec
gin

Mix into a shaker equal parts gin, triple sec and bourbon. I tend to splash an extra bit of triple sec. Shake for 20 seconds and serve in a chilled martini glass. Garnish with an orange twist, raspberries or blueberries.

## Mango Yungueno

4 Traditional Bolivian drink appropriated by privileged Americans. Recipe is from Wikipedia, ultimately. There are three ingredients, two of which aren't readily available in the Northeastern U.S. so replacements have been made.

Posted by: FireHorse. Yield: 1 serving. Prep time: 1 minute.

---

1/4 of a glass ice
1/4 of a glass pisco
1/2 of a glass Newman's Own (TM) Orange Mango Tango cocktail

Fill glass about a 1/4 full of ice cubes. Pour pisco into glass until it's at about the same level as the ice. Fill glass with Newman's Own Orange Mango Tango cocktail drink. (Any citrusy juice or punch would work just fine.) Stir. Enjoy. Repeat.

## Gay Mule

5 Like a Moscow Mule, but with flavor. A variation on the Moscow Mule, but with Bajan rum for better flavor, and no stupid hipster copper mug.

Posted by: haukehaien. Yield: enough for 1 moron or 2 lightweights. Prep time: 2 minutes.

---

1 bottle (8 ounces) Fever Tree ginger beer
2 ounces Mount Gay Eclipse rum
1/2 ounce lime juice
1 lime wedge

Pour rum and lime juice into tall glass and stir to mix. Fill glass with ice. Add ginger beer, garnish with lime wedge.

## The Fruit Loop

6 A fruity summer cocktail from when I used to tend bar. Women would come up and not have any idea what they wanted to order, or men would come up and ask for something for a woman. I came up with this. Easy to make and very refreshing.

Posted by: Shaolin_10304. Yield: 1 serving. Prep time: 2 minutes.

---

2 ounces Stolichnaya Orange vodka
10 ounces 7UP
1 maraschino cherry

Fill a Collins glass with ice. Pour 2 ounces of Stoli Orange vodka. Fill glass with 7UP. Serve with a cherry and a straw. Enjoy.

## The Bitter Old Man

7 Not your dad's gin & tonic. I'm a big fan of G&Ts and wanted to make my own version of the classic. Perfect for a warm summer evening with friends and fellow morons.

Posted by: Shaolin_10304. Yield: 1 serving. Prep time: 2 minutes.

---

2 ounces Tanquerey No. 10 gin
8 ounces tonic water
2 dashes Angostura bitters
1 lime wedge

Fill a rocks glass with ice. Add two dashes of bitters. Stir bitters in ice to coat. Pour 2 ounces of Tanqueray No. 10 gin. Fill glass with tonic water. Serve with a lime wedge.

## Fjellbekk

8 Norwegian for "mountain stream." My wife and I toured Norway for our honeymoon and we asked the bartender at our hotel in Oslo for an original Norwegian drink. He made us the "Fjellbekk". It is pronounced "feel beck" and means "mountain stream" in Norwegian. The wife liked it so much that she continues to ask me to make it for her when she wants something other than wine. After enjoying it, raise your battleaxe high and shout, "Til Valhall!!"

Posted by: Assassin6. Yield: 1 serving. Prep time: 1 minute.

---

2 ounces aquavit
1 tablespoon sweetened lime juice
3 ounces Sprite

Add the aquavit, lime juice, and Sprite together in a highball glass. Top with crushed ice, stir the concoction, and drink until you have a smile on your face thinking about pillage and plunder. The amount of lime juice added will depend on the quality of the aquavit used. Play around and have fun with the recipe.

## Bajan (Barbadian) Rum Punch

9 The legendary, most authentic rum punch. From totallybarbados.com.

Posted by: runner. Yield: 1 – 20 servings. Prep time: fast.

---

1 measure lime juice, freshly squeezed
2 measures sugar syrup (place 2 measures of sugar in saucepan with little water and cook until sugar has dissolved)
3 measures dark Caribbean rum (Mount Gay, preferably)
4 measures passion fruit juice (or water)
dash bitters
dash fresh grated nutmeg

Combine sugar syrup and lime juice. Add rum and passion fruit juice/water. Serve with plenty of ice, a dash of bitters and grating of nutmeg. If using passion fruit juice instead of water, reduce sugar syrup slightly.

***Chef's Notes:***
"Punch comes from the Indian word 'panch' which means five. The five refers to the five ingredients of sour, sweet, strong, weak and spice. The poem for rum punch goes: One of sour, two of sweet, three of strong and four of weak, a dash of bitters and a sprinkle of spice, serve well chilled with plenty of ice."—totallybarbados.com.

## Pina Coladas

| 10 If you like . . . . I took a bad recipe and made it better. |
|---|

Posted by: RoyalOil. Yield: 4 servings. Prep time: 5 minutes.

---

1/2 cup cream of coconut
1/2 cup pineapple juice
1/2 cup rum
2 – 3 tablespoons crushed pineapple
3 – 4 cups finely crushed/shaved ice
pineapple wedges

Add a cup of ice to blender. Add in cream of coconut, pineapple juice, crushed pineapple and rum. Lightly blend for 2 – 3 seconds. Add rest of ice and blend. Add more ice until blender can barely circulate to the top of the container. You should have a very thick smoothie at this point. Pour into glass. Garnish with pineapple wedge (optional). Drink.

***Chef's Notes:***
You know why the pina colada you get at the bar sucks? Because they use coconut milk. Do not make that watery abomination. I find the cream of coconut at a market that caters to Hispanics. You will need it warmed and well-stirred/shaken before using as the coconut oil will congeal and separate. For extra coconut flavor, use a coconut flavored rum. (I'm not sure Valu-Rite carries that flavor.) I have a Margaritaville blender I use. It has an ice bowl on top and shaves the ice into the blender below. Yes, you can add more rum. I recommend it but some of my guests are lightweights. I've also made variations adding strawberries or bananas with good results.

## Smoky Manhattan Moron

11 The drink of choice in the smoky back room where we guide the economy. Recipe mostly lifted from the amazing head bartender at the Trummers on Main Restaurant, Clifton, Virginia. The best drinks are passed along via oral tradition.

Posted by: Semper Why. Yield: 10 servings. Prep time: 35 minutes.

---

4 cups smoked whiskey
10 splashes dry vermouth
30 dashes bitters
20 marachino cherries

Smoke your whiskey. This involves putting 4 cups of whiskey in a flat bakeware (corningware or pyrex) and refrigerating it for 15 minutes. While the whiskey is cooling down, heat your smoker to 225 degrees F and get your wood chips ready. When the smoker is hot, place the bakeware and your wood chips in the smoker for 15 minutes. Remove and pour into a bottle. Adjust the amount of wood chips and time in the smoker to taste.

Make your Manhattans: in a cocktail shaker, put ice, 2 shots of smoked whiskey and a splash of vermouth. Shake a dash of bitters into a martini glass, add two cherries. Shake and strain the drink into the glass over the cherries. For variety, substitute dark cherries or liberal tears.

***Chef's Notes:***
Smoking whiskey depends a bit on your taste. Be warned that after 15 minutes in the smoker, you'll start to cook off the alcohol.

## Velvet Hammer with a Motor

12 Ice cream drink for adults. This is an after dinner drink my dad, C. W. Oakes, would make. Very fond memories of this and his recipe for Dubonnet.

Posted by: Ann Fitzgerald. Yield: 2 – 4 servings. Prep time: 10 minutes?

---

1 quart vanilla ice cream
2 jiggers brandy
1 jigger Cointreau
1 jigger white creme de menthe

Blend or whip. Serve in chilled long stemmed glasses.

***Chef's Notes:***
My husband worked his way through college as a bartender. He had never heard of putting brandy in a velvet hammer. That is what Dad used to call a "motor."

## Martha Stewart's Classic Eggnog

13 Guaranteed to even put Ace to sleep! From www.marthastewart.com.

Posted by: ShainS. Yield: 8 servings. Prep time: 20 minutes.

---

6 large eggs, separated
3/4 cup superfine sugar
2 cups whole milk
3 cups heavy cream
1/2 cup bourbon, preferably Maker's Mark
1/4 cup dark rum, preferably Mount Gay
1/4 cup Cognac, preferably Remy Martin Grand Cru
freshly grated nutmeg

In a very large bowl, beat yolks until thick and pale, then slowly beat in the sugar. Whisk in milk, 2 cups cream, bourbon, rum, and Cognac. Cover, and refrigerate for up to 1 day. Just before serving, beat whites until stiff peaks form. Fold whites into eggnog. Whisk remaining 1 cup cream until stiff peaks form, and fold into eggnog. (Alternatively, you can fold half the whipped cream into eggnog, and top with remaining half.) Sprinkle with nutmeg.

***Chef's Notes:***
Actually gets better with each additional day it sits in the refrigerator (to a point).

## Boozy Irish Cream

14 It puts the covfefe in your coffee! Mornings at the Bartending School in Tennessee sometimes get off to a sputtering start, especially if the instructor was doing too much field research the night before. One morning a hair of the dog that bit me was in order, so I brewed up a couple of shots of espresso but had nothing to spike it with. Thus was born this hangover helper!

Posted by: Malcolm Tent. Yield: 24 servings (1 ½ ounce shots). Prep time: 5 minutes (sober).

---

2 cups Jameson Irish Whiskey (80 proof)
1 14-ounce can Borden's sweetened condensed milk
1 cup heavy cream
2 teaspoons instant espresso powder
2 tablespoons real vanilla extract
½ ounce (1/2 packet) instant dark chocolate hot cocoa mix

Reserve 2 ounces of Jameson Irish Whiskey in a glass with 3 – 4 ice cubes to chill. Add remaining ingredients into blender. Set blender to medium speed and blend for 3 – 4 minutes or until smooth, while drinking chilled Jameson. Store in airtight bottle and refrigerate for 2 hours before consuming.

***Chef's Notes:***
This Irish cream must be kept in the fridge because it contains real dairy products. Will keep for about two months if it lasts that long! A periodic shaking between uses may be required.

## GoK's Moron Margarita

15 This is how you make a margarita. A grizzled oldtimer I met down by the boat launch at the big pier on the Sassafras taught me how to make these while explaining exactly which strains of California grass he was smoking with the one-armed Aztec he learned it from while surfing the Ranch in Santa Barbara in the summer of 1974.

Posted by: Ghost of Kari. Yield: 1 serving. Prep time: 4 minutes.

---

half a lemon
half an orange
1 jalapeno
1 ounce blanco tequila
1 ounce reposado tequila
1 ounce Cointreau
1/4 cup salt
4 cubes ice

Grab a large tumbler. Use the half an orange to wet the rim of your glass and salt it. Put the ice in the glass. Juice the orange and lemon halves and pour the juice over the ice. Add the three shots while explaining knowingly to your drinking partner that this blend of aged and unaged tequilas is the only way to truly capture the fiery essence of the noble agave plant. Slice the jalapeno into thin rounds and float two in the glass. Stir. Serve.

***Chef's Notes:***
Makes one margarita. Use the other halves of the orange and lemon to make another one. Do not substitute triple sec for Cointreau; you already bought two bottles of tequila to make these damn things.

## Collect Call of the Cthulhu

16 AKA the Cthulhu-tini. The last cocktail you'll drink (that night)! Taffey Lewis served this at the Snake Pit Bar in the Fourth Sector.

Posted by: All Hail Eris. Yield: 1 serving. Prep time: 5 minutes.

---

1 tiny pickled octopus
2 1/2 ounces gin or vodka
1/2 ounce dry vermouth
1/2 ounce olive or pickle brine

Have your manservant make this while you mingle at the Miskatonic U. mixer.

## Haymaker's Switchel

17 A drink for a really hot day of work. From Imogene Wolcott's *The Yankee Cookbook*, but initially from a neighbor lady who told me about haying and harvesting wheat when she was a girl.

Posted by: Kindltot. Yield: 16 eight-ounce servings or 8 sixteen-ounce servings. Prep time: mixing time only.

---

1 gallon water
2 cups sugar
1 cup molasses
1 cup vinegar (whatever you have on hand)
1 teaspoon ground ginger

Mix in a pail. One of the tricks of working with molasses is to grease your measuring cup first, it runs off better and faster.

### *Chef's Notes:*

When I was a kid, the lady I knew would tell about growing up in Eastern Oregon, and one of her memories was about being a little girl taking pails of this stuff out to the men working in the field. Per other research on it, the ginger was added because it was considered that the vinegar and cold water would chill the stomach too much and cause cramps, and the ginger would counteract this by being warming. I usually just make it by the pint or quart, and add a couple tablespoons of molasses and a couple tablespoons of vinegar by eye and drink that down, but that is not a proper recipe. It does a really good job of cutting the phlegm, and will re-hydrate you.

A further note, an old friend of the family who grew up in the 1940's in Scotland said they made something similar and he thought it went back to Roman "posca." His wife, who grew up on a farm in Alberta, looked at us funny and said that when she was a kid they drank tea.

## Vodka Mojito: Low Carb & Sugar-Free

18 Tasteh! Doesn't taste like liquor is even involved! This recipe was found on Pinterest and submitted by KetoGasm.

Posted by: SandyCheeks. Yield: 1 serving. Prep time: 2 minutes.

---

1 slice lime
6 – 7 fresh mint leaves
2 tablespoons lime juice
2 packets Splenda or other no-sugar sweetener
1 shot vodka
splash club soda (make sure it's "diet!")

Using a muddler or other utensil, smash fresh mint leaves with lime and Splenda. Fill glass with ice of preference. Add vodka. Finish off with club soda. Garnish with a lime slice and mint. 3 net carbs.

***Chef's Notes:***
The blunt end of a wooden spoon is a good substitute for a "muddler."

## Coffee Cream

19 We don't need no steenking Starbucks! Got this from a website years ago, don't remember which one. But it's really simple.

Posted by: Jay in Ames. Yield: 15 servings. Prep time: 3 minutes.

---

1 pint half and half
1 can sweetened condensed milk
1 tablespoon vanilla

Mix 'em all in a blender, and keep it in the fridge. Mix as much or as little as you like in your coffee. Enjoy!

## Sweet/Spicy Tequila Cocktails

20 Don't remember where I found this, but it's damned good, especially in the summer with all things grilled.

Posted by: Jane D'oh. Yield: 6 servings, or 4 for thirsty morons. Prep time: 25 minutes (plus chilling).

---

1/2 cup sugar
1/2 jalapeno pepper, stemmed and seeded
5 cups chopped fresh pineapple
1/2 cup tequila blanco
lime wedges
demerara sugar

Combine sugar with 1/2 cup water in a medium saucepan and cook over medium heat until sugar dissolves. Remove from heat. Add jalapeno and set aside for 15 minutes to infuse the syrup, then remove the pepper and discard. Cool syrup completely. Pour the syrup into a blender and add the pineapple and tequila. Blend until very smooth. Transfer to a pitcher; refrigerate until ready to serve, at least an hour. Moisten rims of 4 to 6 glasses with lime wedges, then dip in demerara sugar, fill with ice and then pour in cocktail.

***Chef's Notes:***
If you love heat, use a whole jalapeno and leave the seeds in. Not for the faint-of-heart morons.

## Brazilian Lemonade

21 OK, it doesn't have lemons in it. Shut up. Still a damned fine drink, with or without alcohol. I'm not entirely sure where this came from—I found it on a handwritten card in a recipe collection in the house.

Posted by: WitchDoktor, AKA VA GOP Sucks. Yield: 2 – 3 servings. Prep time: 5 minutes.

---

9 tablespoons lime juice
1 cup water
1 cup coconut milk
3 tablespoons sweetened condensed milk
1/4 cup sugar
1 cup ice

There are two ways to make this—the easy way and the more involved way. For the easy way: mix the lime juice, coconut milk, sweetened condensed milk, and water in a blender. Add the ice and blend. For the involved way: instead of using lime juice, take 3 whole limes and cut them into quarters. Put them in your blender and pulse them like crazy until you have mutilated lime rinds with a kind of slurry. Pour through a strainer into a bowl. Take the juice and put back into the blender, adding enough water to come up to 1 and 1/2 cups of liquid. Add the remaining ingredients *except* the ice and blend until smooth, then add the ice and pulse it until it's a drinkable consistency. Best served in a highball with a shake straw. To get fancy, rim a highball with sugar and serve it margarita-style.

***Chef's Notes:***
The difference between the two methods is a bit fuller taste if you use whole limes—you get built-in zest and a somewhat different mouthfeel. It does take a bit longer, and on a hot day you may not want to go to the trouble. I found this also works really well with rum—don't use the expensive stuff, just plain old Bacardi or whatever will be fine.

## Margarita Jello Shots

22 Perfect for "Quatro de Cinco" (thanks, Obama). From *Food Network Magazine* (May 2014).

Posted by: Jane D'oh. Yield: depends. Prep time: 3 hours.

---

two 1/4 ounce packets unflavored gelatin powder
1/2 cup cold tequila
2 1/2 cups bottled margarita mix
flaky sea salt for garnish

Sprinkle the packets of unflavored gelatin powder over the cold tequila in a bowl; set aside. Bring margarita mix to a boil, pour over the tequila-gelatin mixture and stir until the gelatin dissolves. Pour into an 8-inch square pan and refrigerate until set, about 3 hours. Cut into small cubes; sprinkle with flaky sea salt just before serving.

## My Mexican Uncle's Margarita

23 Whoo-hoo! Uncle Albert gave this recipe to me in the 80's.

Posted by: Cicero Kaboom! Kid. Yield: heh. Prep time: 1 minute.

---

ice
6 ounces tequila
6 ounces frozen concentrated limeade
6 ounces triple sec

Fill a blender with ice you get from a bag. Pour tequila, triple sec and frozen concentrated limeade into the blender. Blend. Fill with ice and blend again. Don't judge me, I like these.

The 6 ounce tequila measure is simply a guideline, not a law. When limeade came in those little 6 ounce cans we used that as our measuring device.

## Honey Badger

24 Honey Jack Cocktail. I think some version of this was on Bar Rescue.

Posted by: Aviator. Yield: 1 serving. Prep time: 1 minute.

---

¾ ounce fresh lemon sour
1 ½ ounces Simply Apple cider
¾ ounce Amaretto DiSaronno
1 1/2 ounces Jack Daniel's Tennessee Honey
2 dashes Fee Brothers whiskey barrel-aged bitters

Shake with ice and strain over fresh ice cubes. Garnish with a swath of lemon peel and freshly grated cinnamon.

## Cranberry Liqueur

25 Base for a sweet Cosmopolitan. Found this in a cooking magazine many years ago. Not sure which one anymore, however this recipe can be found all over the internet.

Posted by: enough caffeine. Yield: 1 quart. Prep time: 3 weeks.

---

2 cups sugar
1 cup water
12 ounces cranberries
3 cups vodka

Combine sugar and water in a medium saucepan, cook over medium heat for 5 minutes or until the sugar dissolves. Remove from heat and cool completely. Place cranberries in a food processor, process 2 minutes or until finely chopped. Combine sugar mixture, cranberries and vodka in large bowl. Pour the mixture into clean jars, seal with lids. Let stand 3 weeks in a cool, dark place. Shake jars every other day. After 3 weeks strain the mixture through a cheesecloth-lined sieve into a bowl. Discard the solids. Carefully pour the liquid into clean bottle or jars. Store refrigerated for one year. Use in place of cranberry juice to make a sweet-style Cosmopolitan.

***Chef's Notes:***
Vodka can be doubled to reduce the sweetness of the finished Cosmopolitan. Do not use a cheap vodka, use what you would buy for a standard Cosmopolitan. The finished liqueur is a beautiful red color.

# Raspberry Tom Collins

| 26 My variation on a classic Tom Collins. |
|---|

Posted by: Aviator. Yield: 1 serving. Prep time: 2 minutes.

---

1 ½ ounces Old Tom gin
1 ounce fresh lemon juice
½ ounce simple syrup
seltzer water
6 red raspberries

Place raspberries and simple syrup in a mixing glass and muddle. Add other ingredients except seltzer water and give a quick shake with ice. Strain into a Collins glass with ice. Top with seltzer water, garnish with a whole raspberry and a lemon slice.

***Chef's Notes:***
Old Tom gin is much closer to the original gin at the time of this cocktail's invention. Many recipes call for club soda, but the original drink was made with seltzer water and does not add the salt of club soda.

# Blushing Valkyrie

| 27 Invented by my wife, who didn't like the Valkyrie and improved it. |
|---|

Posted by: Surellin. Yield: 1 serving. Prep time: 25 minutes.

---

2 shots vodka
1/2 shot lemon juice
1/2 shot raspberry syrup

Shake in a shaker until cold. Serve with a slice of lemon in a martini glass.

## Grilled Lemonade with Bourbon

28 For a non-alcoholic version, omit bourbon and add an additional 1/2 to 1 cup cold water.

Posted by: Jane D'oh. Yield: 12 normal servings; morons??? Prep time: 25 minutes.

---

1/2 cup water
1/2 cup honey
1 1/4 cups sugar, divided
2 sprigs rosemary
6 pounds lemons, halved
1 cup bourbon
6 cups cold water

Build a two-zone fire in a charcoal grill, by placing coals on one side of grill. Combine 1/2 cup water, honey, 1/2 cup sugar, and rosemary in a disposable aluminum pan. Place pan on grill grate over side without coals and close lid. Cook 10 minutes, remove pan from grill, and set aside to cool. Place remaining 3/4 cup sugar on a plate. Twist cut side of each lemon half in sugar, place halves on grill over hot coals. Grill until sugar is caramelized, 2-4 minutes, remove from grill and let cool. When lemons are cool, squeeze juice into a medium pitcher (they should yield 3 cups of juice). Pour in grilled syrup, discarding rosemary sprigs. Add bourbon and 6 cups cold water. Stir and refrigerate until chilled. Serve over ice, garnished with grilled lemon slices.

## Spencer Cocktail

29 Classic, high-octane refresher. Adapted from *The Savoy Cocktail Book* by Harry Craddock (1930).

Posted by: Love Gun. Yield: 1 serving. Prep time: it's a drink.

---

1 ½ ounces good dry gin
¾ ounce apricot brandy
3 teaspoons orange juice
1 dash Angostura bitters

Chill glasses in freezer well ahead of time. Pour gin, brandy, orange juice, and bitters into a cocktail shaker over heavy ice and shake hard to mix. Strain into well-chilled martini or other small glass. Garnish with a thin slice of orange zest twist, if desired.

***Chef's Notes:***
"Very mellifluous. Has a fine and rapid action. For morning work."—Harry Craddock

## Cranberry Margarita

30 Good for the holidays. Recipe came from Epicurious.com.

Posted by: Aviator. Yield: 1 serving. Prep time: 2 minutes.

---

1/2 ounce fresh lime juice
1 ounce orange juice (fresh is best)
1 1/2 ounces tequila (blanco or reposado)
2 ounces homemade cranberry jam (see below)
1 tablespoon kosher salt
1 tablespoon sugar
1 ½ teaspoons Chinese five-spice powder

Mix salt, sugar, and five-spice powder on a small plate. Rub rims of old-fashioned glasses with lime wedge; dip in salt mixture and fill glasses with ice. For each cocktail, combine 1/2 ounce lime juice, 1 ounce orange juice, 1 1/2 ounces tequila, and 2 tablespoons cranberry jam in a cocktail shaker; fill with ice. Cover and shake until outside is frosty, about 30 seconds. Strain into prepared glass.

***Chef's Notes:***
For cranberry jam: add ¾ cup fresh cranberries, ¼ cup sugar, 2 teaspoons fresh orange juice, and ¼ cup water to a medium saucepan. Bring to a boil, then reduce heat and simmer for 30 – 40 minutes, stirring occasionally, until thick and jammy. Remove from heat, mix in 1 teaspoon finely grated orange zest, let cool. May be made 5 days ahead; cover and chill. I have also substituted Tajin seasoning for the Chinese five-spice seasoning with a tasty result.

## Drunk Apple Pie

31 Finally! A cocktail that tastes like apple pie! When I was bartending a few years ago, we had to come up with a specialty cocktail. This was my submission, but it was passed for another.

Posted by: josephistan. Yield: 1 serving. Prep time: 2 minutes.

---

1 ½ ounces Fireball (or similar) whisky
1 ½ ounces caramel apple liqueur
1 dash Godiva chocolate cordial (or creme de cacao)

Mix the whisky & caramel apple liquor together first, then add the dash of chocolate liqueur to that. Serve in a glass over ice.

## Bachelor Eggnog

32 A simple uncooked eggnog recipe. This is a derivation of other basic eggnog recipes found online. Chi's favorite.

Posted by: Miley, the Duchess. Yield: 1 serving if you're planning to get drunk. Prep time: 10 minutes plus 3 hours to chill.

---

6 eggs
1 1/2 cups milk
1 1/2 cups heavy cream
6 tablespoons sugar
1 tablespoon vanilla
½ - ¾ teaspoon freshly ground nutmeg

Beat the eggs, then add the sugar and beat well. Add the vanilla and nutmeg and continue to beat. Slowly add the milk and cream. Chill for 3 hours. Add as much liquor as you'd like, depending on how quickly you plan to get drunk. Bourbon is best. WARNING: this goes down more quickly than you'd ever imagine. I'd recommend a double batch.

***Chef's Notes:***
You can just use milk if the cream is too much or you don't have any in the fridge. You can also substitute brown sugar.

## Margaritas

33 Best recipe I've ever tasted! From Cook's Illustrated.

Posted by: Miley, the Duchess. Yield: 4 – 6 servings. Prep time: 15 minutes plus overnight.

---

1/2 cup fresh lime juice
1/2 cup fresh lemon juice
4 teaspoons lime zest
4 teaspoons lemon zest
1/4 cup sugar
pinch salt
1 cup blue agave tequila reposado
1 cup triple sec

Mix everything except the alcohol in a large measuring cup, stir to dissolve the sugar, and store in the refrigerator 4 – 24 hours. Strain to remove the zest, and add the alcohol to the juice mixture. They suggest serving over 2 cups of crushed ice. Use your own judgment.

## The Velvet Hammer

> 34 One and done. From Aunt Rose.

Posted by: Aunt Ralph. Yield: 4 moron servings. Prep time: 2 minutes.

---

1 cup brandy
1/2 cup triple sec
1/2 cup white creme de cacao
1 quart vanilla ice cream

Combine ingredients in blender. Blend until smooth. Serve in lowball glasses. Best enjoyed while seated.

## Smoking Bishop

> 35 Christmas drink. Adapted from a 2002 NPR interview with Cedric Dickens, great grandson of Charles Dickens. A Victorian classic that features annually in the RMBS household. I would comment on its keeping qualities, but the question has never arisen.

Posted by: RedMindBlueState. Yield: 15 – 20 servings. Prep time: 15 minutes active, 24 hours total.

---

5 oranges
1 grapefruit
36 cloves
1/4 pound sugar
2 bottles claret
1 bottle ruby Port

Pre-heat oven to 350 degrees F. Wash the fruit and bake on a rimmed baking sheet until brownish, turning once, about 1 hour. Stud each fruit with 6 whole cloves (it helps to make a starter hole with a toothpick). Put fruit into a nonreactive bowl, add the sugar and pour in the claret—not the port. Cover and leave in a warm place for 24 hours (on top of a radiator is good). Cut fruit in half and squeeze the juice into the wine, then strain. When ready to serve, add the port and heat until gently steaming. DO NOT BOIL!

***Chef's Notes:***
"'A merry Christmas, Bob,' said Scrooge, with an earnestness that could not be mistaken. 'I'll raise your salary, and endeavour to assist your struggling family, and we will discuss your affairs this very afternoon, over a Christmas bowl of smoking bishop, Bob!'"

## Ferrous' Rye Buck

36 A twist on a summer cocktail favorite. This drink was made for me at a local bar called Single Barrel. According to the bartender, this is a take on a Moscow Mule, but with a different liquor & garnish. Enjoy!

Posted by: Ferrous. Yield: 1 serving. Prep time: 5 minutes.

---

2 ounces rye whiskey
8 ounces good ginger beer (such as Bundaberg or Reeds)
1 lemon wedge
1 lemon peel shaving
4 ice cubes
1 highball glass

Place your ice in your highball glass. Using a sharp knife, shave off part of the lemon peel (ideally, this shaving should be at least 1 inch long and half an inch wide). Squeeze the lemon juice over the ice, making sure to leave out the seeds, then discard the lemon wedge. Or don't. It's your call, really, cause you're about to have a drink. Add your 2 ounces of bourbon. Rub the inside part of the lemon peel around the edge of your glass, then add to the drink. Fill the rest of the glass with ginger beer, and enjoy.

***Chef's Notes:***
According to the bartender, any drink with lime & ginger beer is a mule, while lemon and ginger beer is a buck. Feel free to vary liquors and amounts. Cheers!

## Covfefe

37 A pirate's version of Irish coffee. I love the idea of Irish coffee, but prefer the taste of spiced rum over whiskey, so I found something I like.

Posted by: Old Dominion Mom. Yield: 1 moron serving. Prep time: 1 minute.

---

2/3 mug coffee
½ - 1 shot Captain Morgan Silver Spiced Rum
1 – 2 shots Ryan's Irish Style Cream Liqueur

Stir and enjoy hot or cold.

## Apfelwein

38 German hard cider. This is an apple wine recipe from homebrewtalk.com.

Posted by: GrogNerd. Yield: 100 servings. Prep time: 1 to 3 months.

---

5 gallons apple juice (NO PRESERVATIVES!)
2 pounds dextrose/corn sugar or cane sugar
5 grams Montrachet wine yeast

You will need a 5-gallon carboy (I use a Better Bottle), a carboy cap or stopper with airlock, and a funnel. First sanitize the carboy, airlock, funnel, stopper or carboy cap. Open one gallon bottle of apple juice and pour half of it into the carboy using the funnel. Open one bag of dextrose/sugar and carefully add it to the now half full bottle of apple juice. Shake well. Repeat with the second gallon of apple juice. Pour in the mixture of apple juice and dextrose from both bottles into the carboy. Add all but 1 quart of the remaining 3 gallons of apple juice to the carboy. Open the packet of Montrachet yeast and pour it into the neck of the funnel. Use the remaining quart of juice to wash down any yeast that sticks. I am able to fit all but 3 ounces of apple juice into a 5-gallon Better Bottle. You may need to be patient to let the foam die down from all the shaking and pouring. Put your stopper or carboy cap on with an airlock and fill the airlock with cheap vodka. No bacteria will live in vodka and if you get suckback, you just boosted the abv.

It will become cloudy in a couple of days and remain so for a few weeks. In the fourth week, the yeast will begin to drop out and it will become clear. After at least 4 weeks, you can keg or bottle, but it is ok to leave it in the carboy for another month or so. Racking to a secondary is not necessary. It ferments out very dry. Apfelwein really improves with age, so if you can, please let it sit in a carboy for up to 3 months before bottling or kegging, then let it sit even longer.

## Irish Cream

39 A wonderful cold-weather or holiday drink. This delightful recipe came from a co-worker in Mount Vernon, Ohio, decades ago.

Posted by: Ladylibertarian. Yield: 10 servings. Prep time: 10 minutes.

---

1 3/4 cup of your favorite hooch: whisky, rum, bourbon, Scotch, etc.
14-ounce can sweetened condensed milk
1 cup cream (not milk or half & half)
4 eggs
2 tablespoons chocolate syrup
2 teaspoons instant coffee granules
1 teaspoon vanilla extract

1/2 teaspoon almond extract

Blend all ingredients in a blender until smooth. If you lack a blender, I'm sure that whisking the ingredients in a bowl will work. Just make sure the eggs are VERY well blended. Serve over ice. Store tightly covered in refrigerator for up to 1 month. Stir before serving.

## Hot Spiced Cider

40 Great cold-weather drink. I believe this was a recipe from Kroger about 30 years ago.

Posted by: Ladylibertarian. Yield: 12 – 20 servings. Prep time: 5 minutes.

---

1 gallon apple cider
2/3 cup sugar
2 teaspoons allspice
2 teaspoons whole cloves
2 – 3 cinnamon sticks
5 thin orange slices

Combine all ingredients in large sauce pan or crockpot. Heat. This is a staple drink for my family at Christmas. It makes the house smell WONDERFUL!

## Wassail

41 Mulled ale to warm you on a cold day. I tried various recipes for wassail, but was never satisfied. I ended up experimenting in order to get that balance between sweet flavorfulness and aromatic depth.

Posted by: The Political Hat Yield: 10 8-ounce servings. Prep time: 90 minutes.

---

72 ounces (six 12-ounce bottles) brown ale
half of a 750 ml bottle Madeira
4 apples and/or pears
1 cup brown sugar
6 – 8 ounces honey
1 – 2 tablespoons whole cloves
1 – 2 tablespoons whole allspice
1 – 2 tablespoon crystallized ginger
2 – 3 cinnamon sticks
1 blood orange
6 – 12 dashes bitters

In a slow-cooker/crock-pot, combine a half bottle (about 375 ml) of Madeira and five 12-ounce bottles of decent brown ale. Add one sliced blood orange and a cheesecloth (or other) spice pouch soaked in bitters and containing whole cloves, whole allspice, cinnamon sticks, and crystallized ginger, in equal amounts and according to preference. Heat on high. In an oven safe pan or container fill four cored apples and/or pears, of your diverse or uniform choice, with the brown sugar and honey. Add the last bottle/12 ounces of brown ale to the pan and bake for about 40 minutes at 350 degrees F. After baking add the apples/pears and liquid/sugar from the pan to the slow-cooker/crock-pot. Allow to heat for about 30 minutes. Add more bitters to taste if desired. Serve.

***Chef's Notes:***
The sweetness can be adjusted by adding more or less brown sugar. A regular orange can be substituted for a blood orange if the latter is not available.

## Excellent Brunch Punch

42 A punch mild enough to serve early in the day (!) and tasty enought to add sparkle to any occasion. This recipe was typed up on an old-fashioned recipe card, using an old fashioned typewriter. It looks like the type of card that would be in the type of recipe box owned by the type of woman who took great pride in home-making—a lost art, I believe. The name "Gloria Thaman" is typed on the upper right corner. I don't know who Gloria is, as I got this recipe card from my friend, Brenda. But thank you, Brenda, and thank you, Gloria, because this punch rocks.

Posted by: Tired Mom. Yield: 25 regular servings; maybe 8 or so moron servings. Prep time: a few minutes.

---

2 1/2 cups Southern Comfort
2 1/4 quarts 7UP
6 ounces fresh lemon juice
1 6-ounce can frozen orange juice
2 6-ounce cans frozen lemonade
sliced oranges and lemons

Chill ingredients. Mix in punch bowl, adding 7UP last. Add drops of red food coloring as desired (optional—and why in the hell would you do that? But that's what the recipe card says, anyway). Stir lightly. Add orange and lemon slices. If desired, can be mixed in advance, but add 7UP just before serving. The day before I serve this punch, I usually make ice rings for it. You can cut the bottom off a 2-liter soda bottle—cut about 4 or 5 inches from the base of the bottle—wash, fill with water and a few maraschino cherries for prettiness, and pop in the freezer. The shape of the base of the bottle makes a nice "flower" ice ring.

# Elle's Cinderella Tea

| 43 Liquid dessert. Recipe is from my evil not-stepmother, Mommie Dearest. Idk how to spell Mommie. Is it Mommy? |
| --- |

Posted by: L, Elle.    Yield: one pot of tea.    Prep time: 5 minutes.

---

2 tea bags, or loose black tea
3 – 4 whole cardamom seeds
heavy whipping cream to taste
sugar or artificial sweetener to taste

Fill teapot with boiling water to capacity. Add 2 teabags or loose black tea if preferred. Crush cardamom seeds and add to teapot. Allow tea to steep to desired strength. Pour tea through strainer into mugs or teacups. Serve with 1 tablespoon heavy whipping cream and 1 teaspoon sugar/sweetener per cup of tea, or to taste. Enjoy! Then thank me for the pleasure of this experience.

***Chef's Notes:***

You can experiment and try different types of tea to change the flavor. This recipe is for a basic black tea as a base and springboard so you understand what the standard flavor should be.

# Dessert

*Our desserts, ah now none can compare*
*They're just simply delicious, I swear*
*Peach cobbler, I've found*
*Tastes best when it's round*
*The implication of course? Pie are square!*

# Cakes

## Apple Crisp

44 Apple crisp, a yummy dessert. This is Mom's recipe, that I suspect she got from *Better Homes Cookbook* way back when.

Posted by: Kindltot. Yield: 4 to 6 servings. Prep time: 10 minutes to prep, 45 to cook.

---

2 pounds (5 to 6 cups coarsely chopped) apples
1 tablespoon butter, chopped up
1 tablespoon brown sugar
1/2 cup rolled oats
1/2 cup brown sugar
1/4 cup flour
1/4 cup butter
dash salt

Core and coarsely chop summer apples (Gravensteins or other sweet apples are best, there is no need to peel them unless you want to) and put into a 10" x 6" x 2" pan. Dot with the chopped up tablespoon of butter and sprinkle with the tablespoon of sugar. Mix the oats, ½ cup brown sugar, flour, salt and ¼ cup butter together until they make coarse crumbs. Spread the crumbs over the apples. Bake at 350 degrees F for 40 - 45 minutes. Serve with vanilla ice cream or just cream. You can add any spice you want—most recipes call for apple pie-like seasonings.

## Brown Sugar Sour Milk Nut Cake

45 Damned fine and filling dessert (skip dinner). Recipe is from Martha Craney Wiberg (my Gramma).

Posted by: tcn. Yield: probably a dozen or so servings. Prep time: a bit.

---

1 1/2 cups brown sugar
1/3 cup shortening or butter
1 egg
1 cup sour milk or buttermilk
1 cup nuts (walnuts or pecans)
2 cups flour
1 teaspoon cinnamon
1/2 teaspoon cloves
1/2 teaspoon allspice
1/2 teaspoon baking soda
1/2 teaspoon salt

Mix it like a cake. Don't bother to whip the egg whites—just toss the egg in with the sugar and shortening. Bake in 9 x 13 or two small rounds, about 45 minutes at 350 degrees F. (25-28 minutes for two 9 inch round pans_Best with chocolate buttercream frosting. Cut in small pieces—this one is filling.

## Rum Cake

> 46 Not for kids. Who doesn't have a version of this?

Posted by: Euro.    Yield: 8 servings.    Prep time: 80 minutes.

---

1 box lemon cake mix
1 box instant lemon pudding
4 eggs
1/2 cup cold water
1/2 cup vegetable oil
1/2 cup gold rum
1/2 cup butter
1/4 cup water
1/2 cup white sugar
3/4 cup gold rum

Preheat oven to 325 degrees F. Grease and flour large bundt pan. Mix cake, pudding, ½ cup water, oil, eggs, and 1/2 cup rum. Pour into bundt pan and bake about 60 minutes, or until pick test is clean. Gently pierce cake and cool before removing from pan. For glaze: mix butter, 1/4 cup water, and sugar in saucepan. Stir over low heat until butter and sugar melt. Increase heat and bubble about 5 minutes. Stir in ¾ cup rum and remove from heat. Pour over pierced cake and let it soak in.

## Dark Fruitcake

> 47 One of the ONT's favorite holiday baked goods is fruitcake. Yes, fruitcake. Mamma Misanthropic used to make it for Papa Misanthropic and her favorite son. Now Mrs. Mis. Hum. makes it using the same old time-tested recipe from The Electric Company-Home Service Bureau 1954 cookbook.

Posted by: Misanthropic Humanitarian.    Yield: 7 pounds.    Prep time: 2 - 3 weeks.

---

1 cup butter
1 cup sugar
5 eggs
1/2 cup molasses
1/2 cup sour milk
1/4 cup grape juice
2 cups all-purpose flour
1 teaspoon mace
1 teaspoon cinnamon
1 teaspoon cloves
1 teaspoon allspice
1 teaspoon nutmeg

1/2 teaspoon baking soda
1/2 pound citron
1/2 pound chopped pitted dates
1/2 pound candied orange peel
1/2 pound candied cherries
1 pound seedless raisins
1/2 pound almond slices
1 pint brandy or your choice of whiskey or rum.
New clean cotton dish towels (flour sack towels)

Have ingredients at room temperature. Line greased pans with waxed paper. Grease paper. Cream butter well. Add sugar gradually. Add eggs one at a time, beating well after the addition of each. Add molasses, sour milk and grape juice. Dredge fruit and nuts with part of flour. Sift remainder of flour, spice and baking soda together. Combine with first mixture. Add floured fruit and mix well. Spoon into pans. Bake at 275 degrees F. See time chart below.

Cool cakes completely. Soak dish towels in brandy (Mamma Misanthropic's special touch). Wrap completely cooled cakes in brandy-soaked towel. Wrap with cellophane wrap, then aluminum foil and place in cool dry location for 2 – 3 weeks. Dig in and enjoy.

Time chart for baking:
1 – 2 pound fruit cakes: about 90 minutes per pound
2 – 4 pound fruit cakes: about 60 minutes per pound
4 – 8 pound fruit cakes: about 45 minutes per pound
8 – 12 pound fruit cakes: about 30 minutes per pound
Over 12 pound fruit cake: about 20 minutes per pound

## Funny Cake

48 Pennsylvania Dutch Funny Cake. Another recipe from Grammy Janet Boyer.

Posted by: Tonypete. Yield: one 9-inch pie. Prep time: 1 hour.

---

1 unbaked pie shell
1/2 cup sugar
1/4 cup shortening
1 egg
1/2 cup milk
1/2 cup sugar
1/4 cup shortening
1 egg
1/2 cup milk
1 teaspoon baking powder
1 cup all-purpose flour
1/2 teaspoon vanilla

First layer: mix 1/2 cup sugar, 1/4 cup shortening, 1 egg and 1/2 cup milk together and pour into unbaked pie shell. Second layer: mix 1/2 cup sugar, 1/4 cup shortening, 1 egg, 1/2 cup milk, the baking powder, flour and vanilla together. Pour over first layer.

Bake at 350 degrees F for approximately 40 minutes.

## Granny's Butter Rum Cake

49 Dedicated to Ben Had . . . my favorite cake that Granny made.

Posted by: concrete girl. Yield: 12 servings or so. Prep time: 1 hour plus.

---

1 cup butter
2 cups sugar
4 eggs
3 cups flour
1 teaspoon salt
1 teaspoon baking powder
1/2 teaspoon baking soda
1 cup buttermilk
2 teaspoons vanilla

*For rum sauce:*
1 cup sugar
2 tablespoons rum or rum extract
1/4 cup water
1/2 cup butter

Preheat oven to 350 degrees F. Grease BOTTOM ONLY of bundt pan. Cream butter and sugar. Add eggs, 1 at a time. Sift flour, salt, baking soda and powder, add to buttermilk. Stir in vanilla. Pour into bundt pan. Bake 50 – 55 minutes; test for doneness by inserting a knife—if it's clean, it's done. Meanwhile, prepare rum sauce: heat sugar, water, and butter until melted. Remove from heat and stir in rum. When cake is done, remove from oven and prick top with fork. Pour on warm sauce and cool well before removing from pan. Sprinkle with powdered sugar and enjoy!

## Apple Walnut Cake

50 Delicious picnic cake or at home served w/ice cream. My mother's recipe, written down on an index card.

Posted by: washrivergal. Yield: 6 servings. Prep time: 1 hour 30 minutes.

---

2 cups sugar, divided
1/2 cup butter, softened
8 ounces cream cheese, softened
1 teaspoon vanilla
2 eggs
1 1/2 cups flour
1 1/2 teaspoons baking powder
1/4 teaspoon salt
2 teaspoons cinnamon
1/4 teaspoon nutmeg
3 cups peeled and chopped apples
1 cup walnuts
½ cup brown sugar, packed
3 tablespoons butter
½ teaspoon vanilla
1 tablespoon heavy cream

Mix 1/2 cup sugar, cinnamon, and nutmeg with chopped apples. Set aside. Beat 1 1/2 cups sugar, ½ cup butter, cream cheese, and 1 teaspoon vanilla for 3 minutes. Beat in eggs, one at a time. Combine flour, baking powder, and salt. Blend into sugar/butter/cream cheese. Stir apple mixture into batter. Stir in nuts. Pour into greased 9 x 13 baking pan. Bake at 350 degrees F for one hour, or until cake pulls away from sides and middle bounces to touch. For the glaze, combine brown sugar, 3 tablespoons butter, ½ teaspoon vanilla, and heavy cream in a saucepan. Bring to boil over medium heat, stirring constantly. Cook 3 to 5 minutes. Pour immediately over still hot cake, then let cake cool completely.

## Fresh Blueberry and Peach Pound Cake

51 Fat Free (*shifty eyes*). Found somewhere on teh interwebs years ago.

Posted by: Jane D'oh. Yield: 1 10" cake Prep time: 25 minutes.

---

1/2 cup unsalted (room temperature) butter
4 ounces (room temperature) cream cheese
2 cups sugar
5 large (room temperature) eggs
1/4 cup peach brandy, schnapps, or nectar
2 cups all-purpose flour
1 teaspooon baking powder
1/4 teaspoon salt
1 1/4 cups diced fresh peaches
1 cup fresh blueberries

Generously grease and sugar a 10" tube or bundt pan (I use a bundt pan). Beat butter and cream cheese at medium speed for about 2 minutes or until creamy. Gradually add the sugar and beat for 5 to 7 minutes. Add the eggs one at a time and beat until the yellow just disappears. Stir in the brandy. Combine the flour, baking powder, and salt; add to the butter mixture beating at low speed just until blended. Gently fold in the peaches and blueberries. Pour into pan and bake at 325 degrees F for 1 hour and 25 minutes. Cool in the pan for 15 minutes, remove, and cool completely on wire rack. I made this for my MIL's 92nd birthday, and everyone loved it. Gild the lily and serve with peach ice cream.

## Perfect Texas Sheet Cake

52 Sinful. I have had this recipe for nearly 40 years. It came from a co-worker in Mount Vernon, Ohio. You will get a perfect cake every time if you follow the directions exactly.

Posted by: Ladylibertarian. Yield: 12 servings. Prep time: 1 hour.

---

1 stick (1/2 cup) butter
1 stick (1/2 cup) margarine
1 cup water
3 tablespoons unsweetened cocoa powder

2 cups flour
2 cups sugar
1/2 teaspoon salt
1 teaspoon baking soda
2 eggs
1 teaspoon vanilla extract
1/2 cup sour cream

*For icing:*
1 stick (1/2 cup) butter
6 tablespoons milk
3 rounded tablespoons unsweetened cocoa powder
2 teaspoons vanilla extract
1 pound box confectioner's sugar

Bring to boil the butter, margarine, and cocoa powder. Sift together the flour, sugar, salt, and baking soda. Add the hot liquid mixture to the dry ingredients, along with the eggs, vanilla and sour cream. Line an 11 x 17 jelly roll pan with foil. Grease the foil. Pour in cake mixture. Bake in a preheated 350 degree F oven for 20 minutes, NO LONGER.

For the icing: melt butter with milk and cocoa powder, boil for 2 minutes. Add vanilla extract and a powdered sugar. Ice slightly cooled cake while icing is warm. Sprinkle top of cake with chopped pecans, if desired. Serve cake with vanilla ice cream. OMG.

## Bananas Foster

53 The dessert to finish you off. Mimics the Bananas Foster from an upscale Houston restaurant. Recipe was worked out at home with hints from our waiter. Serve this after a good meal and watch people groan since they must eat it all. So good.

Posted by: Dave at Buffalo Roam. Yield: 6 servings. Prep time: 1 hour.

---

1 (18-1/4-ounce) package yellow cake mix
3 eggs, divided
8 ounces cream cheese
1 ½ cups butter, divided
1 (16-ounce) box powdered sugar
1 teaspoon vanilla
3 bananas
1/4 cup good rum
1/2 teaspoon nutmeg
1/2 teaspoon cinnamon

Heat oven to 350 degrees F. Combine the cake mix, one egg and 1/2 cup softened butter and mix well with your electric mixer. Pat the mixture in the bottom of a buttered 13 by 9 baking pan. In a large bowl beat the cream cheese until smooth. Add the other eggs, vanilla, 1/2 cup butter and beat well. Add the powdered sugar and mix well by hand. Spread it over the cake batter and bake for 40 min. The center will be a little gooey. Melt the last 1/2 cup of butter in a small frying pan. Slice the bananas and lightly fry them in the butter. Add the nutmeg and cinnamon. When the bananas are soft add the rum and cook off the alcohol. Flame it for more flair if you like. Serve over the gooey cake with whipped cream on top of it all.

## Aunt Jean's Cheesecake

54 You think you know cheesecake? Get outta here. This is my mother's recipe that she tweaked with each preparation till it was cheesecake perfection.

Posted by: Cannibal Bob. Yield: servings for 8 average morons or 1 serving for Ace. Prep time: 30 minutes.

---

2 8-ounce packages cream cheese
1 cup sugar
4 egg yolks
2 level tablespoons flour
1 pint sour cream
1 teaspoon vanilla
1 cup graham cracker crumbs
1/2 stick (1/4 cup) butter

Separate eggs, set aside egg whites. Mix together cream cheese, sugar, egg yolks, flour, sour cream, and vanilla. Beat egg whites until stiff, then fold into cheese mixture. For the crust: melt butter, mix in cracker crumbs. Press into bottom of 9" springform pan and bring up on sides about 1/4 inch. Pour in cheese mixture. Bake 1 hour at 325 degrees F then turn off oven. Let cool in oven 1 hour. DO NOT OPEN DOOR. Serve warm, at body temperature, or cooled in the fridge. You may serve with fruit compote of your choice or fresh chopped strawberries.

## "Green Stuff" (named by my office staff)

55 Extremely retro, and delicious, quasi cheesecake recipe. This recipe, at least 50 years old, came from one of my mother's long-time friends who was head dietician at Stanton Hospital (which no longer exists). It was served in the doctors' dining room for dessert. This does take some work, and probably sounds bizarre, but it is damn good. An excellent recipe for St. Pat's parties. I made it one year for an office potluck and have not been allowed to stop making it since. Can (in fact, should) be made in advance. It doesn't taste of creme de menthe at all, but I figure this qualifies it as a Moron dessert.

Posted by: Dr Alice. Yield: 12 servings. Prep time: 1 hour.

---

3-ounce package lemon Jello
14 tablespoons boiling water
2 tablespoons green creme de menthe
3 tablespoons lemon juice (bottled OK)
5 drops green food coloring
1 stick (1/2 cup) butter, melted
9 ounces vanilla wafers, crushed
3 tablespoons powdered sugar
8 ounces cream cheese, softened
1 cup granulated sugar
1 tablespoon vanilla
20-ounce can crushed pineapple, drained
1 can evaporated (NOT condensed) milk

Chill the can of evaporated milk, beaters and bowl before whipping. Easiest way to measure the water is to fill a 1 cup measure with water and then take out two tablespoons. Add the boiling water to Jello along with lemon juice, food coloring and creme de menthe. Stir thoroughly to ensure Jello is dissolved, then set aside to cool to room temperature. When cool, whip gelatin thoroughly before adding other ingredients. Mix wafers, powdered sugar and melted butter. Place on bottom of 13x9 in pan, reserve some crumbs for topping. Beat together cream cheese, sugar and vanilla. Mix in pineapple. Mix with whipped jello; whip the evaporated milk and fold into other ingredients. (Do not use nonfat evaporated milk—it won't whip.) Pour over crust, sprinkle crumbs over and chill.

## Buttermilk Cake

56 Pound cake with a lemon and orange juice glaze. My mom and dad were married for 64 years. She passed last month so I can't ask where she got the recipe. It's an old-fashioned Southern pound cake that dad requested for his birthday every year.

Posted by: Mamawolf. Yield: 10 to 12 servings. Prep time: 2 hours to completion.

---

1 1/2 cups oleo or margarine
2 1/2 cups white sugar
3 1/2 cups all-purpose flour
1/2 teaspoon salt
1 cup buttermilk
1 tablespoon lemon extract
1/2 teaspoon baking soda
1 teaspoon water
4 large or extra-large eggs
Juice and zest of 2 lemons
Juice of 1 orange
1 cup sugar

Cream oleo and 2 ½ cups sugar, beat eggs one at a time. Add milk, soda dissolved in water and lemon extract. Add flour last, gradually beating until batter is fluffy. Pour into greased tube pan. Bake 1 hour, 30 minutes at 325 degrees F. For the glaze: combine the lemon juice and zest, the orange juice, and 1 cup of sugar. Dissolve all and pour over cake when you remove it from the oven. Use skewer or ice pick to poke holes in cake before glazing. Let stand 15 minutes before removing from pan.

## Ann's Plum Tart

57 Changed from Marian Burros's plum tart recipe. Easy and delicious.

Posted by: Ann Fitzgerald. Yield: 8 servings. Prep time: 20 minutes, baking time one hour.

---

1/2 cup softened butter
3/4 to 1 cup sugar
1/4 teaspoon almond extract
1 cup flour
1 teaspoon baking powder
pinch of salt
2 eggs
1/2 cup chopped pecans
24 halves of pitted purple plums
Sugar, lemon juice, cinnamon to sprinkle on top

Preheat oven to 350 degrees F. Cream butter and sugar well. Add almond extract. Add flour, baking powder, salt and eggs. Beat well. Spoon batter into a springform pan, 8 inch up to 10 inch. Sprinkle batter with chopped pecans. Place plum halves skin side up on top of batter. Sprinkle lightly! with lemon juice. Sprinkle with about 1 teaspoon of sugar and 1 teaspoon of cinnamon. Bake 50 to 60 minutes. Remove from oven and cool.

## Carrot Cake

58 Moist and delicious carrot cake with cream cheese frosting. This has been handed down from mother to daughter for years in my family.

Posted by: Mamawolf. Yield: 8 – 10 servings. Prep time: 25 minutes.

---

4 eggs
1 1/2 cups vegetable oil
2 cups all-purpose flour
2 cups granulated sugar
2 teaspoons baking powder
2 teaspoons baking soda
2 teaspoons cinnamon
1 teaspoon salt
1 teaspoon vanilla
3 cups grated carrots
1/2 cup chopped pecans

Mix dry ingredients, then add cooking oil and stir well. Add eggs and vanilla; mix into batter. Add carrots and nuts and stir well to mix. Pour into 3 or 4 cake pans. Bake 45 minutes to 1 hour in a 300 degree F oven. Frost with cream cheese frosting.

*Cream Cheese Frosting*
1 16-ounce box powdered sugar
1/2 to 1 stick (1/4 – ½ cup) softened butter
8 ounce package cream cheese, softened
1/4 teaspoon salt
1 teaspoon vanilla

Beat butter and cream cheese until lumps are gone. Beat in powdered sugar slowly until incorporated. Add salt and vanilla extract. Beat until light and fluffy. Spread between layers and on sides of cake. Don't cheat and use canned frosting. There is a special circle in hell devoted to people who use canned frosting on homemade cake.

***Chef's Notes:***
You can substitute applesauce for up to 1 cup of the oil for a cake with less fat. I also add in some ginger, cloves, nutmeg and allspice because I like a spicier cake.

## Easiest Cake

59 Easy upside-down cake, from my mom.

Posted by: Nora.    Yield: 6 servings.    Prep time: 30 minutes.

---

1 can any desired fruit pie filling
1 box dry cake mix—the cheaper and lumpier the better
1 stick (1/2 cup) butter

In a baking pan or dish—roughly 9 x 12—empty can of pie filling. Spread the pie filling to make an even layer. Take the dry cake mix and shake it over the pie filling and be sure to cover all the pie filling. Cut the stick of butter into even pats and spread on top of the cake mix. Bake according to the time on the cake mix box—if it says bake at 350 degrees F for 25 minutes, etc., then follow those instructions. Enjoy! Especially good with plain vanilla ice cream.

## Best Carrot Cake

60 Seriously. This is the best carrot cake. Ever. Recipe is originally from *Southern Living* magazine, October 1997. You can find it on the internet on myrecipes.com if you search for "best carrot cake."

Posted by: NavyMom.    Yield: serves 1, unless you're forced to share.    Prep time: quite a while but it's worth every minute.

---

2 cups all-purpose flour
2 teaspoons baking soda
1/2 teaspoon salt
2 teaspoons ground cinnamon
3 large eggs
2 cups sugar
3/4 cup vegetable oil
3/4 cup buttermilk
2 teaspoon vanilla extract
2 cups grated carrots
1 2/3 cups flaked coconut
1 cup chopped pecans or walnuts

Line 3 (9-inch) round cake pans with wax paper; lightly grease and flour wax paper. Set pans aside. Stir together first 4 ingredients. Beat eggs and next 4 ingredients at medium speed with an electric mixer until smooth. Add flour mixture, beating at low speed until blended. Fold in carrot and next 3 ingredients. Pour batter into prepared cake pans. Bake at 350 degrees F for 25 to 30 minutes or until a wooden pick inserted in center comes out clean. While it's baking, make Buttermilk Glaze. Drizzle Buttermilk Glaze evenly over layers; cool in pans on wire racks 15 minutes. Remove from pans, and cool completely on wire racks. Spread cream cheese frosting between layers and on top and sides of cake.

*Buttermilk Glaze*

1 cup sugar
1 1/2 teaspoons baking soda
1/2 cup buttermilk
1/2 cup butter
1 tablespoon light corn syrup
1 teaspoon vanilla extract

Bring first 5 ingredients to a boil in a large pot over medium-high heat. Boil, stirring often, 4 minutes. Remove from heat, and stir in vanilla. Pour over hot carrot cake.

***Chef's Notes:***

I usually bake this in a 9x13 pan, and have found that using the entire buttermilk glaze over the cake makes it a little too soggy for my taste. I use maybe 2/3 to 3/4 of the recipe.

## Grandma's Rhubarb Cake

61 Moistest cake west of the Mississippi. My grandma gets credit for this one. Growing up in Iowa it was always one of my favorite things to eat and I'm happy to be able to share it with family and friends now. Grandma did not part with recipes easily.

Posted by: westminsterdogshow. Yield: 6 – 8 servings. Prep time: 1 hour.

---

2 cups chopped rhubarb
1 lime, zested
1 cup milk
2 tablespoons apple cider vinegar
1 1/2 cups brown sugar
1/2 cup butter
1 egg, beaten
2 cups flour
1 teaspoon baking soda
1/2 teaspoon salt
1/4 cup sugar
1 teaspoon cinnamon

Combine the rhubarb, 1 tablespoon flour, and lime zest. Set aside. Combine milk and vinegar. Set aside. Cream brown sugar and butter. Add egg and beat well. Sift together remaining flour, soda and salt. Add alternatively with milk until mixed. Fold in rhubarb and pour into a greased 9 x 13 pan. Combine sugar and cinnamon and sprinkle on top. Bake in a 350 degrees F oven for 35 - 40 minutes. Eat until gone.

## Poor Man's Cake

62 Raisins, cinnamon, nutmeg & clove cake. My grandmother's recipe!

Posted by: mpfs. Yield: 16 servings. Prep time: 45 minutes.

---

2 cups sugar
2 1/2 cups raisins
2 cups water
2 tablespoons shortening
1 teaspoon salt
1 teaspoon ground cloves
1 teaspoon nutmeg
2 teaspoons cinnamon
1 teaspoon baking soda
3 cups flour

Preheat oven to 350 degrees F. Grease and flour a bundt pan. Combine the sugar, raisins, water , shortening, salt, ground cloves, nutmeg and cinnamon in a medium saucepan on stovetop. Boil for two (2) minutes. Set aside and let cool. Once raisin mixture is cool add flour and baking soda. Hand-mix thoroughly. Pour into bundt pan and bake for 1 to 1 1/2 hours or until cake tester comes out clean. Let cool and enjoy!

## Grandma Dorothy's Mayonnaise Cake

63 Delicious, easy chocolate cake. This is my mother's recipe. Published once before in the *Augustana Lutheran Church Centennial Cookbook.*

Posted by: NavyMom. Yield: servings for 5 Morons. Prep time: 25 minutes.

---

3 cups flour
1 1/2 cups sugar
3/4 cup cocoa
2 1/4 teaspoons baking soda
pinch salt
3/4 cup mayonnaise
1 1/2 cups cold water
1 teaspoon vanilla
1 teaspoon espresso powder (optional)

Preheat oven to 350 degrees F. Grease and flour a 9 x 13 pan. Sift flour, sugar, cocoa, soda and salt. Blend mayonnaise with water and vanilla (and espresso powder, if using). Combine with dry ingredients and beat well until smooth. Bake 25 – 30 minutes, or until a toothpick comes out clean.

# Apple "Sand" Cake

64 German/Austrian dessert. Recipe is from a Youtube video from the series "Frisch Gekocht" on Austrian Broadcasting Corporation (ORF), one of Austria's national channels. Recipe translated and adapted from the Austrian language by me.

Posted by: Katja. Yield: 12 slices. Prep time: 25 minutes.

---

16 tablespoons butter, divided
3 cups all-purpose flour, divided
1 cup powdered sugar, divided
1 teaspoon cinnamon
zest from 1/2 lemon
2 eggs, separated
1/3 cup sugar
salt
5/8 teaspoon cream of tartar
3/8 teaspoon baking soda
6 small apples, peeled and cored
1/4 cup slivered almonds
additional butter for apples (at least 1 tablespoon)
additional cinnamon and sugar for apples
additional powdered sugar for sprinkling

For crust: melt 6 tablespoons of butter, and knead with 1 1/2 cups flour, 1/3 cup powdered sugar, cinnamon, and lemon zest to form a dough. Press into bottom of 9" springform pan. For cake: in one bowl, mix 10 tablespoons butter with egg yolks and 2/3 cup powdered sugar until foamy. In another bowl, mix together egg whites, sugar, and a pinch of salt. Combine the two mixtures together by hand, then fold in 1 1/2 cup flour, cream of tartar, and baking soda. Pour the entire mixture over the crust, and even mixture out.

Halve and remove seeds from 4 – 6 apples (size will determine how many will fit). Cut a crosshatch pattern on the rounded sides of the apple halves, then arrange the halves so that they cover the dough. Once this is done, brush the apples with melted butter, covering them lightly but completely. Sprinkle almond slivers and cinnamon sugar on top. (Cinnamon sugar can be made by combining ¼ cup sugar with 1 tablespoon sugar.) Bake in convection oven at 325 degrees F for 45 – 55 minutes, the cake being done when the dough portion of the cake allows for a toothpick inserted into center of cake to come out clean. Set to cool for at least 10 minutes, then, if desired, sprinkle top with powdered sugar. Release from springform pan and serve.

## Gushka's Fruit Crisp

65 Versatile deliciousness so simple even a moron can do it! Ok, this is an adaptation of several recipes from several sources to get it to taste and have the consistency of Grammie's original Apple Betty.

Posted by: Gushka can haz kittehs what plays fetch! Yield: 9x9 panful. Prep time: depends on the cook.

---

enough fruit to fill your pan—the fruit you like; apricots and blueberries light Pops up, but Grimmy likes just about anything
1/2 cup white sugar
three tablespoons? cinnamon
½ cup cherry juice (or cider if using apples or pears)
1 ½ sticks (3/4 cup) softened butter
1 cup brown sugar
1 cup flour
1 cup or more Quaker oats
¼ teaspoon vanilla
¼ teaspoon baking powder
¼ teaspoon baking soda
¼ teaspoon salt

Ok, heat up the damn oven to around 375 degrees F, or less if your oven runs too hot. Get out your aluminum foil because you will want to cover your treat for about 20 to 30 minutes of the baking time. I like 20 minutes, Pops likes 30. Depends on how brown you want it. Spray baking spray (like Pam) on the pan. Cut up your fruit and add the white sugar and cinnamon to taste. I mix them in a little bowl till it's the right sugar to cinnamon ratio and then sprinkle it on the fruit until you are happy with it. I like more cinnamon, and not a ton of sugar. You can do this in bowl or in the pan you wish to use. Like a lot of fruit? Use a bigger pan! Remember to cover and cook longer depending on depth of fruit. Some methods call for water in with it (yuck) or cherry juice (better!). It depends on what you are using as the fruit. Believe me, I don't care what kind of fruit you cut up, if you use cherry juice people go nuts. Unless it's apple, or pears, then use cider.

Ok, this is a kind of topping I remember as a cup, a cup, and a cup. You put your softened butter in a bowl and you whisk it with the brown sugar and vanilla. Sift your flour and the salt, baking soda and baking powder into that. You like cinnamon? Go ahead! Add some! I do it here with the sifted dry goods. Grimmy likes cinnamon.

Ok, next you should have what appears to be some kind of cookie dough. I use my hands to smash in the oats, or you can cut them in with a biscuit thing—but do you really want to dirty that? It was gramma's! Do it by hand. You're supposed to use a cup but I always use more. Like it crunchier? Use more. I do, maybe a cup and a half. Crumble evenly over the top of the fruit and tuck it under its aluminum foil blanket for the first half of the cooking. It should take about an hour. It might need more—or less; please check without opening oven, it lets out the heat. This is (I think) my half recipe—one 9 x 9 square baking dish or a skimpy rectangle, but it can be stretched. Ice cream or heavy whipping cream is lovely with this.

***Chef's Notes:***
As you can see, I kind of eyeball this recipe. I love substitutions, and cook time varies depending on type of fruit used. Bloobs and blackberries take less time to become beautiful. Nectarines and plums take a little more, and hard peaches and apples the most.

## Mother Curmudgeon's Old Fashioned Cheesecake

> 66 My mom, Eva Curmudgeon, had this incredible cheesecake recipe. She used to bake all the time and inherited a family cheesecake recipe that she tinkered with until this recipe resulted. I suggest you try it plain the first time and gussy it up with fancy-schmancy toppings on future attempts.

Posted by: Hank Curmudgeon. Yield: one cheesecake. Prep time: 45 minutes to 1 hour; bake time 1 to 1 ¼ hours.

---

*Cheese Filling:*
3/4 cup sugar
6 tablespoons butter
5 eggs, separated
4 tablespoons flour
1 tablespoon grated lemon zest
2 tablespoons sour cream
1/2 teaspoon baking powder
3 tablespoons pure vanilla extract
15 ounces ricotta cheese
1 tablespoon fresh lemon juice

*Dough:*
1 stick butter +2 tablespoons (10 tablespoons in all)
1/4 cup sugar
3/4 cup unbleached flour
1 egg yolk (reserved from above)
1 teaspoon grated lemon zest
1 teaspoon pure lemon extract

Preheat oven to 350 degrees F. First separate the eggs, reserving one yolk separately from the others (you will have four yolks in one bowl and the fifth yolk in another). Keep all five egg whites together; beat the whites stiff—keep beaten egg whites cool. In small mixer bowl prepare dough by adding all other dough ingredients and mix until dough forms a ball. Presto evenly onto bottom and sides of 10-inch springform pan.

To make the filling, first beat softened butter and sugar until fluffy, then add, one by one, all the other filling ingredients, beating well. Last, fold in very gently the beaten egg whites. Pour cheese mixture into dough covered springform pan; even out with a spatula. Bake for one hour at 350 degrees F. After baking for an hour the cheese filling should be dry, but give it the toothpick test before removing from the oven.

# *Pies*

## Southern Chess Pie

67 Very old Southern recipe, sort of like a combination of pecan pie filling and custard. Delicious. Recipe is from my sister's mother-in-law, Julia Bailey Headden, since deceased, who said it was an old family recipe.

Posted by: Akua Makana. Yield: 6 servings. Prep time: 15 minutes + baking time.

---

3 eggs
1 cup sugar
1 stick butter, melted
1 tablespoon white vinegar
2 heaping teaspoons vanilla
2 tablespoons cornbread mix
unbaked pie shell

Preheat oven to 350 degrees F. Beat eggs until light. Beat sugar into eggs. Add melted butter, vinegar, vanilla, and cornbread mix. Pour into unbaked pie shell (Marie Callendar's is the closest to homemade). Bake for 10 minutes. Reduce heat to 300 and bake 30 minutes more. Cover with foil. Bake about 20 minutes more (check every 5 minutes or so) until a knife comes out clean. The original recipe called for cornmeal, but I found that the blue box of cornbread cornmeal mix is better.

## Chocolate Bourbon Pie

68 Chocolate and Bourbon—oh, my Pa liked his bourbon. There was never any left after we made this pie.

Posted by: Euro. Yield: 8 servings. Prep time: 25 minutes.

---

3 beaten eggs
1/2 cup Lite Karo syrup
1/2 cup white sugar
1/4 cup dark brown sugar
1/4 cup butter, melted
2 tablespoons all-purpose flour
1 teaspoon vanilla
4 tablespoons bourbon
1 cup chopped walnuts
1 cup dark chocolate chips
one 9" pie shell, unbaked

Mix eggs, Karo, sugars, butter, and flour until well-blended. Stir in vanilla and bourbon, then nuts and chocolate. Pour into unbaked pie shell. Bake about 40 minutes at 375 degrees F, until pie is set. Let cool, then splash some more bourbon on top of pie.

## Berks County Shoo-Fly Pie

69 Wet bottom shoo-fly pie. Recipe is from Grammy Helen Fenstermacher Boyer.

Posted by: Tonypete. Yield: two 9-inch pies. Prep time: 1 1/2 hours.

---

2 cups brown sugar
2 eggs, beaten
1 cup dark Karo syrup
2 cups water
1 teaspoon baking soda
3 cups all-purpose flour
1 cup brown sugar
1/2 cup butter
pinch salt
2 unbaked pie shells

Mix 2 cups brown sugar and eggs. Add syrup and water to eggs mixture—bring all to a gentle boil and immediately remove from heat. Add baking soda to mixture, stir. Pour into 2 unbaked pie shells. Combine flour, 1 cup brown sugar, 1/2 cup butter and salt and mix until crumbs come together. Add crumb mixture on top of liquid bottom. Bake at 350 degrees F for 55 to 60 minutes.

## Rhubarb Pie

70 Oh, my goodness. Peaches was the best cook. My mother, Millie Oakes, made this for us because Dad loved rhubarb. Yankees are always surprised that folk from Georgia know and love rhubarb. Dad was from the north Georgia mountains where rhubarb loved the cold weather.

Posted by: Ann Fitzgerald. Yield: 8 servings. Prep time: 50 minutes.

---

pie crust for covered pie
4 cups cut-up rhubarb
1/4 teaspoon salt
3/4 cup sugar
Juice of half lemon
4 tablespoons unsalted butter

Preheat oven to 400 degrees F. Mix rhubarb, salt, sugar, and lemon juice; pour into pie shell. Cut the butter in small pieces and dot over the rhubarb filling. Cover with remaining dough. Bake for 30 to 40 minutes. You can adjust sugar and lemon to taste.

## Peanut Butter Pie

71 Bring a friend, you can't eat 1 slice by yourself. Stolen from The Original Oyster House, in Mobile, Alabama. They have the recipe posted on their website, so they obviously don't care who has it.

Posted by: harbqll. Yield: more than you'd think. Prep time: an hour, I guess, plus chilling time.

---

8 ounces cream cheese
8 ounces Kool Whip (must be, not just whipped cream)
1 cup smooth peanut butter (not chunky, trust me)
8 ounces powdered sugar
3/4 cup mini chocolate chips
1 oreo pie shell

Mix cheese, peanut butter, and sugar until smooth. Add Kool Whip, mix until smooth. Mix in chocolate chips. Pour into pie shell, refrigerate a couple hours. Serve topped with Kool Whip. OK, or real whipped cream, if you must. I've also done this using little chocolate dessert cups.

## Blueberry Pie

72 Thanksgiving dessert. Original sources - *Strictly Blueberries* cookbook, copyright 1993, by the Delta United Methodist Church. For the crust, I use the "Traditional American Pie Crust Recipe," generous version, from *King Arthur Flour 200th Anniversary Cookbook*, copyright 1991. Only with butter.

Posted by: Nancy at 7000 ft. Yield: servings for 8 morons. Prep time: at least an hour, depends on how fancy you make the piecrust.

---

4 ½ cups frozen and thawed blueberries
4 teaspoons lemon juice
1/2 cup sugar
1/2 cup King Arthur (KA) Flour pie filling enhancer
1/2 teaspoon cinnamon
1/4 teaspoon ground nutmeg
1/8 teaspoon salt
1 teaspoon grated lemon peel
2 tablespoons butter
1 egg
1 tablespoon water
1 Generous Pie Crust recipe

Prepare pie crust. Split pie dough in two and shape into flat discs, one larger than the other to line the pie dish, the other to go on top. Wrap separately in plastic wrap and chill at least an hour. Sort, rinse and drain blueberries. Blot extra moisture out with paper towels, transfer to a 3 quart bowl. Sprinkle lemon juice over berries. Mix the next six ingredients and pour over your berries, tossing gently. Set aside. Preheat your oven to 450 degrees F.

Take the larger of your two pie crust discs and roll out to fit your pie dish. Line the pie dish with pie crust. Make an egg wash, mixing 1 egg with 1 tablespoon water. Brush bottom of pie crust with egg wash and set aside. Dump berry mixture into pie dish. Smooth down a bit, heaping slightly in the center. Dot with butter. Retrieve the smaller of the two pie crust discs and roll out. Cut some vent holes in it (I have a small bear-shaped cookie cutter I use, making the bears march around in a circle). Lay crust on top of pie, trim to fit, then flute the edge. Brush with egg wash (I also stick some extra dough bears that have been cut out to the top with the egg wash.) Bake at 450 degrees F for ten minutes, then reduce heat to 350 degrees and bake for 30 to 35 minutes until crust is light golden brown. It is best served warm with whipped cream or vanilla ice cream.

***Chef's Notes:***

4 ½ cups blueberries for a 9" pie, 5 cups if you are using a deep dish Polish pottery baker. If you do not know how to make pie crust, I urge you to get a copy of the KA Flour 200th anniversary cookbook (they sell them used on eBay), with all the instructions you will ever need on how to make and shape a pie crust.

# Navaho Peach

73 Better than peach pie. This is a modified version of a recipe given to me by my sister-in-law who said she acquired it from a friend. I feel certain this friend must be Elizabeth Warren as they are both screaming liberals and the recipe is "Navaho" Peach. ;-P

Posted by: RusticBroad. Yield: 6-8 servings. Prep time: 35 – 40 minutes.

---

4 – 5 cups peeled, sliced peaches
1/3 cup sugar
1 tablespoon cornstarch
1 tablespoon lemon juice
2 tablespoons pine nuts, toasted

1/3 cup sugar
1/3 cup cornmeal
1/3 cup flour
1/4 cup butter, melted

Mix together first 1/3 cup sugar and cornstarch. Toss with the peaches. Pour peach mixture into pie plate and sprinkle with lemon juice. Mix together pine nuts, second 1/3 cup sugar, cornmeal and flour. Pour in melted butter and mix until crumbly. Spread over peaches. Bake 25 minutes at 375 degrees F.

## Husband Bait

74 He came for the pie, and stayed for the fine, perky elbows. From *Bon Appetit*, circa 1990; it was a special dessert issue of some sort.

Posted by: Tammy al-Thor. Yield: 1 husband (or 6 – 8 servings). Prep time: about half an hour, not including refrigeration time.

---

1 cup graham cracker crumbs (15 crackers?)
1/4 cup sugar
1/4 cup (1/2 stick) unsalted butter (cut into pieces and softened)
8 ounces cream cheese, softened
1 cup creamy peanut butter (DO NOT use old-fashioned or freshly ground)
1 cup confectioner's sugar
2 tablespoons unsalted butter, softened
1 tablespoon pure vanilla extract
1/2 cup heavy cream, well-chilled
1/2 cup heavy cream
6 ounces semisweet chocolate, chopped

For graham cracker crust: Preheat the oven to 350 degrees F, with a rack in the lower third. In a medium bowl, combine the graham cracker crumbs, sugar and ½ stick butter until well blended. Press evenly into a buttered 9-inch pie pan, reaching up to but not over the rim. Bake until lightly browned, about 10 minutes. Cool the crust completely on a wire rack. For the filling: beat the cream cheese and peanut butter with an electric mixer at medium speed until well blended. Add the confectioner's sugar, 2 tablespoons butter and vanilla and continue beating until fluffy. Whip the ½ cup chilled heavy cream until not quite stiff. Fold a large spoonful of the whipped cream into the peanut butter mixture to lighten it; gently fold in the remainder. Carefully spoon the filling into the cooled crust, spreading evenly. Loosely cover the pie and refrigerate until firm, about 3 hours. (You can put it in the freezer, if you'd like to speed it up.)

For the fudge topping: bring the remaining ½ cup heavy cream to a simmer in a small, heavy saucepan. Add the chocolate and stir until smooth. Set aside to cool to lukewarm. Gently spread the topping over the cooled pie. Refrigerate until firm, about 3 hours. (This pie can be made 1 day ahead; cover it loosely with wax paper or plastic wrap and refrigerate.) Cut the pie into wedges and serve cold.

## Washington State Centennial Pie

75 Better than cheesecake! This is a recipe that my late husband Jeffrey created on his own. He loved to cook and decided to name it after the state centennial in 1989.

Posted by: notsothoreau. Yield: 6 servings? Prep time: 30 minutes.

---

8 ounces cream cheese
2 ounces chocolate
1/4 cup flour
2 cups half and half
1 cup sugar
yolks of 3 eggs
1 – 2 teaspoons vanilla
precooked pie shell

Prepare precooked pie shell (bake at 450 degrees F for 15 minutes). In a double boiler, combine cream cheese and chocolate. In a separate pan, scald half and half. Blend flour with 1/2 cup of the half and half, then add to the scalded half and half and whip well. Add scalded half and half to cream cheese and chocolate mixture. Add sugar to the mixture and whip well. Let heat for 5 minutes, then cook over medium heat for 20 minutes, whipping frequently. Mix the yolks of 3 eggs with 2 tablespoons of the mixture, then add this to the mixture. Cook 3 minutes, whipping constantly. Add 1 – 2 teaspoons of vanilla. Whip well and pour into pie shell. Chill and serve 24 hours after filling. This really does taste better after aging for 24 hours.

## Grandmother's Fried Pies

76 Simple and delicious. My grandmother was a ranch wife and the ranch cook. Nothing fancy ever but it was always good and plenty of it. Small children and adult men love these things.

Posted by: Lester. Yield: servings for 5 Morons. Prep time: 25 minutes.

---

3 cups flour
1 teaspoon salt
1/2 cup margarine
1/2 cup shortening like Crisco or lard
1 well-beaten egg
1/2 cup chilled water
fruit or custard filling

Mix flour and salt. Cut in with pastry blender or by hand the margarine and then the shortening. (You can use a mixer or a food processor but do not overprocess.) Add in the beaten egg and mix in well, then the water. Form into a ball, cover and set into fridge for 30 minutes. Roll out dough on floured cool surface to 1/8 inch thickness. Cut into 5 inch squares or circles. Add cold fruit in the center. Moisten edges with water, fold over, press edges with fork or crimp with fingers. Fry in shortening at 375 degrees F. You can deep-fry or pan-fry and flip them over until nicely brown, usually about two minutes. Drain on paper towels. Best eaten the same day. You can make your own fruit filling by cooking apples, fresh berries or peaches, or use canned pie filling or even good quality fruit preserves.

# Fresh Strawberry Pie

77 I like pie! This recipe was sent to me from a friend that worked at a restaurant in town where these pies were made and piled a mile-high with fresh whipped cream!

Posted by: Cicero Kaboom! Kid. Yield: 8 servings. Prep time: mere minutes.

---

1 baked pie shell
2 cups water
2 cups sugar
4 tablespoons corn starch
1 6-ounce package strawberry Jello
1 quart fresh strawberries
whipped cream

Bring water, sugar and corn starch to a boil. Add Jello and stir to dissolve. Chill 10 minutes or so. Wash and slice strawberries, leave the small ones whole. Put berries in pie crust and pour the Jello mixture over them, filling the crust just not quite to the top. Chill for a couple of hours. Have fun with the whipped cream. You need as deep a pie pan as you can find for this recipe, or use a few more berries and make TWO pies.

# Dutch Apple Crisp Pie

78 This is apple pie dessert nirvana, plain and simple. All accolades go to a lady I used to work with 20 years ago. Thanks, Betty, wherever you are!

Posted by: Lady in Black—Death to the Man Bun. Yield: enough for 6 regular people or 1 Michael Moore. Prep time: 15-20 minutes.

---

2 1/2 pounds (approximately 3 large) Granny Smith apples
1 cup sugar
2 tablespoons flour
1/2 teaspoon nutmeg
1/2 teaspoon cinnamon
1 tablespoon lemon juice
1/2 cup flour
1/2 cup butter
1/2 cup walnuts, chopped
(1) 9" pie crust, not deep-dish
heavy whipping cream (optional)

Preheat oven to 400 degrees F. Peel and slice apples thinly. Mix 1/2 of sugar with 2 tablespoons of flour, nutmeg and cinnamon. Toss flour mixture with sliced apples. Pour into pie pastry shell and sprinkle lemon juice over apples. Mix remaining sugar with 1/2 cup flour and cut in butter until mixture is crumbly. Sprinkle mixture over apples. Bake for 45 minutes. (I usually put a piece of foil on the bottom rack to catch any drips.) Remove pie and sprinkle chopped walnuts on top. Bake for an additional 5 – 10 minutes, or until walnuts are a little browned. Cool for a while. For true decadence, pour heavy whipping cream (unwhipped) on top of warm slices.

## Fudge Pecan Pie

79 Easy. I've used this since I married long ago so the actual origin is unknown. It has been published in various church cookbooks with myself as the contributor.

Posted by: Jazzuscounty. Yield: 8 servings. Prep time: 15 minutes prep/45 – 50 minutes oven.

---

2 one-ounce squares baking chocolate
1 stick (1/2 cup) butter
2 eggs
1 cup sugar
1/4 cup flour
2 teaspoons vanilla
1/2 cup pecans, chopped
1 pie shell

Melt the chocolate and butter in the microwave. Mix flour and sugar, then add to chocolate/butter mixture. Add in the beaten eggs but make certain the mixture is cool enough for the eggs. Stir in the vanilla, then add the pecans. Pour into shell and bake at 350 degrees F till firm. In a regular oven it takes 45 – 50 minutes. It will firm in 30 minutes in a convection oven.

***Chef's Notes:***
I quit using the chocolate squares long ago and started using cocoa and oil. Either works well. Easy to make and it can be made with one bowl.

## Don's Peanut Butter Pie

80 Rich refrigerator cream pie. Served at the Concord Hotel (closed since 1990). I used to be a baker there in the 80s.

Posted by: DonP. Yield: 10 servings (it's very rich). Prep time: half hour or less.

---

1 pint heavy cream
4 tablespoons powdered sugar
18-ounce jar GOOD peanut butter
1 1/4 cups powdered sugar
2 tablespoons vanilla
2 chocolate crumb pie crusts
1 or 2 ounces shaved sweet chocolate

In a large chilled bowl, whip the heavy cream to soft peak, then blend in the 4 tablespoons powdered sugar; put it in the fridge while you prepare the next step. In another bowl, mix the rest of the powdered sugar with the peanut butter and vanilla, beat until smooth. Start mixing in the whipped cream, about a quarter or so at a time. When everything is blended together, whip on high for a few minutes. Pour finished mix into the pie shells, and chill them overnight. I usually top the pies with some shaved chocolate. Recipe works well half-size for 1 pie, but I always make two—one for guests, one for me.

### *Chef's Notes:*
Harder math—slice the pie in half, then go 2" over, slice in half again, then slice the big piece in half, then cut both halves again. 10 pieces.

## Lizzy's Coconut Macaroons

81 Deceptively simple, always a hit. Great cookie for the gluten-avoidant types. Recipe from my grandmother.

Posted by: Lizzy. Yield: depends how much you like 'em. Prep time: 25 minutes.

---

1/2 can sweetened, condensed milk
3 cups shredded coconut
1 teaspoon almond or vanilla extract

Preheat oven to 300 degrees F. Grease cookie sheets or line with parchment paper. Mix sweetened condensed milk, extract and shredded coconut. Drop by teaspoons on prepared cookie sheets, about 1 ½ inches apart. Bake until a delicate brown, about 15 minutes. If they seem not to be baking completely, increase to 325 degrees F. Remove carefully and cool on a wire rack. Store in airtight container at room temperature.

## Mama Caniac's Mama's Oatmeal Cookies

82 Oatmeal cookie recipe from my maternal grandma.

Posted by: Ashley Judd's Puffy Scamper. Yield: a couple dozen, hell I can't count. Prep time: 12 minutes if you don't stop to fap.

---

1 cup (2 sticks) melted butter
2 eggs
1 teaspoon vanilla
1/4 teaspoon baking soda
1/4 teaspoon salt
1 cup flour
3 cups oats
1 cup brown sugar
1 cup sugar

Preheat oven to 375 American degrees, don't know what this is in faggy Celsius. Mix all the shit together. Form into balls, place balls on greased cookie sheet and bake for 12 minutes, but at the 5 minute mark see if they are getting brown around the edges; if they are, remove them and cool a minute or so before shoving them into your gaping maw. Wash your dirty mitts before making these. My Grandma's cookies deserve better than your grimy hands touching them.

## Josh's PB Cookies

83 Peanut butter cookies. It's a Tonypete family recipe.

Posted by: Tonypete. Yield: 16 cookies. Prep time: 20 minutes.

---

1 cup peanut butter
1 egg
1/2 cup old-fashioned oats
1/2 cup sugar

Preheat oven to 350 degrees F. Mix all ingredients. Roll into 1 inch balls. Place balls onto ungreased cookie sheet. Press tops of balls with fork dipped into sugar. (Press twice - right to left and top to bottom, making a cross.) Bake 10 – 12 minutes. Remove and cool on a rack. Double this recipe—they go fast.

## Chocolate Crinkles

84 Very good, easy chocolate cookies. From Peg Bracken's *I Hate to Cook Book*. Very witty, great illustrations, wonderful recipes. I recommend it.

Posted by: Dr Alice. Yield: approximately 30 cookies. Prep time: 20 minutes plus chilling/baking time.

---

2 squares unsweetened baking chocolate
1/4 cup cooking oil
1 cup sugar
2 eggs
1 teaspoon vanilla
1 scant cup flour
1 teaspoon baking powder
1/4 teaspoon salt

Melt the chocolate in the oil over low heat. Stir in the sugar, eggs and vanilla, then sift or mix together and add the flour, baking powder and salt. Put in the fridge to chill. (At least an hour but I like to do this the night before and bake the next day.) Just clap the lid on the pan and stick it in the fridge. Next day scoop out small amounts (maybe 2 teaspoons) and roll into balls between dampened palms of hands. Roll the balls in powdered sugar, place on baking sheet. I highly recommend use of parchment paper. Bake at 400 degrees F for ten minutes—don't overbake! If your oven runs hot, set it low. I make these every year at Christmas and they are always well received.

## Sarah's Oatmeal Cookies

85 Oatmeal cookies with a secret ingredient. I took a basic recipe and revised it. This was so long ago, forty years or so, that I cannot remember where I got the original recipe.

Posted by: SarahSue. Yield: 10 servings. Prep time: 25 minutes.

---

1-3/4 cups flour
1 teaspoon baking soda
1 teaspoon baking powder
1/2 teaspoon salt
2 teaspoons cinnamon
1/2 teaspoon ginger
1/2 teaspoon nutmeg
1/4 teaspoon cloves
2 sticks (1 cup) butter
1 cup brown sugar
1 cup white sugar
2 large eggs
1 teaspoon vanilla
1 cup raisins
3 ½ cups whole oats
1 tablespoon blackstrap molasses

Put raisins in bowl, cover with water and microwave for two minutes. Let sit and cool. Cream butter, sugars, eggs and vanilla. Add flour, baking soda, baking powder, salt, molasses and spices, a little at a time until mixed. Add raisins and oats. Drop by spoonfuls on ungreased baking sheet. Bake at 350 degrees F for ten minutes.

## The Best Fruit Bars

86 Ever wonder what you are going to do with all that freeze-dried fruit you stored for the Hillary presidency? From the missus.

Posted by: Muldoon. Yield: depends on how hungry you are. Prep time: 10 minutes.

---

2 eggs
3 tablespoons all-purpose flour
3 tablespoons almond flour
1/2 cup real butter
1 cup crushed freeze-dried apples
1/2 cup crushed freeze-dried berries, any kind
1/4 to 1/2 cup crushed freeze-dried coconut melts or another sweet fruit
1 teaspoon vanilla
3 tablespoons granulated honey
splash of salt, or not

Mix all ingredients together. Spread mixture into an 8" square pan, scone pan, or something similar. Bake at 375 degrees F (400 degrees F if at high altitude) for 15 minutes. Top with little dab of clotted cream or sweet cream and fresh berries. Or eat plain. There are many variations that would work well.

## No Fail Sugar Cookies

87 This recipe is great when using complex cookie cutters. I found this recipe on the HeroGear website, herogear.us. I made a couple of very minor adjustments (recommending bakers sugar, lining baking sheet with parchment paper, how long to chill dough).

Posted by: NavyMom. Yield: approximately 5 dozen. Prep time: 20 minutes.

---

6 cups flour, sifted then measured
3 teaspoons baking powder
1 teaspoon salt
2 cups unsalted butter, room temperature
2 cups sugar (preferably fine baker's sugar)
2 eggs
2 teaspoons vanilla extract

Preheat oven to 350 degrees F. Cream butter and sugar. Add eggs and vanilla; beat until incorporated. Whisk dry ingredients together and add to butter mixture. Mix until the dough comes together with no crumbs at the bottom of the bowl; do not overmix. Chill—see Hint 1 below. Roll to desired thickness and cut into desired shapes. Bake on ungreased or parchment paper-lined baking sheet for 8 to 10 minutes or until just beginning to turn brown around the edges. This recipe can make up to 5 dozen 3" cookies.

Hint 1: rolling out dough without the mess—rather than wait for your cookie dough to chill, take the freshly made dough and place a glob between two sheets of parchment paper. Roll it out to the desired thickness, then place the dough and paper on a cookie sheet and pop it into the refrigerator. Continue rolling out your dough between sheets of paper until you have used it all. Chill the dough until you can hold it on one hand without it bending. Re-roll leftover dough and repeat the process! An added bonus is that you are not adding any additional flour to your cookies.

Hint 2: To roll the dough evenly, use rolling pin rings (available on Amazon or at bakery supply shops) on your rolling pin. Or lay chopsticks on the counter a little less than your rolling pin width apart. Place the dough between them and roll the rolling pin on the chopsticks.

## Best Brownies

> 88 Yes, they are. I do not like true brownies so much—too gooey.

Posted by: Helena Handbasket. Yield: 18 brownies. Prep time: 1 hour.

---

8 ounces (2 cups) cake flour
2 3.9-ounce packages Jello chocolate pudding
2 teaspoons baking powder
1 4-ounce bar Ghirardelli semi-sweet baking chocolate
2 sticks (1 cup) butter
1 cup (4 ounces) light brown sugar
2 eggs
2 tablespoons half-and-half or heavy cream
2 teaspoons vanilla
1 11.5-ounce package Ghirardelli milk chocolate chips, refrigerated

Heat oven to 350 degrees F. Sift flour, pudding and baking powder in large bowl. Melt baking chocolate and butter in double boiler. Beat eggs lightly in a mixing cup and add enough half-and-half or heavy cream to fill to 2/3 cup; add vanilla and beat in. Add egg mix to dry ingredients. Mix brown sugar in with butter/chocolate over double boiler, then add to batter. Mix chocolate chips into batter and pour into 13x9 pan. Bake brownies for 35 – 40 minutes. Allow 10 – 15 minutes to cool and set.

## Texas Oatmeal Cookies

> 89 My extended family's favorite. Contributed by Polly Elliot to *Sharing Our Best*—local (Monmouth, IL) Heritage United Presbyterian Church cookbook, 1993, with an added ingredient by ME.

Posted by: booknlass. Yield: 2 dozen cookies. Prep time: 20 minutes.

---

1/2 cup Crisco
1/2 cup butter or margarine
1 cup granulated sugar
1 cup brown sugar
2 eggs
2 cups flour
1 1/2 teaspoons baking soda
3/4 teaspoon cinnamon
1/2 teaspoon salt
2 cups oatmeal
1 to 1 1/4 cups chocolate chips
1/4 cup Heath bits

Preheat oven to 350 degrees F. Soften and cream together Crisco and butter. Mix in both sugars. Add eggs, and stir well to blend. Sift together dry ingredients except oatmeal and chocolate chips and Heath bits. Add the dry mix to creamed butter; blend well. Stir in oatmeal and chips and bits. Bake on ungreased cookie sheets for 8 to 10 minutes.

## Butter Cookies with 3 variations

90 Tasty! This recipe is adapted—not published.

Posted by: lurkerssj. Yield: many. Prep time: 10 minutes plus refrigeration time.

---

1 cup unsalted butter
1 cup sugar
1 egg
1 tablespoon vanilla extract
1/2 teaspoon kosher salt
1 3/4 cups unbleached flour

Butter and egg should be at room temperature. Preheat oven to 375 degrees F. Line baking sheets with parchment paper. In a stand mixer or hand held, cream butter and sugar together for about 5 minutes. Add egg and when incorporated, add vanilla. Add flour and salt and beat until just incorporated. Suggested! chill overnight, or at least for a few hours. Drop by teaspoonful onto baking sheets, and bake 7 – 8 minutes, until edges are slightly brown. Cool on racks.

Variation 1: add quality pecan half on top of each cookie before baking.
Variation 2: add 1/4 cup minced crystalized ginger and the zest of one orange at the time vanilla extract is added.
Variation 3: add 1 cup Heath Bits o' Brickle toffee bits at the time vanilla extract is added. It is critical to use parchment paper for the toffee bits variation—no amount of butter on a cookie sheet can make this work.

## Florentine Cookies

91 Blue-ribbon prizewinner at the Utah State Fair, 2006 (yes, really). The original recipe is from an early 1980's edition of *The New York Times International Cookbook,* edited by Craig Claiborne. I made a couple of changes. This recipe really did win a blue ribbon at the Utah State Fair. My daughter was living there at the time and she entered these cookies in the competition. And yes, she still has the blue ribbon!

Posted by: Annalucia. Yield: enough for 5 or 6 regular people, or 1 teenaged boy. Prep time: 30 – 45 minutes.

---

1/2 cup granulated sugar
1/2 cup heavy cream, unwhipped
3 tablespoons unsalted butter
1/8 teaspoon salt
1/3 cup all-purpose flour
3/4 cup chopped dried apricots
1 1/4 cups chopped almonds
8 ounces semisweet chocolate
2 tablespoons unsalted butter

Preheat oven to 350 degrees F. Combine sugar, whipping cream, butter and salt in a saucepan; stir over heat until butter has melted and the whole thing is beginning to bubble. Remove from heat and set aside. Add flour, apricots and almonds to the saucepan, mix well. LET SIT FOR AT LEAST FIVE MINUTES—this is so the batter will thicken, which makes for a nice-shaped and reasonably firm cookie. If you don't let it sit, you will get a runny mess when you spoon it on the cookie sheet. Once the batter has thickened up a bit, drop by spoonfuls onto a greased cookie sheet, or one covered with parchment paper. Doesn't matter how big you make them but leave at least a couple of inches between the dollops; they will spread. Bake 10 – 15 minutes; remove from oven when they're browning around the edges. Let them cool on the pan, because they have to firm up before you move them to the cooling rack—do it too soon and they'll fall apart. Once they are completely cool, you may ice them. For the icing, melt the semisweet chocolate and 2 tablespoons unsalted butter; stir until smooth, then ice cookies.

***Chef's Notes:***

Original recipe called for candied chopped orange peel in the batter, and gave a recipe for candying your own. I substituted apricots because you can only find candied orange peel around here at Thanksgiving and Christmas, and making the peel myself was too much trouble. The icing recipe originally called for a couple of tablespoons of heavy liqueur (e.g. Cointreau) for flavor. I find that adding liquid to melting chocolate immediately causes it to seize up (that is, turn into a paste), and you want a smooth, flowy icing. A couple of drops of vanilla, or orange or almond extract, will do the job just as well.

## Caramel Filled Chocolate Cookies

| 92 The cookie that sold our house (seriously). |
|---|

Posted by: Jane D'oh. Yield: 48 cookies Prep time: 25 minutes.

---

2 2/3 cups flour
3/4 cup unsweeted cocoa powder
1 teaspoon baking soda
1/2 cup, plus 1 tablespoon sugar, divided
1 1/2 cups firmly packed brown sugar
1 cup softened butter or margarine
2 teaspooons vanilla
2 eggs
1 cup chopped walnuts, divided
1 9-ounce package, or 48 pieces chocolate covered chewy caramels, such as Rolo
4 ounces white almond bark

Preheat oven to 375 degrees F. In a small bowl, measure flour, cocoa, and baking soda; blend well. In a large bowl, beat 1/2 cup sugar, brown sugar, and butter or margarine until light and fluffy. Add vanilla and eggs; beat well. Add flour mixture; blend well. Stir in 1/2 cup of the walnuts. Chill dough for about 10 minutes for easier handling. Meantime, in a small bowl, combine remaining 1/2 cup walnuts and 1 tablespoon sugar.

For each cookie, lightly flour your hands and shape about 1 tablespoon of dough around 1 caramel candy, covering completely. Press one side of each cookie ball into walnut mixture. Place nut side up, 2" apart, on ungreased cookie sheets. Bake for 7 – 10 minutes or until set and lightly cracked. Cool 2 minutes on cookie sheets, then remove to wire racks to cool completely. Melt almond bark in small saucepan over low heat, stirring constantly until smooth. Drizzle over cookies, either with a spoon, or using a plastic bag with a tiny corner cut off. Or, leave off the almond bark drizzle—they're just as good without it.

## Mom's Orange Cookies

93 Unusual cookie which will make everyone who tastes them regard you with love and awe. Ever since I was a wee tad, Mom made these cookies. I've never tasted their like elsewhere. Maybe a family recipe?

Posted by: naturalfake. Yield: a lot. Prep time: unknown.

---

1 cup Crisco
1 ½ cups sugar
2 eggs
juice and grated rind of 1 large orange (or 2 small)
1 cup buttermilk (or sour milk)
4 cups flour
3 teaspoons baking powder
1 teaspoon baking soda
1 teaspoon vanilla extract
2 tablespoons butter
juice of 1 orange
grated rind of 1/2 orange
enough confectioner's sugar to make icing stiff

Cream shortening, add sugar, well-beaten eggs, orange juice and rind. Stir baking soda into buttermilk. Sift flour and baking powder, and add alternately with buttermilk. Add vanilla. Mixture should be stiff. Let stand 15 minutes. Drop by teaspoonful on greased pan. Bake at 350 degrees F until very light brown. For icing: cream 2 tablespoons butter, add the juice of 1 orange and grated rind of 1/2 orange. Add confectioner's sugar, enough to make the icing stiff enough to spread on cookies when they are cool. If you pack these cookies for shipping, storage, or gifting, be sure to pack between layers of wax paper.

## Elfrieda's Rum Balls

94 Moronically simple to make, magically delicious. Grandma's recipe. She was a German farm girl, therefore this recipe is nothing but win in the flavor category.

Posted by: naturalfake. Yield: unknown. Prep time: unknown.

---

3 cups vanilla wafers
1 cup sifted powdered sugar
1 ½ cups finely chopped nuts (walnuts, pecans, hazelnuts)
1 ½ tablespoons cocoa
2 tablespoons white Karo syrup
Generous 1/2 cup rum

Crumb vanilla wafers (3 cups = one 12-ounce box) in food processor and put in a big bowl. Chop nuts in food processor until fine. Mix dry ingredients (wafers, powdered sugar, nuts and cocoa) with hands. Stir Karo into rum and add to dry mixture. Mix well with hands. Roll by hand into bite-size balls, one inch or so in diameter, then roll in additional powdered sugar.

## Oatmeal Cranberry Cookies

95 Thick chewy "breakfast cookie." Adapted from the Smitten Kitchen.

Posted by: lin-duh fell. Yield: lots of cookies. Prep time: about 45 minutes.

---

1 stick (1/2 cup) butter
2/3 cup brown sugar
1 egg
1 teaspoon vanilla extract
3/4 cup flour
1/2 teaspoon baking soda
1/2 teaspoon baking powder
1/2 teaspoon ground cinnamon
1/2 teaspoon ground nutmeg
1/2 teaspoon kosher salt
1 1/2 cups rolled oats
3/4 cup dried cranberries or raisins
½ cup walnut or pecan pieces (optional)

Combine flour, baking soda, baking powder, spices, and salt in a bowl, then set aside. In a large bowl, cream butter and sugar. Then add egg and vanilla until smooth. Stir the flour mixture into the butter mixture and then add the oatmeal and nuts, if using. Chill covered dough for about an hour or up to 24 hours. The longer you chill the dough, the better the cookie turns out. Heat oven to 350 degrees F. Line a baking sheet with parchment. Scoop out the dough into about 1 – 2 tablespoon portions and place onto baking sheet about 2 inches apart. Bake for 10 – 12 minutes until edges are golden. Cool for 5 minutes then transfer to a rack to cool completely. Enjoy with a glass of milk!

## Best Sugar Cookies Ever

96 Fifty+-year old recipe for incredible sugar cookies. My mother (1924-2007) baked these cookies for as long as I can remember, at least 50 years.

Posted by: jayhawkone. Yield: 90+. Prep time: 10 – 15 minutes.

---

3/4 cup Crisco
1 1/2 cups sugar
1/4 teaspoon salt
2 eggs
1 teaspoon vanilla extract
1 teaspoon almond extract
1/2 teaspoon baking soda
3 tablespoons sweet or sour cream
3 cups flour

Cream Crisco, sugar, salt, eggs, and vanilla and almond extracts with mixer until light and fluffy. Dissolve baking soda and sweet or sour cream, then add to creamed mixture at low speed [if using milk instead of sweet or sour cream, add additional one cup of shortening (not recommended)]. Blend in flour. Roll into balls 1 to 1 1/2 inches round, and bake at 375 degrees F for 8 – 10 minutes.

## Coconut Macaroons

97 It's just not Passover without macaroons. Found on a package of coconut ages ago; I've dressed it up quite a bit since then.

Posted by: Stewed Hamm. Yield: 24. Prep time: 15 minutes.

---

1 can (14 ounces) sweetened condensed milk
1 egg white, whipped
2 teaspoons vanilla extract
1 1/2 teaspons almond extract
1 package (14 ounces) flaked coconut
1/2 cup coconut powder

Preheat oven to 325 degrees F. Line baking sheets with parchment, set aside. In a large bowl, combine condensed milk, egg white, extracts, coconut, and coconut powder. Mix well. Place rounded spoonfuls or quenelles onto prepared baking sheets. Slightly flatten each mound with a spoon. Bake 20 – 25 minutes or until lightly browned around edges. Immediately remove from baking sheets to prevent sticking. Cool on wire racks. Store at room temperature. These are great as-is, but are fantastic when drizzled with dark chocolate.

### *Chef's Notes:*
If the quenelles aren't compact enough, the liquid will drain out of the macaroon before it's done cooking, and you end up with a pile of coconut in a rubbery puddle. So be sure to work them a bit with your spoons before you drop them on the baking sheet.

## Chocolate Chocolate Chip Cookies

98 A soft and cakey cookie. Adapted from Alton Brown's Puffy Chocolate Chip Cookie recipe.

Posted by: Grannysaurus Rex. Yield: 48 cookies. Prep time: 1 hour.

---

- 2 cups all-purpose unbleached flour
- 1/4 cup cornstarch
- 1/2 cup unsweetened cocoa powder
- 1/2 teaspoon table salt (or 1 teaspoon kosher salt)
- 1/1/2 teaspoons baking powder
- 1/2 cup butter-flavored shortening
- 1/2 cup butter, room temperature
- 1 cup light brown sugar, packed
- 3/4 cup white granulated sugar
- 2 large eggs
- 1 tablespoon cold, strong coffee
- 1/1/2 teaspoons pure vanilla extract
- 2 cups semisweet or bittersweet chocolate chips

Sift together the flour, cornstarch, cocoa powder, salt, and baking powder and set aside. Combine the shortening, butter, sugar, and brown sugar; cream until light and fluffy using either a stand mixer or handheld mixer. Add the eggs 1 at a time to the creamed mixture. Then add coffee and vanilla. With the mixer set to low, slowly add the dry ingredients to the bowl and combine well. Stir in the chocolate chips. Chill the dough at least 30 minutes or even overnight. When ready to bake, preheat the oven to 375 degrees F. Line cookie sheets with parchment paper. Using a 2-tablespoon cookie scoop, portion the dough onto the prepared sheets. Bake for 10 minutes or until golden brown and puffy, checking the cookies after 5 minutes. Rotate the baking sheet for even browning. Cool cookies on a rack.

### *Chef's Notes:*
I don't have four cookie sheets. I find it works best for me to cook four batches of 12 cookies. This allows a cookie sheet to cool off slightly before portioning the next batch.

# Chef Jeff's Magic Brownies

99 The best ever! This was developed by my late husband Jeffrey. It does not contain marijuana, but there's no reason that you couldn't add it!

Posted by: notsothoreau. Yield: 12 servings. Prep time: 30 minutes.

---

7 tablespoons butter
2 ounces unsweetened chocolate
6 tablespoons milk
1/2 teaspoon baking soda
1 cup sugar
1 egg
1 cup plus 2 tablespoons flour
1 teaspoon baking powder
1/4 teaspoon salt
1 tablespoon vanilla
1/2 cup nuts, if desired

Melt chocolate and butter in a double boiler. In a separate bowl, beat egg until light. Combine sugar, baking soda, flour, baking powder and salt. Add egg, milk, vanilla and chocolate/butter mixture to the dry ingredients. Mix well. Grease and flour (using the 2 tablespoons of flour) a small (8 x 8 inch) square baking pan. Add the nuts to the mixture if desired and pour into the pan. Bake at 375 degrees F for 30 minutes.

# Hermit Cookies

100 A cookie any guy will love. My mom always made these from a recipe she found in a community cookbook. I have since seen it many times since so it must not be copyrighted!

Posted by: Nicole. Yield: 2 dozen. Prep time: 25 minutes.

---

3/4 cup butter
1 1/2 cups brown sugar
1 cup raisins
1 cup chopped dates
1 cup chopped walnuts
2 eggs
1 1/2 teaspoons vanilla
2 cups flour
1/2 teaspoon baking soda
1/2 teaspoon baking powder
2 tablespoons milk
1 teaspoon cinnamon
1/2 teaspoon nutmeg

Preheat oven to 375 degrees F. Cream butter and sugar. Add eggs and vanilla. Add the raisins, dates and walnuts. Mix the baking soda with milk and add. Add baking powder and mix well. Add the flour and mix. Place on cookie sheet using scoop of choice. I use the 2-inch dispensing scoop and get 2 dozen. Bake for 12 minutes or until golden brown. I have substituted figs for the dates and changed up the nuts. I get asked for this recipe whenever I serve them.

## Crispy Crunchy Brownie Bites

101 Thin light crispy chocolate bites. Recipe is from instructables.com (copycat of Sheila G's brownie brittle).

Posted by: lurker. Yield: 24 servings. Prep time: 30 minutes.

---

1/4 cup margarine
1/2 teaspoon salt
1/2 cup all-purpose flour
1/2 cup powdered sugar
1/4 cup natural cocoa
1 teaspoon baking soda
1 teaspoon coffee crystals (optional)
1/3 cup water
2 tablespoons meringue powder
1/4 cup granulated sugar
1/4 cup mini chips (chocolate, peanut butter, caramel)

Preheat oven to 300 degrees F. Line jelly roll pan or half-sheet pan with parchment and spray with vegetable oil spray. Microwave margarine until melted, then add salt. Butter tends to make baked goods spread so texture will be different if using butter rather than margarine. Combine flour, powdered sugar, cocoa, and baking soda; set aside. Combine coffee crystals (if using) with water and pour in base of stand mixer. Add meringue powder, mix slowly until combined then on high. Slowly add sugar, whisk until very stiff peaks form and are held inside beaters/whisk. Sift dry ingredients into meringue. Fold in until about 3/4 combined. Add margarine, fold until just combined. Pour onto parchment-lined pan and spread thin (slightly thicker than 1/8 inch) using offset spatula. If using jelly roll pan it will completely fill pan, if using half-sheet pan it will be more free form and not fill the whole pan. Sprinkle with mini chips. Bake for 25 minutes. Remove from oven and score into desired size. Place back in oven and bake another 15 minutes. Turn off oven and allow to cool in oven. Remove and break along scored lines.

### *Chef's Notes:*

Meringue powder can be found at Amazon, Michael's, Jo-Ann's, etc. I haven't tried Dutch-process cocoa, but it may alter lift given by soda. I suspect with very little trouble this could be made gluten free by using rice flour rather than all-purpose flour, but have not tried that.

## Ginger Biscuits

102 The best ginger cookies. I don't remember where I got the original recipe. I have been baking it for years and just kept increasing the spices.

Posted by: EA the lurker. Yield: 50 cookies. Prep time: 20 minutes to mix plus baking time.

---

2 cups sifted flour
1/2 teaspoon salt
3 teaspoons ground ginger
3/4 teaspoon ground cloves
2 teaspoons baking soda
3/4 cup butter, room temperature
1 1/4 cups white sugar
1 egg, beaten
1/4 cup molasses

Preheat oven to 350 degrees F. Sift together dry ingredients. Cream together butter and sugar until fluffy, add egg and molasses and mix well. Mix in dry ingredients gradually until just blended. Drop by teaspoonful onto ungreased cookie sheet, bake 15 minutes, then move cookies to cooling rack. Keep the dough cold by putting the unused dough in the refrigerator between batches. Parchment paper on the cookie sheets makes it easier to move the cookies to the cooling rack and makes cleanup easier.

## Deer Droppings

103 No-cook peanut butter cookies; amusing for Christmas parties. Sorry, this Moronette cannot recall where she found this recipe.

Posted by: WOWpromo. Yield: servings for 20 Morons. Prep time: 20 minutes.

---

1 cup creamy peanut butter
1 cup honey
1 cup thin Chinese noodles
1 cup salted peanuts

Place peanut butter in large microwaveable bowl. Microwave for one minute on high until soft. Add honey to peanut butter and blend well. Add Chinese noodles and peanuts and stir gently until evenly mixed. Place wax paper on a large cookie sheet pan. Scoop heaping tablespoons of peanut butter mixture and drop on wax paper. They should be the size of a cookie and look like they just came out of Rudolph. Refrigerate overnight. Remove from wax paper and enjoy. Save leftovers in a container and store in refrigerator. Kids think these are hysterical.

## Ranger Cookies

104 Bet you can't eat just one! A common and popular recipe in the western U.S.

Posted by: Legally Sufficient. Yield: 6 dozen. Prep time: 15 minutes.

---

1 cup brown sugar
1 cup sugar
1 cup oil
2 eggs
1 teaspoon vanilla
2 cups flour
1 teaspoon baking soda
1/2 teaspoon salt
2 teaspoons cinnamon
2 cups corn flake cereal
3/4 cup oatmeal
2 heaping cups chocolate chips

Preheat oven to 350 degrees F. Sift dry ingredients together (flour, soda, salt and cinnamon) and set aside. Add brown sugar, sugar, oil, eggs and vanilla to a mixing bowl and mix well. Add the sifted dry ingredients in batches, mixing well after each addition. Add corn flakes, oatmeal, and chocolate chips, mixing well after each addition. Use small scoop to place dough on cookie sheets lined with parchment paper, or on ungreased cookie sheets, and flatten to about 1/2 inch thickness. To flatten the dough, I lay a rectangle of waxed paper over about six mounds of dough and use my chicken pounder to gently squash each heap of dough. The dough can also be rolled into balls and flattened with a fork. Bake 8 to 10 minutes.

## Snickerdoodles

105 Always a big hit, and so easy to do. I got this recipe from my friend Shithead in college. We sold these cookies and used the proceeds for food and books. Back then we used butter-flavored Crisco, which has since been reformulated and isn't useful any more.

Posted by: Steck. Yield: 5 dozen. Prep time: 30 minutes.

---

1/2 cup butter
1/2 cup lard
1 1/2 cups sugar
2 eggs
2 1/8 cups flour
2 teaspoons cream of tartar
1 teaspoon baking soda
1/2 teaspoon salt
2 tablespoons sugar
2 teaspoons cinnamon.

Cream butter, lard & 1 ½ cups sugar; add eggs & sifted dry ingredients (flour, cream of tartar, baking soda, and salt). This can all be done with a bowl and a fork, no appliances needed. Chill the dough for a while unless you're in a hurry. Pull out gobstopper/walnut-sized chunks, roll into balls, then roll balls into a mixture of 2 tablespoons sugar and 2 teaspoons cinnamon. Place about 2 inches apart (labor saving trick) on ungreased cookie sheet—the cookies have plenty of grease in 'em already. Bake at 400 degrees F until tops start cracking and cookes are lightly browned but still soft (about 7 minutes ).

***Chef's Notes:***
Only do one cookie sheet at a time unless you know your oven *very* well; don't leave 'em in the oven any longer, don't make oven any hotter. Dough can be kept for later, if you can resist eating it raw.

## Sour Cream Drop Cookies

106 AtomicPlaygirl's mom's famous cookies! Recipe is from my mom.

Posted by: atomicplaygirl. Yield: ~60 cookies. Prep time: 25 minutes.

---

1 cup softened butter
1 ½ cups white sugar
2 whole eggs
3 ½ cups all-purpose flour
1/2 teaspoon baking soda
1/2 teaspoon salt
1 teaspoon nutmeg
(generous) 1/4 cup sour cream
raisins and/or nuts to taste (optional)
60 halves candied cherries
coloured sugar sprinkles

Cream butter and sugar in a mixer on medium until you achieve a light consistency. Add eggs, beat well. Gradually add dry ingredients and sour cream; mix well. Add nuts/raisins (if using) and mix until incorporated. Drop by teaspoonfuls onto ungreased cookie sheet. Sprinkle on coloured sugar, place cherry half in the centre. Bake at 350 degrees F for approximately 12 minutes; let dry on cooling rack. These cookies spread a fair amount. This is a great Christmas cookie; add a touch more nutmeg if you enjoy that flavour (I do!). My mom's recipe says you can use brown sugar instead of white, but I have never done so.

## Struffoli/Pignolata

107 Traditional fried honey balls (because after all the GAINZ, you owe it to yourself . . .). You'll see this recipe calls for leaf lard. This is what my grandma made every year for Christmas. My mom at 93 still insists on making a batch or three every year because it "wouldn't be Christmas without it!"

Posted by: RondinellaMamma. Yield: a bunch. Prep time: 2 hours.

---

2 ½ cups flour
4 large eggs
1 egg yolk
1/4 cup leaf lard
1/2 tablespoon sugar
dash salt
1/2 teaspoon grated lemon peel
1 1/2 cups honey
1 teaspoon grated orange peel
2 tablespoons colored nonpareils

Place the flour on a board and make a well. Put the eggs, egg yolk, leaf lard (if you can't find leaf lard, use Crisco vegetable shortening), sugar, salt and lemon peel in the well and mix thoroughly, working the dough with your hands until it is smooth and springy. Roll out long thin cylinders of dough and cut into pieces that are about the size and shape of marbles. Fry the small balls of dough in hot oil until they are golden brown. Remove them from the oil and let them drain on paper towels. When all the dough pieces are fried, put them in a deep bowl. Heat the honey to melt it, add in the orange peel and then pour over the fried dough balls. Sprinkle the nonpareils over the top of the honey balls. When serving, scoop some honey balls out into a small bowl for each guest.

***Chef's Notes:***
These are a tradition from Christmas to Carnevale and St Joseph's Day. During those times of the year, keep at room temperature in a covered dish. If you don't want to fry the dough in oil, use lard or vegetable shortening.

## Biscotti con Pignoli / Pine Nut Cookies (or what to do with the egg whites left over from the zabaione recipe...)

108 Chewy almond paste cookies with pine nuts. This is a standard recipe. It should look like this anywhere ( any cookbook or website) you check. If it doesn't, then they are taking you for a ride.

Posted by: RondinellaMamma. Yield: 3 dozen cookies. Prep time: 1 hour.

---

8 ounces almond paste
1 cup sugar
2 egg whites (from large eggs)
3 ounces pine nuts

Crumble the almond paste into a mixing bowl and add the sugar. Then mix together until it is like a fine sand (if you have a heavy duty mixer, use a paddle to do this). Then add the egg whites to the almond paste and sugar and beat for about three minutes, until the mixture is thick and smooth. The mixture should hold its shape, it should NOT be liquid-y. If it is, add small amounts of almond paste to thicken it. Line cookie sheet with parchment paper and either put the almond paste mixture in a pastry bag and pipe out 1 – 1 ½ inch drops about an inch apart or drop it onto the parchment-lined cookie sheet by rounded teaspoons, also 1 – 1 ½ inches apart. Sprinkle the pine nuts onto the cookies and gently press them into the cookies. Heat the oven to 375 degrees F and bake the cookies for about 15 – 20 minutes or until the cookies are lightly browned. Once they are out of the oven, let them cool before removing the parchment. If it sticks to the cookies, lightly wet ( a spray bottle works well) the back of the paper and then gently peel it off the cookies.

***Chef's Notes:***
This is the part where MATH comes in! (Apologies in case anyone said there wouldn't be any.) This famous cookie has a very basic recipe which can be embiggened depending on how many cookies you wish to make. For every (approximately) 3 dozen cookies wanted, use the quantities listed above. This recipe can easily be doubled.

## Dove Chocolate Nut Butter Cookies

109 Easy, fabulous, can-be-awesome sandwich cookies. Derived from "Peanut Butter Drops" cookie recipe from the *Gluten-Free Gourmet* by Bette Hagman, published by Henry Holt & Co, 1990.

Posted by: Milady Webworker. Yield: about 2 dozen cookies. Prep time: 30 minutes.

---

2 eggs
1 cup nut butter
1 cup sugar
1 bag dark chocolate Dove candies

Preheat oven to 350 degrees F. Beat eggs. Add sugar and nut butter, and mix until thoroughly combined. Drop by small spoonfuls on ungreased cookie sheets. Place one unwrapped Dove chocolate in the middle of some or all of the cookies. For sandwich cookies leave half without chocolates. Bake in preheated oven 10 to 12 minutes. Cool on rack. For sandwich cookies place one plain cookie upside down on top of one chocolate cookie while still warm and press lightly. Makes about 2 dozen 2 inch cookies.

***Chef's Notes:***
You can think of this more as a formula than a recipe. For each egg use 1/2 cup each nut butter and sugar. After that there are many possibilities. We've made these with homemade or commercial peanut, almond or sunflower seed butter. A combination of granulated and brown sugars works well. You could even use milk chocolate Dove candies, but why would you? These store and travel well; individually wrapped cookies are reported to last a long time if lost in your bag. Otherwise, they are gone much too quickly.

## Oatmeal Crisps

110 Best oatmeal cookies ever created. Family recipe from who-knows-where.

Posted by: Tonestaple. Yield: 1 serving if you're me. Prep time: 30 minutes plus.

---

1 cup butter
1 cup brown sugar
1 cup granulated sugar
2 eggs
1 teaspoon vanilla extract
1 1/2 cups all-purpose flour
1 teaspoon salt
1 teaspoon baking soda
1/2 cup chopped walnuts
3 cups rolled oats

Cream butter & sugars. Stir in eggs and vanilla. Sift flour, salt, and soda together. Stir into mixture. Stir in walnuts and oats. Roll into tubes about 1½ inch in diameter. Wrap in waxed paper and refrigerate for at least two hours. Preheat oven to 375 degrees F. Slice cookies about ½ inch thick and lay out on cookie sheet. Bake for about 10 minutes. Remove to rack to cool.

### *Chef's Notes:*

Only communists ruin perfect oatmeal cookies with raisins. Also, it is a scientific fact that this is the best cookie dough ever and when you take the rolls out of the refrigerator to bake, you are required to cut off the irregular ends and devour them on the spot.

## Kristiana Kringle

111 A family favorite for decades. Almondy pastry for any occasion. Especially good for evening coffee after dinner or at breakfast.

Posted by: Thursby. Yield: 10 to 12 servings. Prep time: 15 minutes prep, 75 minutes bake and cool.

---

2 cups flour, divided
2 sticks (1 cup) butter, divided (one should be cold)
2 tablespoons plus 1 cup cold water
3 eggs
2 teaspoons sugar, plus additional for sprinkling on dough
1 teaspoon vanilla extract, divided
1 teaspoon almond extract, divided
1 cup powdered sugar
1 tablespoon butter
lightly toasted slivered almonds (optional)

Cut ½ cup cold butter into 1 cup flour till it resembles coarse corn meal (like you're making pie dough). Add enough cold water to hold the dough together, about 2 tablespoons. Divide in half and press onto parchment lined baking sheet in 14" x 3" strips. Lightly sprinkle with sugar. In a medium saucepan combine 1 cup water and 1/2 cup butter; heat to boiling point and remove from heat. Add 1 cup flour all at one time and mix till smooth. Add the eggs one at time mixing till thoroughly smooth. Add 2 teaspoons sugar, ½ teaspoon vanilla extract and 1/2 teaspoon almond extract mixing thoroughly. Pile evenly over strips using all the mixture and bake at 375 degrees F for 45 minutes till golden brown. Let cool and ice with powdered sugar combined with 1 tablespoon butter, 1/2 teaspoon vanilla extract and 1/2 teaspoon almond extract. For a little extra crunch, sprinkle with lightly toasted slivered almonds. Slice and enjoy. If you want a different flavor you may substitute almond extract for all vanilla, maple or anything else you may want to try.

## Haystacks

112 Easy and delicious, butterscotch and peanut butter on chow mein noodles. Father used to make them every Sunday. From North Alabama, but I suspect this or something similar is found everywhere.

Posted by: Moron Robbie. Yield: 40+ cookies. Prep time: 1+ hour.

---

1 1/2 cups butterscotch chips
1 cup peanut butter
1/2 of a 5-ounce can chow mein noodles
1/2 cup peanuts

Melt and mix the butterscotch and peanut butter together, by microwave or stove, just do it low and slow and stir often. Once it's melted you dump and stir in peanuts, then the chow mein noodles. Some will break and that's good. Don't worry if they all do. It won't matter. You can scoop them out with a spoon and dump them on wax paper on your counter to cool, or you can put the wax paper on something that you can slide into your fridge for them to be ready faster. I like them on the counter, personally, because they get really creamy and gooey when they've mostly set up. The fridge makes them harden too fast and you'll miss that window. I've tried it with Rice Krispies before, too, and it turned out pretty tasty. Experiment.

## Cornflake Crunchies

113 Cornflakes, sugar, peanut butter . . . yeah, that's about it. Another Sunday afternoon treat from my father.

Posted by: Moron Robbie. Yield: varies with size of cookies. Prep time: 25 minutes.

---

6 cups cornflakes (don't skimp)
1 cup corn syrup
1 cup sugar
1 cup peanut butter

Heat sugar and corn syrup over medium heat, stirring constantly, until it boils. Turn off the heat, add the peanut butter and stir some more. Slowly add the cornflakes, stirring constantly. Drop tablespoons (or larger) onto wax paper on counter to cool. Either creamy or crunchy peanut butter works.

## Shortbread Chocolate Chip Cookies

114 So good I got a marriage proposal from someone I had never met after he tasted these. Even though I'm only 29 per the AoSHQ Style Guide, I have had this recipe for over 35 years. It came from a family friend who had cut it out of a newspaper, who knows when.

Posted by: bluebell. Yield: about 6 dozen cookies. Prep time: 20 minutes.

---

2 cups butter, softened
2 cups powdered sugar
2 teaspoons vanilla
1/2 teaspoon salt (1 teaspoon if using unsalted butter)
4 1/2 cups flour
2 cups chocolate chips
1 cup chopped walnuts or pecans, optional

The butter must be very soft, but not melted. Cream the butter and powdered sugar, then blend in the vanilla and salt. Gradually stir in the flour. The dough will be stiff. Stir in the chocolate chips and the nuts, if using. Shape into 1" balls, and place them 2" apart on ungreased cookie sheets. Flatten with a fork to 1 1/2" rounds. Bake at 350 degrees F for about 15 minutes, until they get just the tiniest bit tan around the edges. Remove to cool on a rack.

### *Chef's Notes:*

The original recipe said to sprinkle the tops of the still-warm cookies with 3 tablespoons powdered sugar put through a strainer, but I have never done that. I do, however, put nuts in these cookies—usually pecans—unless I know someone has a nut allergy.

## Peanut Butter Chocolate Chip Cookies

115 Dedicated to CBD, so that he will take my name off the List o' Shame, and because he was a tremendous help with this cookbook project, but mostly so that he will take my

name off the List o' Shame. I have had this recipe hand-written on an index card in my recipe box for decades. I have no idea from whence it came, but I have never seen another recipe exactly like it.

Posted by: bluebell. Yield: 4 dozen cookies. Prep time: 20 minutes.

---

1 1/4 cups flour
3/4 teaspoon baking soda
1/2 teaspoon baking powder
1/4 teaspoon salt
3/4 cup peanut butter
1/2 cup butter, softened
1/2 cup sugar
1/2 cup packed brown sugar
1/2 teaspoon vanilla
1 egg
5 tablespoons milk (if necessary)
6 ounces (1 cup) chocolate chips

Preheat oven to 375 degrees F. Combine flour, baking soda, baking powder, and salt, then set aside. In a large bowl, combine peanut butter, butter, sugar, brown sugar, and vanilla, then beat until creamy. Beat in egg, then gradually add the flour mixture, mixing well. If dough seems too stiff, add milk, a tablespoon at a time, up to 5 tablespoons (I don't use the milk). Stir in chocolate chips. Drop by level tablespoons onto ungreased cookie sheets. Bake 10 to 12 minutes.

***Chef's Notes:***
CBD says you might need to chill the dough a bit before baking, if it's too soft. Listen to him. In spite of being a Yankees fan, he does know a thing or two about cooking.

## White Chip Orange Dream Cookies

116 Great cookies, from my grandma, Catherine.

Posted by: Farmer. Yield: 5 dozen cookies. Prep time: 15 minutes.

---

2 1/4 cups flour
3/4 teaspoon soda
1/2 teaspoon salt
1 cup butter, softened
1/2 cup sugar
1/2 cup brown sugar
1 egg
2 – 3 teaspoons grated fresh orange peel
2 cups white morsels

Combine flour, soda, and salt, set aside. Beat butter, sugar and brown sugar, then add egg and beat well. Add flour mixture and mix well. Add orange peel and white morsels, and blend. Drop by teaspoonfuls onto an ungreased cookie sheet. Bake at 350 degrees F for 10 – 12 minutes until edges are golden brown. Remove to racks and cool.

## Peppermint Chocolate Brownies

117 I bastardized some infantryman's recipe while my husband was stationed in Germany, and I was learning to cook.

Posted by: Jillybeans68    Yield: 1 serving if you have no self-control.    Prep time: 35 minutes.

---

2/3 cup unsweetened cocoa
2/3 cup shortening
2 cups white sugar
4 large eggs
1 teaspoon vanilla extract
1 1/4 cups all-purpose flour
1 teaspoon baking powder
1 teaspoon salt
1 cup or more crushed peppermint candy (optional)

Preheat oven to 350 degrees F. Grease 9 x 11 baking pan with Pam spray. Melt cocoa and shortening in large saucepan over medium heat, stirring over heat until shortening is mostly melted, then remove from heat. Stir the sugar into the saucepan, then add the eggs and vanilla to saucepan as well. In a separate bowl, mix the flour, salt and baking powder. Add dry ingredients into the saucepan. Once all ingredients are blended, spread into greased pan. For a special treat, you can add crushed peppermint over the top of the brownie batter. Bake for 25- 30 minutes. At 25 minutes, check to see if brownies are pulling away from the edges of the pan; if they are, remove from oven, and rest pan on baking rack to cool. Otherwise bake for the full 30 minutes. Remove pan and place on baking rack to cool. I prefer Penzeys' or King Arthur Flour's Double Dutch cocoa, but you can use any Dutch cocoa for baking.

## Coconut Milk Ice Cream

118 Easy keto non-dairy sugar-free frozen treat. Recipe is from my own kitchen. There are many versions of this on the internets, which I looked up later. Super-simple, obvious recipe.

Posted by: Emily. Yield: 4 moron servings. Prep time: 5 minutes.

---

1 can full fat coconut milk
1/2 cup berries of your choice
healthy sweetener such as stevia, to taste
dash lime or lemon juice

Put the berries in a bowl and mash with a fork. Add the can of coconut milk. If it has separated in the can (is a bit lumpy), microwave for a minute or two in a glass bowl. Add sweetener and lime or lemon juice to taste. Freeze.

***Chef's Notes:***
This makes good popsicles. Could be processed in an ice cream maker to keep ice crystals from forming. Or, just pour into a flat container and freeze. Modify by adding flavors of your choice instead of the berries and lime/lemon juice!

## Homemade Ice Cream

119 Better than Bluebell Homemade and that's saying a lot. Grandpa milked two cows: a Guernsey for milk to drink and a Jersey for the cream content for grandma's butter. We used the Jersey milk for this ice cream, too.

Posted by: Dave at Buffalo Roam. Yield: 1/2 a gallon is a serving, right? Prep time: 15 minutes.

---

6 eggs
3 cups sugar
1/2 teaspoon salt
1 tablespoon flour
3 cups condensed milk
1 tablespoon vanilla
1 quart milk

Beat the eggs, pour in everything except the quart of milk (for now) and mix well. Pour it into your old crank ice cream maker and fill with that reserve quart of milk to within 1-1/2" from the top. Put cracked ice and IC salt in the wooden IC maker and crank until it's stiff. It helps to have a small child sit on the ice cream maker while you crank it, especially if it is a grandchild. The old folks used to cover the whole top of the ice cream maker, ice and all, with a croaker sack so the ice cream would harden further. It was torture waiting. This is vanilla but fresh Fredericksburg peaches blended in is acceptable.

## Mandarin Orange Parfait

120 Mrs. Salty's dessert for nice people we host at home. From my wife's college roommate in (----) [date redacted as classified top secret].

Posted by: NaCly Dog. Yield: 4 – 6 servings. Prep time: 5 hours.

---

one 3-ounce package lemon gelatin (I use sugar free)
one pint vanilla ice cream
one 11-ounce can mandarin oranges (light syrup or own juice)

Dissolve gelatin in ½ cup boiling water. Soften ice cream in large bowl. Pour gelatin over ice cream and beat with electric mixer until smooth. Drain oranges; reserve 10 sections. Fold remaining oranges into gelatin mixture. Pour into serving bowls (parfait glasses). Top with orange sections. [She covers the top of the glasses with Saran Wrap, but not sure if this is needed.] Place in freezer. Remove from freezer 2 – 4 hours before serving in order to soften oranges. A easy-to-make hit every time. Long-handled spoons help with the presentation in parfait glasses.

## Almond-Crusted Chocolate Torte

121 Delicious and unique ice cream dessert. Always a red-letter day in my childhood when my mother made this. Recipe is from Peggy Card (aka dearly departed Cricketmom).

Posted by: Cricket. Yield: 12 servings. Prep time: 20 minutes prep time, plus minimum 4 hours freezing time.

---

1/2 cup butter
1 cup flour
1/2 cup sugar
1/2 cup chopped almonds
1 1/2 quarts chocolate ice cream (Breyers or other high quality)

1 cup whipping cream
1/4 cup golden rum (or 1 tablespoon rum flavoring)
1/2 teaspoon almond flavoring

Melt butter in large skillet. Stir in flour, sugar and almonds. Cook over medium heat until mixture is golden and crumbly (6 – 8 minutes). Reserve 3/4 cup crumb mixture. Pat remaining mixture into buttered 9-inch springform pan. Freeze 1 hour. Soften ice cream slightly in chilled large bowl. Beat whipping cream cream until soft peaks form. Gently fold rum and whipped cream into softened ice cream. Spoon into springform pan. Freeze for 1 hour. Sprinkle top with reserved crumb mixture. Return to freezer for a minimum of 2 hours. Can be made ahead and stored up to 2 weeks. Enjoy!

## Fresh Peach Ice Cream

122 Perfect for a gel-type freezer. This is wonderful with fresh blueberry and peach pound cake. Or by itself.

Posted by: Jane D'oh. Yield: 1 quart. Prep time: 15 minutes, plus overnight chill.

---

1 cup fresh (or frozen) peaches
3/4 cup sugar, divided
2 cups half-and-half
1 cup whipping cream
1/2 cup peach preserves
1/4 teaspoon almond extract (optional)

In a food processor, process peaches with 1/4 cup of the sugar. (I don't process too finely.) Refrigerate in an air-tight container. In a heavy 3-quart saucepan, combine remaining 1/2 cup sugar with half-and-half, whipping cream, and peach preserves. Bring to a simmer over medium heat. Remove from heat when the first bubbles begin to form around the edge of the pan. DO NOT let mixture boil. Remove from heat, add almond extract if desired (I use it—it enhances the flavor of the peaches), place in an airtight container, and refrigerate overnight. Add pureed peaches to chilled milk mixture and pour into a gel-type countertop freezer. Freeze according to manufacturer's directions. Ice cream will be soft. For firmer ice cream, place in the freezer for several hours or overnight.

# Easy Eclairs

123 Family reunion tomorrow? No biggie! You won't seem like an asshole if you bring these. My grandmother taught me this. No idea where she got it. Its like crack to small children and PMSing women.

Posted by: Mouseslayer. Yield: 20 servings? Cut them smaller and more can eat. Prep time: 10 minutes.

---

1 pound graham crackers
1 can? jar? idk what its called chocolate frosting for cakes
2 boxes French vanilla INSTANT pudding
3 cups milk, 2%. Like NORMAL people
1 8 oz tub? jar? Cool Whip, or generic

Get a 9x13 pan or two 9x9 pans. I prefer 9x9 pans; that way I can take one and eat the other at home. If you're at risk for diabetes use a 9x13 pan. Pour instant French vanilla pudding mixture into a large mixing bowl. Add 3 cups milks. Whisk rapidly. Whisk in the Cool Whip. Make one layer of graham crackers in your pan(s). Spoon 1/2 (1/4 if 2 pans) of your pudding/Cool Whip mixture into pan. Make another layer of graham crackers. Spoon the rest of the pudding mixture in. Make another layer of graham crackers. Microwave tub of frosting for like 1 minute 30 seconds. CAREFULLY pour frosting over top layer of graham crackers. That stuff's hot, so be careful. Angle the pan to make the frosting flow and cover all graham crackers. Don't try and use a spatula; you'll just fark up the crackers. Throw in fridge overnight.

***Chef's Notes:***
Graham is apparently spelled that way. Least my computer says so. I don't trust the thing.

# *Other*

## Killer Keto PB Fudge

124 Low sugar, high fat. I made it up.

Posted by: xanderphife. Yield: servings for 2 – 4 Morons. Prep time: 5 minutes.

---

2 scoops peanut butter
1/2 cup heavy whipping cream
Small handful chocolate chips

In a microwave safe container, combine ingredients. Microwave for 30 – 45 seconds on high, depending on appliance strength. Check to ensure chocolate is melted and mix together. Let stand 1 – 2 minutes and enjoy. It's super rich, super good. I love peanut butter!

## Coconut Candy

125 My mom's traditional coconut candy. My mom used to make this as a treat during our school holidays (when we were in Malaysia). It's a fun dessert to make with the kids (lots of stirring!).

Posted by: IC. Yield: 10 – 15 servings. Prep time: 60 – 80 minutes.

---

3 cups finely grated fresh coconut
1 cup sugar
1 cup condensed milk
1 teaspoon butter
1/2 teaspoon pink food coloring
2 teaspoons essence of vanilla (vanilla extract)

Mix all ingredients in a pot over low to medium heat. Stir well. Keep stirring (continuously) until contents stick together and sugar crystallizes (this would take about an hour or so). Line a square baking pan with butter or non stick liner. Spread contents into pan and even it out to about an inch in thickness by pressing on it with a ladle or any other flat serveware. While it is still hot, cut into bite-size squares. Once cooled, it can be stored in a container. This is a sweet coconut dessert but you can modify it to reduce the amount of coconut and/or sugar and even the color!

## MorePappy's Fudge

126 Irresistible chocolate peanut butter fudge. This is my great-grandfather's fudge recipe. He used to make it every year during the holidays and after he passed away, my mom and I worked for years to figure out the technique to get the texture right. The consistency is different than a usual gooey and soft fudge, it is more dry and crumbly and just melts on your tongue.

Posted by: DangerGirl33 and Her 1.21 Gigawatt SanityProd (tm). Yield: depends on how much fudge one Moron can eat. Prep time: 20 minutes (plus cooling time).

---

1 1/2 cups sugar
1/4 cup unsalted butter
5 ounces evaporated milk
1/4 teaspoon salt
7-ounce jar marshmallow creme (fluff)
12-ounce bag semi-sweet chocolate chips
1 teaspoon vanilla extract
16-ounce jar natural peanut butter (oil poured off)

Line a 9x13 inch baking pan with parchment paper or very lightly grease pan with cooking oil. Combine sugar, butter, evaporated milk, salt and marshmallow creme in a heavy saucepan. Bring to a boil over medium-high heat while stirring. Cook for five minutes, stirring constantly, making sure mixture is constantly bubbling. It will turn a light golden color. Remove mixture from heat and stir in chocolate chips and vanilla extract until completely combined. Add peanut butter and swirl into the chocolate mixture. Pour into prepared pan and chill until cooled, then cut into squares.

***Chef's Notes:***
It is important to pour the oil off the top of the peanut butter to achieve the proper texture. You can also completely incorporate the peanut butter into the fudge mixture. We like to keep it as a swirl, so you get parts where there is more peanut butter flavor.

## Aloha Snackbar Jello Salad

127 Peaches and cream layered salad. From *Taste of the South* Magazine.

Posted by: Jane D'oh. Yield: 12 servings. Prep time: 15 minutes, plus at least 5 hours refrigerated.

---

2 (3 ounce) packages peach-flavored gelatin
1 1/2 cups boiling water
1 (29 ounce) can sliced peaches in heavy syrup, drained and juice reserved, finely chopped
1 (16 ounce) container sour cream

2 (8 ounce) containers peach-flavored yogurt
1 (16 ounce) container frozen, non-dairy whipped topping, thawed
Garnish: sliced peaches, toasted sliced almonds

In a medium bowl, combine gelatin and boiling water; stir until gelatin is dissolved completely. Add reserved peach syrup and sour cream. Whisk until smooth. Add peaches to gelatin mixture, stirring to combine. Pour mixture into an ungreased 13 x 9 x 2 inch pan. Refrigerate until set, at least 4 hours. In another medium bowl, fold together yogurt and whipped topping until well combined. Gently spread yogurt mixture over gelatin layer. Refrigerate for 1 hour. Garnish with sliced peaches and toasted almonds if desired.

## Fresh Blueberry Galette

128 So easy a moron can do it! Cut this out of a cooking magazine years ago.

Posted by: Jane D'oh. Yield: 6 moron servings. Prep time: 45 minutes.

---

1 pound (3 cups) fresh blueberries
2 tablespoons cornstarch
1 tablespoon fresh lemon zest
1 tablespoon fresh lemon juice
1/4 teaspoon ground cinnamon
1/4 teaspoon salt
1/2 cup, plus 1 teaspoon sugar
1 9-inch refrigerated pie crust (from one 15-ounce package)
1 tablespoon cold, unsalted butter
1 large egg, lightly beaten

Preheat oven to 425 degrees F and place rack in middle position. Line a large baking sheet with buttered foil, or use Silpat or parchment. Stir together blueberries, cornstarch, zest, juice, cinnamon, salt, and 1/2 cup sugar in a large bowl until combined. Unfold pie crust onto baking sheet. Spoon blueberry mixture onto center of dough, leaving a 1 1/2" border around edge. Fold edge over 1 inch, pleating dough. Dot filling with butter pieces. Lightly brush dough with some beaten egg and sprinkle with remaining teaspoon of sugar. Bake until filling is bubbling and pastry is golden, about 25 – 30 minutes. Cool slightly on baking sheet on a rack. Serve warm. Delish served with lemon sorbet or vanilla ice cream.

## Apple Blackberry Cobbler

129 September's perfect dessert. My mom made this one up after sending my Sis and I out to pick the fruit. In retrospect it was as much to get us out of the house as it was to have delicious dessert.

Posted by: tms. Yield: 5 moron servings. Prep time: 15 minutes, plus 25 minutes bake time.

---

1/2 cup butter
2 1/2 cups brown sugar, divided
2 cups all-purpose flour
4 teaspoons baking powder
1 teaspoon cinnamon
1/2 teaspoon ginger
1/4 teaspoon cloves
dash black pepper
1 teaspoon vanilla
1 1/2 cups milk
2 1/2 cups diced apples
3 cups blackberries

Preheat oven to 350 degrees F. Melt butter into bottom of a 9 x 13 cake pan. In mixing bowl stir together 2 cups brown sugar, flour, baking powder, vanilla, milk and spices. Pour onto melted butter. Coat fruit mixture with remaining sugar and pour on top of batter, evenly distributing across pan. Bake until batter crisps through the fruit and is golden brown. Serve with ice cream or whip cream. Recipe can be used with any ratio of apples to blackberries. A tart, crisp apple is preferred.

## Aunt Camille's Almond Cake Squares

130 Very rich dessert. This is the special dessert of my mother-in-law's sister. She was a terrific lady and a very good cook. This cake is extremely rich. Serve with coffee or tea. Excellent for baby showers or the like. It is like eating almond candy mixed with butter. Yum.

Posted by: Lester. Yield: many. Prep time: 30 minutes.

---

1 cup butter
3/4 cup sugar
1 large egg
1/2 cup almond paste
1 teaspoon almond extract
2 cups sifted flour
1/4 cup sliced almonds

Beat softened butter and sugar with mixer until fluffy. Separate the egg retaining the white. Add the yolk to the butter mixture and combine. Add the almond paste to the mixture. Since it is solid add slices of it to the mixture to help it combine better. Add extract. On low speed add in the flour by 1/2 cups until it is all mixed in and only slightly lumpy. Take the mixture and press into a 8x8 pan. Beat the egg white lightly, brush on the top of the mixture in the pan, and add the scattering of sliced almonds. Bake at 350 degrees F for 30 minutes until lightly browned. Let cool completely. Cut into 1 ½ inch squares. Note: 1/2 cup almond paste is roughly a half of an 8-ounce package of almond paste. Do not use marzipan. This recipe can be doubled very well.

## Heavenly Salad

131 NOT your grandma's whipped-cream-and-canned-fruit salad. My family's traditional Christmas dessert, which my grandmother made for decades. She got the recipe from a woman in her town who catered on the side. Every bridal shower in town featured this lady's chicken salad, hot biscuits and Heavenly Salad.

Posted by: Dr Alice Serves Lots - 12 or more Prep time: 90 minutes

---

1 large can diced pineapple
1 large can white Royal Anne cherries in juice
2 cups mini marshmallows
½ - ¾ cup broken pecans
¼ - ½ cup slivered almonds
3/4 cup whipping cream
3 egg yolks
one or more lemons, juiced
1/4 cup flour
few grains salt
1/4 cup sugar

Drain pineapple and cherries, keeping the juice. Seed cherries if needed, and set fruit aside. For the cooked dressing: combine 1 cup each of the cherry and pineapple juices with lemon juice, beaten egg yolks, and flour which has been mixed with sugar. Whisk till smooth, cook in double boiler till thick. Taste and add more lemon juice if needed. It should be moderately tart to compensate for sweetness of the marshmallows. When thick, cool thoroughly and combine with whipped cream. Combine fruits, marshmallows and nuts in large bowl with completed dressing; cover and refrigerate 24 hours. Stir once or twice during this time.

### *Chef's Notes:*

This takes a little work but can be made in advance and lasts several days. It's the dressing that makes this salad. The contrast of tastes and textures is remarkable. Please use fresh lemon juice; it makes a difference.

## Chilled Strawberry Soup

132 Easy and contains alcohol, like many 'ettes. This was from *Taste of Home* magazine a very long time ago.

Posted by: nerdygirl    Yield: 2 servings.    Prep time: 5 minutes.

---

1 pint hulled strawberries
1/3 cup white wine
2 tablespoons sugar

Put ingredients into food processor or blender. Puree until smooth. Put into bowls and chill.

## Lemon Posset

133 Best dessert ever! From *Cook's Illustrated.* Recipe by Annie Petito.

Posted by: Harry Oburn.    Yield: 6 servings.    Prep time: 30 minutes.

---

3 cups heavy cream
1 cup sugar
1 ½ tablespoons lemon zest
9 tablespoons lemon juice

Pour cream into a saucepan. Measure depth of cream with a ruler. The cream is going to be reduced to original volume (3 cups) and the ruler will be used to measure when this is done. Add sugar and lemon zest and bring to a boil over medium heat while stirring with spoon. Once it is at a boil, continue boiling and stirring until mixture is reduced to 3 cups (or original depth as measured by the ruler). Depending on the size of the saucepan, you may need to reduce the heat while boiling to avoid boilovers. After reducing to original volume, remove from heat and stir in lemon juice. Let sit for 20 minutes and strain to remove lemon zest. Pour into ramekins and refrigerate uncovered for at least 3 hours. On serving, let sit at room temperature for 10 minutes before serving.

## Mom's Peanut Butter Fudge

> 134 Gotta love a recipe with only four ingredients. Mom made this during the holidays from around 1980 until her arthritic hands prevented her.

Posted by: Cicero Kaboom! Kid. Yield: enough for a family. Prep time: 30 minutes.

---

4 cups granulated sugar
2 cups smooth peanut butter
1 cup whole milk
1 13-ounce jar marshmallow cream
1 – 2 cups very coarsely chopped walnuts, optional

Cook sugar and milk to soft ball stage. QUICKLY add peanut butter and marshmallow cream and nuts, if using. Stir it fast while still hot! You will need a he-man wooden spoon to stir this. Pour into a large square cake pan and let it cool. Cut into squares with a sharp spatula. Keeps well between layers of wax paper in a Tupperware.

## Peanut Butter Fudge

> 135 Best. Fudge. Ever. My grammy's famous fudge recipe. I still make it every year to include in my Christmas cookie baskets.

Posted by: shinypie. Yield: 5 Moron servings. Prep time: 10 minutes.

---

2 cups sugar
3 tablespoons butter
1 cup evaporated milk
1 cup mini marshmallows
1 1/3 cups creamy peanut butter
1 teaspoon vanilla

Bring sugar, butter, and milk to a rolling boil over medium heat, stirring constantly. Boil for 5 minutes. Remove from heat and add marshmallows, peanut butter, and vanilla. Stir till marshmallows are completely melted. Pour onto greased baking sheet. Cool completely before slicing. I usually use a 9 x 13 baking sheet but you can go smaller if you like thicker fudge.

## Mom's Five-Cup Old-Fashioned Heavenly Hash

136 A light dessert or side dish. My mother and her mother made this recipe for decades. I'm not sure where it originated. When I was young, my mom and her mother served this for dessert on Christmas Eve, a meal that was light, in advance of the BIG DAY!

Posted by: Ladylibertarian.    Yield: 8 – 12 servings.    Prep time: 10 minutes.

---

11 ounce can mandarin oranges, well drained
16 ounce can pineapple chunks, well drained
1 cup flaked coconut
1 cup miniature marshmallows
1 cup sour cream

Mix all ingredients. Cover and chill in refrigerator for at least two hours. Keeps well.

## Gelato allo Zabaione

137 Delicious Marsala wine custard ice cream, but without using an ice cream machine. In my family, my grandmother, mother and aunts used any excuse to feed their children and husbands egg custard because it's good for you! If it had Marsala wine in it, they reasoned that it's even better for you! Usually zabaione is served warm, but this is a way to enjoy it in the hot summer months. (Who am I kidding, we make it like this in the winter, too.)

Posted by: RondinellaMamma.    Yield: servings for 8 Morons.    Prep time: 2 hours (allows for cooling).

---

6 egg yolks from large eggs
6 tablespoons sugar
3/4 cup Marsala wine
2 cups heavy cream

Use a double boiler: bring the water in the bottom pot to a simmer. In the top part of the double boiler (away from the bottom pot), add egg yolks and sugar and whisk them until they are very thick, creamy and lemony-looking (about 5 minutes). Now place the top of the double boiler over the bottom pot of simmering water; add the wine to the sugar and egg mixture; and whisk until it is thick like a hot custard. Take it off the heat and let it cool. Whip the cream until stiff peaks form. Take the cooled wine custard and fold it gently into the whipped cream. Put this mixture into a covered container and pop it into the freezer for at least 4 hours or overnight. To serve: let the frozen zabaione sit out for a few minutes (5?) and then scoop it out as if it were ice cream and serve it with some homemade cookies. Serve smallish portions as it is a very rich dessert.

***Chef's Notes:***
This recipe has a strong Marsala kick. Regular zabaione uses much less so if you are wary about using the entire 3/4 cup, you can cut back the wine to 1/2 cup.

## 'Nanner Pudding

138 'Nanner Pudding, duh. Adapted from Alton Brown's recipe for refrigerated banana pudding on foodnetwork.com.

Posted by: DangerGirl33 and Her 1.21 Gigawatt SanityProd (tm). Yield: 8 – 10 servings.
Prep time: 3 hours.

---

3/4 cup granulated sugar
3 tablespoons cornstarch
1/4 teaspoon kosher salt
2 large eggs
1 large egg yolk
2 cups whole milk
3 tablespoons unsalted butter, cut into 6 pieces and chilled
1/2 teaspoon vanilla extract
3 ripe bananas, peeled and sliced into 1/4-inch rounds
1 tablespoon freshly squeezed lemon juice
2 tablespoons granulated sugar
1 cup heavy whipping cream, very cold
45 – 60 vanilla wafers

Combine the 3/4 cup of sugar, cornstarch and salt in a 3-quart saucepan. Add the eggs and egg yolk and whisk to combine. Add the milk and whisk until well combined, about 30 seconds. Cook over medium heat (it will bubble but shouldn't hard boil) until the mixture becomes thickened. Remove from the heat and whisk in the butter, 1 piece at a time, being sure each piece is fully incorporated before adding the next. Whisk in the vanilla extract. Cover the surface of the pudding with a round piece of parchment and refrigerate 2 hours. Toss the banana slices with the lemon juice in a small bowl and set aside. Spread a small amount of pudding in the bottom of a bowl or deep dish. Cover with a layer of vanilla wafers, followed by a layer of banana slices. Spoon 1/3 of the remaining pudding on top of the bananas and repeat, ending with a layer of pudding. Put the whipping cream and 2 tablespoons sugar into a large bowl and beat with a mixer on high just until stiff peaks form. Spoon the whipped cream over the top of the pudding and spread to cover completely. Top with some vanilla wafers. Refrigerate for 30 minutes before serving. Store, covered, in the refrigerator for up to 3 days.

# Bread

*As any poor baker should know*
*Desperation can lay you down low*
*You might say at the least*
*West is west, yeast is yeast*
*I only did it 'cause I kneaded the dough*

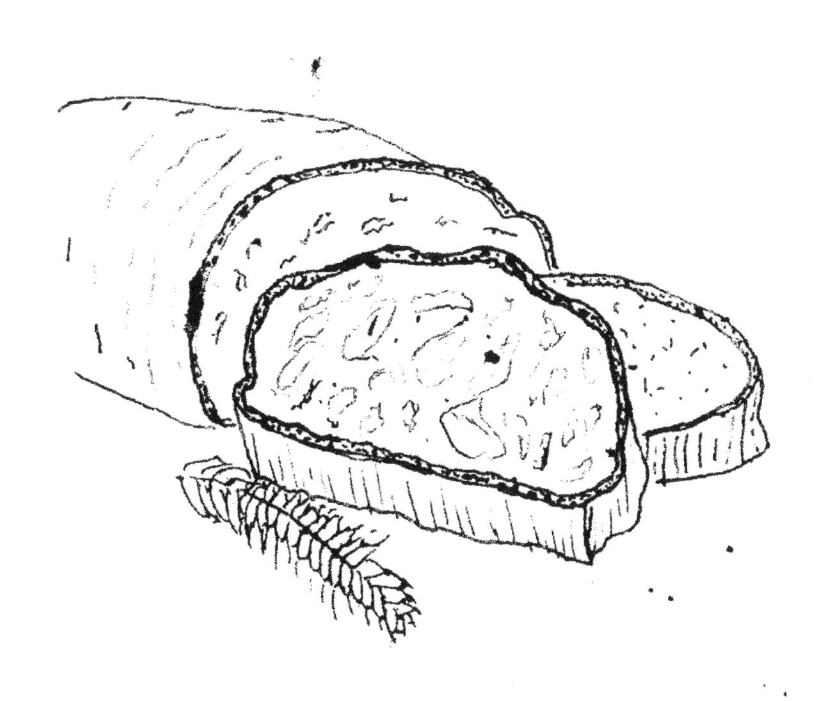

## Tonypete's Semolina Sesame Bread

139 Semolina bread with sesame seeds—a Tonypete family recipe.

Posted by: Tonypete. Yield: one big loaf. Prep time: 3 hours.

---

2 1/2 teaspoons active yeast
1/4 cup warm water, 110 degrees F or less
1 tablespoon olive oil
1 cup water
2 1/2 cups durum wheat or semolina flour
3 teaspoons salt
1/3 cup sesame seeds

In a measuring cup dissolve the yeast in the ¼ cup warm water. Let it stand until creamy, about 10 minutes. Whisk the olive oil and the cup of water together. Put the flour and salt in the bowl of a food processor with the knife blade. Pulse 2 or 3 times to mix the dry ingredients. With the machine running pour in the yeast mixture and then the water/oil mixture. Process for about 45 seconds after the dough comes together. Knead on a floured surface until the dough feels smooth. (Or you can make the dough by hand in a large bowl. Put the wet ingredients and the salt in a large bowl and mix in the flour a cup at a time until the dough forms. Knead it until the dough is soft and silky smooth.)

Form the dough into a ball and put it in a lightly oiled large bowl. Cover tightly with plastic wrap and then a kitchen towel. Set aside in a warm place to rise until double in size, 60 – 90 minutes. Press the dough down and put it on a floured work surface. Flatten the ball with your fingers to form a rectangle. Tightly roll the dough to form a cylinder; the loaf should be about 10 inches long and 6 inches in diameter. Wet the top of each loaf, sprinkle with sesame seeds and press the seeds in with your fingers. Cover loosely with plastic wrap and then a towel to keep the loaf from drying out. Set aside to double in size, 60 – 90 minutes.

Sprinkle corn meal on a baking sheet. Place the loaf on the sheet and make 3 slashes on the top with a sharp knife. Slide the loaf onto a baking stone or place the sheet on the stone. (If you do not have a stone, put the sheet on the lowest rack of the oven.) Spray the loaf several times with water. The moisture helps the bread expand before the crust sets.

Place in oven preheated to 425 degrees F. After about 10 minutes reduce the heat to 400 degrees F and bake in the dry oven until the loaf is golden brown and sounds hollow when you knock on it, about 25 – 30 minutes. Cool loaf on a wire rack for 20 minutes before slicing. Butter while still warm.

## Mrs. Ibguy's Acclaimed Challah

140 Outstanding challah for all occasions. This is Mrs. Ibguy's original recipe.

Posted by: ibguy. Yield: 1 braided loaf. Prep time: 2 hours (plus resting) (dough resting, notmoron's) (although . . .).

---

1 cup warm water
3 large eggs (divided)
1/3 cup olive oil
1/4 cup white sugar
1/4 teaspoon salt
3 1/2 cups bread flour
2 1/2 teaspoons instant yeast
1 tablespoon sesame and/or poppy seeds

Add water, 2 eggs, and the rest of the ingredients except seeds to bread machine in the order listed. Set machine for pizza mixing (mine is a Cuisinart, and this setting mixes and goes through the first rise in 1 hour 30 minutes). Watch mixing of ingredients to assure a smooth dough. Add more water or flour to adjust if necessary. Remove dough from machine. Punch down to deflate, place in an oiled bowl and turn to coat. Cover with plastic wrap and refrigerate overnight.

Preheat oven to 170 degrees F for last rise. Grease baking sheet thoroughly. Remove dough from bowl and cut into three equal pieces. Roll into foot-long ropes. Braid, folding ends under and pinching to secure. Place braided loaf on cookie sheet. Put in oven, turning off oven afterward for last rising. Set timer for 30 minutes.

At the end of last rising, remove bread from oven. Preheat oven to 350 degrees F. Lightly beat remaining egg in a small bowl. Brush risen loaf with egg and top with seeds. Bake in preheated oven on the middle of rack for 22 minutes. Loaf will be thoroughly brown and risen. Remove from baking sheet and cool thoroughly before slicing. Loaf freezes well if wrapped in plastic wrap and aluminum foil tightly.

### *Chef's Notes:*
For the bread machine step, you could—instead—mix in a mixer with a dough hook, then knead with the dough hook for 15 minutes.

## Super Easy French Farmhouse Bread

141 Someone will think you are a gourmet. From my sister Robin.

Posted by: tcn. Yield: 1 to 8, depending upon hunger level. Prep time: 18 – 24 hours.

---

1 pound flour
1/2 teaspoon salt
1/4 teaspoon yeast
1 3/4 cups cool water

Mix dry things together in a big bowl. Mix in water with a fork. It will be very sticky. Cover the bowl with a towel and let it sit for 18 to 24 hours. During the time it sits, occasionally fold the dough over on itself with a rubber spatula, once an hour or less, and it should take no more than 30 seconds. If you forget or go to sleep, no worries. It isn't necessary, just good practice.

When you want to bake it, preheat a big cast iron pot or a baking stone in a 450 degree F oven for about 20 minutes. Then rub a little butter in the pot, and dump in the dough. Beauty is not a virtue here—just dump it in. Put the lid on (or a metal bowl over it, if on a stone) and bake it for 30 minutes at 450 F. Then take the lid or bowl off, and bake it for 25 more minutes. If you double the recipe, then add about 5 minutes. When it is fresh from the oven, it will be sticky to cut. If you let it sit the moisture will even out and make it easier to slice.

***Chef's Notes:***
I cook this in a round glass casserole dish and it turns out just fine. Also, don't stick with white flour—add some other stuff once in a while. You can also stud it with baked garlic cloves right before baking, or do any other fancy-ass stuff to it. It is hard to ruin this bread.

## Lace Curtain Irish Soda Bread

142 Upscale version of the traditional pan. Concocted by my Gran, Bridget McMahon, because, "Sure now we're Americans we can afford butter and sugar."

Posted by: IrishEi. Yield: 1 loaf. Prep time: 5 minutes.

---

3 cups all-purpose flour
1/2 cup sugar
1 tablespoon baking powder
1 teaspoon baking soda
1/4 pound (one stick) butter, melted
1 cup raisins (optional)
1 cup buttermilk

Preheat oven to 375 degrees F. If you haven't got a traditional stoneware baking pan, grease and flour an 8" cake pan. Sift flour, sugar, baking powder, and baking soda together in a large bowl. Add melted butter and blend as much as possible. Raisins may be added at this time if desired. Add buttermilk a little at a time and mix until a sticky dough forms.

With floured hands, shape into a ball and press gently into prepared pan. Dip a serrated knife into flour, and cut a cross about 1/4" deep into top of the loaf. Bake for 40 to 50 minutes until toothpick inserted in the middle comes out clean, and loaf sounds hollow when tapped.

### *Chef's Notes:*
Do not overwork the dough! It will be sticky and messy.

## Oatbread

> 143 This one'll kick your ass. Got this from my Czech grandmother. It's awesome.

Posted by: harbqll. Yield: 1 loaf. Prep time: an hour I guess?

---

1 1/2 cups warm water
1 packet dry yeast
2 tablespoons honey
1 1/2 cups rolled oats, or quick steel cut oats, or a combination of the two
2 1/2 to 3 cups all purpose flour (feel free to use some oat flour here too)
1 tablespoon salt
2 tablespoons butter, actual real butter, how many times do I have to say it?
1/3 cup dates, diced
1/3 cup candied orange peel, diced
1/3 cup apple, diced
some coarse oats, for topping

Mix warm water, yeast and honey in a large bowl. Allow to do its thing for about 5 minutes. Add oats, 1 cup flour, salt, and butter. Combine thoroughly, then add fruit. Work mixture until evenly distributed. Gradually add remaining flour until you have a ball of dough. Turn out the dough on a floured countertop, and knead for about 5 minutes. You want a ball that bounces back when poked. Place in a greased bowl and cover with a dish towel. Allow to rise until doubled in size.

Punch down and divide in two. Roll both into loaves of desired shape, wet the tops, and sprinkle with rolled oats, or dip into a dish of oats. Score the tops with a sharp blade. Allow to rise again until doubled in size. Bake at 400 degrees F for about 30 minutes, until golden brown. Allow to cool 10 minutes (assuming you can contain yourself that long) then devour. Serve with apple butter, or just butter.

## Best White Bread Ever

144 Better than the spongy stuff; also better than the artisan stuff. This is the "Basic White Bread" from the 1974 edition of *The Joy of Cooking* with my own (slight) variations.

Posted by: Annalucia. Yield: 2 one-pound loaves. Prep time: it varies.

---

2 cups water, milk, or a mixture of the two
2 tablespoons butter
2 teaspoons yeast
1 1/2 teaspoons salt
2 tablespoons sugar
6 cups (roughly) King Arthur Bread Flour, or similar

Combine water/milk, butter and sugar in a saucepan; heat and mix until the butter melts. Set aside to cool until lukewarm (about 100 degrees F). Add yeast and 1 cup flour; combine and let stand for about 10 minutes. Then add salt and the rest of the flour, and keep kneading (either by hand or in a stand mixer) until the texture is firm and no longer sticky, but not dry or lumpy. Cover with clean cloth, set in some mildly warm place (e.g., an oven that hasn't been turned on, or an ordinary kitchen counter in bright weather) and let rise for an hour or so.

Punch down, divide in half, give each loaf an extra knead to smooth it out. Place each in a greased 8 ½ x 4 ½ inch loaf pan, cover and let rise until the tops of the loaves are just starting to stick out of the pan. Give each loaf a slash or two on the surface (this encourages "ovenspring," or a good rise at the beginning of baking) and bake at 350 degrees F for about 50 minutes. Flip baked loaves out onto a cooling rack, and try to let them cool down before you tear into them.

Chef's Notes:
The original recipe called for all-purpose flour, but I prefer it with higher-protein bread flour—it makes a firmer loaf. Yeast is persnickety. If the liquid is too cold, it won't activate; if it's too hot, the yeast will be killed and you won't get a rise. Aim for about 100 degrees F—if it feels slightly warm to the touch, that's what you want. Milk makes a tender loaf; water makes a crustier one (as in French bread). You pick.

# Cheddar Beer Bread

145 This is the delicious bread served with the Asiago Cheese Dip at the Rock Bottom Brewery in Arlington, VA. This bread is especially fantastic when toasted. Along with the Asiago Cheese Dip, this is our attempt to recreate these appetizers at home.

Posted by: WitchDoktor, AKA VA GOP Sucks. Yield: 4 mini loaves. Prep time: a while.

---

2 1/2 cups beer (light lager works well)
4 1/2 cups flour
1 teaspoon baking powder
1/2 cup sugar
pinch salt
4 tablespoons chopped green onions
1 1/2 to 2 cups shredded cheddar cheese

Preheat oven to 325 degrees F. Lightly grease 4 mini loaf pans. Pour beer into a large bowl and add half the flour, mixing well. In another bowl, add the baking powder, sugar, and salt with the other half of the flour and blend completely. Add this mixture to the beer/flour mixture and blend. Add in the green onions and cheese. Divide the dough between the four loaf pans. Bake for one hour or until the bread is lightly browned—you may need to bake a bit longer depending on your oven. Let bread cool completely and remove from loaf pans. Do not wrap loaves until completely cooled or it will sour. Serve warm or as toasted slices, especially with the asiago cheese dip (see Appetizer chapter for recipe).

# *Fruits and Nuts*

## Honey Bread

146 A sweet and spiced quick bread from *The Fanny Farmer Cookbook*, 1979 edition.

Posted by: right wing yankee. Yield: 1 loaf. Prep time: 80 to 90 minutes.

---

2 cups white flour
1 teaspoon baking powder
1 teaspoon baking soda
1 teaspoon salt
1/2 teaspoon cinnamon
1 teaspoon ginger ground
1/2 cup honey
1 egg, slightly beaten
1 cup milk or light cream

Preheat the oven to 350 degrees F and butter a loaf pan. Combine dry ingredients in a large bowl, then add honey, egg, and milk (or cream if you choose). Beat with an electric beater for about 20 minutes (if you skimp on the amount of time, the bread with be a bit tough). Pour batter into the pan and bake for 45 to 50 minutes, until a toothpick inserted into the center comes out clean. The top will rise unevenly and form deep cracks during baking. Remove from pan and cool on a wire rack. Best served warm with butter.

***Chef's Notes:***
This is not a 'pretty' bread—as stated in the directions, it will rise unevenly, making a loaf that looks like a mountain. But the taste makes up for its odd appearance.

## Dildo's Banana Bread

147 It's bread, made from bananas and other shit. Duh. Modified beyond all recognition from somebody whose name I have forgotten.

Posted by: CharlieBrown'sDildo. Yield: 1 loaf. Prep time: 5 minutes.

---

4 – 5 overripe bananas
1 cup granulated sugar
2 extra-large eggs
1 teaspoon vanilla extract
3/4 cup (1 1/2 sticks) unsalted butter (melted and cooled)
2 cups all-purpose flour
1 teaspoon kosher salt

Preheat oven to 350 degrees F. Butter a 9 by 5-inch loaf pan. With an electric mixer, or even better, a stand mixer fitted with a whisk, whip the bananas and sugar together for a few minutes on the highest speed that won't splatter banana on your ceiling; the goal is to blend the sugar thoroughly into the bananas and get some loft into the mixture. Slow the speed to medium-low and add the eggs and vanilla; mix for 30 seconds or so and then slowly (especially if you didn't have time to allow it to cool) add the butter. Mix in the dry ingredients at low speed for a few seconds, just until you can't see any dry flour. Using a spatula, scrape the sides and bottom of the bowl down and finish mixing by hand.

Pour the batter into the buttered loaf pan. Whack the pan on the counter and then give it a bit of a shake until the batter is level. Place the pan on a baking sheet to catch any overflow and bake for about 1 hour and 10 minutes. "About" is the important word here. After about an hour take a quick peek at the loaf. If it looks wet at the top then bake it for a few more minutes. Just make sure not to overcook it.

I actually don't like banana bread very much, but it is positively awful when it's overcooked and dry. I make this for the little brats, who seem to devour it, especially when it is slightly underdone. They like banana bread more than they like raw bananas, so every time I buy bananas they carefully do not eat the last four, hoping that I will make this crap. It works. I hate being manipulated by children.

This also works fantastically as muffins. Use paper baking cups in the muffin tin and decrease the cooking time to about 30 minutes. And remember, the word about means about.

## Pumpkin Bread

148 Is it bread or is it a cake? Who cares, it's delicious! Got this recipe from a work friend ~25 years ago. Friend would return from home with loaves of her mom's pumpkin bread to share.

Posted by: Lizzy. Yield: 1 loaf. Prep time: 1 hour 45 minutes.

---

2 1/4 cups flour
2 teaspoons baking powder
2 teaspoons baking soda
1/2 teaspoon salt
1/2 teaspoon cinnamon

1 1/2 cups sugar
3/4 cup vegetable oil
3 eggs
1 cup canned pumpkin
1/2 cup chocolate chips

Preheat oven to 350 degrees F. Grease and flour a tube pan. Mix together the flour, baking powder, baking soda, salt and cinnamon. In a separate bowl, mix together the oil and sugar. Beat in eggs one at a time, then mix in the pumpkin. Slowly mix in the flour mixture, and then add the chocolate chips. Pour the batter into the tube pan and bake for 1 hour 15 minutes.

### *Chef's Notes:*

You can also add chopped nuts.

## Punkin' Bread

149 Just like Mamaw's. It's my recipe, but Mamaw's was very similar. She baked hers in one-pound coffee cans.

Posted by: Cicero Kaboom! Kid.    Yield: 2 loaves.    Prep time: 1 hour plus.

---

2 cups all-purpose flour
1 teaspoon baking powder
1 teaspoon baking soda
3/4 teaspoon salt
2 eggs
1/2 cup or just less vegetable oil
1/3 cup water
1 teaspoon vanilla extract
3/4 teaspoon cinnamon
1/2 teaspoon nutmeg, ground or fresh grated
1 cup packed brown sugar
2 cups pumpkin*
1/2 cup chopped pecans (optional)
1/2 cup golden raisins (optional)

Mix flour with soda, baking powder and salt. Set aside. Whisk eggs, oil, water in a large bowl. Add spices, vanilla and sugar. Beat well. Add pumpkin, mixing well. Stir dry ingredients into batter. Fold in nuts and raisins, if using. Pour into 2 greased 8 x 4 x 3 loaf pans or muffin tins filling half-way to top. Bake at 350 degrees F for an hour (loaf pans) or until it tests done with a toothpick (no goop sticks to it when inserted in the middle). Cool on racks before slicing.

### *Chef's Notes:*

* Pumpkin: slice, peel and cube a real one. Barely cover with water, add a little salt and bring to a boil. Cook just a minute or so until tender. Drain and mash. Any orange-fleshed squash will do. Canned pumpkin is just perfectly fine.

## Mom's Banana Nut Bread

150 Banana bread baked with Mom's love! This recipe is from Mom.

Posted by: Mrs. Mis. Hum. Yield: 1 loaf. Prep time: 10 minutes to prep; 1 hour to bake.

---

1 cup sugar
2 eggs
1/2 cup butter
1 teaspoon baking soda
Dash salt
2 cups flour (all-purpose)
2 tablespoons buttermilk
3 large bananas
1 cup walnuts (chopped)

Combine sugar, eggs, butter and stir well. Sift together flour, baking soda and salt and add to first mixture. Add buttermilk and walnuts. Add mashed bananas last of all. Bake at 375 degrees F for 1 hour.

## Grandma Schmidt's Old-Fashioned Stollen

151 The classic German Christmas bread! My dear Grandma Schmidt was born in Milwaukee in 1904; didn't learn to speak English until she was 9. Her family always had made stollen, as did most German families. This recipe comes from a Wisconsin Electric Power Company holiday cookbook. for employees.

Posted by: Tom Servo. Yield: 3 loaves. Prep time: 1 hour + rising time.

---

2 packages active dry yeast
1/4 cup warm water
1 1/2 cups whole milk
1/2 cups sugar
1 1/2 teaspoons salt
3/4 cup butter
2 cups + 4 cups sifted all-purpose flour
3 eggs, beaten
1/2 teaspoon ground cardomom
1/2 cup seedless dark raisins
3/4 cup sliced candied cherries
1/2 cup diced citron

Soften active dry yeast in warm water. Scald milk; stir in sugar, salt, and butter, cool to lukewarm. Mix in 2 cups flour, yeast, eggs, cardomom, and fruit. Add enough remaining flour to make a stiff dough. Knead on floured surface; place in greased bowl; grease top of dough, cover. Let rise until doubled (note: proper rising is absolutely crucial to success!). Punch dough down; cover and let rest 10 minutes. Divide into 3 equal parts. Shape each piece into a 10 x 8 oval, and fold lengthwise. Place in greased shallow pans. Let rise until doubled (second rising). Bake at 350 degrees F about 30 minutes. Frost with vanilla icing (I prefer cream cheese icing) and decorate if desired. (I stick cut pieces of green and red candied cherries into the icing.)

***Chef's Notes:***
Sometimes I don't use the citron and use more candied cherries—be sure to use both green and red! It is a very yeasty bread—serve hot, thickly sliced and with plenty of butter.

## Cheese Blintz Coffee Cake

152 Little crescents of cream cheesy/cinnamon happiness. Handed down from my mom's friend Fran.

Posted by: bebe's boobs destroy. Yield: 20 crescents. Prep time: Depends on how fast you roll. Figure at least an hour.

---

2 packages (10 rolls each) buttermilk biscuits
1 8-ounce block cream cheese
1/2 cup sugar
3 tablespoons cinammon
1/3 cup finely chopped pecans or walnuts
1/3+ cup melted butter

Mix sugar, cinammon & chopped nuts. Cut cream cheese block into 20 pieces. Flatten each biscuit, then place a piece of cream cheese & a spoonful of sugar mixture in center. Fold biscuit over filling, pinching together to seal. Spread first 10 biscuits in a layer in well greased tube pan. Drizzle melted butter over layer, and sprinkle sugar mixture over layer. Repeat with second layer. Bake at 350 degrees F for approximately 25 minutes, then flip into a large greased pie pan & bake for approximately 10 more minutes.

***Chef's Notes:***
You want to make sure the biscuits cook completely, but be careful not to burn the outer surface of the biscuits.

## Jule Kage

153 Scandinavian Christmas bread. Passed from grubby hand to grubby hand of filthy Scandis for decades or more (not really). So far as I know, this came out of my mother's family and they are only 50% Scandi. This makes an excellent toast; serve with butter.

Posted by Krebs v Carnot: Epic Battle of the Cycling Stars (TM). Yield: 1 regular loaf. Prep time: 2 hours.

---

2 cups milk, whole or 2%, lukewarm
2 teaspoons salt
3 teaspoons yeast, dissolved per instructions
4 tablespoons shortening
1/4 cup candied cherries, chopped
1 cup raisins
1/4 cup citron, chopped
3/4 cup (or less) granulated sugar
1 teaspoon ground cardamon
1 or 2 large eggs
6 to 7 cups flour

Mix together milk, salt, shortening and sugar. Add dissolved yeast, allow to cool slightly. Add egg(s) and mix well. Blend in fruits and mix. Add 1/2 cup of flour and mix to form spongy mass. Add in remaining flour, 1 cup at a time, then knead. Once all flour is mixed in, allow dough to rise twice, kneading in between risings. Form into loaves and place in greased bread pan. Allow to rise one last time for an hour, then bake in pre-heated oven at 350 degrees F for between 30 and 40 minutes. Remove from oven, then bread pan and allow to cool on wire rack.

## World- Famous Rich Dough Dinner Rolls

154 Served to acclaim all over the world. My mother's recipe, but I think it was her mother's. I've inherited its fame in my family. I've served these in Europe, Asia, the Middle East, North America, Central America and the Caribbean to extravagant compliments.

Posted by: Delilah. Yield: about 3 dozen rolls. Prep time: about 4 hours.

---

2 packages active dry yeast
1/2 cup warm water (~110 degrees F)
1/2 teaspoon sugar
1 1/2 cup milk at room temperature
1/4 cup shortening, melted and cooled
2 eggs, beaten
5 cups flour
1/2 cup sugar
2 teaspoons salt

Stir yeast into warm water and ½ teaspoon sugar, set aside to rise. Mix dry ingredients in a large bowl. Pour in all the liquids, and stir. Dough will be very wet. Cover with a clean towel and let rise in a warm spot until double in bulk. Punch down, turn out of bowl and let rest for 5 minutes. Knead in additional flour to make a very soft dough. Form into rolls and put on greased baking sheets. Cover and let rise again until double in bulk. Bake 12 – 15 minutes at 375 degrees F. Brush tops of rolls with melted butter. Rolls take about 4 hours to make. If you make 1 1/2 times the recipe, you will have enough for dinner rolls and cinnamon buns.

To make cinnamon rolls: roll out remaining dough into a rectangle. Brush dough generously with soft butter, sprinkle with brown sugar, cinnamon (cloves, nutmeg, and chopped nuts if desired). Roll dough up along the long edge. Use a thread to cut into ½ - 1 inch rolls. Place on greased baking sheet. Let rise until double. Bake at 375 degrees F for 15 – 18 minutes. Drizzle with powdered sugar glaze.

### *Chef's Notes:*

The milk, eggs and tiny bit of sugar makes the dough rich and wet. Be gentle! The cinnamon rolls are so much more tender than the "famous" food court type.

## Baking Powder Biscuits

155 So light and fluffy.

Posted by: Tonestaple. Yield: 8 biscuits. Prep time: 15 minutes prep; 12 or so for baking.

---

2 cups all purpose flour
3 teaspoons baking powder
1/2 teaspoons salt
1/3 cup Crisco, lard, or butter
7/8 cup whole milk

Preheat oven to 450 degrees F. Sift and resift the three dry ingredients a total of 3 times to make sure everything is completely mixed. Cut in the fat with a pastry cutter or two knives until it's the size of small peas. Make a well in the middle of the ingredients and pour in the milk. Mix only long enough to get everything well stuck together.

Dump it out on a well-floured board and knead with floured hands until the dough seems smooth rather than sticky. This is not a long process. To knead the dough, push in on it with the heel of your hand and then fold it over towards your hand. In other words, make a dent in the dough and fold it in half. Give it a quarter turn, and repeat. Keep doing this until the dough is smooth, but don't overdo it.

Pat the dough out until it's less than 1 inch thick and cut with a biscuit cutter. Place on a baking sheet and bake for 10 to 12 minutes until they are golden brown. If you know what's good for you, break them open and put butter in the middle immediately so the butter will melt and drip and make an unholy delicious mess.

### *Chef's Notes:*

I have taken up weighing my dry ingredients. It's tidier—don't have to wash the measuring cups—and, in theory, more accurate. Lately I have been making these with butter but Crisco is also good. I just don't like the taste of the lard but there's no accounting for taste. I have also used half and half for the liquid when I've been out of milk and it works, but don't be a commie and use something awful like 2% or worse. Under no circumstances can you use a rolling pin on these. You will end up with flat hard hockey pucks and since I warned you, you can't blame me. Don't skimp on the flour for the kneading. Using my biggest biscuit cutter I only get about 8 out of the batch, but you can probably double it safely—you can most recipes. Or you can use a smaller cutter.

## Pollard Dinner Rolls

156 One-hour buttermilk dinner rolls. Great-grandma Pollard was the originator of this recipe.

Posted by: Dave at Buffalo Roam. Yield: three big pans of rolls. Prep time: 1 hour.

---

4 1/2 cups flour
1 1/2 cups buttermilk, lukewarm
1/2 cup melted shortening
1/2 cup sugar
2 cakes yeast
1/2 cup warm water
1/2 teaspoon baking soda
1 teaspoon salt

Crumble yeast cakes into the warm water and let stand until dissolved. Add warm buttermilk. Add sugar and shortening and sift in the flour, soda and salt. Beat smooth and let stand covered for 20 minutes. Turn onto your floured board, knead and make into rolls. We make them small. Place in greased pans, cover with cloth and let them rise about 30 minutes. Bake at 325 degrees F until the tops brown.

***Chef's Notes:***
Lots of butter of course. It makes about three pans for us. My son always claimed a pan as his birthright.

## Better Buns

157 For your better meat. I needed something to hold my grilled ground beef patty so that my chess pieces wouldn't get all greasy.

Posted by: GolfBoy. Yield: 8 buns. Prep time: 3 1/2 hours.

---

1 cup tepid water
1 package active dry yeast
1 pinch sugar
3 1/2 cups flour
1 teaspoon brown sugar
1 1/2 teaspoons salt
1 egg
4 tablespoons (1/2 stick) melted butter
1 teaspoon vegetable oil
3 tablespoons milk

Add yeast and a pinch of sugar to the tepid water, and let stand for 10 minutes until frothy. Mix flour, salt and brown sugar in large mixing bowl. Beat egg and milk together. Add yeast mixture, beaten egg, and melted butter (cooled) to the dry ingredients. Fold together until well mixed. Let stand 15 minutes. Knead dough 5 to 10 minutes, adding more milk or flour if necessary, until smooth and no longer sticky. Shape dough into a ball, coat lightly with oil, cover with plastic wrap, and let rise 50 minutes.

Tamp down dough lightly into a flat square. Fold into thirds, repeat. Cut dough into 8 equal portions. Shape each portion into a ball by folding repeatedly toward a single point, pinch to seal the seam. Arrange rolls seam-side down on parchment-lined baking sheet. Cover with lightly oiled plastic wrap, and let rise 1 to 1 1/2 hours, or until nearly doubled in volume.

Preheat oven to 425 degrees F. Bake until the internal temperature reaches 197 degrees F according to a probe thermometer, approximately 15 minutes.

***Chef's Notes:***
To get a great dough for cinnamon rolls, increase the amount of sugar to 3 tablespoons.

## Perfect Buttermilk Biscuits

158 It will do something in your mouth, but never apologize. From my wife's family. These are the butteriest, flakiest, most delicious biscuits ever in the history of ever. IF you do them right.

Posted by: imp. Yield: ~16 3" biscuits. Prep time: 20 minutes.

---

4 cups all purpose flour (not sifted)
2 tablespoons baking powder
2 teaspoons salt
1 1/2 cups buttermilk
1/2 pound (2 sticks) butter

The following order is important, because you want the butter as cold as possible but still workable. Also, the instructions are detailed, because this is the way to make good biscuits, not dry or rubbery crap (plus, you are all morons and need to be reminded how to breathe properly).

Put butter in freezer when you begin to make the biscuits, not before. Preheat oven to 425 degrees F. Mix dry ingredients. Measure buttermilk and set aside. Generously grease 2 9x9 baking pans (use different butter from what's in the freezer, or spray canola if you are a heathen). Remove butter from freezer and cut it lengthwise on both sides, keeping the long pieces together. With the stick in its original shape, cut 1/4 inch cubes of butter and drop them in the flour, gently moving them as you add them to make sure they are separated from each other. Do this for both sticks of butter. Then, using a heavy-duty pastry cutter (not forks), cut the butter into the flour until it is all a coarse meal (no pieces of butter larger than a BB). Scrape the flour cutter frequently with a table knife to make sure all the butter is incorporated well. Add the buttermilk slowly while stirring to get it evenly distributed. When the dough starts to form a large mass, take your hopefully-washed hands and start to make a ball of dough. Work the dough gently until you get a dough that is not sticking to your fingers, and the buttermilk has been worked all the way through. Place the dough down and go wash your hands again, you filthy curs.

Flour a piece of waxed paper or a cutting board and keep a little extra flour on hand. Place the dough on the floured surface and roll it out with a rolling pin until the dough is about 3/4 inches thick (1 inch is too thick, 1/2 inch too thin). Take a 3" floured biscuit cutter and cut out biscuits, placing them in the greased pans as you go, evenly spaced (touching is OK, unlike in colleges nowadays). When the dough needs to be reformed, squish it together and re-roll it gently, then cut more biscuits until the dough is used up (there might be a little scrap left to make a mini biscuit, or eat it raw like paste like Uncle Joe). Once the biscuits are in the pans, put them in the hot oven and bake for 11-12 minutes, checking every 30 seconds toward the end. Make sure the sides look completely dry and the tops are a nice, golden brown (not just getting brown). Depending on your oven, you may have to rotate after 10 minutes, but do it quickly, the oven needs to stay hot. The biscuits might cook as long as 14 minutes, but shouldn't be much longer than that unless your thermostat in the oven is broken.

Remove, and slather with jam, or make sandwich with thick ham, sausage and/or bacon, or just fill it with more butter and salt for pure decadence. Butter!

## Dragonknitter's Easy Biscuits

> 159 Anyone-can-make biscuits. This is a recipe I originally saw on Allrecipes.com, but I haven't been able to locate it again for this submission. I changed it to fit ingredients I have in my pantry, and I have been making it from memory, so it's mine now.

Posted by: Dragonknitter. Yield: 7 – 8 large biscuits. Prep time: 30 minutes.

---

3 cups self-rising flour or substitute*
1 1/2 cups cold buttermilk
1/2 cup (1 stick) butter

Measure the self-rising flour or substitute* into a decent-sized mixing bowl. Cut in the cold butter until small pea-sized lumps throughout. Place bowl in freezer until the oven is preheated to 400 degrees F, with a cast iron skillet or other metal pan in it. When the oven and skillet have reached full temperature, remove the bowl from the freezer, add cold buttermilk just to hold the dough together and mix. Turn out onto floured board, pat into about ¾ - 1 inch thick slab, cut out rounds of dough, and set aside. Pull out hot skillet, place on heat safe surface or the top of your stove, quickly swipe inside of skillet with butter or spray with cooking spray, and arrange the cut biscuits in it. Place back in oven quickly, and bake until golden on top, about 20-25 minutes, depending on your oven and heat. Remove and serve hot, with your favorite biscuit toppings (butter and honey?) on the side. Makes 7 – 8 large biscuits with a large 2 ½ - 3 inch round cutter, but you can adjust this any way you like. Even a Moron can do it!

***Chef's Notes:***
*You can make your own self-rising flour which is what I usually do: 3/4 cup regular flour, 1 teaspoon baking powder, 1/4 teaspoon (or a bit less if you prefer a less salty dough) salt. You will need to make four batches of this substitute for this recipe. I got it off the internet somewhere as an alternative, if you don't keep SRF on the shelf. Also, if you don't have buttermilk, add the juice of half a lemon to enough whole milk to make 1 ½ cups total liquid.

You can adjust this recipe easily for a larger amount, just keep the ratio the same—it easily becomes 1 ½ recipes, 2 recipes, etc. The key to this is the cold ingredients. The cold butter and cold dough quickly heating and flaking in the hot baking dish and hot oven is what gives tender flaky biscuits, not kneading the dough, so the less handling the better.

I never thought I could make homemade biscuits until I found this recipe.

# *Other*

## Tonypete's Pizza Dough

160 Everyday pizza dough. Adapted from a recipe by Laura Vitale.

Posted by: Tonypete. Yield: 2 10-inch pizzas. Prep time: 3 hours.

---

3 1/2 cups all-purpose flour
1 1/2 tablespoons salt
1 teaspoon sugar
2 tablespoons extra-virgin olive oil
1 1/3 cups warm water -- about 110 degrees F
1 envelope yeast

Add the yeast to warm water and set aside for 5 - 10 minutes. In the bowl of a standing mixer fitted with a dough hook, mix together the flour, salt, sugar and olive oil. Stir the yeast in the water to make sure it's all dissolved and add it to the flour mix. With speed set to medium, mix everything until combined. Reduce speed to low and mix for 10 minutes.

Oil 2 bowls with olive oil and set aside. Divide the dough into 2 pieces and form into 2 balls. Place each of the balls into the oiled bowls and brush the tops with olive oil. Place a piece of plastic wrap on top of each bowl and put into a warm place. Rest until doubled in size—about 2 hours.

Heat oven to 475 degrees F. Take each ball of dough and place onto baking sheet and gently push out dough to desired size. Top with favorite toppings—done! Bake for about 20 minutes.

## Sticky Wicket's Versatile Moron-Proof Bread

161 Idiot-proof, easy, delicious, and versatile bread recipe. My recipe, developed over a number of years. But, like all bread recipes that already share a limited number of ingredients and preparation/baking styles, similarities with existing published recipes can't be ruled out.

Posted by: Sticky Wicket. Yield: 12 buns/5 bowls/2 loaves. Prep time: 2 ½ hours.

---

3 1/2 cups all purpose flour or bread flour
1 cup very hot tap water
2 medium eggs
1/4 cup sugar
2 1/2 heaping teaspoons instant dry yeast
1/2 teaspoon salt

Combine dry ingredients in a large mixing bowl. Add eggs, and stir in with a fork. Pour in hot water, and mix with a fork or spatula. If using a stand mixer with dough hook (preferred), knead for 8 minutes, adding flour or water a tablespoon at a time to achieve a stiff pliant dough. If kneading by hand, knead for 10 minutes. Resultant dough should be stiff, hold its shape when held in your hand—no sagging!—finger poked into it should leave a depression. Lightly grease a large plastic bowl. Place dough in bowl, turning once to coat. Cover with plastic wrap, and leave at room temperature to rise until dough has more than doubled (about 40 minutes to an hour). Turn dough out onto a very lightly floured surface, and deflate gently. Divide dough into two equal pieces (except for bread bowls).

For hamburger or hot dog buns, roll each piece of dough out into a log shape, cut into six even pieces, shape gently with your hands, and place on a lightly greased baking sheet. Let rise in room-temperature oven for 20 minutes. Gently press down on hamburger buns. Let rise another 20 minutes. For bread bowls, roll dough out into a log shape. Cut into five equal pieces. Roll each piece into a ball (a bit larger than a baseball, but smaller than a softball). Place balls of dough on a lightly-greased baking sheet. Mist with warm water, then place in room-temperature oven to rise for about thirty minutes. For loaves, shape each piece of dough into a rounded rectangle. Place rectangles onto separate lightly-greased baking sheet. Spritz each loaf with warm water, and place in a room-temperature oven to rise for about 30 minutes. Place three ½-inch deep slanted cuts across the top of each loaf, spritz again with warm water, and return to room temperature oven to rise for another ten to fifteen minutes.

BAKING: remove your risen buns/bowls/loaves from the oven, spritz with warm water, and set aside. Preheat oven to 375 degrees F for 15 minutes. Do not rely on your oven's preheat timer. If you have a baking stone or bricks, place them in the oven to preheat. For gas ovens, the lowest rack is reserved for a shallow pan of water. For electric ovens, we're just going to dash a cup of water over the heating elements. Why? Because steam. Steam condenses on the cooler surface of your baking bread, keeping it soft, and pliant as your bread expands during the baking process. It also helps in the formation of a crisp, proper crust.

When oven is ready, slide your baking sheets in, and immediately toss in a cup of water over the heating elements on the bottom of the oven (electric), or put in your shallow pan of water (gas). Bake for about 20 minutes. Check for color. Buns, and rolls should be lightly browned on top, and can be removed to a cooling rack. Bread bowls and loaves should be baked an additional ten minutes for a darker crust, a uniform golden brown. Using oven mitts, flip them upside down, and thump your finger against their underside. It should sound hollow, and drum-like. Remove to cooling rack.

***Chef's Notes:***
Unlike a lot of bread recipes, this one uses eggs, and quite a lot of sugar, which is like steroids for yeast, (hence, the short rise times). If you're patient, and want flavors to develop

properly, cut the sugar in half, and add ten to fifteen minutes to rise times. Buns can be brushed lightly with melted butter after they're removed from the oven to soften their crusts, (usually not needed). Crumb texture is very soft, like store bought bread. Crusts are well developed, and 'crackle' when gently squeezed. Best served the day baked, but will keep at room temperature for three days. I use this recipe for making Indian Fry Bread too, which is a departure from accepted recipes (though I reduce sugar to 1 1/2 tablespoons, otherwise the bread is too sweet). This recipe is hard to mess up, and when your bread is baking, your house smells amazing!

## German Pancakes

162 Breakfast, hangover mitigation. From a battered 3x5 card of unknown origin.

Posted by: Luke. Yield: 4 servings. Prep time: 5 minutes.

---

8 tablespoons (1 stick) butter
6 eggs
1 cup milk
Pinch (about 1/4 to 1/2 teaspoon) salt
1 cup flour
Dash vanilla (optional)
Dash cinnamon (optional)

Get down a 9"x13" baking pan. Unwrap the stick of butter, and drop it in the pan. Put the pan in the oven and set the oven for 400 degrees F. Get out a mixing bowl. Crack the eggs into the bowl and discard the shells. (Doing this first makes it easier to fish out shell fragments if you're still drunk. Or just clumsy.) Dump the rest of the ingredients into the mixing bowl. Mix with either a mixer or a whisk. (You're trying to incorporate air bubbles into the mix, so a wooden spoon won't do. But a fork will work in a pinch.) Once the oven is preheated, pour the mixture into the melted butter at the bottom of the pan. Give it a quick shake to distribute everything a bit more evenly. Close the oven door, and set the timer for 30 minutes.

Go to ace.mu.nu and read the morning thread. Or the art thread. Or whatever it was Ace was talking about in the afternoon. Or make bacon. Maybe coffee, if you like that sort of thing. When the timer rings, pull the pan out, and set it on something that won't melt. Let it cool for a minute or two. Then take a sharp knife, and cut it into eight pieces. Put it on plates, and serve with maple syrup.

### *Chef's Notes:*

So easy Amanda Marcotte could do it! (But she really should be making a sandwich instead. Or maybe a pie.)

# Mexican Cornbread

163 Spicy-Cheesy Cornbread from my mother.

Posted by: Penelopeisfirst. Yield: 2 8" skillets. Prep time: 15 minutes.

---

2 eggs, beaten
2 cups cheddar/taco cheese
1 can sweetened creamed corn
1 cup milk
1 cup self-rising corn meal
1/3 cup flour
3 stalks green onion, chopped
2 pinches salt
2 tablespoons vegetable oil
10 – 12 slices pickled jalapeno

Preheat oven to 400 degrees F with 2 8" iron skillets inside. While oven is preheating, place all ingredients into a large mixing bowl. Mix ingredients thoroughly. Once oven is preheated and skillets are hot, oil bottom of each skillet and pour half of the cornbread mix into each. Bake for 25 minutes at 400 degrees F, then bake for additional 20 minutes at 350 degrees F. Remove from oven and let cool before removing from skillet.

*"But first..."*

# Snacks & Appetizers

*Appetizers! Wow, these are awesome.*
*How the subtle aromas do blossom!*
*But due to matters expedient*
*You may find the ingredients*
*Include at least one road-killed possum.*

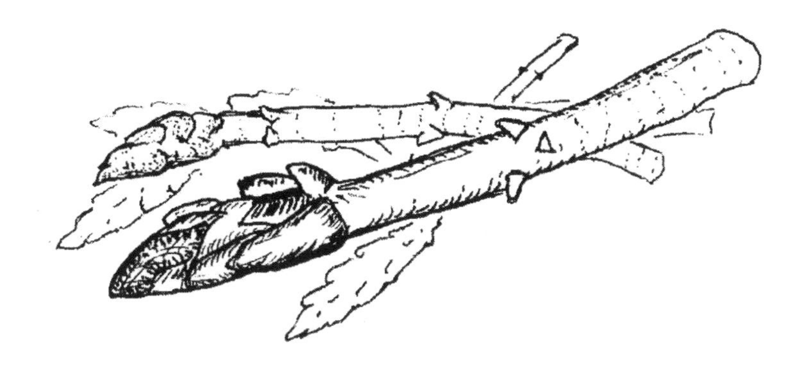

## Mr Methane Chip Dip

164 Great going down, nasty coming out! You will be nobody's friend the next day.

Posted by: exsanguine.    Yield: 30 servings.    Prep time: 1 hour.

---

4 8-ounce packages cream cheese
2 pounds spicy Italian sausage
2 16-ounce jars Pace Picante Hot Sauce
3 tablespoons cayenne pepper
2 bags Tostito's Scoop corn chips

Place the 4 blocks of cream cheese into a crock pot. Brown the Italian sausage and add to crock pot when done. Add Pace and cayenne to pot. Heat on high for 1 – 2 hours, stirring often until it is at a creamy consistency. Serve with the Scoop chips right out of the pot.

## Barf in a Bowl

165 Hot dip for corn chips. Also, a disguise for raw veggies! I got this recipe from a neighbor, who held it close to the vest until she moved to the opposite end of the state. Just before she left, she shared it with all the moms in my 'hood. "Barf in a Bowl" is the name my kids affectionately gave to this appetizer because it looks rather unappetizing as it is being made. However, don't let the name fool you—it is deee-lish!

Posted by: Tired Mom.    Yield: enough for a buncha morons.    Prep time: 25 minutes.

---

1 tube Jimmy Dean hot pork sausage
1 brick (8 ounces) original Philadelphia cream cheese
Two cans original Rotel tomatoes
2 cups shredded cheddar cheese
corn chips and/or an assortment of raw veggies

Brown tube of sausage in a large pan on medium high heat, breaking up the sausage into tiny crumbles; once fully cooked, drain grease from the meat, wipe grease from pan. Return pan of meat to the fire and reduce heat to medium; add brick of cream cheese and two cans of Rotel tomatoes (now is a good time to turn on the oven, preheating to 300 degrees F). Stir ingredients together as cream cheese melts. Once cream cheese is fully melted, transfer contents of pan into oven-safe casserole dish. Sprinkle top generously with shredded cheddar. Pop into the oven for 10 – 15 minutes (check at 10 minutes). When cheese on top is fully melted and mixture is bubbly, pull from the oven and serve with corn chips.

***Chef's Notes:***
To trick children into eating vegetables, hide the corn chips and serve with an assortment of raw carrots, peppers, snow peas, celery—the more colorful the better!

## Black Bean and Cilantro salsa

166 Food of the gods. This is completely my own recipe.

Posted by: Stephen Price Blair. Yield: 4 servings. Prep time: 30 minutes.

---

1 can crisp corn
1 can black beans
1 cup chopped red onion
3 lemons
1 tablespoon olive oil
½ cup chopped red bell pepper
½ cup finely chopped cilantro
1 tablespoon chopped jalapeno
1 teaspoon salt
½ teaspoon pepper

Mix all ingredients together. Let rest in refrigerator for five minutes or more for the flavors to settle. Eat with tortilla chips, on meats or tacos, or by the spoon.

## Simple Salsa

167 Hot tasty salsa for your chips and whatever else. Watched my mom and abuelita make it.

Posted by: Fastfreefall. Yield: 2 – 5 servings. Prep time: 25 minutes.

---

5 jalapenos
2 habaneros
3 cloves of garlic
thick slice onion
big pinch cumin
salt to taste
pinch cilantro
16-ounce can peeled tomatoes

Roast the jalapenos and the habaneros so they get a nice char. Roast the garlic for a light char. Snip off stems and first milimeter of ends of peppers. Place all items into blender: the peppers, cumin, onion, garlic, big dash of salt, a pinch of cumin and peeled tomatoes.

***Chef's Notes:***
This works without cilantro if it grosses you out. Many variations exist.

## Crack Dip

168 Dip so good it should be a controlled substance. This recipe was given to me by a colleague at the American Embassy in Athens. She brought it to the First Annual Chili Cookoff, which I got roped into organizing, and I thought it should have won. Chili purists demurred, saying something with chicken and velveeta had no right to an award. Jerks. Anyway, I have served this dip all over the world, and a friend at another locale dubbed it Crack Dip, because he couldn't leave the giant slow cooker full of the stuff.

Posted by: Moki. Yield: 1 – 10 servings, depending on the addictive personalities of your guests. Prep time: 45 minutes to prep the chicken, 30 minutes for the dip.

---

1 to 2 pounds boneless, skinless chicken breasts
2 tablespoons olive oil
1 teaspoon each salt, pepper, garlic powder, onion powder
1/2 teaspoon cumin
one 2-pound block Velveeta cheese product
one 10-ounce can Rotel tomatoes
one 4.25-ounce can chopped black olives
one 4.5-ounce can chopped green chilies

For the chicken: place oil in a glass baking dish, sprinkle with the salt, pepper, garlic and onion powders, and cumin. Roll chicken breasts in the seasoned oil, cover with foil and bake at 375 degrees F for about 45 minutes. Remove from oven, cool for ten minutes, then shred, discarding cartilage. Set aside.

For the dip: in a large dutch oven, place the Velveeta, cut into small chunks, the rotel, olives and green chilies. Mix over medium heat until Velveeta begins to melt. Add shredded chicken, and continue to stir gently until Velveeta is completely melted, and the ingredients are combined. Serve immediately with corn chips or crudites (but really, why bother?) or pour into the ceramic container of a slow cooker, cover and refrigerate for up to two days. An hour before service, place the ceramic container into the slow cooker heating element, and turn on low, stirring occasionally.

## Blender Hummus

169 Hummus from a handed-around recipe. Authentically Turkish, I am told.

Posted by: Kindltot. Yield: it's a dip. Prep time: 15 minutes.

---

16-ounce can garbanzo beans
2 cloves garlic, peeled
4 tablespoons lemon juice
2 tablespoons tahini, roasted type
1/4 cup reserved bean liquid
1/2 teaspoon salt
2 tablespoons olive oil
ground paprika to taste

Drain the garbanzo beans, reserving the liquid. Put everything but the paprika and the olive oil into the blender and whomp it up to a paste. Spoon the paste into a shallow bowl and shake paprika over it, and add the olive oil on top. You often find it garnished with parsley. You can add whatever you want to this; I have seen pine nuts, extra pepper, lots and lots of garlic. It is mostly a dip so serve it with pitas, toasted bread, or naan.

## Asiago Cheese Dip

170 I *love* the cheese dip at the Rock Bottom Brewery in Arlington, VA. This is our attempt to recreate that dip at home. Be sure to add the sun-dried tomatoes at the very end, or else you'll wind up with pink dip. You can substitute sun dried tomato paste. This is an original recipe from my family, based on the cheese dip from Rock Bottom brewery.

Posted by: WitchDoktor, AKA VA GOP Sucks. Yield: 8 – 10 servings. Prep time: 30 minutes.

---

1 cup mayonnaise
1 cup sour cream
4 ounces cream cheese, softened
1/2 cup + 2 tablespoons shredded asiago cheese
1/2 cup sliced green onions
1/2 cup sliced mushrooms
1/4 to 1/2 cup sun dried tomatoes (4 ounces)

Preheat oven to 350 degrees F. Reconstitute sun-dried tomatoes in water and then drain well. Squeeze water from tomatoes, then julienne into fine strips. Combine mayonnaise, sour cream, cream cheese, ½ cup of the asiago cheese, green onions, and mushrooms, saving the 2 tablespoons of asiago, and mix well. Fold in sun dried tomatoes. Place in an oven-proof container, top with remaining asiago cheese, and bake for 15 – 20 minutes or until bubbly. Serve hot with toasted cheddar beer bread (see Bread chapter).

## Yogurt Cheese

171 Turn plain yogurt into soft cheese in your home. Many places suggest this system, but I learned it from my mom.

Posted by: Christopher R Taylor. Yield: it varies. Prep time: 4 – 8 hours.

---

1 pint plain yogurt
1 filter
½ teaspoon salt
1 strainer

Take the strainer and put it over a container it will stay in, but not touch the bottom of. Give at least half inch of clearance. Line the strainer with cheesecloth or a coffee filter, so that it fills the strainer. Spoon the plain yogurt into the center, so it doesn't touch the sides or overflow, as much as possible. This works best with non-flavored, plain yogurt. Leave for at least 4 hours, in the refrigerator, but overnight is best. The excess liquids will drain out over time, leaving a thicker, more solid substance like soft cheese. The longer it strains, the thicker, up to a point. This has little flavor, but you can add dill weed, citrus, peppers, garlic powder, or whatever sounds good. Mix well and store in a closed container for a few hours, or a day for best results. Great for crackers or a dip, it's a nice spread.

## (Everything in the) House Dip

172 Two simple ingredients as a base for any flavor point in your larder. The recipe is mine, all mine. There are only two food groups: chips and dips. Everything else is a nutritional supplement.

Posted by: markreardon. Yield: 1 – 50 servings. Prep time: moments only.

---

pint(s) sour cream
tablespoon(s) low sodium Better than Bouillon Chicken base

For each pint of sour cream (use a good sour cream, not the watery store brands) add one heaping (heaping is important, at least to me) tablespoon of the low sodium chicken base. This combination gives the bulk and flavor-carrying power that you need to make any flavor point for a dip. Add two tablespoons (from a jar) of crushed garlic and you have "DEATH BY GARLIC" dip. OR add a teaspoon of chopped chives for a delightful mild chive dip. OR add a teaspoon of curry powder or paste for a chicken curry dip. Keep it simple, use anything in your larder. If you must use a vegetable other than potatoes, slice them to assure a chip shape to maximize the dip experience.

## Kahlua Pecan Brown Sugar Baked Brie

173 I got this recipe from www.noblepig.com.

Posted by: Tami. Yield: 6 – 8 servings. Prep time: 30 minutes.

---

1 whole wheel of Brie (19 ounces)—President Brie is best for this recipe
1 cup Kahlua
1 cup packed light brown sugar
1 cup whole or chopped pecans
crackers of your choice

Preheat oven to 350 degrees F. Carefully slice off the top off the rind of the Brie BUT do NOT completely remove. Bake for 15 minutes. When the Brie is done baking, the top can be easily removed to expose the creamy cheese. While the Brie is baking, in a medium saucepan combine the Kahlua and brown sugar and bring to a boil, then simmer for 10 – 15 minutes or until a syrupy consistency is made. Throw the pecans in for 2 minutes at the end to warm them through and completely cover with the sauce. Remove the Brie from the oven and completely remove the top rind. Pour Kahlua sauce over the Brie.

***Chef's Notes:***
Let the sauce cool some before pouring it on the Brie. If it's too hot, it will be too runny and turn the Brie into a gloppy mess. If the sauce becomes too thick due to cooling, reheat it a tiny bit.

## Buffalo Chicken Dip

174 I found this on Allrecipes.com, but there are similar recipes all over the internet.

Posted by: Tami. Yield: 20 servings. Prep time: 20 minutes.

---

1 – 1 1/2 pounds shredded chicken (I use the breast from rotisserie chicken)
2 8-ounce packages cream cheese, softened
1 cup ranch or blue cheese dressing, or 1/2 cup each
3/4 cup pepper sauce i.e., Frank's RedHot
1 1/2 cups shredded cheddar cheese (I shred a block of cheddar cheese)
celery/carrots/crackers for dipping

Preheat oven to 350 degrees F. Heat chicken and hot sauce in skillet over medium heat, until heated through. In bowl combine cream cheese and dressing(s). Layer in a baking dish as follows: cream cheese/dressing mixture on bottom of dish, then shredded chicken and hot sauce mixture, and finally the shredded cheddar cheese on top. Bake for 20 – 25 minutes. You can substitute whatever cheese you might prefer for this dish.

## Plain Ol' Hummus

175 Simple homemade hummus, just your standard hummus recipe.

Posted by: ThePrimordialOrderedPair. Yield: 1 serving for a really fat hummus lover. Prep time: 30 minutes.

---

1 can (15.5-ounce) chick peas/garbonzo beans
3/4 teaspoon salt
1/2 teaspoon garlic paste, OR 2 medium cloves of garlic
1 1/2 teaspoons pure lemon juice
1/2 cup tahini paste

Nothing could be simpler than making awesome tasting hummus: strain juice out of can of chick peas into cup, and keep cup of juice. Put chick peas into food processor and blend at high speed until fairly smooth. Add a little of the chick pea juice if you want to make the blending easier. I usually blend this part for 5 minutes or so, sometimes longer. Add salt, lemon, and garlic (either garlic paste or the two minced cloves—the paste is easier). Blend some more—a minute or two—to make sure everything is mixed through. Add the tahini paste and blend further. This might be very dry and could ball up as you are blending it, so start adding juice from the cup of chick pea juice to thin it out. Blend some more, adding chick pea juice until it's very smooth and a little bit thinner than you like—it will thicken a touch in the refrigerator. You can't over-blend so err on the longer side, the smoother the better. I usually end up putting about 3/4 of the chick pea juice into the hummus. Adding the chick pea juice is all about making the blending easier and achieving the thickness you want, so more or less is totally up to you. Done. You now have hummus that's better than anything you will buy in the store. Put it into a container and refrigerate.

## Olivada

176 Olive dipping sauce. No idea where this came from. I've had it forever. Predates my computer.

Posted by: Wenda (sic) Yield: lots and lots. Prep time: 5 minutes.

---

3 cups pitted black olives, preferably Kalamata
2 cloves garlic
2 tablespoons capers, rinsed and dried
1/4 cup good olive oil

Drop the garlic through the feed tube of a food processor to chop it. Add capers and olives and chop all coarsely. Pour in the olive oil while pulsing the machine, until the mixture is blended. Process until smooth. Serve with crackers or veggies. This keeps for a looooooong time. It can also be used as a pasta sauce with shrimp or scallops.

## Jolo's Salsa

177 Tasty hot salsa. This recipe is mine.

Posted by: Jolo. Yield: 30 servings. Prep time: 30 minutes.

---

10 pound can diced tomatoes
26-ounce can whole hot marinated jalapeno peppers
1 large yellow onion
2 green bell peppers, cored
2 red bell peppers, cored
5 garlic cloves
1 lime—zest and juice
2 tablespoons sugar
1 – 3 big squirts Sriracha hot chili sauce

Chop the garlic and the onion. Next core and chop the green and red bell peppers. Drain and chop the can of whole hot marinated jalapeno peppers. Drain and chop the can of tomatoes. Add the sugar and lime. Add 1 big squirt of Sriracha hot chili sauce. Stir well and put lid on the bucket. Place in refrigerator for 12 hours. Taste and add more Sriracha hot chili sauce if desired. Add cilantro to taste if you want. I do most of the chopping/cutting with a food processor. I dump everything in a 1 gallon plastic ice cream bucket after it gets chopped.

## Salsa Negra

178 This needs to be made at least hours before serving; overnight is best! My Tia Rosa gave me this receta when I was whining about there not being a Baja Fresh within a thousand miles of the Ozarks. This is a great salsa for chip-dippin' , tacos, burritos, hash browns, scrambled eggs or anything else you can think of.

Posted by: Tammy al-Thor. Yield: a goodly bowlful. Prep time: 10 minutes to chop, 45 minutes (?) of cooking.

---

10 – 12 Roma tomatoes
2 – 3 teaspoons fresh lime juice
1/2 large onion, roughly chopped (chunks are fine, no small dice necessary)
2 tablespoons roughly chopped garlic
1 can chicken broth
2 – 3 tablespoons oil (olive oil is fine)
1/2 bunch cilantro (no stems)
large tomato, diced
salt and pepper to taste

Turn on broiler, or set oven to at least 450 degrees F. Cover cookie sheet with foil and spray with non-stick spray. Cut Roma tomatoes in half on the long side and lay them on the cookie sheet with the cut side facing up. Salt them. Put those suckers under the broiler or in that hot oven and cook them til they are totally black on the top. I don't mean charred, I mean as black as the SCOAMF's heart. Half hour? 45 minutes? I have no idea, you know your oven better than I do; just keep an eye on them, and make sure the tops get black as sin. None more black. In the meantime, put the garlic, lime juice, onion, oil, and a few tablespoons of broth in a food processor and puree til the mixture gets to the texture that you like for your salsa. Transfer to serving bowl. Once your tomatoes have gotten as black as the scorched earth around Shrillary McPantsuit's campaign headquarters, let cool for a few minutes, then put them in the food processor with some more broth and puree them to the same texture as the other mixture. Add this to the onion mixture and stir together. Chop up your large tomato and the cilantro, add to the mixture. Stir some more and add some broth if it seems too thick. Add salt and pepper if needed. Some of my brothers add jalapenos at this point, but as much as I like super spicy food, I prefer this salsa without the heat.

## Commander Betty's Dip

179 Simple comfort-food chip dip of the Greatest Generation. This was probably a widely-used recipe in the 1950s/1960s. I got it from a friend I met through volunteering at a military museum. She was a classic of the Greatest Generation. Tough, wise, served as a Navy nurse in WWII and went on for a whole career, in which her natural command presence had her in charge of hospital wings and sections of hospital ships. I submit this because it's very good, very simple and easy to make, and to honor the memory of Commander Betty and her colleagues who won The Big One and served through America's golden age of prosperity and power.

Posted by: rhomboid. Yield: 6 – 8 servings. Prep time: 15 minutes.

---

16 ounces sour cream
1 small can chopped black olives
8 – 12 scallions
1 5-ounce jar Hormel's dried beef

Chop dried beef into small pieces. Dice scallions. Add beef, scallions, and chopped olives from can to sour cream. Mix well, then refrigerate. Serve with chips, crackers, or vegetables.

## Jalapeno Dip

180 Jalapeno cheese dip that is always a hit! Got this from a friend many years ago.

Posted by: AnnaS. Yield: enough for a group. Prep time: 10 minutes.

---

block of Cracker Barrel Vermont sharp white cheddar
1 cup of mayonnaise
1/3 to 1/2 block of Velveeta
All the juice and half the peppers from a jar of sliced jalapenos

Put all in a food processor and process. Viola! Great dip. Serve with tortilla chips. Wonderful the next day heated and served over baked potatoes or green beans.

## RMBS's Mom's Skorthalia

181 A classic Greek garlic dip, from a family recipe.

Posted by: RedMindBlueState. Yield: approximately 3 cups. Prep time: 15 minutes.

---

6 large garlic cloves
1/2 loaf 2-day-old Italian or other dense white bread, crusts removed
1 teaspoon salt
1 egg
1 1/2 cups vegetable oil
1/2 cup olive oil
1/3 cup white vinegar

After removing crusts, soak bread in water. Remove, and squeeze very dry. Add garlic cloves and salt to food processor, and process until garlic is very finely minced. Add soaked, dried bread and process together with garlic until well blended. Add egg, and process until well blended. With the processor running, slowly add oil until the mixture forms a smooth white emulsion that resembles mayonnaise. If using grape seed oil, the full amount called for may not be needed, as it emulsifies extremely well. Add vinegar and process until well blended. Refrigerate. Will thicken after chilling.

***Chef's Notes:***
Not for the faint of heart. This will kill vampires at 1,000 meters. It goes very well as a dip for vegetables, and for salty chips, and as a sauce for grilled meats. Do not substitute for the blend of oils. This recipe will not work well, if at all, with all olive oil or all vegetable oil.

## Sveti's Crab-n-Cheese Dip

182 Hot crab dip good for games, parties and pot-lucks. I got the recipe from Svetlana Kocherginskaya, a Russian post-doc I knew in grad school 20+ years ago. Been a family favorite ever since.

Posted by: Mrs. Scrood (my husband posts, I lurk). Yield: 10 regular servings, maybe 4 moron servings. Prep time: 30 minutes maybe?

---

12 ounces cream cheese
1 cup sour cream
1 cup crab meat
1 cup cheddar cheese
1/2 teaspoon (or to taste) garlic salt
1 loaf French baguette

Allow cream cheese to soften at room temp and chunk up the crab meat to medium-small pieces. Preheat oven to 375 degrees F. In large bowl mix cream cheese, sour cream, crab meat, garlic salt and 1/2 of the cheddar cheese. Pour mixture into pie pan, spread evenly in pan, sprinkle top with remaining cheddar cheese. Bake for 15 – 20 minutes until cheese is melted and lightly browned on top. Slice French baguette on bias in thin slices. Serve dip warm from oven with bread. Stand back as Horde scarfs down immediately; try not to lose a finger in the frenzy.

***Chef's Notes:***
Imitation crab meat works well too if on a budget. Use a French baguette, not that soft floppy stuff sold in some grocery stores. Or crackers are good too. DO NOT serve just before a meal you spent all day slaving over. Horde will eat all the dip and not eat the gorgeous meal you have ready (speaking from experience here).

## Salsa

183 Mild or hot, depending on the peppers you use. From my American friend in Sweden.

Posted by: Miley, the Duchess. Yield: 1+ quarts. Prep time: 30 minutes.

---

2 1/2 pounds Roma tomatoes
3 medium cooking onions
1/2 bunch cilantro
1/2 jar banana pepper rings
2 cans El Paso salsa fresca
1 small can tomato sauce
1/2 cup oil
1/2 cup white vinegar
3 tablespoons sugar
2 teaspoons salt

Chop everything into small pieces and mix (I only uses the cilantro leaves without the stems). Allow to set in fridge at least overnight to allow flavors to blend and develop. Keeps for a long time in the fridge, but is usually gone before it ever has a chance to go bad! For those of you who find cilantro to be disgusting, you can substitute Italian parsley and chopped chives.

## Dill Dip

184 The only thing this abysmal cook can make with repeated success. My mother gave me this recipe so I could make my own and quit pestering her. Since I ate a bag of Ruffles potato chips daily, I made it often.

Posted by: kathysaysso. Yield: 16 ounces, so 1 serving. Prep time: 24 hours from start to finish.

---

8 ounces Best Foods mayonnaise
8 ounces sour cream—full fat
4 tablespoons dill weed
1 tablespoon Beau Monde seasoning
1/4 teaspoon onion powder
1/4 teaspoon celery salt
1/4 teaspoon garlic powder

In a bowl, mix the mayo and sour cream together. Throw in the spices, and mix them around as well. Put it in the refrigerator (make sure to cover the damned bowl—you're not a heathen!) for at least two hours, but it will taste much better if you can leave it in there for an entire day. The dip will also taste better if you use a metal bowl rather than a plastic bowl. Don't have a metal bowl? Maybe your dog's dish is metal. Borrow it. Think outside the box!

## Smoked Salmon Dip

185 Best damn salmon dip this side of the Rockies. I have been making this dip for over ten years. It did start as a recipe but has been mine since then.

Posted by: westminsterdogshow. Yield: 3 cups. Prep time: 30 minutes.

---

8 ounces cream cheese, softened
1 cup sour cream
1/4 cup whipping cream
1 lemon, zest and juice
3 garlic cloves, minced
2 tablespoons fresh dill, chopped
1 teaspoon Worcestershire sauce
1 teaspoon black pepper
1/2 teaspoon red pepper sauce
1 teaspoon Old Bay seasoning
1 pound smoked salmon
2 tablespoons fresh chives

Combine cream cheese, sour cream, whipping cream, lemon zest and juice in food processor until smooth. Add remaining seasonings and combine well. Transfer to serving bowl, fold in salmon and garnish with chives. Cover and chill. Serve with crudities, crossing or crackers. If you do have any leftovers (doubtful), it actually freezes well and makes a great ravioli filling.

## Ruthless's Guacamole Dip

186 Avocado dip with a punch. This was based on various recipes I had seen, going back a half century or so, and with my own touches.

Posted by: Ruthless. Yield: 4 – 6 servings. Prep time: 10 minutes.

---

2 ripe avocados, mashed
1 medium tomato, chopped fine
1 cup small curd cottage cheese
juice of one lime
¼ cup mayonnaise
4 tablespoons jalapeno pepper slices, chopped
2 – 3 dashes Tabasco sauce
Cilantro as garnish

Mix all ingredients except cilantro and place in serving bowl. Garnish with chopped cilantro leaves. Serve with corn tortilla chips. Goes great with Valu-Rite Margaritas.

## Fondue de Suazo Especial de Rosier

187 Appetizer, snack, or meal. A favorite alternative to C-Rats left over from Vietnam when the mess hall in Central America was closed or shut down for various violations. Ingredients vary depending on what was sent to the PX from the PX in Panama, and if one could get to the village for fresh vegetables.

Posted by: Scotch and Tritium. Yield: 1 – 10 servings. Prep time: 15 minutes.

---

1 large jar Cheez Whiz
1 can Spam
1 large jar salsa
1 large onion
hot sauce to taste
1 large tomato
1 large bag chips, any kind

Dice onion and tomato. Finely cube Spam. Combine all ingredients in some sort of vessel that won't melt, heat until Cheez Whiz will drip from a spoon. Add hot sauce to taste. Serve with chips, or just eat with a spoon if chips are unavailable. In CONUS, real meat can be substituted for Spam, Velveeta for Cheez Whiz. Salsa brand is irrelevant. Goes well with Jim Beam and grape soda because that is the only soft drink sent up from Panama when the dish was invented.

## Cuffy's Veggie Dip

188 Slightly salty veggie dip. One of Mom's all-time favorites. Great for all occasions.

Posted by: Cuffy Meigs. Yield: several servings. Prep time: 10 minutes.

---

2/3 cup mayonnaise, not Miracle Whip crap
2/3 cup sour cream, not the wimpy low-calorie crap
1 tablespoon Beau Monde seasoning
1 tablespoon parsley flakes
1 tablespoon minced onions
1 teaspoon dillweed
2 shakes Worcestershire sauce
1 shake Tabasco sauce

Combine all ingredients; cover and refrigerate for two to four hours to let the flavors blend and the onion soften a bit.

## Corn and Bean Salsa

189 Everyone that has eaten this wants the recipe, so here you go. This was given to me by a friend in New England at least 10 years ago. I have modified it to suit our tastes.

Posted by: bluebell. Yield: lots. Prep time: 10 minutes.

---

1 cup finely chopped celery
1 cup finely chopped red onion
1 fresh jalapeno, seeded and finely chopped (or more if you like it hot)
1 roasted red pepper, finely chopped (or you can use a fresh red pepper, either way)
1 15-ounce can black-eyed peas
1 15-ounce can black beans
1 15-ounce can shoepeg (small white) corn, or regular corn
3/4 cup olive oil
1/2 cup apple cider vinegar
1/3 cup sugar

Combine the celery, onion, and both types of peppers in a large bowl. Rinse the black-eyed peas, beans, and corn in a large colander, then drain well and add to the other veggies. Mix the olive oil, vinegar, and sugar in a sauce pan and stir over low heat until the sugar dissolves. Let cool a little, then pour over the salsa and refrigerate. To serve, lift the salsa out with a slotted spoon into a bowl and serve with Tostitos "Scoops" chips.

## Deviled Ham and Cheese Dip

190 My grandmother Catherine's recipe.

Posted by: Farmer. Yield: enough. Prep time: 15 minutes.

---

1 4.5-ounce can deviled ham
1 3-ounce package of cream cheese, softened
2 tablespoons chili sauce
1/4 cup mayonnaise
dash of salt
few drops of Tabasco or Worcestershire sauce

Mix thoroughly in a food processor. Chill for an hour or more. Remove a little before serving.

## Pico de Gallo Salsa

191 Rob's best salsa recipe evah! It's mine. I have been growing capsicum as a hobby for many, many years. You could imply this recipe was culturally appropriated, but that would be retarded.

Posted by: Cicero Kaboom! Kid. Yield: One serving. Make your own salsa, moron! Prep time: the time it takes to drink one beer.

---

2 – 10 serranos
1/4 cup onion
2 Roma tomatoes
1 – 2 garlic cloves
1/4 cup cilantro
scant 1/8 cup good oil
2 tablespoons red wine vinegar
1 tablespoon fresh lime juice
pinch coarse salt

Stem and seed the peppers under running water. Smash the garlic or run through a press. Chop the peppers, onions, garlic, tomato and cilantro in order, chopping each additional item into and with the previous items, blending the flavors and making the first items choppier into smaller pieces/parts. Place into a bowl and add the oil, vinegar, lime juice and salt. Stir well to combine. A small splash of raspberry balsamic vinegar takes this dish to a new level of deliciousness.

## Cucumber Salsa

192 A cool and savory salsa or stand alone side dish. I've modified this to taste but the original recipe comes from the Pepper Fool's website (www.pepperfool.com) and recipe for "Grilled Ono and Cucumber Salsa"

Posted by: Coop. Yield: 10+ servings. Prep time: 2 hours.

---

4 cucumbers
8 Roma tomatoes
1 large red onion
1 bunch cilantro
2 large limes
2 cloves minced garlic
6 or to taste jalapenos
1 tablespoon vinegar
1 teaspoon coarse sea salt or to taste

The bulk of the work is dicing everything to about a ¼ to ½ inch dice. But . . . peel the cucumbers. Remove the pulp and seeds from the tomatoes. Finely mince the garlic cloves. Remove seeds and pulp from the jalapenos. Avoid as many cilantro stems as possible. I prefer a little coarser chop for appearance. Mix all chopped/diced ingredients in a large bowl. Season with sea salt to taste and squeeze lime juice (bottled juice is fine) and a little vinegar and then let it sit in the refrigerator for several hours before serving. This is great over rice or cold pasta or even as its own side dish. It will keep for several days but it will need to be drained periodically for a fresher look or appearance.

## Beefy Dip for Vegetarian Morons

193 Multi-use vegetarian beef-like stuff. Modified from a recipe I got off a soup can years back. Had to accommodate both a Hindu and a vegetarian at work on a pot luck and this worked well.

Posted by: Colonel32. Yield: 4 – 8 servings. Prep time: 5 minutes.

---

one package beefless ground
one can tomato soup
1/2 cup shredded cheese
picante salsa to taste (Valentina's preferred)

Empty contents of beefless ground into a skillet. Heat ground on medium-low until thawed. This can be accelerated with a little water and higher heat but can scorch the ground. If necessary drain off any excess water from step 2. Add contents of one can of tomato soup and picante sauce to the beefless ground. Stir contents of the pan to ensure everything is coated and raise to high heat. As soon as the contents start to bubble, stir once more, then cut down to low/simmer. Add cheese to the contents and let sit on simmer for 5 minutes. Et voila! Place contents into serving bowl. It is desirable to make sure the cheese ends up mixed in at this step rather than resting on top.

***Chef's Notes:***

Feel free to use this with your choice of chips (Tostitos Hint of Lime are a nice choice) or add to a burrito or taco in place of regular ground beef. And, of course, beef can be used if you want to skip the weenie vegetarian requirements.

## Salsa de Muse

194 A tomato-based, fresh salsa. Mrs. Muse has been making this salsa for our family for > 20 years. It is actually my recipe that I created by cobbling together bits and pieces of several others. Kind of like Frankenstein.

Posted by: OregonMuse. Yield: ? Prep time: 30 – 45 minutes.

---

5-6 Roma tomatoes
1/2 cup chopped red onion
3 cloves garlic
1 habanero pepper
1/2 teaspoon garlic powder
1 1/2 tablespoons lime juice
1 tablespoon wine vinegar
3/4 teaspoon dried cilantro
3/4 teaspoon salt

Pile everything into a food processor and let 'er rip. Actually, I prefer using one of those hand-cranked salsa makers because the powered food processors usually turn the salsa into soup. The salsa is ready to eat immediately, but tastes a lot better if placed in the refrigerator for 6 – 12 hours so the flavors can meld. Due to the vinegar and lime juice, this salsa will remain fresh for up to 2 – 3 weeks.

***Chef's Notes:***

Substitutions: 4 medium-sized regular tomatoes may be substituted for the Romas. Fresh cilantro may be used instead of dried. If habanero peppers are too hot, serranos or jalepenos may be substituted to bring the heat level down to an acceptable level.

# Mango Jam with Brown Sugar and Cinnamon

195 A delicious spiced mango jam. This was originally from allrecipes.com, but has been so heavily modified that you may as well ignore that origin.

Posted by: Zaklog the Great. Yield: 6 half-pint jars. Prep time: 30 minutes.

---

2 2/3 pounds mango, peeled and diced
1 1/2 cups water
4 tablespoons lemon juice
1 1/2 cups brown sugar
1 1/2 cups white sugar
1 teaspoon ground cinnamon
1 package pectin

Put the mango chunks and the water in a pot and cook over medium heat until mango is soft. Add lemon juice, sugars, and cinnamon and stir until dissolved. Add pectin and stir until dissolved. Pulp the mango with a potato masher or, preferably, an immersion blender. Continue cooking on medium heat until the mixture will gel on the back of a chilled plate (10 to 15 minutes). Remove from heat and transfer to whatever storage you prefer. If canning, carefully follow standard canning procedures. I always can preserves whenever I cook them. The process is not complicated, but must be done carefully. You can find general instructions for this process online or in numerous cookbooks.

## Rye Toast with Cheese

196 Awesome and unusual appetizer. This recipe has been in my family for ages. I have no idea where it originated, but I've never seen it in a cookbook.

Posted by: MallardDuckLintBrush. Yield: 1 – 100 servings. Prep time: 20 minutes.

---

1 package Rosen's (or other cocktail) light rye squares
1 package any white melting cheese—I use baby Swiss
4 tablespoons mayonnaise
1 tablespoon dried tarragon
1/2 teaspooon cayenne pepper

Lightly toast the rye squares. You want them to be firm enough to stand up to the mayonnaise, but not fully toasted. Spread a thin layer of mayonnaise on each square. Sprinkle each square with tarragon. Lightly sprinkle each square with cayenne pepper. Top with cheese. Return squares to toaster or broiler and cook until cheese is lightly browned and bubbly. Serve hot. I find that cheese slices are easier to use, but grated cheese works as well.

## Spam Musubi

197 Hawai'ian treat made easy. Sushi rice recipe from www.japanesecooking101.com.

Posted by: Militant Bibliophile. Yield: 3 servings. Prep time: 60 minutes.

---

1 cup sushi rice
1 can Spam
3 tablespoons rice vinegar
3/4 tablespoon sugar
1/2 teaspoon salt
3 – 5 sheets roasted seaweed

Place the rice in cold water and agitate with your hands until the water becomes cloudy with starch, then drain. Wash the rice 2 – 3 more times and let sit in cold water for thirty minutes. Drain the water and add 1 1/4 cups of fresh water for cooking. Bring to a boil on high heat uncovered, then cover and let simmer on low for 15 minutes. Remove from heat, let stand ten minutes. Combine vinegar, sugar, and salt and mix until fully dissolved (heating helps, but don't boil the vinegar). Fluff the rice and cut in vinegar solution. In a frying pan or griddle, fry spam in cuts of about 1/4 inch thickness. Lay two cuts end for end at one end of a sheet of seaweed. Wet your hands and form the seasoned sticky rice into bullets roughly the size of the spam cutlet. Roll the sheet of seaweed over the two and allow it to conform to the rice. Note: the wetness of your hands and that of the rice should help seal up the seam. Once the seam is no longer in danger of opening, use a sharp knife or scissors to cut the two pieces apart. Conform the ends to the musubi and you've got your snack! Makes 6 – 8 rolls, depending on how generous you are with your rice.

***Chef's Notes:***
Be sure to work with wet hands when forming the rice and rolling the seaweed. It keeps the rice from sticking to you and helps form it into the shape you want, as well as getting the seaweed to adhere.

## Spinach Bacon Cheese Swirls

198 Bacon! Recipe is from my kid

Posted by: Euro. Yield: 4 – 5 servings. Prep time: 30 minutes.

---

large bag spinach
2 cups shredded mozzarella cheese
1 large onion, diced
8 strips soft-cooked bacon
dash garlic
dash salt
pat of butter
large rectangle puff pastry, rolled

Roll out puff pastry into larger rectangle—not so thin as to see through it, though. Saute onions in butter, then add spinach to sweat a bit. Season with garlic and salt. Let cool a few minutes, then add cheese and diced bacon. Mix/toss. Spread onto pastry. Roll up pastry, then slice into "wheels." Bake on greased sheet about 20 minutes at 400 degrees F.

## Dirty Martini Appetizer

199 Like vodka? Like olives? All-righty, then. Variations have been around awhile, don't know who to blame.

Posted by: Full-Metal Spanx. Yield: 6 moron servings. Prep time: 5 minutes.

---

8 ounces cream cheese
3 whole green onions, chopped
8 chopped green olives
3 tablespoons olive juice from jar
1 teaspoon vodka
1/4 teaspoon lemon pepper seasoning

Combine all ingredients and serve with crackers or on celery stalks. Left-overs make great toast spread in the morning.

## Crispy Zero-Carb Wings

200 Crispiest, easiest wings recipe ever courtesy of #science! I got it from thecookful.com.

Posted by: votermom. Yield: 4 moron servings. Prep time: 1 ½ hours.

---

10 chicken wings, cut into drums and flats
1 tablespoon baking powder (not baking soda)
1/2 teaspoon salt

Preheat oven to 250 degrees F (yes, 250 is correct). Cut 10 chicken wings into drums and flats, discard the tips. Put the 20 pieces into a bowl and toss with salt and baking powder. Put wings on a cooking rack on top of a baking sheet and bake for 30 minutes. Increase oven temperature to 425 degrees F and bake for 40 to 50 minutes until brown and crispy. Serve with your favorite sauce.

***Chef's Notes:***
Some people prefer baking powder without "sodium aluminum sulfate" in it, but I don't taste a difference.

## Fancy-Pants Canapes

201 For when royalty visit the trailer. I made these once for company, and they never came back.

Posted by: GolfBoy. Yield: 6 servings. Prep time: 25 minutes.

---

12 slices Wonder bread
1 can Spam
6 slices Kraft American cheese
1/2 cup Miracle Whip

Slice Spam into 12 slices the long way. Apply a layer of Miracle Whip to a slice of bread. Top with two slices of Spam. Add a slice of cheese. Apply a layer of Miracle Whip to another slice of bread. Place slice of bread, Miracle Whip side down, over the cheese. With a chef's knife, trim off bread crusts (save them for meat loaf). Bisect along both diagonals, resulting in four congruent right isosceles triangles. Repeat until the Spam and cheese are used up. Garnish tops with with olive slices, radish roses, etc. Serve before the air conditioner goes out.

***Chef's Notes:***
Velveeta will do in a pinch, but the slices won't be the right size.

## Deviled Eggs

202 Recipe is from the 1960 edition of *Better Homes and Gardens Cookbook*, which was a wedding gift to my mother (she still has it). Recipe sounds simple, but these are damn good deviled eggs. I've been making them for years and they always get eaten. I have a friend who is not fond of eggs, but she will eat these. They are good.

Posted by: Dr Alice. Yield: 12 servings (ha!). Prep time: 30 minutes.

---

6 eggs
2 tablespoons mayonnaise (real mayo!)
1 teaspoon vinegar (distilled or apple cider is fine)
¼ - ½ teaspoon salt
Dash white pepper
1 teaspoon mustard
¼ teaspoon paprika

Cover eggs with cold water in a pot, add dash of salt, and bring to a full boil. Then turn off the heat and let them sit 30 minutes (longer won't hurt). Peel the eggs and cut them in half. Place whites on a serving dish. Now take the yolks and force them through a sieve or grate them finely. This step really does make a difference, you get a better texture. It also allows you to get rid of any bits of undercooked yolk. Combine with all other ingredients. (Incidentally, I find the full 1/2 tsp of salt makes them too salty. I use a very scant 1/2 teaspoon.) Then either spoon the paste into the whites or make a poor man's pastry bag by putting all the yolk mixture into a ziplock bag and cutting off the tip of one corner. Squeeze the mixture into the whites. This saves time if you double or triple the recipe—which I recommend! Finally, sprinkle the filled eggs with additional paprika for color.

## Bocaditos Espanoles

203 Awesomeness distilled into bite-sized oralgasms. From *Seduced by Bacon: Recipes and Lore About America's Favorite Indulgence* by Joanna Pruess. This puts all other hors d'oeuvres to shame. They freeze well and are good to have on hand for impromptu orgies.

Posted by: All Hail Eris. Yield: 24 bocaditos. Prep time: 15 minutes.

---

6 slices (crumbled) cooked bacon
2 cups grated Manchego cheese
1/2 cup cream cheese
1/2 cup dried tart cherries, chopped
1/3 cup roasted and salted almonds, chopped
1 teaspoon smoked paprika
1/2 teaspoon salt
24 phyllo cups

Combine bacon, Manchego cheese, cream cheese, cherries, almonds, paprika, and salt in a food processor and pulse lightly until the mixture is blended but not completely smooth. You should be able to see little bits of the ingredients. Refrigerate until cold. Preheat oven to 350 degrees F. Roll the mixture into 1-inch balls; put one into each phyllo cup. Bake for 10 minutes. Remove, let stand for 5 minutes, and serve warm.

## Donna &&&&&&V's Mustard Shimp

204 Easy, delicious and low-carb. My old boss made this for an office party many years ago. A fine dish for a MoMe, particularly for those 'rons and 'ettes who are into their GAINZZ. Any Moron could make this.

Posted by: Donna&&&&&&V. Yield: 5 moron servings. Prep time: 25 minutes.

---

2 – 2 ½ pounds medium (not jumbo) shimp, cooked, peeled and deveined, tails on (you can use fresh or frozen thawed shrimp)
1/4 cup finely chopped parsley
1/4 cup finely chopped shallots
1/4 cup tarragon vinegar
1/4 cup white wine vinegar
1/2 cup good olive oil
4 heaping tablespoons Dijon mustard
2 teaspoons crushed red pepper flakes
2 teaspoons salt
ground black pepper to taste

If using frozen cooked shrimp, defrost according to directions, let drain and set aside. Mix all the other ingredients in a large bowl. Add the shrimp and stir to coat all of the shrimp. Cover and refrigerate for 6-8 hours. If making the shrimp for an evening party or for dinner, make it in the morning and let it sit but try not to exceed 8 hours by too much—you don't want the shrimp to get mushy!

## Charleston Pickled Shrimp

205 An old Southern classic. This is a *Southern Living* adaptation of a recipe from one of the oldest community cookbooks in the U. S., *Charleston Receipts* by the Junior League of Charleston, SC, printed in 1951. I double this recipe and bring to Christmas dinner at the SIL's every year, and it is devoured.

Posted by: Jane D'oh.    Yield: 12 servings.    Prep time: 23 minutes, plus 1 day for chilling.

---

2 pounds large raw, unpeeled shrimp
3 small white onions, thinly sliced
1/2 cup olive oil
1/4 cup tarragon vinegar
2 tablespoons pickling spices
2 teaspooons salt
1 teaspoon sugar
1 teaspoon Worcestershire sauce
1/2 teaspoon dry mustard
1/4 teaspoon ground red pepper
1/4 cup fresh parsley

Peel and devein shrimp. Cook in boiling water to cover just until shrimp turn pink and opaque, about three minutes. Drain and rinse with cold water. Layer shrimp and onions in a large bowl. Whisk together oil and next seven ingredients; pour over shrimp and onions. Cover and chill 24 hours, stirring occasionally. Stir in chopped parsley just before serving. Serve using toothpicks.

## Charleston Pickled Shrimp

206 An old Southern classic. This is a *Southern Living* adaptation of a recipe from one of the oldest community cookbooks in the U. S., *Charleston Receipts* by the Junior League of Charleston, SC, printed in 1951. I double this recipe and bring to Christmas dinner at the SIL's every year, and it is devoured.

Posted by: Jane D'oh.    Yield: 12 servings.    Prep time: 23 minutes, plus 1 day for chilling.

---

2 pounds large raw, unpeeled shrimp
3 small white onions, thinly sliced
1/2 cup olive oil
1/4 cup tarragon vinegar
2 tablespoons pickling spices
2 teaspooons salt
1 teaspoon sugar
1 teaspoon Worcestershire sauce
1/2 teaspoon dry mustard
1/4 teaspoon ground red pepper
1/4 cup fresh parsley

Peel and devein shrimp. Cook in boiling water to cover just until shrimp turn pink and opaque, about three minutes. Drain and rinse with cold water. Layer shrimp and onions in a large bowl. Whisk together oil and next seven ingredients; pour over shrimp and onions.

Cover and chill 24 hours, stirring occasionally. Stir in chopped parsley just before serving. Serve using toothpicks.

## Kahlua Pecan Brown Sugar Baked Brie

207 I got this recipe from www.noblepig.com.

Posted by: Tami. Yield: 6 – 8 servings. Prep time: 30 minutes.

---

1 whole wheel of Brie (19 ounces)—President Brie is best for this recipe
1 cup Kahlua
1 cup packed light brown sugar
1 cup whole or chopped pecans
crackers of your choice

Preheat oven to 350 degrees F. Carefully slice off the top off the rind of the Brie BUT do NOT completely remove. Bake for 15 minutes. When the Brie is done baking, the top can be easily removed to expose the creamy cheese. While the Brie is baking, in a medium saucepan combine the Kahlua and brown sugar and bring to a boil, then simmer for 10 – 15 minutes or until a syrupy consistency is made. Throw the pecans in for 2 minutes at the end to warm them through and completely cover with the sauce. Remove the Brie from the oven and completely remove the top rind. Pour Kahlua sauce over the Brie.

***Chef's Notes:***
Let the sauce cool some before pouring it on the Brie. If it's too hot, it will be too runny and turn the Brie into a gloppy mess. If the sauce becomes too thick due to cooling, reheat it a tiny bit.

## Blackberry Turkey (or Beef) Meatballs

208 From www.burprecipes.blogspot.com.

Posted by: Tami. Yield: 18 – 20 meatballs. Prep time: 30 – 45 minutes.

---

For the blackberry sauce:
12 ounces (about 4 cups) fresh or frozen blackberries
2 tablespoons butter
1 small yellow onion, finely chopped
1 jalapeno pepper, finely chopped
1 medium clove garlic, minced
2 teaspoons fresh thyme, chopped
4 tablespoons apple cider vinegar
2 tablespoons blackstrap molasses
2 tablespoons (generous) brown sugar
2 tablespoons prepared mustard
½ cup ketchup
½ teaspoon salt

For the meatballs:
3 tablespoons butter
1 large egg
½ cup bread crumbs
¼ cup grated Parmesan cheese
¼ cup chopped parsley
2 medium cloves garlic, minced
¼ cup shallot, minced
1 teaspoon salt
½ teaspoon freshly ground black pepper
1 pound ground turkey

To make blackberry barbecue sauce: puree the blackberries in a food processor or blender until finely blended. Set aside. Melt the butter in a medium saucepan. Add onions and jalapeno and cook over medium heat until the onions have softened and are beginning to brown. Add garlic and thyme and continue to cook for approximately one minute. Add blackberries and allow the mixture to simmer for approximately ten minutes. Add remaining ingredients, bring to a boil, and simmer for ten more minutes. Stir in salt. Remove from heat and strain through a fine mesh strainer to remove seeds. Allow to cool if not using right away. Can be made ahead. Will keep for 2-3 weeks in the refrigerator.

To make the meatballs: place egg into a large bowl and beat until blended. Add bread crumbs, Parmesan, parsley, garlic, shallot, salt and pepper. Mix in the turkey. Shape the turkey mixture into 1 1/4-inch-diameter meatballs. Place on a large plate or baking sheet. Heat the butter in a heavy large frying pan over medium-high heat. When foam dissipates, add the meatballs and saute until browned on all sides, about 5 – 7 minutes. Turn off heat; transfer the meatballs to a plate. Wipe out excess oil. Return all the meatballs to the pan and ladle 2 – 3 cups of the blackberry sauce over the top. Turn the heat to medium-low and simmer, stirring occasionally, until the sauce thickens slightly and the meatballs are cooked through, about 20 minutes. Sauce is also great on grilled chicken, pork, or ribs. These can also be heated in a crockpot.

## Fig and Blue Cheese Savouries

209 Little bombs of flavor. This recipe is by the Runaway Spoon on the Food52 website.

Posted by: lin-duh fell. Yield: about 2 – 3 dozen. Prep time: less than 1 hour.

---

1 cup flour, plus more for kneading
1/2 cup (4 ounces) butter, cut into several pieces
4 – 5 ounces blue cheese, crumbled
fresh ground black pepper, to taste
small jar good quality fig preserves

Preheat oven to 350 degrees F, move rack to center position. Line a baking sheet with parchment. Place flour, butter pieces, blue cheese, and fresh ground pepper (to taste) into a food processor. Process until dough comes together and starts to form a ball. Transfer dough to a floured surface and knead a few times to pull dough together. Break off small pieces, (about a tablespoon each), and roll into a balls. Use a pastry tamp dipped into flour to press the balls down to about 1/8 to 1/4 inch thick (the end of a 1 inch dowel or something similar also works). There should be an indent with a rim. Chill for about 10 – 15 minutes then fill the indents with a bit of the fig preserves. Bake for about 10-15 minutes until the savories are golden and the preserves are bubbly. Let cool for about 10 minutes then transfer to a serving plate. Enjoy!

***Chef's Notes:***
You can freeze these before baking for future use. Just bake them from frozen.

## Marinated Eggs

| 210 Soy sauce marinated soft boiled eggs. Adapted from Christina Tosi. |
|---|

Posted by: lin-duh fell. Yield: 12 eggs Prep time: 45 minutes, total time up to 24 hours.

---

2 ounces warm water
1 – 2 tablespoons honey or agave nectar
1 ounce rice vinegar
1 cup soy sauce
1 clove garlic, crushed
1 – 2 teaspoons Sriracha (optional)
ground pepper
12 eggs, room temperature

In a container that will fit all the eggs in one layer, whisk all the ingredients until blended except the eggs. Set aside. Bring a pot of water that will fit all the eggs to a boil. Gently lower the eggs into the boiling water and gently stir them around for a few seconds. Cook the eggs for EXACTLY 7 minutes. While eggs are cooking fill a large bowl with ice and cold water. When eggs are done, immediately transfer them to the ice bath. When eggs are cool, peel them and then place them in the marinade. Marinate them for at least 3 hours or up to 12 or more hours in the refrigerator. This is where your personal taste comes in. Stir/turn them occasionally so they marinate evenly. Remove from marinade and store in a covered container for up to a week. You can save the strained marinade for a few batches. Enjoy them alone as a snack, with some ramen noodles or rice, on a salad, etc. You can adjust the saltiness by marinating them for more or less time. All the seasonings can be adjusted to your personal taste.

## Low Carb Chicken Wings

| 211 Easy and tasty. From a magazine about 15 years ago—I've adjusted it to my tastes. |
|---|

Posted by: It's me donna. Yield: 20 servings or so with 4 each. Prep time: 20 minutes or so prep, 1 hour cooking.

---

4 pounds chicken wings
3 cups grated Parmesan cheese
3 tablespoons dried parsley
2 tablespoons dried oregano
3 teaspoons paprika
2 teaspoons salt
1 teaspoon black pepper
1 cup melted butter

Preheat oven to 350 degrees F. Separate wings from drumettes, or purchase already separated wings. Combine cheese, parsley, oregano, paprika, salt and pepper in shallow bowl. Line shallow baking pan with foil. Spray foil with cooking spray. Melt butter in shallow bowl. Dip each piece of chicken in the butter, then roll in cheese mixture. Arrange on foil-lined pan and bake 45 – 60 minutes. Great dipped in blue cheese dressing.

## Five Minute Quesadillas

212 Quick, easy quesadillas that any Moron can make, even while drinking Valu-Rite. Recipe came from lots of experimentation, but Pooky had the genius idea for the aioli sauce.

Posted by: pookysgirl. Yield: 1 Moron serving. Prep time: 5 minutes.

---

2 flour tortillas
1 tablespoon your choice of sauce (Ranch, Bacon Ranch, we like to use Stonewall Kitchen Maple Bacon Aioli)
1/2 cup 4-cheese Mexican blend (Sargento)
1/2 cup 6-cheese Italian blend (Sargento)
3/4 cup chicken breast strips
1/4 cup bacon pieces

Put the sauce in the middle of one of the tortillas. Lay the other tortilla on top of it and push down in a circular motion to spread the sauce evenly. Open the tortillas back up and sprinkle in one of the cheese blends. Place the chicken strips evenly across the tortilla and sprinkle in the bacon pieces. Add the other cheese blend and lay the other tortilla (sauce side down!) and press down gently. In an 1100-watt microwave, cooking this takes about 45 seconds. When done, cut in half and enjoy! You can assembly-line these pretty easily if you want to make more than one at a time.

## Academy Award (TM) Meatballs

213 Meatballs with BBQ sauce. Great appetizer. Adapted from a recipe I found on southernfood.about.com. I have tweaked it a bit. I like this recipe because it is not too heavy on the Italian seasonings. The BBQ sauce recipe is from Peg Bracken's *I Hate to Housekeep* book. The first time I made these I served them at an Oscars party, hence the name.

Posted by: Dr Alice. Yield: approximately 6 serving. Prep time: 25 minutes.

---

1/2 cup breadcrumbs
one egg, beaten
one carrot, finely grated
2 teaspoons zested lemon peel
2 teaspoons Worcestershire
2 pounds ground beef (or turkey)

*For sauce:*
1 bottle Heinz chili sauce
2/3 cup water
1/4 cup vinegar (I use slightly less)
1 teaspoon sugar
1 teaspoon prepared mustard
1/2 teaspoon onion or garlic powder or celery salt

Combine all the meatball ingredients and mix lightly with your hands. (Two points here: first, a Microplane grater is great for this recipe if you have one. You want both the carrot and the lemon zest finely shredded. Second, do not overmix or you will have dense, heavy meatballs. Do not want.) Now get out your pan, put in some cooking oil and brown the meatballs. You don't want them fully cooked through, just browned. At this stage you can put them on a cookie sheet and freeze, then bag them and you have ready to go meatballs. Or, have the sauce ingredients of your choice pre-mixed and warming on the stove, then toss in your meatballs and cook for 30 – 45 minutes. Serve with toothpicks. Or on rice for an entree.

To make the BBQ sauce, combine all of the sauce ingredients, simmer 10 minutes or so, then put in the meatballs. I like to use a little less vinegar, maybe 3 tablespoons.

### *Chef's Notes:*

Heinz chili sauce is NOT salsa. It is a mild ketchupy sauce, on the sweet side. Look in the condiments aisle.

## Mushroom Roulade

214 Adapted from the *J. Bildner & Sons Cookbook*, by Jim Bildner.

Posted by: RedMindBlueState. Yield: 10 – 12 appetizer portions, or up to 32 small slices as part of a brunch menu. Prep time: approximately 1 hour.

---

1 ounce dried wild mushrooms
1 pound fresh mushrooms
2 cloves of garlic
1/2 pound cooked lean ham
2 tablespoons butter
2 tablespoons sherry or Madeira
1/2 cup heavy cream
1 ounce cream cheese
1/4 cup chopped flat leaf parsley
6 eggs
1 egg white
1/2 teaspoon each salt, white pepper and nutmeg
2 tablespoons sherry or Madeira
3 tablespoons flour

To make the filling, place the dried mushrooms in a small bowl, and cover with hot water. Let stand for 20 minutes. Chop the button mushrooms finely. Mince the garlic. Dice the ham, or pulse in a food processor for a finer texture. Drain the wild mushrooms, reserving the soaking liquid. Rinse any remaining grit off the rehydrated mushrooms, and chop finely. Strain the soaking liquid through cheesecloth, a fine mesh strainer, or a paper towel; set liquid aside. Heat a large, 12" skillet over high heat, and add the butter. Add chopped fresh mushrooms, salt and pepper to taste, and cook, stirring occasionally until mushrooms have exuded their liquid, about 3 – 5 minutes. Add the reserved mushroom soaking liquid and cook until the liquid has evaporated and the mushrooms have begun to brown slightly. Add the chopped wild mushrooms and cook for about 1 minute, then add the garlic and cook for another minute. Add in diced ham, then stir in sherry or Madeira, cream and cream cheese. Lower heat to medium and stir to melt the cheese. Cook, stirring until the ham and mushrooms are coated. Stir in chopped parsley and remove from the heat.

Preheat the oven to 375 degrees F. Lightly oil a baking sheet (9" x 18") and line with oiled parchment paper. For a smaller sized roll, use two half-sized baking sheets (9" x 13"). Silicone baking mats can be used in place of parchment paper, but must be lightly oiled. Separate the eggs, placing yolks in one large bowl, whites in another. Add the extra egg white to the egg whites and set aside. Place egg yolks, salt white pepper and nutmeg in a stand mixer. Beat until thick and pale. Add sherry or Madeira and continue beating until egg yolks are very thick and almost white. Slowly blend flour into the egg mixture. Beat egg whites until very stiff, but not dry. With a spatula, fold egg whites into egg yolk mixture. Spread the batter into the prepared baking sheets, and bake until lightly brown and puffy, about 12 – 15 minutes. Remove the roulade from the oven and allow to cool for 2 minutes, then invert onto a sheet of plastic wrap and gently peel off the oiled parchment paper. Spread the filling in an even layer over the roulade and, using the plastic wrap to assist, roll up carefully, along the long side. Set the completed roulade seam side down and slice into ½" slices.

### *Chef's Notes:*

This can be made a day in advance and reheated. Made in two small baking sheets, it makes a great item for a brunch menu, and for those on a gluten-free diet, the flour can be omitted and the recipe will still work. Be sure to oil the parchment paper and baking sheet well, or the roulade will stick.

## Ferrous' Sausage Rolls

215 Delicious sausage wrapped in pastry. Everyone who says English food is terrible doesn't know the facts. My British wife made these for me just after we got married. Since then, I've taken the recipe for my own, adapted it and made modifications. This is the original, but feel free to make modifications on your own.

Posted by: Ferrous21. Yield: servings for 6 morons, or 1 very hungry one. Prep time: 1 hour, roughly.

---

1 pound sage-flavored ground sausage
1 pound plain ground sausage
1/2 yellow onion
2 tablespoons black pepper
2 tablespoons garlic salt
1 package puff pastry sheets
1 egg
1/2 cup diced green onions
2 tablespoons ground black pepper

Preheat your oven to 400 degrees F, and remove your puff pastry sheets from the freezer and let thaw, taking care to unfold them from the packaging before they thaw completely. In a large mixing bowl, combine both sausage varieties with green onions, salt & pepper. Using a fine grater, grate onion into sausage mixture and combine. Set aside. Separate puff pastry sheets into 3 identical sections and roll out until roughly double in size. (Flour is handy at this point) Lay out sausage mixture along one long edge of each rolled-out pastry sheet, roughly one inch thick, then roll up into puff pastry, pinching the pastry edges together. At this point, you should have a long pastry log filled with sausage. Cut into 1 inch sections, perforate each section with knife to let air escape. Arrange rolls on a non-stick baking sheet with about 1 inch of space between each roll. In a small bowl, whisk the egg together and and apply as egg wash to individual rolls. Bake in oven until the pastry is a rich golden brown, about 20 to 30 minutes. Serve as soon as practical.

Feel free to play around with different filling as well. This chef has found it practical to substitute the sage sausage for regular sausage and instead of the onion add 4 minced shallots, 1/2 cup of soy sauce, 1/2 cup of rice vinegar and 2 tablespoons of ginger. These rolls travel well and stand up to re-heating, so they work well for events where you can make them ahead of time and re-heat them later. There are plenty of other variations that you can do with the basic recipe. For instance, you can make larger rolls (say, 6 inches long) to take along to sporting events.

## Chicken Crack

216 Best chicken wing that never had a bone. Well, I got it from my wife, but I'm pretty sure she free-styled off the back of a bottle of Frank's RedHot.

Posted by: Captain Ned. Yield: 8 appetizer servings. Prep time: 10 minutes.

---

1 12.5-ounce can chicken packed in water
1 8-ounce brick full-fat cream cheese
1/2 cup chunky blue cheese dressing
1/2 cup Frank's RedHot Sauce
1 cup shredded cheddar cheese
salt and pepper to taste

Put everything in a small saucepan. Heat over low heat until everything is melted and smoogly. Serve immediately or put in crock pot to bring to work next day. Serve with tortilla/nacho chips of personal choice. Scales up easily, and heat easily controlled through the amount of Frank's RedHot used. Pre-packaged shredded cheese works better here as the cornstarch used to keep the cheese from clumping aids in firming up the mix.

## Lorene's Cheese Ball

217 Easy and Delicious. I first had this cheese ball on a Christmas tour of homes in Mount Vernon, Ohio. One of the hostesses served it.

Posted by: Ladylibertarian. Yield: 8 – 12 servings. Prep time: 10 minutes.

---

16 ounces cream cheese, softened
5-ounce jar Old English Sharp Cheddar
2 tablespoons chopped green onion
2 tablespoons chopped green pepper
2 tablespoons chopped green olives

Combine all ingredients. Form into ball. Cover and refrigerate until it is served. Serve with crackers.

## Prosciutto-Wrapped Asparagus

218 Quick. Easy. Delicious. To my knowledge, I came up with it. But based on its simplicity, I didn't split the atom.

Posted by: Gterz. Yield: 5 servings. Prep time: 15 minutes.

---

1/4 pound prosciutto
1 pound asparagus
1/2 cup balsamic vinegar

Boil asparagus until slightly tender but still firm. Remove from boiling water and put in ice bath to stop cooking process. Remove asparagus and wrap each stalk with one slice of prosciutto, lengthwise. Place in skillet over medium heat and gently turn. As the prosciutto cooks it will bind to and reheat the asparagus. The prosciutto should be nicely browned to add a crispy, baconesque texture. While this is cooking, place vinegar in saucepan over high heat. Let the vinegar boil until it becomes viscous and immediately remove from heat to prevent burning. Plate asparagus and lightly drizzle the sauce over the top two-thirds. Enjoy.

## Chicken Bacon Bites

219 Bacon, with chicken! (C'mon, bacon!) I found this recipe online about a decade ago. It was presented in a cartoonish format, rather like "The Oatmeal," but I failed to record the source (sorry!).

Posted by: Krebs v Carnot: Epic Battle of the Cycling Stars (TM). Yield: 6 servings. Prep time: 60 minutes.

---

2/3 cup brown sugar, loosely packed
2 chicken breasts, skinless
1 ½ tablespoons chili powder
1 pound bacon, sliced
1 cup pineapple juice

Slice chicken breasts into cubes about 1 inch per side. Place chicken pieces and pineapple juice in a bowl, cover, and set in refrigerator for two hours. Preheat oven to 350 degrees F. Mix together brown sugar and chili powder in a small bowl. Slice bacon into thirds across the strips. Remove chicken pieces from pineapple juice. Wrap a piece of bacon around each chicken piece and pin it in place with a wooden toothpick. Dunk each wrapped piece in the brown sugar and chili powder mixture and coat it thoroughly. Place pieces on an oven rack or broiling pan. Bake pieces for 40 minutes at 350 degrees F. Remove and serve hot.

### *Chef's Notes:*

Obviously this can serve as a takeoff point for many baked concoctions, as well as exploration of sauces to serve with these. Have at it!

## Cocktail Meatballs

220 A disappearing meatball magic act. Recipe is mine.

Posted by: liz953. Yield: about 50 balls. Prep time: 15 minutes.

---

1 pound ground beef
1/2 of a 4-ounce can water chestnuts
1/4 cup soy sauce
1 egg
1/2 teaspoon Worcestershire sauce
1/4 cup bread crumbs
1/2 teaspoon garlic powder

Finely chop water chestnuts. Combine well with the rest of the ingredients, add salt and pepper to taste.Roll into small meatballs, about an inch in diameter. Bake at 400 degrees F until cooked through, 20-25 minutes. Serve with sweet chili sauce or sweet and sour sauce (and toothpicks). Don't make these large, like Italian meatballs. You want to be able to pop the entire thing into your mouth. Recipe doubles easily. These freeze well after cooking.

## Curry Bites

221 Tasty and curried English muffin bits. A family-gathering favorite of my wife's family.

Posted by: Krebs v Carnot: Epic Battle of the Cycling Stars (TM). Yield: 64 to 96 bites. Prep time: 30 minutes.

---

1 cup shredded cheddar cheese
1/4 cup regular mayonnaise
1/4 cup chopped black olives
2 tablespoons chopped green onion
1/4 teaspoon curry powder
8 English muffins, split

Thoroughly mix first five ingredients together. Place 1 to 1 ½ tablespoons of mixture on one half of an English muffin and spread evenly out to its edges. Place muffin halves on a non air-cushioned cookie sheet. Place sheet in broiler at medium-high setting. Broil until topping is lightly browned. Remove from oven and allow to cool for five minutes on a wire rack. Transfer muffins to cutting board and cut into from four to six pieces. Serve warm.

***Chef's Notes:***
The non air-cushioned requirement for the cookie sheet is important for thorough baking of the muffins.

## Crustless Mini Quiches

222 Low carb, party-pleasing breakfast quiches. Recipe is from Epicurious.com. These transport well for office functions. You can refrigerate them overnight and then reheat them in the microwave.

Posted by: fly gal.    Yield: 48 quiches.    Prep time: 30 minutes.

---

1/2 head broccoli, thick stems removed
6 large eggs
6 egg yolks
2/3 cup whole milk
2/3 cup heavy cream
1 teaspoon kosher salt
1/2 teaspoon black pepper
3/4 cup shredded sharp Cheddar cheese
3/4 cup finely chopped ham
1/2 cup halved grape tomatoes
48 strips bacon (optional)

Preheat oven to 375 degrees F. Lightly spray two 24-cup muffin pans with cooking spray or line with paper liners. Have ready a bowl of ice water. Bring a saucepan of water to boil, add the broccoli and blanch 30 seconds. Drain and transfer immediately to the ice water to stop the cooking. When cool, drain, pat dry and chop coarsely. In a bowl whisk whole eggs, egg yolks, milk, cream, cheese, salt and pepper. To the baking cups, add a few pieces of broccoli and cheese. Pour the egg mixture in each prepared cup, leaving room for pieces of broccoli and a couple halves of tomatoes. Top with extra cheese if desired.
*Optional: Instead of paper liners, line each cup with one strip of bacon. Pre-cook the bacon in the oven for 10-15 mins (or until crispy). Bake until tops are puffy and lightly browned, about 15 minutes. Cool for 10 minutes and arrange on platter.

## Beery Peanut Brittle

223 Sweet, spicy, beer-flavored peanut brittle. This is my own recipe from my food blog, oggi-icandothat.blogspot.com.

Posted by: Oggi.    Yield: 2 servings.    Prep time: 15 minutes.

---

1 cup toasted peanuts
½ teaspoon flaked sea salt
1 teaspoon baking soda
1 tablespoon butter, diced

1 cup sugar
¼ cup light corn syrup
1 cup (fruity or light) beer
1/8 teaspoon chipotle powder

Butter a large baking pan or line with silpat, set aside. Mix first 4 ingredients, set aside. In a large saucepan, mix the beer, sugar, corn syrup, and chipotle powder. Boil over moderate heat for 12 minutes until golden in color. Stir in the peanut mixture and quickly spread on the prepared pan. Let cool and break into small pieces. Store in an airtight jar.

## Dunkers

224 Cookies to be eaten with tea or coffee. This is my grandmother's recipe, her German-born mother taught it to her.

Posted by: Lirio100. Yield: 2 – 4 dozen. Prep time: 2 hours?

---

1 1/2 cups hot water
6 cups granulated sugar
3/4 cups melted lard
1 teaspoon baking soda
1 teaspoon salt
1 teaspoon ground cloves
8 – 10 cups flour

Dissolve the sugar in the hot water. Mix together the lard, baking soda, salt, ground cloves, and flour. Mix the liquid ingredients with the dry, starting with the 8 cups of flour, a 1/2 cup at a time. Test a bit of dough on the cookie sheet--if it spreads add more flour a 1/2 cup at a time. Roll the dough into a log about 2 inches in diameter. Slice into pieces an inch wide, then roll into a ball and place on cookie sheet. Bake at 350 – 375 degrees F for about 10 minutes. Let cool completely.

***Chef's Notes:***
DO NOT eat these unless dunking them into a liquid, such as coffee or tea. They cool hard.

## Grandma Buck's Ebleskivers

225 My Danish rgandmother's Christmas Eve treat. From my maternal grandmother Marie. Recipe found on a handwritten card in her kitchen after she passed away.

Posted by: geoffb5. Yield: a lot. Prep time: a couple hours.

---

1 package dry yeast
1 teaspoon sugar
1/2 cup warm water
4 cups all-purpose flour

1 teaspoon salt
4 large eggs
1 can evaporated milk
1 can warm water

In a cup mix yeast, sugar, and 1/2 cup warm water. Let yeast start working. Mix together in large bowl the flour, eggs, salt, evaporated milk, and can of warm water. Add yeast mixture to bowl. Let mixture rise for 1 hour in warm place covered with a towel. Cook in ebleskiver pan with shortening by putting some shortening in each cup to melt. Then fill each cup 3/4 full with batter. When bottom is browned turn with fork to brown top of ball. A filling such as apple sauce can be added to the ball before turning so as to be inside the pancake ball. Put cooked balls in covered dish and cover warm balls, in layers, with brown sugar. Keep warm till served. Store leftovers in refrigerator. Leftovers are good served warm or cold.

***Chef's Notes:***
This dish requires a special pan called an Ebleskiver pan.

## Quick Potato Pancakes

226 Ultimate comfort food using leftover mashed potatoes. Family recipe.

Posted by: Artisanal ette. Yield: depends on how much mashed potatoes you use. Prep time: depends on how much dough you make.

---

mashed potatoes
flour
salt
butter

Use only traditional creamy, whipped mashed potatoes made with potatoes, milk/cream, butter and salt, and whipped light and fluffy with no lumps. No garlic! Mix mashed potatoes, flour, and salt to taste in a large bowl until dough consistency. It will take more flour than you think; add a bit at a time so that you do not add too much. Roll out large thin (1/8th thick or so) rounds that will fit into a large skillet. Pre-heat skillet, dry. Fry the large, thin pancakes in the hot, dry skillet until browned on both sides. Move the pancake to a dish, and smear both sides with butter (I use small blocks of cold butter on the end of a fork but go ahead and use your fingers if you like!). Eat while fresh from the pan.

## Handkase mit Musik

227 German bar food. Common bar snack in Germany.

Posted by: FaCubeItches. Yield: 4ish servings. Prep time: 30 minutes.

---

10 ounces farmer's cheese
1 large or 2 medium onions, Vidalia preferred
oil and vinegar sufficient to coat
large pinch fennel seeds
1 loaf rye or black cocktail bread

Slice or cube farmer's cheese; size to fit on cocktail bread. Dice onions, put cheese and onions in bowl. Mix oil and vinegar—you just need enough to thoroughly coat cheese and onions; add to bowl. Refrigerate until cold (can be served warm if desired) Spoon mix onto plate or serve directly from bowl. Sprinkle fennel seeds over top (if serving from plate). Serve with cocktail bread—just spoon mixture onto each slice.

## BBQ Artichokes

228 Grilled artichokes. Recipe is from Frank Ostini, Hitching Post Restaraunt, Buellton, CA.

Posted by: CaliGirl. Yield: 4 servings. Prep time: 70 minutes.

---

4 artichokes
4 tablespoons butter
2 tablespoons white wine
4 tablespoons olive oil
2 tablespoons fresh lemon juice
salt and freshly ground pepper to taste

*Dipping Sauce -*
2 cups mayonnaise
4 sun-dried tomatoes
2 teaspoons ancho or pasilla powder
1/2 teaspooon each cayenne pepper, chili powder, paprika
2 large onions
1/4 cup (or to taste) garlic cloves

Preheat outdoor grill to medium heat. Wash artichokes, place in large steamer until heart is tender, about 45 minutes depending on size. Allow to cool. Slice in half and remove chokes with a spoon. Melt butter and olive oil in a pan, add white wine and lemon juice. Keep warm. Grill artichokes about 10 minutes, basting with the butter mixture, and finish with salt and pepper to taste. I grill these over red oak. Artichokes can be cooked a day ahead and refrigerated.

For the dipping sauce, roast onions and garlic in separate foil packets on grill on indirect heat until soft. The onions will take about 30 minutes, the garlic about 1 hour to 1 1/2 hours. In a food processor process mayo, onions, garlic, tomatoes, chili powder, paprika, cayenne pepper, ancho or pasilla powder, and pinch of salt. This sauce may also be made ahead and refrigerated.

## Olive Garden Zuppa Toscana Knock Off

229 Tuscan soup similar to that of the Olive Garden by way of "The Tuscan Recipes" website. Most of the ingredients are probably on hand in the average moron's kitchen. Prep to eating is about one hour. Impossible to eat only one bowl. You can't tell the difference from the Olive Garden's version.

Posted by: Joe S. Yield: 8 servings. Prep time: 20 minutes.

---

1 pound ground Italian sausage
1 1/2 teaspoons crushed red pepper flakes
1 large white onion, diced
2 teaspoons garlic puree
10 cups water
8 cubes chicken boullion
1 cup heavy whipping cream
3 large russet potatoes
bunch kale
4 pieces bacon

Saute Italian sausage and crushed red pepper in a large pot. Drain excess fat, refrigerate while you prepare other ingredients In the same pan, saute bacon, onions and garlic over low-medium heat for approximately 15 minutes or until the onions are soft. Add bouillon cubes and water to the pot and heat until it starts to boil. Add the sliced potatoes and cook until soft, about half an hour. Add the heavy cream and just cook until thoroughly heated. Stir in the sausage let heat through, add rough diced kale to serving bowls and ladle soup on top. Chow!

## Spinach and Egg Appetizer

230 Any vegetable is better with cheese. From the long-gone Gondoliere Italian and Steaks of Oxford, Mississippi.

Posted by: Colonel Kurtz. Yield: 2 moron servings. Prep time: 10 minutes.

---

1 package (8 ounces) frozen spinach
garlic powder to taste
1 large handful shredded mozzarella
grated Parmesan to taste
1 or 2 eggs

Plan ahead, defrost the spinach. Take a frying pan, get it preheating on the stove while you get everything else going. Put spinach into pan, powder it with garlic to taste. Let it cook a bit. Crack 1 or 2 eggs into the spinach, continue stirring as with scrambled eggs. Throw in the shredded mozzarella, stir until eggs are cooked and cheese is melted. Top with grated Parmesan and serve.

***Chef's Notes:***
Lubing the pan helps. Butter, olive oil, even used Italian sausage drippings once. Speaking of Italian sausage, I once did a large batch with Italian sausage and called it an entree.

## Charleston Pickled Shrimp

231 An old Southern classic. This is a *Southern Living* adaptation of a recipe from one of the oldest community cookbooks in the U. S., *Charleston Receipts* by the Junior League of Charleston, SC, printed in 1951. I double this recipe and bring to Christmas dinner at the SIL's every year, and it is devoured.

Posted by: Jane D'oh. Yield: 12 servings. Prep time: 23 minutes, plus 1 day for chilling.

---

2 pounds large raw, unpeeled shrimp
3 small white onions, thinly sliced
1/2 cup olive oil
1/4 cup tarragon vinegar
2 tablespoons pickling spices
2 teaspooons salt
1 teaspoon sugar
1 teaspoon Worcestershire sauce
1/2 teaspoon dry mustard
1/4 teaspoon ground red pepper
1/4 cup fresh parsley

Peel and devein shrimp. Cook in boiling water to cover just until shrimp turn pink and opaque, about three minutes. Drain and rinse with cold water. Layer shrimp and onions in a large bowl. Whisk together oil and next seven ingredients; pour over shrimp and onions. Cover and chill 24 hours, stirring occasionally. Stir in chopped parsley just before serving. Serve using toothpicks.

## How to Properly Roast Your Nuts (Almonds)

232 Experiment to find your ideal shade. Simple family method.

Posted by: Merovign. Serves Oh boy. Prep time: 45 minutes.

---

raw almonds
salt

Preheat oven to 325 degrees F. Arrange uncooked almonds on a baking tray, dense or loose as you like, in one layer. While roasting the almonds (30 minutes, but start checking at 25 or when you smell distinctly almondy roasting smells - they vary a LOT), mix some salt in warm water, basically to saturation. Call it six tablespoons per cup if you're *obsessed* with numbers. Pour the saltwater in a squirt bottle. You may want to cover an area with paper bags to absorb overspray, because when the almonds are done to your taste (be aware they will get a little darker and more roasty/bitter after you take them out), you're going to remove them from the oven and spray them with salt water. Turn once during spraying. You end up with a much stronger and richer-flavored almond than you're ever likely to get from a can (soaking in saltwater before cooking is one of the reasons these are rarely fully roasted). Experiment with cooking times looking for light to dark tan interiors to get a feel for your flavor options. This *can* work with other types of nuts, but not really nut mixes. Your results will vary a lot.

## Nordstrom's Tomato Basil Soup

233 Best damn tomato soup. Adapted from Blake Roger for Serious Eats.

Posted by: lin-duh fell. Yield: 8 servings. Prep time: 60 – 90 minutes.

---

6 tablespoons olive oil
4 large carrots, peeled and diced
1 large onion, diced
2 tablespoons dried basil
2 28-ounce cans whole Roma tomatoes, peeled
1 quart (32 ounces) chicken broth or stock
1 pint heavy cream
salt & pepper to taste

In a heavy-bottomed stockpot, heat oil over medium-high until shimmering. Add onions and carrots, cook until almost soft, about 10 minutes. Add basil and cook until vegetables are completely soft, about another 5 – 10 minutes. Add tomatoes and broth, bring to a boil then turn heat down and simmer for 30 – 45 minutes. Remove from heat and let cool a little then puree in a blender/food processor (in batches) or use a stick blender. At this point you can strain for a silky texture or leave as is. Return to pot and over low heat, slowly stir cream into soup a little at a time. Bring soup to desired temperature and then serve hot. You can garnish this soup with croutons or buttered toasted baguette rounds.

## Egg McMorons

234 A great hearty egg sandwich for REAL men and women. Inspired by Egg McMuffins at McDonalds.

Posted by: qdpsteve. Yield: 1 serving. Prep time: 5 – 10 minutes.

---

1 each egg
2 – 4 thick cheese slices of your choice (I prefer pepper jack)
2 – 9999 slices REAL or Canadian bacon
1 – 4 ounces mayo concoction of your choice
1 Pro-Brexit English muffin

Did you know you can MICROWAVE-fry eggs?? Yes you can! Just splat an egg's innards onto a plate and nuke it for about 45 seconds. If it's not done, keep going 10 seconds at a time until it's warm, firm and appears ready to eat. Once it's done, cut out the yolk heart and its white surroundings in a circular size close to the diameter of your muffins. Of course you can take the leftover egg scraps and place them in your sandwich as well. Open up your muffins and place on them your bacon (you're not at the mercy of the fast food fascists so put on as much as you want!), your cheese, and your sauce (put it on the meat and cheese, not on the muffin itself or it will get soggy). Finally, plop your nuked egg on there. Put it together and enjoy – it's better than what any clown on tv could ever sell you. You'll love it so much, you'll be writing up Top 5 Lists of ways to thank qdpsteve for this recipe!

## Old Bay Pretzel-and-Cheese Cookies

235 Not a sweet cookie. Recipe is from *Dorie's Cookies* by Dorie Greenspan.

Posted by: Aviator.    Yield: 3 dozen cookies.    Prep time: 20 minutes.

---

1 ½ cups all-purpose flour
2 teaspoons Old Bay seasoning
¼ teaspoon salt
12 tablespoons cold butter, cut into 24 pieces
4 ounces shredded sharp cheddar cheese
2 ounces salted pretzels, coarsely chopped

Combine flour, Old Bay and salt in a food processor; pulse to combine, then scatter butter on top of flour mixture. Pulse until dough forms clumps, stopping occasionally to scrape down sides of bowl. Add cheese and pretzels; pulse to combine. Knead dough briefly on a work surface. Divide in half; shape each half into a 9-inch log. Wrap each tightly in plastic wrap; freeze at least 1 hour and for up to 2 months.

Preheat oven to 350 degrees F. Cut dough into 1/2-inch-thick slices (easiest with a serrated knife). Place slices 1 inch apart on parchment-lined baking sheets. Bake 19 – 21 minutes, rotating sheets if necessary for even cooking, or until firm and golden. Cool on sheets 5 minutes, then transfer to cooling racks to cool completely.

***Chef's Notes:***
This is not a sweet cookie and goes great with Bloody Marys or beer. Good with a bit of homemade cranberry jam (For cranberry jam recipe, see recipe for Cranberry Margarita in Drinks chapter).

## Fool's Toffee

236 Easy, tasty toffee recipe—no candy thermometer needed. From the *Colorado Cache Cookbook* by the Junior League of Denver, but it looks like there are other variations of this on the internet.

Posted by: Lizzy. Yield: 5 Moron servings. Prep time: 30 minutes.

---

1 cup butter (do not substitute)
1 cup brown sugar, packed
36 Saltine crackers
11 1/2 ounces milk chocolate chips
1/2 cup chopped pecans

Preheat oven to 350 degrees F. Line a jelly roll pan with foil. Place the single layer of saltines on the pan. Make sure they're close together. Melt the chocolate chips. In a small saucepan, mix the butter and brown sugar, then boil it or 4 minutes. Quickly pour the butter mixture over the saltines, spreading it as evenly as possible. Bake the saltines for 5 minutes. Immediately upon removing the pan from the oven, spread the melted chocolate over the saltines. Sprinkle the nuts over the chocolate. Place the pan in the fridge to cool. When ready to serve, break the toffee into pieces. Store the toffee in the fridge. It's a little tricky to make. And it may not work the first time, but be precise and sequential in your steps and you'll have good results.

## Dill Pickles In a Bucket

237 Dill pickles made fresh from the garden. Original recipe developed by the moron author.

Posted by: bergerbilder. Yield: 100 pickles. Prep time: 25 minutes.

---

1/4 cup non-iodized granulated salt
3 cups white vinegar
approximately 15 fresh pickling cucumbers
1 or 3 large or small stalks fresh dill weed
5 cloves garlic
1 5-quart ice cream bucket with lid
8 cups water

Cut cucumbers into wedges, 6 per cuke (you might want to trim the ends before cutting). Layer into bucket with dill stalks and garlic slices until full. Bring water, vinegar, and salt to boil. Slowly pour the hot brine over cucumber slices until full. Make up any shortage of brine with propotional amount of salt, water, and vinegar. Cover all with bucket lid. Let stand 1 day at room temperature, then refrigerate until cold. Keep refrigerated until all pickles are gone. Cider vinegar can be used, but shelf life is not as long. Using iodized salt will also reduce shelf life.

## Grain-free Granola

238 Granola made without oatmeal or other grains. I developed this recipe myself, because I love granola but am trying to avoid grain-based foods. Rich stuff! A little snack of this goes a long way and keeps you full for quite a while.

Posted by: lauraw. Yield: 10+ servings. Prep time: 40 minutes to an hour.

---

3 tablespoons coconut oil
2 cups flaked coconut, unsweetened
4 cups whole or chopped nuts and/or seeds, your choice*
1 cup dried fruit, chopped**
2 egg whites
1/4 cup honey
1 teaspoon cinnamon
3 teaspoons vanilla extract
1 teaspoon finely grated lemon zest
1/2 teaspoon salt

Preheat the oven to 325 degrees F. Place a sheet of parchment paper in a cookie sheet. Place the coconut oil on the parchment paper and set the cookie sheet in the oven to melt the oil. Mix the coconut and nuts together in a bowl. Place about a cup of the mixture in a blender or food processor and grind it into coarse meal. Return the nut meal to the bowl with nuts. Add the dried fruit and mix all together. In a large clean bowl, whip the egg whites until they form soft white peaks. Add the remaining five ingredients and whip again to incorporate fully. Add the nut mixture to the egg whites and mix thoroughly. Remove oiled pan from oven. Pour granola mix into hot pan and spread it all out over the coconut oil from edge to edge. Flatten it out firmly and evenly with the back of the spatula. Place in the center of the oven and bake for about half an hour, turning pan halfway through cooking time to encourage even browning. If you have a convection oven you may not need to turn the pan. Turn the heat down to 275 degrees F starting at about the fifteen minute mark. Start keeping a close eye on the granola, as nuts can scorch quickly. We're aiming for an even golden brown.

Sometimes toasting the granola takes fifty minutes, sometimes it takes just half an hour. I suspect the difference is in the total moisture content of your original nuts/ egg white mix. Just keep with it. Lift some pieces up with a fork. If the top starts to scorch while the bottom seems raw, move the pan to the bottom rack. And vice-versa. When all is toasted light brown, remove the pan from the oven and let it cool and dry out in place completely. Break it up into chunks and pack in ziploc bags or tins.

* I like a mix of whole pecans and blanched sliced or slivered almonds. Macadamias for holiday treats.
** if I don't feel like chopping dried fruit I just use dried cranberries or dried sour cherries. And use sliced or ribbon-size dried coconut, not the finely shredded stuff. We're trying to mimic the texture of large oatmeal flakes.

***Chef's Notes:***
It's a pain in the ass, but don't be tempted to leave out the lemon peel. You can substitute other citrus zest (they all work) if you like, but the citrus really makes this snack awesome and shouldn't be left out.
If you don't have a zester, just peel some big pieces of lemon peel off with a knife or vegetable peeler and throw them in the blender with the nuts you're going to pulverize in the beginning of the recipe.

## Ukrainian Breakfast Nosh Sandwich

239 Yummy snack to prepare for the workday. Arthur M. from Kharkov taught me this one. Be sure to use real Baltic sprats! One time I cheated and used smoked sardines and everyone knew! We would share this out among 3 to 5 cow-orkers with the morning coffee or strong black tea. nomnomnom!

Posted by: sock_rat_eez. Yield: 3 or 4 servings. Prep time: 20 minutes, more or less.

---

1 big slice rye bread
1 can Riga smoked sprats
1 garlic dill pickle
1 or 2 hard-boiled egg
1 or 2 tablespoons mayonnaise

Place bread on a sheet of foil. Good quality rye bread may be obtained at a Polish or Eastern European deli. Look for the stuff with the fewest ingredients and a label indicating small bakery origin for preference. If a round loaf, use a big middle slice, otherwise 2 may be required. Spread an adequate amount of mayonnaise on the bread. Slice the pickle 1/8 – 3/16 inch thick, radially or lengthwise, and place on the mayo-coated bread, covering it completely. Apply a layer of sprats similarly. Top off with sliced hard-boiled egg. Wrap and take to work to share with your Ukrainian co-workers. To serve, slice into 1 ½ - 2 inch squares.

## Danish Gravad Laks

240 AKA Gravlax. An old Danish family recipe. You'll never pay $6.00 for 4 ounces of packaged lox again!

Posted by: LASue. Yield: 1 – 10 servings. Prep time: 25 minutes + 24-48 hours for curing.

---

1 ½ - 2 pounds salmon fillet, boned, skin on if possible (but works without skin too)
5 tablespoons kosher salt
4 tablespoons brown sugar
1 tablespoon freshly cracked black pepper
1 bunch fresh dill, chopped or whole
1/4 cup lemon vodka, limoncello, vodka or aquavit

If you have a whole salmon, cut it in half, lengthwise (butterfly it). Line a glass baking dish large enough to hold the salmon lying flat, with saran wrap. Leave several inches of saran wrap draped over the ends of the dish. Lay one half of the fresh salmon, skin side down and flesh side up, in the dish. Mix the salt, sugar, and pepper in a bowl. Sprinkle half of the dry seasoning over the salmon, lay on half of the dill, then dot with half of the lemon vodka. Repeat the process on the other half of the salmon using up the remainder of the spices, dill and vodka. (Save a few sprigs of dill for serving.) Place the salmon halves back together, fleshy sides together and skin on the outside. Wrap the fish tightly in the plastic wrap. Place a board or cooking sheet on top of the fish and weigh it all down with a brick or whatever is handy (canned food also works). Put the salmon in the refrigerator for 24 – 48 hours. Turn it over about every 12 hours; re-weigh it down after each turn. To serve, unwrap the fish and rinse the salt mixture off. Using a very sharp, long knife, cut the fish on an angle into very thin slices. Plate the salmon with fresh dill and lemon slices or mustard. Serve as part of a smorgasbord, use it on open face sandwiches, or add it to an omelet.

## Spicy or Not Snack Mix

241 Chex Mix with or without cayenne pepper. Probably off a box of Chex cereal but it's been tweaked many times since then.

Posted by: Boots. Yield: 12 servings. Prep time: 45 minutes.

---

8 cups variety of dry cereal (Chex, Crispex, Life)
1 cup bagel chips
1 cup salted mixed nuts
1 cup mini pretzels
1 1/2 sticks (3/4 cup) butter
1 1/2 teaspoon seasoned salt (Spike or any other)
1 teaspoon onion salt
1 1/2 teaspoon sweet paprika

1/2 teaspoon or more ground cayenne pepper
1 – 2 tablespoons Worcestershire sauce or soy sauce

Combine all the dry ingredients in a large bowl—cereals, nuts, bagel chips, pretzels. Combine all the other ingredients (butter and spices) in a smaller, microwave safe bowl. Microwave the butter/spices for 30 seconds on high, stir, and continue to heat for 10 seconds at a time until the butter is melted. Pour the melted butter over the dry ingredients and mix well. Divide the mixture between two lasagna pans (9x13)—no need to butter the pans as there's plenty of butter in the snack mix. Use a rubber spatula to get all the butter and spices out of the bowl and into the pans. Bake at 325 degrees F for 20 minutes, stirring several times while baking. Cool slightly then serve. Store any leftovers in an airtight container.

***Chef's Notes:***
Butter is better than margarine or cooking oil. Modify the amount of spices to suit your tolerance of spiciness. Start with less and increase the amount the next time if necessary.

## Country Boy's Mom's Homemade Chex Mix

> 242 CB's Ultimate Crack Snack My mom has been making this snack since like forever. It came from my Grandma on my Dad's side, but from there nobody knows.

Posted by: Country Boy. Yield: I dunno, 6 or 7 servings? Prep time: roughly 2 1/2 hours total.

---

3 cups regular Cheerios cereal
3 cups Wheat Chex cereal
3 cups Corn Chex cereal
3 cups Rice Chex cereal
1/2 bag stick pretzels
3 1/2 sticks butter (margarine doesn't work)
5 tablespoons Worcestershire sauce
1 teaspoon onion salt
1 teaspoon garlic salt
1 teaspoon celery salt

Mix the cereal and pretzels together in an aluminum baking pan like they use for turkey or roasts (you know what I mean). In a pan on the stove, melt the butter while adding to it the Worcestershire sauce and salts. After the butter is melted, slowly pour the sauce over the cereal and pretzels, using a large spoon to mix the sauce in with the ingredients as you go. Once it's all mixed together, bake in the oven at 250 degrees F for two hours, stirring the contents every 20 minutes. Enjoy!

## Emergency Raisin Salami Sammich

243 No cooking necessary! Confuse your taste buds! Ace can cook better than me. When I was a kid, this is what I made to eat, if the ingredients were there. I don't know if anything this ridiculous has ever been published in a hoity-toity publication, let alone a common, vulgar one. Mrs. DIG says this sammich is weird. I like the spiciness of the salami combined with the sweetness of the raisins. A nice combo. For me at least!

Posted by: Deplorable Ian Galt. Yield: 1 sammich. Prep time: 2 – 4 minutes.

---

2 slices raisin bread
deli salami, sliced
Miracle Whip to taste

Apply a *thin* layer of Miracle Whip on one side of each slice of raisin bread. Put the salami on one of the slices, and place the other slice on top of the salami, preferably with the mayo on the *inside* of the sammich. A cross section should normally look like this:
(from top to bottom)

Raisin Bread
Miracle Whip
Salami
Miracle Whip
Raisin Bread

# Sides

*Mac and cheese with grilled chipmunk cheeks?*
*Or plumber's soup? It's all full of leeks*
*But you'd best plan ahead*
*'Cause it's often been said:*
*Preparation time? Roughly #two weeks*

# *Starches*

## Hashbrown Casserole

244 Cheesy potatoes. This recipe came from church suppers.

Posted by: ALH. Yield: 8 – 10 servings. Prep time: 10 minutes or so.

---

32 ounces frozen hashbrowns, diced style is best
2 cups shredded cheddar cheese
1 stick (8 tablespoons) butter, melted
1 can cream of chicken soup
1 pint sour cream
1 sleeve Ritz crackers

Mix potatoes, cheese, soup, sour cream and butter in an extra large mixing bowl. Spread in a 9 x 13 glass baking dish. Crumble Ritz crackers, spread evenly on top of potato mixture. Bake at 375 degrees F until gold and bubbly, about 40 minutes. Goes well with breakfast or dinner. I usually serve with ham or sausage.

## Mom's Despair (Spam & Rice)

245 A drunk bachelor go-to classic. I created this one night before starting on my second twelve-pack, but I'm certain other people in other places have done this. I called this "Mom's Despair" because she taught me to cook, well enough that my Dad thought I did as good a job as she did on all the standards, like chili beans, spaghetti, etc. She was pleased with me. When I came up with this, she scowled, told me I was going down a very dark path of error, and to make sure that no one thought she had anything to do with its origin. This dish pairs well with the second twelve pack of the evening.

Posted by: Monty James. Yield: 2 – 3 servings—sometimes 1. Prep time: 30 minutes.

---

12-ounce can Spam
1 box Rice-A-Roni, Uncle Ben's, or other flavored rice or pasta mix
½ to 1 cup frozen or fresh mixed vegetables (optional)
1 or more eggs (optional)
pepper to taste
seasoning salt, or some other dry seasoning mix
marinade of some sort (optional)
flour tortillas (optional)

Remove Spam from can, and rinse the gelatin off. Dry with paper towel. Using sharp knife, cut Spam into cubes of a size which pleases you. Season with dry seasoning of your choice, salt and pepper, or not at all, whatever makes you happy. Brown Spam in frying pan, gently, but try to render as much of the grease out of it as you can. Alternately, you can toss the cubed Spam with some sort of marinade (my favorite is Basque Company Meat Tenderizer) and brown in the oven in a roasting pan at about 325 degrees F. Whichever method you use, don't let it get too overdone. Remove from pan with slotted spoon, and use paper towels to soak up any grease on the meat. Prepare flavored rice mix according to instructions on box. Dump cooked Spam in for about the last ten or so minutes cooking time. Toss thoroughly and eat.

There's a lot of scope for doctoring this up, the basic idea is just Spam and rice. You can put mixed vegetables in the rice while you're cooking it, and when you've added the Spam you will have a nutritionally complete product, after a fashion. Crack an egg into any leftovers, mix well, and fry up some patties for breakfast. Good reason to leave the grease in the pan from the night before. Or put another egg in there and scramble it, roll up in a flour tortilla, and make breakfast burritos. Good hangover remedy. You can vary the ration of Spam to rice, i.e. use a smaller 8-ounce can of Spam, or get one of those 16-ounce cans of DAK Premium Ham. Tabasco is good on this; I also like to put plenty of Worcestershire sauce and cracked black pepper on a big bowl at oh-dammit-thirty in the morning.

## German Potato Salad

246 Warm comfort food. With names in the family tree like Karlson and Thoerwachter, you know this is authentic. Passed down from my wife's grandmother.

Posted by: Rocket Jones. Yield: 16 servings. Prep time: 30 minutes.

---

5 pounds potatoes
12 slices bacon, each cut into eighths
4 tablespoons bacon drippings
1 cup diced onion
2 tablespoons flour
4 tablespoons sugar
2 teaspoons salt
1/2 teaspoon pepper
2/3 cup vinegar
1 1/3 cup water

Boil the potatoes until tender. Drain and slice ¼ inch thick. Cook bacon. Drain (reserving 4 tablespoons drippings), and add bacon to potatoes. Cook onion in reserved drippings until tender. Stir in flour, salt, pepper, and sugar to onions. Add vinegar and water. Bring to a boil, stirring constantly. Pour over potato mixture and mix gently until well coated. Serve warm. Grandma always peeled the potatoes. I don't bother.

## Red Beans, Rice and Andouille Sausage

247 Easy fixings for a covered dish event. This came from the Zatarain's Red Beans and Rice Dinner mix instructions, with specific additions. Easy on the chef and pocketbook, and seems to be a hit when made.

Posted by: NaCly Dog. Yield: 4 – 5 servings. Prep time: 30 minutes.

---

3 cups water
8-ounce Red Beans and Rice Dinner Mix (use the reduced salt version if you want)
12-ounce package Chef Bruce Aidell's Cajun Style Andouille Pork Smoked Sausages (from Walmart)
2 tablespoons olive oil (California Extra Virgin per zombie's recommendation)

Add water, all the red beans and rice mix from the bag, all thinly-sliced (1/4th" to 1/8th") sausage, and the olive oil. Mix well. Bring to boil, then cover and simmer for 25 minutes. Stir occasionally to ensure the rice and beans are not sticking on the bottom of the sauce pan. After 25 minutes, or when the rice is tender, turn off heat. Fluff after 5 minutes. Enjoy.

## Blake's Darn Good Mac & Cheese

248 Mac & cheese recipe created by me. Maybe myself. Or even I. My recipe is so good, it was stolen by a Cordon Bleu trained chef. (Not quite a 1 Pinnochio.) The amount of cheese is merely a guideline. So is the type of cheese.

Posted by: Blake. Yield: servings for 3 people and 4 days of leftover heaven. Prep time: 3 hours.

---

1 cube (stick) salted butter
1 pint half and half
1 16-ounce container sour cream
1 pint heavy whipping cream
1 8-ounce package cream cheese
1/ 2 round smoked gouda
1/2 round smoked provolone
1/2 pound colby jack cheese
1/2 pound medium sharp cheddar
2 tablespoons feta cheese
1 pound medium pasta shells - Barilla
4 tablespoons flour

Boil pasta until slightly tough (al dente); it usually takes 8 or 9 minutes. Drain and let cool. Cools best if spread out in pan that will be used to for final cooking of mac and cheese. Next, make the cheese sauce: all ingredients should go into the pan at the same temperature! First, grate every single scrap of cheese into a large bowl. Put a bit of the half and half aside for later use with the flour. Combine sour cream, cream cheese, butter, heavy cream and half & half in a sauce pan over low heat. Once everything is melted together and the sauce is simmering (should have the occasional bubble), over low heat, start adding the cheese. After the sauce starts to bubble slightly (over low heat!), start whisking in the grated cheese. Slowly add more cheese as it melts into the sauce. After whisking in the cheese, mix together a small amount of flour and half and half, then stir into the sauce. Heat for a bit longer, check carefully around the edges of the sauce pan for any butter than might not have mixed in (whisk more if needed). Pour sauce over shells. Mix or don't mix, as preferred. I personally prefer not to mix, as I like texture and flavor variations. Grate more cheese over the top, put on pellet grill for two hours on high smoke. (This is 225 on my pellet grill.) If you don't have a pellet grill, baking in the oven on 350 degrees F for 90 minutes should do it.

## A Moron's Mighty Mac & Cheese

249 Best comfort food ever. Not sure where we got the recipe—it's the one my mom made while I was growing up and it still tastes great!

Posted by: Lord Squirrel. Yield: servings for 1 Moron or 4 regular folks. Prep time: 30 minutes.

---

6 cups water
1 1/2 cups Creamette's brand elbow macaroni noodles
pinch (or three) salt
ground black pepper to taste
2 tablespoons all purpose ground flour
6 slices Kraft American cheese
1 cup whole milk (no skim or 2%)
1/4 stick (2 tablespoons) salted butter

Bring the water to a boil. I usually add a few shakes of salt to the water. Add the elbow macaroni noodles. Turn down heat a bit (to medium-high) and stir for a few minutes until noodles are nice and tender. Drain the noodles. In a second pot, melt the salted butter on medium heat. When butter is melted, add the flour and a few shakes of salt. Stir until all ingredients are blended together. Add the WHOLE milk. Keep stirring all ingredients until it starts to thicken up a bit. Add 2 slices of American cheese at a time (there should be 6 slices minimum) until they melt into the sauce. Keep adding slices until they are all melted. Dump noodles into a large bowl. Then pour the sauce over the noodles and stir it all together. Season with ground black pepper to taste. Do NOT use anything other than ingredients listed for this recipe—no whole grain noodles or weak skim milk. This is comfort food, so treat it as such!

## Wisconsin-style German Potato Salad

250 Easy potato salad. Adapted from Mrs. JTB's mother's recipe.

Posted by: JTB and Mrs. JTB.  Yield: depends on preferred portion size.  Prep time: 30 minutes.

---

6 medium red potatoes
¼ - ½ cup finely sliced onions (Vidalia or other sweet onion)
4 – 8 strips bacon, cut in small squares
1/2 cup vinegar
4 tablespoons sugar or sugar sustitute
6 tablespoons water
2 tablespoons flour

Cook the 6 medium red potatoes in their skins/jackets until tender. Then peel and slice. (Note: hot when peeling. Can hold in a towel or oven mitt.) Put potatoes in a large bowl. Add onions to potato bowl. In a skillet, cook the bacon (already cut in squares). When the bacon is crisp, add flour to the skillet and stir until flour is absorbed. Add to skillet the vinegar, sugar or sugar substitute, and water. Heat to boiling while stirring. The flour will thicken this sauce a little as it is heated. Pour sauce over potatoes and onions. Stir gently. Can be served warm or cold. Refrigerate. The potatoes will absorb the sweetened vinegar sauce. Same sauce, when cooled, can be used on leaf lettuce.

## Gramma Flora's Dressing

251 Sausage stuffing from Gramma Flora.

Posted by: Tonypete.  Yield: 6 servings.  Prep time: 45 minutes.

---

1 pound Italian sausage, crumbled
3/4 cup diced onion
1/2 cup diced celery
2 eggs
1 1/2 cup milk
4 cups Italian bread crumbs
1/4 cup Romano/Parmesan cheese, grated

Saute sausage, onion and celery until onion and celery are translucent. Mix eggs, bread crumbs, milk and cheese together and then add sausage mixture—mix together. Pour all into greased casserole dish. Bake at 350 degrees F for 35 minutes. Serve as a side with turkey or ham.

## Holiday Potatoes

252 Creamy, cheesy, delicious. I received this recipe from a friend who got it while living in Montana. She called it Montana Potatoes. I renamed it after many years of these potatoes being a holiday (red, green, gold) tradition in my family.

Posted by: jazzuscounty. Yield: 10 – 12 servings. Prep time: 25 minutes/1 hour oven.

---

8 – 10 good sized potatoes, cooked
1 – 2 tablespoons salt
1 large onion, chopped
1 small jar diced pimento
1/2 bell pepper, chopped
1/2 pound Velveeta type cheese, cubed
1 tablespoon dried parsley
1/2 pound butter
1/2 cup milk

While the potatoes boil, chop the onion and bell pepper as well as the cheese. Drain potatoes from large pot and add the salt, onion, pimento, bell pepper, cheese, parsley and butter. Mix together till creamy or if you prefer, with some potato and lumps left. Add milk at the end and mix one more time. Bake in a sprayed 3 quart or 9 x1 3 casserole dish. Bake at 375 degrees F for one hour. I shared this with another friend who used frozen potatoes for a short cut. She said it worked great.

## Grandma's German Potato Salad

253 This German potato salad recipe comes from my grandmother, Mary, who passed in 1971. My mother has been making this since I was a young sprout growing up in Indiana in the 1950's. Mom just turned 95 and last summer was probably the last time that she will make this.

Posted by: Edd Zachary. Yield: 8 – 12 servings. Prep time: 1 hour.

---

10 medium new potatoes
2 teaspoons salt
8 slices bacon, diced
1/2 cup apple cider vinegar
2 tablespoons flour
1 sliced medium onion
pepper to taste
1/2 cup water
1 cup white granulated sugar

Cook potatoes in skin; cool, skin, and slice. Fry bacon until crisp, then drain all but 2 tablespoons grease. Add flour to pan and stir. Add vinegar, water and sugar; cook until thickens and looks clear—may have to adjust sugar and vinegar to taste. Pour over potatoes and onion, add salt and pepper to taste. Heat in crockpot on low for few hours. Serve warm.

## Utica Greens

254 Greens with attitude! Utica Greens are a central NY favorite. I discovered them through my sister who discovered them while attending college in Rochester. The recipe is my own. I picked apart a restaurant serving and made my own approximation. These are greens for people who don't like greens. Spicy and toothsome.

Posted by: WhatWhatWhat? Yield: servings for 6 – 8 Morons. Prep time: 45 minutes.

---

2 pounds (approx. 2 heads) escarole, washed and chopped
1/2 cup + 2 tablespoons olive oil
1/2 cup sliced onion
4 ounces pancetta or prosciutto, chopped
5 cloves chopped garlic
3 hot cherry peppers, drained, seeded and chopped
1/2 cup chicken stock
1/2 cup seasoned bread crumbs
1/2 cup grated Parmesan cheese
salt and pepper to taste

Preheat oven to 400 degrees F. Blanch escarole for 2 minutes in boiling water, drain and run under cold water. In large skillet, heat 1/2 cup olive oil over medium heat. Add onion and pancetta (or prosciutto), cook 5 minutes until onion is softened. Do not brown! Increase heat to medium-high. Add garlic, cook till garlic is golden brown, then add escarole, peppers and chicken broth. Combine thoroughly with wooden spoon and cook until escarole is wilted. Season with salt and pepper. Transfer mixture to 2-quart glass baking dish. In small bowl, combine the bread crumbs and 2 tablespoons olive oil. Spread mixture over the escarole, sprinkle with Parmesan cheese. Bake about 15 minutes until cheese is melted. If you want it hotter, don't seed the peppers, or just remove some but not all of the seeds.

## Unbelievably Easy Rice Pilaf

255 Weird technique, but perfect results every time! Adapted from Alton Brown. I've changed some ingredients, but the technique is all his.

Posted by: Duke Lowell. Yield: 4 servings. Prep time: 5 minutes.

---

1 ½ cups white rice, rinsed and drained
½ cup vermicelli, broken into small pieces
½ cup diced carrots
½ cup frozen peas, thawed
2 cloves garlic, peeled and pressed
1 medium onion, diced
2 ½ cups chicken stock
2 tablespoons salt
1 teaspoon black pepper
2 tablespoons olive oil

Preheat oven to 350 degrees F. In a 4-quart Dutch oven, Le Creuset for you one percenters, over medium heat add olive oil, onions, and carrots. Mildly saute until onions are translucent. Add rice and vermicelli and stir to coat. Crank heat to high stirring frequently. Add more oil if it's sticking. When the rice is golden brown and has a nutty aroma, add garlic, carrots, and peas. Stir for about 30 seconds. Add stock and stir, ensuring nothing is stuck to the bottom. Bring to a boil. Cover with a moist dish towel. Place lid on top of dish towel and fold edges up over the lid. Into the oven for 20 minutes. 20 minutes is the time and the time for cooking shall be 20 minutes. Not 19 nor 22. 23 is right out! Remove from oven and let sit for 5 minutes. Fluff with fork and serve. For plain white rice, combine 2 cups rice, 2 ½ cups water, salt and pepper in Dutch oven. Bring to boil and use the same oven technique. Perfect every time!

## Chipotle Potato Salad

256 Roasting the potatoes adds a nice twist. This is a much-modified recipe from Mesa Grill, a Bobby Flay restaurant.

Posted by: CBD. Yield: 8 servings. Prep time: 50 minutes.

---

4 pounds Yukon Gold potatoes, cut in chunks
1/4 cup Dijon mustard
1/2 cup mayonnaise
2 tablespoons fresh lime juice
2 tablespoons chopped chipotle pepper
1/3 cup chopped cilantro
1/2 red onion, thinly sliced
2 cloves garlic, chopped fine
kosher salt
black pepper
corn oil

Preheat oven to 425 degrees F. Toss potatoes with enough corn oil to coat them and kosher salt to taste, and roast for 25 – 35 minutes until golden brown but firm. Combine the rest of the ingredients in a medium bowl and season with salt and pepper to taste. Place warm potatoes in a large bowl and pour the mixture over potatoes and toss well. Correct seasoning and serve warm.

## Roasted Sweet Potatoes with Apples & Cranberries

257 Fabulous Thanksgiving side. Easy, and sweetened naturally instead of with a lot of brown sugar or marshmallows. Recipe from Courtney Rae Jones at thefigtreeblog.com.

Posted by: Lizzy. Yield: 6 servings. Prep time: 1 hour total.

---

2 tablespoons canola or olive oil
1 large sweet potato, peeled & diced in 1/2 inch cubes
2 medium apples, peeled and cubed
1/2 cup dried cranberries
1 teaspoon ground cinnamon
1/4 teaspoon ground nutmeg
2 tablespoons brown sugar, firmly packed
1 cup pecans
salt, to taste

Preheat oven to 425 degrees F. Combine the brown sugar, cinnamon, nutmeg and a pinch of salt in a small bowl. Place the sweet potato, apple and cranberries in a 1 1/2 quart baking dish. Drizzle with canola oil or olive oil. Sprinkle the sugar/cinnamon mixture over top and mix well to coat. Cover and bake for 30 minutes. Remove the cover and add the pecans. Mix well and bake an additional 15 minutes (or until the sweet potato is tender). You can substitute butternut or acorn squash if you don't have sweet potatoes on hand.

## Persian Rice Salad

258 Unusual side dish which pairs well with grilled Middle Eastern flavor foods. Always gets rave reviews. From *Bon Appetit* in September 2002, credited to Mustard Seed Market & Cafe, Akron, OH.

Posted by: Cricket. Yield: 8 – 10 servings. Prep time: approximately 1 hour.

---

28 ounces vegetable broth
2 cups long grain brown rice
1 1/2 cups roasted salted cashews, coarsely chopped
1 1/2 cups (about 7 ounces) sliced pitted dates
4 green onions, thinly sliced
1/2 cup olive oil (I usually use about 1/3 cup)
1/4 cup fresh lemon juice
1/4 cup chopped fresh cilantro
1/4 teaspoon ground cinnamon

Bring broth to boil in large saucepan over medium-high heat. Mix in rice. Return to boil. Reduce heat to low, cover, and cook without stirring until rice is tender, about 40 minutes. Spread out rice in large baking pan and cool. Transfer rice to large bowl. Add cashews, dates, and green onions; toss to blend. Whisk olive oil, lemon juice, chopped cilantro, and ground cinnamon in small bowl. Add to rice and toss to coat. Season salad to taste with salt and pepper. (Can be made 2 hours ahead. Let stand at room temperature.)

## Ott Family Baked Beans

259 I got this from a cousin who is married to one of the Ott family.

Posted by: Deathknyte. Yield: several servings. Prep time: 20 minutes tops.

---

½ pound bacon
½ ring sausage
½ onion
2 16-ounce cans baked beans
¼ cup molassas
½ cup brown sugar

Use a pot big enough to cook everything in. Chop up the onion, cut the bacon into small bits, quarter to half inch lengths will do, and cut the sausage into thin slices of an eighth inch to a quarter inch in thickness. The onion is very optional but add it to the pot either at the beginning or end of the cooking the bacon and sausage stage, depending on if you want cooked onion. First cook the bacon and sausage in the pot to the consistency that you like it. Add in one-half of the beans to dilute the fat in the bottom. Stir and add in the molasses and brown sugar. Add in the rest of the baked beans. Let it all melt together while stirring for a few minutes. Experiment with different types of baked beans (I use Bush brothers) and different types of brown sugar (I use cane) or molasses. I can't eat onions so I never make it with any.

## Homemade Mac and Cheese

260 Overson family recipe. This recipe came down from my grandmother to my mother, and then on to her children.

Posted by: Zakn. Yield: 7 servings. Prep time: 30 minutes.

---

1 pound large elbow macaroni
1 pound + some extra as sharp a cheddar as you like (I go with extra- extra-sharp)
2 large eggs
a pint or so 2% or whole milk
1/2 teaspoon cumin powder
1/2 teaspoon onion powder/chopped onion (dried) or use fresh
cubed ham (optional)

Boil the macaroni to al dente or a little less than al dente if you want a firmer noodle after baking. While the water is heating up/boiling the macaroni, I like to slice the cheddar into 1/8th inch slices or so. Drain the macaroni and set aside for a bit. If you are using fresh onion/onion powder or some cubed ham, now is the time to mix that into the macaroni. Grease/butter an oven-safe casserole dish. You'll want a deeper one. I have a nice 4-quart oval one that works well for this. Preheat the oven to 450 degrees F. I usually start doing this here because it usually gives it enough time to preheat while I'm doing all the next stuff.

So now that you have the dish greased/buttered, add a layer of macaroni to the dish. A little less than a third of the dish (I always go for two layers). This thing will rise a little, so think of that when you are making that first layer of macaroni. Once you have the macaroni layer down, sprinkle your cumin powder on top. Be careful with the stuff as it is strong and aromatic (dish works fine without it as well). Once that is done, take your sliced cheese and completely cover the layer of macaroni. You'll have to break some of the slices to fit in round areas, but don't be stingy! Cover the whole layer! If you want to use some shredded or chunk cheese to cover edges, go for it. Even some cheddar curd goes well for that if it's available in your area.

Okay, now layer one is done, go ahead and put in macaroni layer two! Leave room for the sliced cheese on top! But fill the dish almost all the way up (remember it's gonna rise). Don't want to have it overflow your dish in the oven! (I always put a foil layer on a pizza pan that I then put the casserole dish on, because I have Moron'd this thing up more than once.) Then add another sprinkle of cumin on top. Take your two eggs, break them and beat them with some of the milk. Once that is done you want to dump that into the macaroni. I like to drizzle it all over the top as even as I can, but it doesn't really matter. You can even use a single egg for this, but I've never tried it with something like no-yolks or something like that. It might work! But we are really going for more of a souffle dish here than a traditional mac and cheese.

Now you want to take the rest of your milk and start pouring it in until you can see it in the macaroni. Not till full, literally just until you start seeing milk through the macaroni. Then stop! Then take the cheese and cover the layer. Side note: You can grind up cheddar goldfishes for some novelty on the top layer. It's not bad. Adds some crunch, but if you do this right, the top layer of cheese should be crunchy enough, but some people like a bready thing on top. Whatever. Goof around with this recipe. It works great with cubed ham, etc. Now we are ready to bake it, uncovered, for 45 minutes. You want the top layer of cheese to be a nice golden brown. Remove from oven and let this thing set for a while. At least a half hour or so. Then serve. This will serve 4 to 6 with plenty of leftovers that will go fast. The top crust is the best part, so we always use a spatula to make 1/2" to 3/4" slices for serving. Take the spatula and separate it from the sides of the dish, then slice down and lift out the goodness.

### *Chef's Notes:*

I personally don't use anything onion related, but the family does when I'm not around. I also don't always use the cumin, but it adds a neat flavor to it which is very unique, just be careful with it. It can really overpower a dish that is vintage comfort food. For things like Thanksgiving where you are preparing many dishes, you can prepare this up to right before where you add the eggs, milk and last cheese layer. Just keep it in the fridge covered with plastic wrap or covered with the casserole dish top. Then when you are ready to cook your stuff like green bean shit that needs a hotter oven, break it out, add your eggs, milk and last cheese layer and toss in the oven.

## Aunt Wally's Bean Casserole

261 Great side dish at a picnic or potluck. Recipe comes from my beloved sister-in-law, Wally Krasniansky.

Posted by: Ladylibertarian   Serves 12   Prep time: 1.5 hours

---

15-ounce can green beans
15-ounce can yellow beans
15-ounce can kidney beans
15-ounce can pork and beans
15-ounce can lima beans
1 can tomato soup
1 small can tomato paste
1 cup brown sugar
1/2 cup chopped onions
1/2 cup diced celery
3 teaspoons prepared mustard
1 pound hot Italian sausage (loose)
½ pound bacon, diced

Brown sausage and saute onion and celery with bacon. Drain some of the grease. Mix all ingredients and place in deep casserole dish. Bake at 350 degrees F, uncovered, for one hour. This is a great substitute for regular baked beans. It also can be a main course.

## My Mexican Rice

262 There will be no leftovers. Adapted from *Sunset Mexican Cookbook,* Winter 1996.

Posted by: Cicero Kaboom! Kid   Yield: 6 servings.   Prep time: 45 minutes.

---

1 1/2 cups long grain rice, basmati is best
2 1/2 cups chicken stock
1 cup canned tomatoes
1 cup chopped onions
2 – 3 cloves garlic, minced
3 tablespoons oil, lard or smalz
lime juice (optional)
chopped cilantro (optional)

Whirl the tomatoes in a blender to make unchunky. Heat the chicken stock to a simmer and hold it at the temperature. Heat the oil or fat until shimmering. Add the rice and keep it moving with a paddle or wooden spoon until it changes color. Add the onions and stir frequently for about 4 minutes. Add the garlic and keep it moving for about a minute. Do not let anything scorch! Add the tomatoes and crank up the heat. Stir frequently until bubbling and beginning to thicken a bit, maybe 2 minutes. Add the hot chicken stock. It should hiss at you when you add it! Stir well, scraping the bottom. Reduce to just barely a simmer. Put on the lid. Cook 25 – 30 minutes. Test for doneness by sticking a fork in there all the way to the bottom. It should be dry and just beginning to brown a bit. Sprinkle with a little lime juice and chopped cilantro if you like and fluff it up.

***Chef's Notes:***
I use a cast-iron chicken fryer (round, very deep skillet) and put aluminum foil over it before putting on the lid so it seals. You can use any heavy, stainless pan with a tight-fitting lid. Roasted, peeled and chopped jalapeno or Anaheim chiles are a nice addition. Add them after the garlic.

## Mom's Rice

263 Steak side dish. My mother always made it with beef tenderloin.

Posted by: Jed. Yield: 4 servings. Prep time: 60 minutes.

---

1 cup rice
2 cans consomme
2 pats butter

Preheat oven to 350 degrees F. Combine rice and consomme in casserole dish. Add butter to top. Bake 1 hour.

## Dyfunctional Family Mashed Potatoes

264 A true family recipe. Recipe comes from a love of tubers and alcohol, coupled with a refusal to go quietly. A holiday favorite!

Posted by: lurks alotte. Yield: 10 servings. Prep time: 1 hour.

---

5 pounds red skinned potatoes
2 cups whole milk
2 sticks butter
1/2 cup flat Italian parsley
1 tablespoon kosher salt
8 – 10 cloves garlic
too much alcohol

Wash potatoes, chop into large pieces. Make a stiff drink. Sigh. Boil enough salted water to cover chopped potatoes, about 1 gallon. Add potatoes to boiling water for 20 minutes. Drain water, leaving potatoes in the pot. Finish your first drink, make your second drink. Finish your second drink. Make your third drink. Add butter to potatoes and begin to mash them with a potato masher clenched in an angry fist. Listen to family members arguing in the next room. Sigh. Once butter is melted and mixed, add milk and stir into potatoes. Break up a fight in the next room. Make another drink, losing count. Add salt and stir. Carefully remove stems from parsley and bruise with the back of the knife, then roughly chop and add to pot.

Add finely minced garlic and stir. Grind teeth, make another drink. Break up fight in next room. Become the next fight in the next room. Make another drink. Taste potatoes; add salt or garlic to taste and serve with a surly remark.

## Melissa's Baby Dutch Yellow Potatoes

265 These are garlic-infused bacon-wrapped baby potatoes. Makes your house smell soooo goooood! My neighbor across the street gave me the idea at a cookout for bacon-wrapped potatoes. I added the garlic olive oil bit.

Posted by: CDR M. Yield: servings for 5 Morons. Prep time: 10 minutes.

---

1 pound bag Melissa's Petite White Potatoes
1 pound bacon
1/4 cup garlic olive oil

First preheat the oven to 400 degrees F. Clean the potatoes. Then you take your bacon and cut the slices in half. Pour some of your garlic olive oil into a small bowl and dip your potato in it. Then wrap a half slice of bacon around the potato and toothpick it on. Place on a baking tray and proceed to the next one. When you are done, place the tray in the oven for about 40 – 50 minutes and prepare for the most divine smell ever in your house. I serve these every time as a side dish for my smoked pulled pork. You can add sour cream and melted cheese as additional topping for your potatoes when served. Sure to be a crowd pleaser!

## Home Made Refried Beans

266 Quick, easy, and flavorful beans. Came up with this on my own out of desperation.

Posted by: Christopher R Taylor. Yield: 3 servings. Prep time: 20 minutes.

---

1 can beans
1 cube beef bouillon
1 tablespoon lard/bacon grease etc.
1 pinch salt
½ teaspoon cumin
½ teaspoon garlic powder

Open the can of beans, pour into a sauce pan and put on low heat. Add in the other ingredients. The beans can be any sort, but pintos and black beans give the most authentic results in my experience. I recommend lard as authentic, but bacon grease is a good substitute, and even margarine can work. You just need some kind of fat added in. When the fat melts, take a potato masher and crush the beans until they are a semi-consistent paste. You'll have some skins and pieces of bean in there, and that's fine. You're looking for the consistency of store-bought refried beans, but it won't reach full thickness until it cools slightly. Try not to boil the beans, and be careful to stir or they will burn on the bottom. Some cheese grated and melted on top gives a nice presentation and flavor.

## Salt Potatoes

> 267 This is the national dish of Syracuse, NY. It supposedly originated at Hinerwadel's, a well-known picnic grove and catering hall. They sell packaged potatoes and salt, but you can just buy them individually.

Posted by: Otto Zilch. Yield: 6 servings. Prep time: 40 minutes.

---

3 pounds new potatoes (very small: 1 1/2 inches diameter or less)
12 ounces salt
4 tablespoons butter (for serving)

Start 2 quarts of water boiling in a large pot (enamel is best, avoid aluminum); add salt as the water heats. Do not skimp on the salt or think you can get away with just a half pound. Syracuse is the Salt City, after all. Meanwhile, wash the potatoes, and pierce each one twice with a fork. When the water comes to a boil, add potatoes, and continue boiling for about 35 minutes. If you have a grill or oven on, finish the potatoes there for about 3 to 5 minutes so they'll develop a nice crust on the outside. Dip in melted butter as you eat them. Suggested pairing: Molson's or other Canadian beer (it's cheaper in Syracuse than in Ontario). For a true New York State Fair meal, serve these with spiedies or Hoffman's coneys.

## Rotmos (Mashed Root Vegetables)

> 268 A delicious and visually appealing alternative to mashed taters, which is especially delicious with brats or other sausage. From my ex-MiL. This is pronounced "root moose."

Posted by: Miley, the Duchess. Yield: 4 – 6 servings. Prep time: 1 hour or less.

---

1 large rutabaga (2 pounds)
6 potatoes (2 pounds)
3 large carrots
3 cups water with a bouillon cube added
5 white peppercorns
5 whole allspice
1 teaspoon salt
4 tablespoons butter
3/4 cup milk

Cut the rutabaga, potatoes and carrots into 1" cubes. Bring the water, bouillon cube, peppercorns, allspice, and salt to a boil. Add the rutabagas and carrots to the pot. The root vegetables take somewhat longer to cook than the potatoes. I typically give them a 20 minute head start, then add the potatoes. Boil vegetables until tender, checking periodically for tenderness. Drain, then fish out the whole spices. Finish by mashing with the butter and milk.

## Creamy Potato Salad

269 Wins every potato salad competition. My mom's family has worked to refine this recipe over the years, but my Uncle Ed really hit the jackpot by whipping the heavy cream a little before mixing it with the mayo.

Posted by: Miley, the Duchess. Yield: 12 - 16 servings. Prep time: 1 hour plus overnight.

---

3 1/2 pounds medium red potatoes
2 cups mayonnaise
1 cup heavy cream
1 – 2 tablespoons yellow mustard
1 teaspoon salt
1/2 teaspoon black pepper
1/2 cup finely chopped celery
1/4 cup finely chopped onion
2 tablespoons finely chopped Italian parsley

Boil the potatoes whole, in their skins, until tender, then cool before peeling. I do not add salt to the water, so if you do, you may wish to adjust the salt in the dressing. For the dressing, whip the heavy cream until thickened but still pourable, and fold into the mayo. Add the rest of the ingredients and mix well. Cut the potatoes into 3/4" pieces and mix with the dressing. Chill overnight to allow the flavors to blend. Don't even think about substituting brown or Dijon-style mustard or you'll ruin it!

## Char's Potatoes

270 The best comfort food. I found out some bad news and VIA's ship was out to sea. My dear friend Char was to have dinner with the admiral's wife. She canceled her dinner date. We sat at the table drinking wine and eating happy pills (York Peppermint Patties). Char went home and grabbed this casserole.

Posted by: Mrs. VIA. Yield: servings for 8 Morons. Prep time: 15 minutes.

---

1 bag frozen hash browns
1 pint sour cream
1 can cream of chicken
3 cups shredded cheddar cheese
1 stick (8 tablespoons) butter

Preheat oven 350 degrees F. In a large bowl mix sour cream, cream of chicken soup, and cheese together. Mix in frozen hash browns; you may need to break them up first. In the meantime, melt the butter. Take the mixture and place in the casserole dish. Drizzle melted butter on top of the mixture. Bake for 90 minutes to 2 hours until golden brown. You can added bacon crumbles and/or green onions.

## Bacon n' Bourbon Dressing

271 A sage based dressing/stuffing that combines different artisan breads with the goodness that is bourbon and bacon. This dressing developed over years of experimenting, and will likely change over time. Tired of soggy/mushy dressing that was horribly bland, I focused on bringing out the flavor of different artisan bread via the power of bacon and bourbon. The nice thing about this recipe is the flexibility: you can experiment with different combinations of different breads to make a unique dish that suits your own palate.

Posted by: The Political Hat. Yield: 6 – 10 servings. Prep time: 90 minutes.

---

2 pounds bacon
2 different loaves artisan bread, cut into chunks
½ cup (or more) butter or margarine
2 fistfuls fresh sage
2 shallots
1 clove garlic
1 red onion
handful crushed black walnuts
1 teaspoon black pepper
1 egg (well beaten)
1 – 2 cups (at least) chicken or turkey stock
2 – 3 jiggers bourbon

Cut bacon up into little bits and cook slowly on low to render out all the fat, preferably in a cast-iron skillet. Once most of the fat has been rendered out, increase heat to medium and add finely diced shallots, finely diced garlic, finely diced onion, and finely diced sage. Cook until onions become translucent. In a separate cast-iron or Teflon-free pan, heat the black walnuts until they start to release their oils. Add bacon mixture and black walnuts to two different loaves of artisan bread and mix thoroughly with black pepper, bourbon, a beaten egg, and enough chicken/turkey stock to keep the mixture moist but not soggy. After mixing, add back to cast iron skillet that has been coated in butter and/or margarine. Cover mixture in a thin layer of butter/margarine and cover the pan with aluminum foil. Bake in oven until preferred consistency is reached (at 375 degrees F for 30 minutes, depending on the oven). Serve directly out of the cast-iron skillet with the rest of the bourbon to wash it down.

***Chef's Notes:***
This recipe is meant to get the most out of different artisan breads, and the breads one chooses can vary. I, myself, never use the same two types of artisan bread, so it's like a new dish with a unique taste each time.

## Canellini Bean Salad

272 Simple Italian antipasto style bean salad. Created by me! =)

Posted by: atomicplaygirl. Yield: 4 servings. Prep time: 5 minutes.

---

1 15-ounce can canellini beans, rinsed and drained
1 peeled medium shallot bulb, very thinly sliced
2 tablespoons chiffonade of mint leaves
1/4 cup white wine vinegar
1 ½ tablespoons olive oil
salt and pepper

Pour vinegar into a small bowl and slowly add the olive oil as you beat the vinegar with a fork or whisk. Add a good pinch or two of salt and grind or two of pepper. Add shallots to vinegar mixture and stir. Drain canellini beans and rinse briefly under water; allow to drain again, shake to remove excess water. Add beans to the bowl along with the mint. Mix and serve immediately. I serve this as part of an antipasto plate with salami, roasted veggies/garlic, cheese and fruit. Add a little more olive oil and salt to remove some of the pungent flavour of the vinegar, if you don't like it.

## LizLem's Fancy Potatoes

273 Elegant-looking yet hearty potato dish, great for parties. My own invention, a hodepodge of so many things I like. "Created by Diane" has a recipe for roasted holiday potatoes that I think I used as a base idea, then improvised from there.

Posted by: LizLem. Yield: 6+ish servings. Prep time: 2-2 ½ hours.

---

5 pounds potatoes
1/4 cup extra virgin olive oil (plus a little extra to brush on top later)
1 teaspoon minced garlic
1 teaspoon garlic powder
1/2 teaspoon salt (or to taste)
1/4 teaspoon pepper (or to taste)
1/4 cup fresh chopped rosemary, thyme, oregano

Preheat oven 375 degrees F. Infuse/mix in the minced and powdered garlic to the olive oil; set aside. Wash potatoes and cut off heels. Slice the potatoes 1/8" thin using a knife, grater or mandoline. Pat dry and put into mixing bowl. Mix in with your hands the garlic-infused olive oil, salt, pepper, and herbs until potatoes are evenly coated. Grease glass baking pan with olive oil. Arrange potatoes in rows, curved outer skin visible on top. (If larger potato pieces were sliced to get evenly sized, place sliced end down on bottom of dish.) Varied heights of potatoes is encouraged for visual appeal. It is easiest to grab a small stack at a time and then snugly fit the stacks together till you have a full row of potato spanning the long length of the dish. (I prefer doing potato rows in the baking dish, about 3-4 rows per dish, because it's easier and still pretty. But a circular baking dish can be used as well, the potatoes forming a larger outer circle, then the rest making smaller and smaller circles inside.) Sprinkle any extra herbs on top. Bake uncovered one hour. Remove from oven, brush top with a little olive oil, cover with foil and bake until fully cooked. Bake an extra half hour if pieces are larger. If pieces are thinner and even, can get away with 10 – 15 minutes. Brush once more with a little oil for sheen, sprinkle a little more salt and pepper on top. Ready to be served!

### *Chef's Notes:*

Any type of potato can be used. I like the red ones for this best, but Yukon and sweet potato would also work. You can even mix different potato types for a higher pretty quotient. I prefer more herbs than less, so be generous with the herbs. More a rounded ¼ cup than a flat one. The key to this baking properly is consistently even sizes of potatoes. If they are all 1/8" thin and if the larger middle pieces are halved to be the same size as the smaller end pieces, everything bakes fast and even. If there are varying sizes or if potatoes are closer to ¼" size, more baking time will be required. If you bake it with four pounds or less of potatoes, all the other ingredients about the same, only requires an hour of baking time.

# *Fruit and Veggies*

## Cranberry Dream

274 Jello—give in to it. Saw it in maybe *Better Homes* a long time ago, and have adlibbed it since. Kids like this as an alternative to plain cranberry sauce with turkey. You can use whole berry sauce.

Posted by: Euro. Yield: 8 servings. Prep time: a while.

---

1 1/2 cups boiling water
1 8-serving box cranberry or raspberry Jello
1 16-ounce can cranberry sauce
1 1/2 cups cold water
1 11-ounce can mandarin oranges
1 1/2 cups graham cracker crumbs
1 stick (8 tablespoons) melted butter
1 8-ounce box cream cheese, room temperature
1 8-ounce tub Cool Whip, optional

Stir boiling water into jello until dissolved. Stir in cranberry sauce until melted. Refrigerate 1 1/2 hours, then stir in drained oranges. Return to fridge. Combine crumbs and butter, press into bottom of 13 x 9 dish. Bake 10 minutes at 325 degrees F. Let cool. Beat cream cheese until smooth, stir in Cool Whip. Pour Jello mixture on top of crust. Top with cheese/Cool Whip mixture. Chill 3 hours or overnight.

## Lebanese Spinach

275 Can be used as topping on rice, in spinach pies, in scrambled eggs, etc. JTB's Lebanese grandmother made spinach pies using refrigerated biscuit dough instead of filo dough. These pocket-sized triangles of deliciousness were a hit with the grandkids. Unfortunately, she did not give us her recipe. The closest one we found is this recipe, which we adapted, from "Filo Triangle" in *Middle Eastern Cooking* by Rose Dosti. Also known as Sambousik.

Posted by: JTB and Mrs. JTB. Yield: depends on use. Prep time: 15 minutes.

---

1 (10 – 16 ounce) package frozen chopped spinach, thawed
1/4 cup olive oil
1 small onion, chopped
1/4 cup crumbled feta cheese
3 – 8 tablespoons lemon juice, to taste

1/4 teaspoon sumac from good spice shop
salt and pepper to taste
1 package refrigerated biscuit dough

Thaw spinach. Squeeze dry after thawing and fluff to separate. Heat olive oil in a medium skillet. Add onion. Saute 1 minute. Add spinach, stir a minute or two. Add remaining ingredients except biscuit dough. Lemon juice should be added to taste—original recipe calls for 3 tablespoons. JTB's family uses 8 tablespoons (quite tart). Mix thoroughly. Use in rice, scrambled eggs, pasta, etc. If making spinach triangles/pies, separate each biscuit from refrigerated biscuit roll. Flatten each biscuit. Spoon spinach mixture on dough. Fold over into half-moons. Seal edges by pinching or pressing down edges. Follow directions on biscuit package regarding whether to grease baking pan and for length of baking time.

***Chef's Notes:***
Important: do not use sumac from the wild. Use that ingredient only if purchased from a spice shop. The sumac is optional. Lightly sauteed pine nuts can also be added.

## Shirley's Cranberry Relish

> 276 Never buy that canned shit again. In med school, I had T-day dinner with a fellow student's family. Her aunt had prepared this. I managed to talk her out of the recipe, with the proviso that, if I ever passed it on to anyone, I would give her full credit. So I present you with SHIRLEY SANDOSKI'S unbelievably awesome cranberry sauce.

Posted by: harbqll. Yield: way more than you think. Prep time: overnight.

---

1 package/bag fresh cranberries (they're a standard size)
2 granny smith apples, not peeled
2 oranges (save the peel of one orange)
1 1/2 cups sugar
2 boxes raspberry jello (sugar-free only)
1 ½ cups boiling water
1 ½ cups cold water
1 cup chopped pecans
8 ounces crushed pineapple, well drained

Combine cranberries, apples, oranges (with that reserved peel!), and sugar in food processor. Grind and let sit to meld for 10 minutes. Unless you have an unreasonably huge food processor, you'll have to do this in batches, and mix them together when complete. Dissolve raspberry jello in 1 1/2 cups boiling water in whatever mold you plan to use. Once dissolved, add 1 1/2 cups cold water. Add pecans and pineapple to Jello. Add cranberry mixture to Jello. You can mix it all up, or leave it as is so the pineapple and pecan will be at the top of the mold when inverted. Up to you. Place in fridge overnight to set. I hope you got a BIG jello mold. Otherwise use two. Or cut the recipe in half, if you're a hippie.

## Roasted Vegetable Mix

277 A fantastic side dish. You know how they say the best recipes are the ones you steal? This is one of those. I found it on a hotel buffet (the hotel is now out of business) and have been making it ever since. Very easy to recreate.

Posted by: Dr Alice. Yield: servings for 4 Morons. Prep time: 10 minutes plus cook time.

---

15-ounce can garbanzo beans, drained
1 large onion
1 – 2 zucchinis
1 – 3 tomatoes, depending on size
1 garlic clove
olive oil
salt and pepper

Drain the garbanzos, thickly slice the zucchini, thickly slice the onion, dice the tomatoes (how many depends on size and type, plus your taste for tomatoes). Toss all on a cookie sheet or roasting pain with olive oil, salt, pepper. Roast at 400 degrees F for about 20 minutes. Turn once during this time. This is really good. All sorts of roasted vegetables will work. You need onion, something sharp (tomato, bell pepper), something green (zucchini, broccoli), something starchy or sweet (potato, carrot, beets, garbanzos). Have fun with it.

## Cucumber Slaw

278 Making a big damn deal out of the simplest dish in the kitchen. I got this from Mom and bitter experience, but mostly . . . .

Posted by: Stringer Davis. Yield: servings for 4 Morons. Prep time: 20 minutes "if you fix it right."

---

one big (he said) cucumber
about half a large onion
few tablespoons Greek yogurt
maybe some sour cream
a generous dollop mayonnaise
Marzetti's slaw dressing
several heavy shakes dill weed

A side-dish salad serving can be made from one cucumber, about the size your husband thinks his man-part is. If company is coming, use a second one, about the size it really is. Use a vegetable peeler to make shallow, long stripping cuts (on the cucumber, you awful person) and remove all the green and yellow. Now comes the dangerous part: using an 8- or 10-inch chef's knife, cut that cucumber on a safely-mounted cutting board into paper-thin slices, just as thin and transparent as you can. A chef's knife has a belly-shaped blade, not straight. The reason for this is that you finish each slice with a little rocking motion against the board, making sure each piece is separate without chunking the cuke. It's an art. Do not bleed in the salad.

Slice about a third of the cucumber, then flip the slices with a grand artistic movement into a clean bowl, one size bigger than you think you need. Sprinkle this first layer heavily with dried dill weed (not dill-seed; they are different spices). Then do the next third of the fruit and add it to the bowl. This layering process is important in how the slices absorb flavors, and helps when you start tossing the mixture. Add mayonnaise, Greek (sheep's milk) yogurt, and Marzetti's slaw dressing, by single spoonfuls and in roughly equal parts, to each successive layer as you continue slicing.

Now do the same cut to the center section of a large onion. Cut across each thin onion slice once (twice if the onion's really big), and use your clean fingers to shred the individual long onion fibers into the bowl. Don't just chop the onion—these long shreds add a high-toned texture. When it looks like you have enough, add a little more! Top the mixture with another dusting of dill, and stir the ingredients gently with the rubber scraper we usually call a spatula. After mixing, transfer to a smaller container if you need to (scrape it all out!), cover with a snap-top or saran wrap, and store in the refrigerator. An hour is about the minimum; overnight is better. Before serving, use a spoon to give the whole thing another little toss to mix fluids and flavors.Don't spill any; you'll have to lick it up.

## Easy Creamed Spinach

279 Easy creamed spinach (basic and advanced). The basic recipe came from a guy I played rugby with while going to school; the 'advanced' developed over the years since then. The basic is so easy, even Moronic college students and/or their non-cooking grandmothers can make it, yet so good that people *will* ask you for the recipe. It is super-easy to make and double/triple/etc. when needed.

Posted by: Duncanthrax. Yield: 6 servings. Prep time: 5 to 20 minutes.

---

2 10-ounce packages frozen chopped spinach
1 package cream cheese
1 medium onion, chopped
1 clove garlic, minced
1 tablespoon olive oil
1/2 teaspoon kosher salt
1/4 teaspoon black pepper (preferably fresh ground)

For the basic version: put the two packages of spinach (either frozen or thawed) in a pot on medium heat. When the spinach has heated to the point that the liquid in the pot is just starting to bubble, put the package of cream cheese in the pot. Stir while the cheese melts. Remove from heat when hot. Transfer to serving dish. For the 'advanced' version: thaw the spinach. Heat the olive oil in a large skillet over medium heat. Add the onion, garlic, salt and pepper and stir until soft, about 6 to 7 minutes. Add the cream cheese, and stir until melted. Add the spinach to the sauce, and cook until heated through, approximately 3 to 4 minutes. If desired/needed, a small amount of milk can be added to adjust consistency.

## Hrothgar's Bacon Zucchini

> 280 Hey, it's got bacon! Basically an old family recipe of unknown and unknowable antiquity or provenance!

Posted by: Hrothgar. Yield: scalable Prep time: 30 minutes.

---

2 – 3 really fresh zucchini
4 – 6 strips thick-cut bacon
1/2 to 1 Vidalia onion

Use kitchen shears to cut bacon into roughly 1" squares, and toss in a large frying pan on low to medium heat, stirring frequently. You may need to add a little bacon grease. Chop onion coarsely to get approximately 1" squares. The onion will blend into the background so you could probably use a whole one. Wash and thinly slice zucchini in exactly 5 mm (+/- 0.05 mm) rounds. Once the bacon has just started to brown, toss in the onions and saute them. Note the bacon does not need to be fried to a crisp and is acting more like fatback in the recipe. Once bacon and onions have been cooked, but not overdone, throw in the zucchini slices. If possible, you want to have all the slices very lightly seared in the bacon grease, but this is not critical. Keep stirring the zucchini until you see signs of it browning and beginning to go limp. I add a small amount of water at this point, put a lid on the pan and check it every now and again. You can also add salt and pepper to taste, but it really doesn't need much seasoning (thanks to the bacon). The zucchini should be limp, but retain the integrity of identifiable slices. Over-cooking will result in a mush, albeit a very tasty mush!

## Pineapple Casserole

> 281 Pineapple with a cheesy, crispy crunch. I can't say who invented this dish. My mom made it for every special occasion for at least the last 30 years.

Posted by: Mamawolf Serves 6 Prep time: 15 to 20 minutes.

---

1 20-ounce can pineapple chunks, drained
1/2 cup sugar
3 tablespoons flour
1 cup grated cheddar cheese
1/2 cup crushed Ritz crackers

1 stick (8 tablespoons) melted butter

Mix flour and sugar together and pour over pineapple chunks in a greased baking dish. Add cheese and sprinkle crackers crumbs over top. Pour melted butter over all. Bake at 350 degrees F for 30 minutes. I have also made this with thinly sliced apples in place of the pineapple. It is an easy side dish and goes great with ham.

## Roasted Garlic Cauliflower Goat Cheese Puree

282 No, seriously. This is GREAT. My wife, "Giggles," aka the Kitchen Witch, put this together for her "Daring Cooks Challenge" on her blog, thekitchenwitchblog.com. We serve it with Cowboy Steak with Red-Eye Gravy (recipe can be found in the Main Courses section).

Posted by: McGyver. Yield: servings for 2 Morons. Prep time: 15 minutes.

---

1 large head cauliflower, cleaned and cut up
1 head roasted garlic, peeled
2 tablespoons cream
2 tablespoons melted butter
4 ounces goat cheese
salt and pepper to taste

In microwave steamer bag or microwave safe bowl, steam cauliflower for 5 minutes or until it's tender. To a food processor add the cauliflower and remaining ingredients, pulse 3 to 5 times and then puree. Add more cream if you like a thinner puree.

## Pai Huang Gua ("Smashed Cucumbers")

283 Classic Chinese side dish. This is a classic street food dish in China; there are a million versions, but this is how I like it.

Posted by: Wiz427. Yield: servings for 4 Morons. Prep time: 10 minutes.

---

4 small pickling cucumbers
4 – 6 cloves garlic, minced
1/4 teaspoon pickling salt
3 tablespoons Chinese black vinegar (Kong Yen brand from Taiwan is best)
2 tablespoons sesame oil (3 tablespoons if not using hot sesame oil)
1 tablespoon hot sesame oil (optional)
1 teaspoon hot sauce, preferably chili garlic or sambal oelek

Wash cucumbers and trim ends. Wrap in plastic and smash cucumbers until they split. Unwrap and coarsely chop into large chunks. Mince garlic. Salt cucumbers and garlic in a bowl, drizzle liquids one at a time and mix with a spoon. Serve immediately. Adjust the amount of heat and garlic as you like.

## Deborah's Cranberry Relish

284 Best cranberry relish you have had in your life!! My good friend Debbie gave this to me years ago. She is an amazing cook, and friend. I always make huge amounts and can for friends.

Posted by: SatRose. Yield: servings for 6 – 10 Morons. Prep time: 25 minutes.

---

2 12-ounce bags cranberries
1 cup cold water
1 cup sugar
1 cup coarsely chopped walnuts
2 cups drained canned mandarin oranges
1 cup apricot jam
1/2 cup raspberry jam

Cull bad cranberries. Chop walnuts coarsely, set aside. Combine cranberries, water and sugar in a saucepan. Boil slowly 6 minutes or until ALL cranberries have burst. Add walnuts, mandarin oranges, apricot jam and raspberry jam. Boil slowly for 5 minutes. This can be frozen. I have put into plastic containers, and glass canning jars (but do not water seal, like when you can homemade jam). Don't use freezer bags, they don't do well. Thaw when you wish to serve. The jam and oranges balance the tartness of the cranberries. Adjust for your taste after first batch!

## Andy's Good Ol' Slaw

285 Cole slaw which is mine, mine, all mine.

Posted by: Agitator. Yield: 10 to 15 servings. Prep time: 20 minutes to prepare, an hour to sit.

---

1 large head of cabbage
2 teaspoon salt
1/2 teaspoon ground pepper
1/4 teaspoon celery seed
2 cups apple cider vinegar
1 cup sugar
1/2 cup salad oil
1/2 bell pepper, seeded
1/2 small sweet onion
5 or 6 baby carrots

In a large bowl, finely shred cabbage. A mandoline is tailor-made for this, just watch your fingers. By finely, I mean less than 1/16" thick. Set aside. Combine all other ingredients in a blender. Grate, grind, or whatever until the baby carrots are in very small pieces. Pour mixture over the shredded cabbage. Stir well. Allow to sit in the refrigerator for at least an hour before serving. Great with fish, pork, or grilled chicken. Keeps a long time, it just gets tarter with age. For GAINZ, substitute Splenda volume for volume for the sugar.

## Sherry McEvil's Strawberry Cranberry Relish

286 This is a NO FAIL recipe for anyone, even non-cooks. It is a great recipe to take to a Thanksgiving dinner. I usually double or triple the recipe, it's that good.

Posted by: Sherry McEvil. Yield: 6 – 8 servings. Prep time: 25 minutes.

---

1 16-ounce bag frozen strawberries
1 12-ounce bag fresh cranberries
1 3-ounce box strawberry gelatin
1/2 cup pecan pieces
1/2 cup orange juice concentrate, thawed
1 1/2 cups sugar
1 cup water

Boil the water and pour it over the strawberry Jello and sugar in a bowl large enough to contain all the ingredients. Stir until the gelatin and sugar are dissolved. Stir in the orange juice concentrate and the nuts. Chop the washed cranberries in a food processor. I add the SLUSHY strawberries, a big spoonful at time, along with the whole cranberries to help the processor chop the cranberries more evenly. Add the cranberry/strawberry mix to the other ingredients in the large bowl, stirring them into the other ingredients. Chill for 4 – 6 hours before serving. It is better if it is allowed to chill overnight.

## Hrothgar's Easy Baked Onion

287 A tasty side dish, if you like onions. I saw something like this and there are many such recipes, but this is my variant reduced to moronic simplicity.

Posted by: Hrothgar. Yield: 1 – 2 servings. Prep time: 35 minutes.

---

1 sweet onion, preferably Vidalia
Lea & Perrins Worcestershire sauce to taste
soy sauce to taste (I use organic)
lemon pepper to taste
Lowry's seasoning salt to taste

Cut top and bottom off onion, then slice in half across the rings. Orient the two onion halves so they look like bowls and cut them crossways so you have six segments, being careful not to cut them all the way through. Place on tinfoil in a lightly greased baking dish so the crossway cuts are visible. Sprinkle seasonings on top as desired. Drizzle Worcestershire sauce and soy sauce across the top and allow to soak in. I think wine would also be tasty but it's too much like work. Same thing for a bit of EVOO (extra-virgin olive oil) drizzled across the top. Bake for 30 minutes for limp but slightly crunchy onions, but you could go longer. These go remarkably well (and simultaneously) with my baked pork chop recipe (in the Main Courses chapter). I prefer Vidalia onions but any sweet onion does reasonably well.

## Pasta and Zucchini Noodles with Almond-Mint Pesto

288 Light, healthy and delicious. Someone got us a spiralizer for a wedding present so I came up with a recipe to utilize it. This is a great side dish that can become main with addition of chicken or shrimp.

Posted by: westminsterdogshow. Yield: 2 servings. Prep time: 30 minutes.

---

1 cup fresh mint leaves
1/4 cup toasted almonds
1 lemon, zest and juice
1 tablespoon + 1 teaspoon olive oil
1 tablespoon water
3 ounces fusilli pasta
1 large zucchini (spiralized or grated lengthwise)
1/2 cup frozen peas
red chili pepper to taste
2 ounces feta cheese

For pesto, in food processor place the mint, almonds, lemon zest and juice and a pinch of salt. Pulse until finely chopped. Add 1 tablespoon olive oil, pulse again, and add water as needed for thick, spreadable consistency. Cook pasta to package directions, al dente. Heat 1 teaspoon olive oil in large skillet over medium heat. Add zucchini and peas and cook for one minute. Add pasta, toss and cook for two minutes. Remove from heat, add pesto and finish with chili and feta.

## Broccoli Ramen Noodle Slaw

289 Not as bad as it sounds! Adapted from a family recipe.

Posted by: WeaselWoman. Yield: servings for 5 – 10 Morons. Prep time: 25 minutes.

---

1 16-ounce bag broccoli slaw
2 packages chicken ramen noodles
1 bunch of green onions, chopped
1 cup unsalted peanuts
1 cup sunflower seeds
1/2 cup white sugar
1/4 cup vegetable oil
1/3 cup apple cider vinegar

Crush ramen noodles. Mix slaw, broken ramen noodles and green onions. Wisk together sugar, oil, vinegar and seasoning packet from ramen noodles. Pour liquid over slaw and toss to mix evenly. Refrigerate until served. Top with peanuts and sunflower seeds before serving. Peanuts are optional. Can easily be doubled or tripled for larger groups. Sounds weird but it's really good!

## Dad's Warm Red Cabbage Slaw

290 Great side dish with pork. This recipe comes from my dad's mother. Dad's parents came to this country from Austria before WWI.

Posted by: Ladylibertarian. Yield: 8 – 12 servings. Prep time: 30 minutes.

---

1 smallish red cabbage
1 pound bacon, diced
1/2 cup white vinegar
1/2 cup water
1 teaspoon salt
1 teaspoon pepper

Fry diced bacon in skillet. Do not drain. Add sliced cabbage, vinegar, water, salt and pepper. Simmer until cabbage is tender. A tablespoon or so of sugar can be added if you want a sweeter slaw.

## Bachelor Corn Fritters

291 Simple dish for non-chefs. The only thing my mother could make that I would eat.

Posted by: auscolpyr. Yield: 4 or more servings. Prep time: at least 15 minutes.

---

12 ounces canned corn (cream or nibblets)
4 favorite type of peppers (serrano, jalapeno or whatever)
3 cups favorite type of cooking oil
1/2 cup milk (whole)
1 cup flour
1 teaspoon baking powder
1 pinch salt
1 teaspoon chili powder
1 teaspoon paprika
1 squirt honey

1 pinch cinnamon

2 eggs

Mix (sift?) the dry ingredients, add the milk, eggs, corn and chopped peppers and stir until you have a thick pancake batter with bubbles on top. Optional, put in a fridge for an hour or more but if hungry, it's ready for a deep fry (or for those without a deep fryer, like me, have a deep pan ready with cooking oil). When the oil is hot (test with a drip of the batter), use a tablespoon to drop batter in the fryer (or pan/pot); turn after a minute or so and then remove to a paper towel-lined plate after another minute. Repeat until batter is gone. The main thing is the corn and batter. Use whatever peppers, seasonings and sweeteners you like. I like a thicker batter so I usually leave the batter in the fridge overnight.

# Fresh Packed Garlic Dill Pickles

292 My favorite for any occasion! I derived this recipe empirically to duplicate the pickles served at The Bagel, an outstanding Jewish kosher restaurant on West Devon Avenue in Chicago's West Rogers Park neighborhood, after they closed.

Posted by: sock_rat_eez. Yield: 1 to 12 servings. Prep time: 20 minutes.

---

4 to 6 pickle cucumbers
3 to 5 cloves garlic
2 heaping tablespoons salt
1 good sized branch fresh dill

Peel cucumbers. Thinly (1/8" - 3/16" thick, lengthwise) slice, or cut lengthwise into quarters or sixths, cucumbers. In a wide mouth quart Mason jar, add salt. Thinly slice garlic, as above. Crumple up the dill and place in bottom of jar. Holding the jar on its side, load as much cucumber as will fill the jar to the top. Add cold water to fill the jar completely. Place lid and ring on jar and tighten. Shake to mix the salt. Place jar in refrigerator. It will help to make a uniformly salty and garlicky pickle to shake and invert the jar every few hours. After 24 hours +/- they are ready to enjoy! Note that I like them salty, and strongly garlicky—your tastes may differ. Feel free to modify the proportions! The original ones from The Bagel were not as strongly seasoned as mine, to the best of my decades-old recollection. These must be kept refrigerated! When they start getting translucent around the edges, finish them off, they are nearing their lifespan, typically 10 – 14 days.

***Chef's Notes:***

These are great to use in my Ukrainian Breakfast Nosh Sandwich (recipe in the Snacks and Appetizers chapter). If you don't like or can't eat pickles made with vinegar these are for you!

## Spinach Salad with Apples, Avocado and Bacon

293 The only salad our kids will ask for. Original recipe from epicurious.com, submitted by reader Jeff Edmunds.

Posted by: Snowybits    Yield: 6 – 8 servings.    Prep time: 20 minutes.

---

1/2 cup olive oil
1 tablespoon honey
1/8 cup apple cider vinegar
1 tablespoon fresh lemon juice
1 1/2 teaspoons dry mustard
1/2 teaspoon smoked paprika
1/2 teaspoon ground ginger
dash or two cayenne pepper
1/2 pound bacon, cooked, drained and roughly chopped
2 6-ounce bags baby spinach
2 medium apples (anything sweet and crisp, I use Honeycrisp), halved, cored and thinly sliced
2 or 3 green onions, thinly sliced
2 ripe avocados, scooped out and cubed
1 cup chopped and toasted pecans

Whisk oil, honey, vinegar, lemon juice, dry mustard, smoked paprika, ground ginger and cayenne in small bowl. Salt and pepper to taste. Combine spinach, apple, green onions, avocado, bacon and pecans in large bowl. Drizzle salad with dressing and toss to coat. Extra bacon and/or pecans can be sprinkled on top. I am constantly improvising with this salad. I may grate fresh ginger instead of powdered, or use red onion, or use Dijon mustard. You get the idea!

## Adriane the Ethnic Food Critic's Hawaiian Sunomono

294 A cucumber, and pineapple side dish from *Sunset Magazine*, July 2012.

Posted by: Adriane the Critic . . . .    Yield: 6 servings.    Prep time: 20 minutes.

---

3 medium/2 large cucumbers, sliced thin
1 20-ounce can pineapple chunks, cut in half
1/6 – ¼ red onion, minced
1 tablespoon fresh mint, finely snipped
1 tablespoon fresh basil, finely snipped
1 splash, if necessary mirin (sweet rice vinegar)

Mix everything together and chill. Makes about 6 cups.

***Chef's Notes:***
Great with Bar-B-Q chicken and grilled fish. For me, crushed pineapple is a little too soupy, but YMMV. Original recipe called for shiso (also called perilla)—which I did not have—and

helpfully explained it was an herb in the mint and basil family. The grocery up the street had fresh mint and fresh basil, so I said 'Why not?' and have never looked back. I use some syrup from the canned pineapple, which for some people is too sweet. If so, try a splash of mirin to tart it up a bit and make it more like Japanese sunomono. If you prefer to peel cucumbers before slicing, no recipe adjustment is needed.

## Steamed Asparagus, Smothered and Covered

295 Turn a perfectly healthy vegetable into an instant heart attack! Mom and Dad were using this recipe (with canned asparagus), probably before I was born. It was a staple of our Thanksgiving and Easter dinners as far back as I can remember. When responsibility for making the dish was handed off to me, I ditched the canned version and opted for freshly steamed asparagus. The whole family was amazed at the difference. Dad and Mom have been gone for a few years now, but I carry on the tradition and serve this asparagus dish every Thanksgiving.

Posted by: EyeTest. Yield: 8 servings. Prep time: 1 hour—divided: 30 minutes prep, 30 minutes cooking.

---

3 bundles fresh asparagus
2 cups medium white sauce (modified recipe)
1/2 to 1 cup shredded cheddar cheese
2 boiled eggs, sliced
cooking spray
salt and pepper

4 tablespoons butter or margarine
4 tablespoons flour
1/4 teaspoon dry mustard
ground black pepper
1 cup milk
1 cup vegetable broth (canned or from concentrate)

PREPARE ASPARAGUS (This step can be done the day before)
Rinse asparagus in cold water. Break off and discard tough ends. Break asparagus stalks into 1-1/2 inch pieces (or leave whole and trim stalks to uniform length for a more elegant presentation). Arrange pieces in steamer basket in a single layer and place over boiling water. Steam 9 minutes or until a fork easily pierces the stalks. If storing overnight, put in a container, sprinkle with a little salt, toss lightly, cover and refrigerate. Lightly coat the inside of casserole dish with non-stick cooking spray. Dump asparagus pieces (or arrange whole stalks) into the baking dish. The dish should be no more than half full.

For the white sauce: in a cup, combine dry ingredients. In a medium saucepan, melt butter over medium heat. Add dry ingredients to the saucepan, stirring to achieve a smooth paste. Reduce heat and gradually whisk in 1 cup milk and 1 cup vegetable broth, stirring constantly to dissolve any lumps. Return to medium heat and stir constantly until sauce is thickened and bubbly. Pour sauce evenly over asparagus. Bake in oven at 350 degrees F until asparagus is hot and sauce is bubbling, about 30 – 40 minutes (depending on whether the asparagus was cold or room tempetature). Remove from oven and sprinkle shredded cheddar cheese over the sauce. Return to oven for a few minutes to melt the cheese. Just before serving, arrange boiled egg slices on top of cheese. Serve warm. To save time, you could buy a packet or two of powered white or bearnaise sauce mix from the grocery store instead of making it from scratch. But I've never tried that.

## Hoosierma's Creamy Corn

> 296 Killer corn for your BBQ dinner. I'm an Indiana girl, so I have a LOT of corn recipes—this is a mix of several of them. Also a pinch of The Pioneer Woman.

Posted by: hoosierma. Yield: 4 – 6 servings. Prep time: 1 hour.

---

6 ears corn on the cob
1/4 cup butter
1/2 brick (4 ounces) cream cheese
½ - 1 pound freshly shredded quesadilla cheese
splash to lots more jalapeno juice or diced jalapenos
1/4 cup cojita cheese (optional)
1/4 cup (ish) half and half
salt and pepper to taste

Preheat oven to 350 degrees F. Shuck and wash corn. Cut corn off of cobs and "milk" the cobs (use the back of a knife and scrape all the juice off the cob—it is the really sweet part!). Cut cream cheese and butter into cubes and mix into corn (I usually microwave until it melts). Stir in rest of ingredients, pour into a baking dish and bake for 30 minutes, or until corn is tender and dish is bubbly. This is a great recipe—add or subtract whatever you like; used diced jalapeno or just the juice.

## Lobster Salad

297 Created this after one of a lifetime of diving trips in the Florida Keys. Helps stretch a few tails for a crowd.

Posted by: mc.  Yield: 20 servings.  Prep time: 45 minutes.

---

6 Florida lobster tails
2 pounds tricolor rotini
1 medium purple onion
5 stalks celery
1/2 fresh red pepper
1/2 fresh yellow pepper
½ cup fresh tarragon leaves, chopped (no stems)
2 skinned red apples
3 tablespoons Dijon mustard
32 ounces mayonnaise
1 cup honey or agave nectar
1 cup (optional) craisins

Boil the tails in salted water without overcooking (they should be just turning red). Remove tails from water and add the rotini to the water. Cook and drain. Let the tails cool, split the shells and remove the meat. In a large mixing bowl add mayo, chopped tarragon, mustard, honey, salt and pepper and mix well. Chop celery, peppers, onion, skinned apples, craisins and lobster to bowl and mix. Follow with rotini and mix. You can adjust any of the ingredients to taste.This works with chicken breast or shrimp just as well.

## Gazpacho Salad

298 Great summer salad for a bbq or picnic. This was a reader submission to *Cooking Light* magazine ~20 years ago. I don't have her name and the recipe is not available on their site's recipe archive.

Posted by: Lizzy.  Yield: 8 servings or so.  Prep time: 30 minutes.

---

3 cups seeded, chopped tomatoes
1 cup peeled, chopped cucumber
1 cup chopped green bell pepper
1/4 cup thinly sliced green onion
1/4 cup chopped Bermuda onion
2 tablespoons fresh basil
2 tablespoons + 1 teaspoon red wine vinegar
1 teaspoon olive oil
1 teaspoon Dijon mustard

1/8 tsp *each* salt and pepper
2 cloves garlic, minced

Combine all of the chopped vegetables in a bowl. Set aside. Make the dressing by combining the basil, vinegar, oil, mustard, salt, pepper, and garlic. Mix dressing into vegetables and chill for 1 hour before serving. Best to serve the same day as it is prepared; it can get watery if left in the fridge overnight.

## Big V's Coastal Carolina Coleslaw

> 299 Low salt variant of the classic. My SIL's father has a very low salt diet so I have been making these versions of OBX foods.

Posted by: Big V. Yield: around 10 servings. Prep time: 20 minutes.

---

1 medium-sized head cabbage (green)
1 medium-sized head cabbage (purple)
1 tablespoon mustard powder
Mrs. Dash Table Blend to taste (use as salt and pepper)
2 tablespoons mayonnaise
1/2 cup apple cider vinegar

Core and slice the 2 cabbages into very thin strips. Mix in a large bowl with the vinegar. Toss in the mustard powder and Mrs. Dash. Cover and let sit in the fridge for 10 minutes. Uncover and stir in the mayo, then recover and chill till ready to serve. Some folks add shredded carrots to this or minced onions but I prefer my coleslaw to be simple. Olive oil can be used instead of mayo but I prefer the texture you get with Dukes.

## Avocado Ranch Dressing

> 300 Ranch dressing done up all green. My own recipe, modified from Mom's ranch dressing classic.

Posted by: Christopher R Taylor. Yield: about 2 cups. Prep time: 10 minutes.

---

1 cup mayonnaise
½ teaspoon salt
½ teaspoon pepper
1 tablespoon lemon juice
2 tablespoons milk
1 avocado

Mix milk, mayo, lemon juice, salt, and pepper in a container. De-pit and scoop out meat from avocado, and mash in a bowl to smooth consistency. Then mix avocado into the dressing until well blended to a pleasing green hue. This can be done with other vegetables, for instance a can of green chiles and some cilantro and cumin makes a terrific Mex-themed dressing. Blending up a peeled cucumber (without the seeds) makes a very light, cool dressing. Adding some herbs such as parsley, lemon thyme, or chives spices up the mix.

## Mazza's Salad

301 Easy garlicky salad that goes with everything This is a variation of a wildly popular salad in central Ohio. The original was created by Mazza's Restaurant in Mount Vernon, Ohio. The restaurant has been closed for about 15 years.

Posted by: Ladylibertarian. Yield: 1 – 20 servings. Prep time: 10 minutes.

---

1 cup good olive oil
1 tablespoon white vinegar
1 tablespoon salt
1 teaspoon pepper
5 – 10 garlic cloves
1 cup crumbled gorgonzola cheese
1 head lettuce or romaine lettuce

The dressing is easiest made in a blender or food processor. I use a blender. If you have neither—no problem—just whisk well in a bowl. Combine all ingredients except gorgonzola cheese. Blend or whisk until smooth. If whisking, use garlic press to incorporate garlic. Add gorgonzola cheese at the end and blend gently so there are some pieces visible. Clean and chop head or romaine lettuce in the quantity needed. Dress with amount of dressing desired (a little more is better than a little less). The traditional way to serve this is wilted, but many people object to that presentation, so I dress the lettuce right before serving. Dresssing keeps for two months in the refrigerator.

***Chef's Notes:***
Use gorgonzola cheese only. Bleu cheese just doesn't taste right. Also, this is not an ideal salad to eat on a first date.

## Cabbage Salad Dressing

302 Simple and tasty cole slaw dressing, from my Grandma Margaret.

Posted by: Mrs. Mis Hum. Yield: servings for 6 Morons. Prep time: 10 minutes.

---

2/3 cup vinegar
1/2 cup salad oil
1/2 cup sugar
1 teaspoon ground mustard
1/2 teaspoon celery seed
dash salt and pepper

Combine all ingredients in a saucepan. Boil dressing 1 minute; pour over cabbage salad mixture while hot.

## Broccoli Slaw Salad

303 Tart, but a bit sweet, this crunchy slaw goes great with BBQ. From theperfectpantry.com.

Posted by: no nic, but lurker for many years. Yield: 4 – 6 servings. Prep time: 15 minutes.

---

1/4 cup sliced raw almonds
1 12-ounce package broccoli slaw
1/2 cup dried cranberries
3 tablespoons extra-virgin olive oil
3 tablespoons white vinegar
3 tablespoons honey
3 tablespoons plain Greek yogurt
1 1/2 teaspoons Dijon mustard
1/4 teaspoon kosher salt
1/4 teaspoon fresh black pepper

In a small dry nonstick frying pan, toast the almonds over medium heat, shaking pan frequently, until just starting to brown. Remove from heat and set aside to cool. Add the broccoli slaw and cranberries to a large mixing bowl. Combine remaining ingredients in a large measuring cup or mixing bowl. Whisk together until the dressing is smooth and emulsified. Pour the dressing over the broccoli slaw. Let sit for at least 30 minutes or up to 4 hours, stirring occasionally to redistribute the dressing that will settle on the bottom of the bowl. On warm days, refrigerate until ready to serve. Just before serving, stir in the toasted almonds. Serve at room temperature or cool.

## Marinated Broccoli and Cauliflower Salad

304 Great for a party or buffet. Kinda zingy. From my mom, who is thrilled that little children will voluntarily eat the onions in this salad. If sweet onion is not available in winter, use a small regular onion, diced. Marinate a little longer.

Posted by: KT. Yield: 12 – 20 servings. Prep time: 30 minutes.

---

Good Seasons Italian salad dressing seasoning mix (buy the 4-pack)
4 large or 6 medium carrots
1 medium to large sweet onion
3 to 4 pounds broccoli
1 large head (3 pounds) cauliflower
2 cans (each 3.8 ounces dry weight) sliced black olives
fresh ground pepper to taste

Prepare an 8-ounce cruet of dressing per directions on seasoning packet. Use cider vinegar. I substitute extra vinegar for the water because marination draws moisture from the veggies. Peel and thinly slice carrots. Sprinkle with water. Microwave just until easily pierced by a fork, stirring every 15 seconds. Set aside to cool. In a very large bowl, pour first cruet of dressing over bite-sized slices of onion. Add bite-sized broccoli florets and sliced tender, peeled stems. Add enough additional prepared dressing to leave a skiff of dressing on the bottom of the bowl when tossed. Toss in bite-sized cauliflower florets, carrots, drained olives and pepper. Cover and marinate for 2 – 3 hours, tossing occasionally. Refrigerate leftovers. Toss leftovers (in marinade) with angel hair cabbage or other shredded greens.

## Can't Beet That Salad

305 Roasted beets with sauteed beet tops. From the kitchen of Emmie.

Posted by: Emmie. Yield: 6 servings. Prep time: 1 ½ hours.

---

1 bunch beets with fresh tops
olive oil
salt and pepper

Cut tops off of beets and reserve. Clean beets and wrap in foil. Roast in 350 - 400 degree F oven until easily pierced with a knife. Depending on oven temperature and size of the beets, this may take 30 to 90 minutes. While beets are roasting, clean beet tops and trim off tough stems and discolored areas on the leaves. Chop into bite-sized pieces. Add just enough olive oil to coat the bottom of a wide skillet and heat over medium heat. Add beet tops. Season with salt and pepper and toss until coated with oil and cook until wilted. Transfer to serving bowl. When beets are finished roasting, remove foil and allow to cool enough to handle. Peel the beets and cut into pieces that will fit nicely on a fork. (I cut them into sticks measuring approximately 1/4 by 1/4 by 3/4 inches.) Add the beet roots to the tops in the serving bowl and toss to mix. Serve cold or at room temperature. Golden beets have a more delicate flavor and I prefer them for this recipe, but if red beets have fresher-looking tops, I use those instead.

## Rhomboid's Signature Roast Walnut Salad

306 Green salad with walnuts, walnut vinaigrette, and other goodies. Origin is a little murky. Sister-in-law's sister reported a fantastic roasted walnut salad at some catered event, and also said that World Market sells a great roasted walnut oil. I put this together with the idea of putting bits of fruit in a green salad (done by several chains these days). Added cheese for salty counter-point. Voila!

Posted by: Rhomboid. Yield: servings for 4 Morons. Prep time: 15 minutes.

---

1 bag mixed greens or spinach salad (pre-washed)
1 cup roasted walnut oil
1/3 cup balsamic vinegar
2 tablespoons Dijon mustard
1 teaspoon crushed or minced garlic
1 teaspoon fresh ground black pepper
1/2 teaspoon salt
1/2 cup crumbled blue cheese (any type) or feta
1 cup roasted walnut pieces
1/2 cup dried cranberries

For vinaigrette: add mustard, salt, pepper, garlic, and balsamic vinegar to a medium or large mixing bowl. Slowly add walnut oil, whisking vigorously, so that mixture emulsifies. For walnuts: put walnut pieces (break up whole walnuts if that's all you can find) on a cookie sheet or in an oven-proof dish. Bake at 350 degrees F for 6 – 8 minutes, watching closely to avoid charring. Let cool. Final assembly: put salad greens in large bowl. Add cranberries, roasted walnut pieces, and crumbled cheese. Add vinaigrette, toss, and serve.

***Chef's Notes:***
Roasted walnut oil: look for La Tourangelle, sold in fancier grocery stores, or any other brand roasted walnut oil. Any blue cheese will do, or feta, as long as they are in crumbled form.

## Marinated Tomato and Cucumber Salad

307 To celebrate summer tomatoes, cukes and sweet onions. From my mother-in-law, who made a big bowl of this salad to lift the spirits of friends during an out-of-town hospital vigil. It worked.

Posted by: KT. Yield: 6 servings. Prep time: 20 minutes.

---

1 8-ounce cruet prepared Good Seasons Italian Salad Dressing
1 small to medium sweet onion
1 small to medium green bell pepper
1 1/2 pounds young, tender cucumbers
2 pounds meaty, ripe tomatoes
fresh ground black pepper to taste

Prepare salad dressing per directions on the seasoning packet, substituting extra cider vinegar for the 3 tablespoons of water. Pour into a large bowl. Slice onion and remove a few rings from the centers of the slices. Cut up the rest. Add to the dressing with seeded and sliced green pepper. Allow to sit for about half an hour. Peel cucumbers unless skins are sweet and tender. Cut in chunks. Toss into veggies and dressing. Blanch tomatoes (if necessary), peel and cut in chunks. Toss into veggies and dressing. Add pepper to taste. Allow flavors to blend for an hour or two. Toss occasionally. Serve in bowls with good bread, sandwiches, poultry or bacon. Grow or buy less-juicy tomatoes like Roma or tasty Oxheart types for this recipe. Do not refrigerate.

## Texas Caviar

308 A delicious and healthy appetizer, and side dish. Great for potlucks, since it's vegan and gluten-free. Great dish for Southern New Year's day tradition of black-eyed peas. Adapted from *The Homesick Texan* by Lisa Fain.

Posted by: Duncanthrax. Yield: 8 to 12 servings. Prep time: 20 minutes + at least 4 hours to chill.

---

4 cups cooked (or 2 16-ounce cans) black-eyed peas
1 bunch green onions
1 can (or 4 Romas) Rotel tomatoes
2 medium to large jalapenos
1 medium ripe avocado
1 can white corn
1 bunch cilantro
1 large bell pepper (yellow, orange, or red, in that order)
1 tablespoon (each) fresh oregano, Tabasco sauce, Worcestershire sauce
1 large lime
3/4 cup olive oil
3 cloves (at least) fresh garlic
1 teaspoon fresh ground black pepper
½ teaspoon salt

Cook the fresh or dried black-eyed peas, or drain and rinse the canned black-eyed peas. Drain the Rotel tomatoes, or chop the 4 fresh Roma tomatoes. Wearing gloves, finely chop the jalapenos. (If less heat is desired, remove the seeds and the supporting structures they're on from the interior first. Absolutely wear gloves for this!) Slice the green onions thinly. Finely chop the bell pepper, oregano, and cilantro. Press or finely mince the garlic. Peel and cube the avocado. In a large bowl, mix all ingredients together, along with pepper and salt, and chill for 4 to 8 hours before serving.

***Chef's Notes:***
This recipe is easy to double or triple. If doing so, adding different colors of bell pepper (yellow, red, orange) makes it even more festive. Ingredients like black beans, other types of corn, red onion, etc. are fun, as well. You may substitute Italian dressing for the olive oil, if desired.

# Herbed Watermelon-Feta Salad

309 I got this from allrecipes.com.

Posted by: Tami. Yield: 12 cups. Prep time: 40 minutes.

---

8 cups seedless watermelon, cubed
1 cup thinly sliced red onion
1 cup thinly sliced fresh basil
1 cup chopped fresh cilantro
1/2 cup finely chopped mint leaves
6 tablespoons fresh lime juice (juice of 2 large limes)
1 4-ounce package crumbled feta cheese
3 tablespoons olive oil
2 tablespoons balsamic vinegar (you can try different balsamic vinegars, i.e. raspberry balsamic)
salt and pepper to taste

Combine all ingredients in a large bowl and gently mix. I know this sounds like weird ingredients to put together but it was really good!

# From the Grill

*I was looking for something to eat*
*And discovered an Ace of Spades treat*
*Now say what you will*
*You should fire up your grill*
*As they say, you just can't beat our meat*

## Santa Maria Style BBQ Tri-Tip

310 BBQ tri-tip from CaliGuy. Just what it sounds like. I have no idea who I stole this from. I've been making it for a long time.

Posted by: CaliGirl.    Yield: enough for 4 – 5 morons.    Prep time: 1 1/2 hours.

---

Approximately 3 – 4 pounds tri-tip roast with fat
4 tablespoons (or to taste) garlic salt
3 tablespoons fresh ground pepper
3 tablespoons sea salt

Remove roast from refrigerator 30 minutes before grilling. Season with spices. We roll the roast in a pan containing the spices. Heat grill with direct and indirect heat. Place roast fat side up over direct heat and sear for about 10 minutes. Turn roast over and sear other side until brown. Move roast to indirect heat and continue cooking until thermometer reads 130 degrees. Let roast rest 15 minutes before carving.

***Chef's Notes:***
We BBQ over red oak. You can purchase red oak chips online from Susieqbrand.com.

## Grilled Cilantro Chicken

311 The Platonic ideal of grilled chicken. I am about as derivative as they come, but this one sprang from my head, sort of like Athena from Zeus!

Posted by: CBD    Yield: 8 servings.    Prep time: 75 minutes.

---

1 cup rough chopped cilantro
4 tablespoons Dijon mustard
1 1/2 tablespoons kosher salt
several grinds black pepper
4 cloves garlic, minced
3/4 cup chopped onion
1 seeded jalapeno
1/2 teaspoon ancho chile powder
2 ounces balsamic vinegar
2 ounces honey
1/2 cup olive oil
4 – 5 pounds skin-on chicken thighs and breasts

Blend until smooth all ingredients except the olive oil (and chicken...duh!). Continue blending while drizzling olive oil into the mixture so that it emulsifies and gets nice and thick. Use more oil if necessary. Cut the chicken breasts in half. Into a big bowl dump the chicken and the emulsified marinade. Coat well and refrigerate for one day, tossing it once or twice if you are really bored or obsessive-compulsive.

Clean and oil the grill, and preheat it to about 300 degrees F. Lay the chicken skin-side up on the grill, as far from the flame as possible. The goal is indirect heat. Cook for 30 minutes with the top down (the grill's. . . not yours), shooting for that magic 300 degrees F. If your grill heats unevenly move the chicken around once or twice. After 30 minutes, flip the chicken and cook for an additional 20 – 30 minutes. Check the internal temperature for your preferred degree of doneness, then move the chicken to direct heat to crisp and brown it, moving and flipping until all pieces are evenly browned. Remove from grill and allow to rest for 10 minutes before serving.

***Chef's Notes:***
The emulsified marinade sticks to the chicken during cooking and adds a really nice complexity of flavor that is worth the trouble.

## Yummy Wings

312 Wings with the right kick. This recipe came from experience & experiment.

Posted by: 75olds. Yield: 3 – 4 servings. Prep time: 5 minutes.

---

30 – 35 chicken wings
24-ounce bottle Goya mojo criolla marinade
12-ounce bottle Robert Rothschild Anna Mae's smoky sweet chipotle BBQ sauce

Put thawed wings in a gallon ziplock bag, empty mojo sauce in bag and marinate in fridge for 2 hours to overnight. Then grill wings with indirect method after searing to get the grill marks. After 25 – 30 minutes, baste with Anna Mae's sauce for a couple minutes. Put cooked wings in a bowl, pour in more sauce and shake to coat. Serve with blue cheese and ranch dressings. Enjoy.

## Filipino Lechon Manok (grilled chicken)

313 From Cicero Kaboom! Kid wife.

Posted by: Cicero Kaboom! Kid. Yield: 4 – 6 servings. Prep time: 5 hours.

---

1 dead bird of 4 pounds weight
1/4 cup soy sauce
2 tablespoons fish sauce
1 tablespoon brown sugar
1 teaspoon salt
2 teaspoons lime juice
1/4 cup water
1/2 cup thinly sliced onion
6 cloves garlic, mashed or minced
1/4 teaspoon fresh cracked black pepper
1 bundle lemon grass, kinda folded and tied up

Dry bird with paper towels. Place in a gallon zip-lock bag that is in a large bowl. Mix all ingredients except lemon grass and pour onto the bird. Remove most of the air from the bag and shake it up a bit to distribute the goodies. Put the bag back into the bowl and put the whole deal into the refrigerator overnight or at least 3 hours. Remove the bird, let it drain briefly while you get the grill going. Stuff the lemon grass bundle into the bird and cook over offset heat for an hour or hour and a half until it's done.
Eat with rice. Fight over the wings.

***Chef's Notes:***
Add one or three hot Thai Chili peppers sliced into rings to the marinade

# Grilled Turkey

314 The original WeaselFamily recipe passed down through countless generations.

Posted by: Weasel. Yield: 5 – 6 servings. Prep time: 30 minutes – 2 hours.

---

one 12-14 pound whole turkey
cooking oil
salt/pepper
butcher's twine and poultry needle

Rinse turkey, remove bags of innards from inside and pat dry. Using butcher's twine and poultry needle, sew closed neck and body cavity openings. Tie legs together and fold wings under. Coat entire bird with cooking oil and salt & pepper to taste. Cook on charcoal grill using indirect method approximately 2 hours or until temperature probe pops up. Let stand 15 minutes before carving. Turkey turns very dark brown and outer meat is pinkish (but not uncooked) from grill.

***WeaselNotes:***

Indirect grilling method—Weber-style charcoal grill: Place aluminum foil disposable drip pan on center of lower charcoal rack. Fill with 2" water or beer. Pile 30 – 40 briquettes on either side of drip pan and light. Place grilling rack with handle openings over briquette piles. Add briquettes during cooking—approximately 5 – 6 on each side every 30 minutes until turkey is done.

## SuperChops!

315 Delicious grilled pork loin chops with Vidalia onion wrapped in bacon. This was something my parents made up for camping trips when I was a kid. It's been a staple of summer grilling in our family ever since.

Posted by: Grendel. Yield: 1 moron serving. Prep time: 30 minutes.

---

one 3/4 inch thick boneless pork loin chop
3 slices thick-cut bacon
one 1/4 inch slab Vidalia or sweet onion
½ teaspoon Lawry's seasoned salt
1/3 teaspoon ground black pepper
1 slice Kraft American cheese singles

Lay out three slices of bacon in a star/asterisk pattern on a paper plate. Place the boneless pork loin chop in the center of the bacon. Place a slab of Vidalia onion on the top of the pork chop, then pull the ends of the bacon up and over the top of the chop and onion to form a bacon-wrapped morsel of pork and onion deliciousness. Secure the package together for grilling by placing three toothpicks through the bacon and onion into the chop.Prepare your grill at 300 degrees F. When the grill is at temperature, add the superchops, onion side down and season with the Lawry's seasoned salt and black pepper. Be extra-careful to watch for flareups as the bacon will produce lots of grease initially. After 5 – 7 minutes flip the chops. Allow the grill to increase in temperature to about 350 degrees F. The key is to keep the temperature low enough at first to allow the heat to penetrate the onion and the chop enough to be done (I cook to 135 degrees F in the center) without torching the bacon black. Once the chops reach the desired temperature in the center, remove the toothpicks and add one slice of cheese to each (onion side up) chop. Close the grill lid and allow one or two minutes for the cheese to melt, then serve and enjoy THE MOST DELICIOUS PORK CHOP IN THE UNIVERSE!

## Grilled Pork Tenderloin with Corn Relish and Tomato Salad

316 Fresh and simple but totally delicious. Stumbled upon this fantastic recipe on the *WSJ's* Slow Food Fast section.

Posted by: TeezFoSheez. Yield: 4 servings. Prep time: 45 minutes – 1 hour.

---

1 ½ pounds pork tenderloin
1/2 cup olive oil
3 large heirloom tomatoes, cut into wedges
5 tablespoons scallions, thinly sliced
2 teaspoons minced garlic
2 tablespoons roughly chopped fresh mint
2 teaspoons apple cider vinegar
3 ears sweet corn, shucked
2 tablespoons minced shallots
kosher salt
fresh cracked pepper
leaves from 2 sprigs of fresh rosemary, chopped

Light grill and slice tenderloin into four equal rounds. Brush meat all over with 1 tablespoon of olive oil and season with a pinch of salt, pepper and the chopped rosemary. Cover and set aside at room temperature. Make tomato salad by combining the following in a large bowl and set aside: tomato wedges, 2 tablespoons of scallions, half the minced garlic, all the chopped mint, 1/2 teaspoon vinegar, 3 tablespoons olive oil, and a pinch of salt and pepper. Grill corn over medium-high heat, turning often until charred all over, about 3 – 4 minutes. Meanwhile, grill pork over medium-high heat until charred slightly on the outside and medium temperature within. Let meat rest 5 minutes before serving.

Make the corn relish: cut kernels off corn and transfer to a bowl. Combine them with the following, and toss together: 5 tablespoons of oil, 1 ½ teaspoons of vinegar, remaining minced garlic, remaining scallions, all the shallots, and a pinch of salt and pepper. Serve pork with relish spooned on top or on the side with the tomato salad on the side.

## GMan's Ribs

317 Smoked baby back ribs. The rub was initially pulled from allrecipes.com, I think—but it's been modified a bit. The rest is just experience.

Posted by: GMan. Yield: 3 racks of ribs, so 3 - 8 servings? Prep time: 7+ hours.

---

3 racks of baby back ribs
½ cup yellow mustard
2 tablespoons salt
1 tablespoon cinnamon powder

1 tablespoon powdered ginger
2 tablespoons white sugar
2 tablespoons brown sugar
2 tablespoons black pepper
2 tablespoons white pepper
2 tablespoons onion powder
1 tablespoon garlic powder
1 tablespoon chili powder
1 tablespoon paprika (not smoked!)
1 tablespoon cumin powder
1 cup butter
¼ cup brown sugar

The evening before cooking, soak any wood chips or chunks you may be using to smoke your ribs, in water.

Approximately 1 hour before cooking, prepare the rib racks (remove membranes, etc). Stir all the rub spices together (salt through cumin powder) until uniformly mixed. Coat ribs generously with yellow mustard, or a dressing of your choosing. Generously coat ribs with the rub mixture on all sides and let stand for an hour at room temperature. Meanwhile bring your cooking device up to temperature. You will be cooking the ribs at between 220 and 250 degrees F. For best results, you're going to want the temperature not to vary more than a few degrees in either direction during the cooking time. After the ribs have rested for an hour, place them in your smoker/on your grill. If you are using wood chunks or chips to smoke, start these now as well. Cook the ribs for 3 hours. You may add more wood for smoking if you like, but I don't find it necessary.

While the ribs are cooking, melt the butter and stir in the ¼ cup brown sugar. After the ribs have cooked for 3 hours, take them off the heat, place them on a double layer of aluminum foil (the Texas crutch) and drizzle about half the butter and brown sugar mix over them. Wrap them in the foil and place back on the heat for 2 more hours. After 2 hours, remove the ribs from the foil, drizzle the remaining butter and brown sugar mix over them and put them back on the heat for 1 more hour. Pull the ribs from the heat and test for doneness by flexing them or the toothpick test. I wrap them in foil and let them rest for at least a half hour after cooking. Enjoy!

## Cheese Biscuits with Bacon-Sausage Gravy

318 Breakfast on the grill. From *Chile Pepper* magazine.

Posted by: Jane D'oh. Yield: 4 – 6 servings. Prep time: 5 minutes, plus cook time 25 minutes.

---

4 slices peppered bacon
One 16-ounce package hot (or mild) breakfast sausage
1/3 cup flour
4 cups milk
salt to taste
2 ½ teaspoons coarse-ground black pepper
1 16-ounce can biscuit dough
1 cup shredded pepper jack cheese

Place cast iron skillet on grill and preheat to 400 degrees F. Cook the bacon until crisp, then drain on paper towels. When cool, crumble. Add the sausage to the skillet and brown. Using a slotted spoon, remove the sausage and set aside. Add the flour to the reserved drippings in the skillet and stir continuously to make a roux, until thickened and tan in color. Add the milk and continue to stir as the gravy thickens. Season with salt and pepper. Add the bacon and sausage to the gravy and stir to combine. Place the biscuits on top of the gravy and top with shredded cheese. Increase grill temperature to 450 degrees F, cover the grill, and cook for 10 – 12 minutes, until the biscuits are puffy and lightly browned and the cheese is melted. Serve hot.

***Chef's Notes:***
This can be cooked in the oven, after cooking the gravy and sausage and making the roux on the stove top. Adjust oven temperature so as not to overcook biscuits.

## Don Q's Hawaiian BBQ Ham

319 Great for parties. Recipe developed by trial and error, while throwing parties in Hawaii . . . .

Posted by: Don Quixote. Yield: 20 servings. Prep time: 3 – 4 hours.

---

spiral-sliced bone-in half ham
BBQ sauce
teriyaki sauce
mustard
honey

Combine 4 parts teriyaki sauce, 4 parts BBQ sauce, and 1 part mustard. Mix thoroughly. Taste; if too tart, add honey to taste. Open a beer, pour about 4 parts beer into the sauce to make it a bit more liquid . . . drink the rest of the beer. Take a spiral-sliced bone-in half ham, and use a brush to slather the sauce in between the various spiral slices, and outside of the ham—note, the more between slices, the better. Drink another beer (truly, this is part of the traditional method of preparation).

This is best done on a Weber dome-type grill. Build a fire with briquettes and let it burn down to no flame . . . while drinking more beer. Take a sheet of aluminum foil, and place it on the grill in the center, just large enough for the ham to sit on, flat side down (yes, one or two slices will get overdone, but there is plenty more). Cook slowly, for a couple of hours, until the ham is thoroughly warm throughout, periodically basting with sauce. (I often, an hour or so in, put even more sauce between the slices—messy, but fun.) Remove from fire; let sit for 10 minutes or so, then slice down the length of the bone, to 'slice' the ham. Great to serve with sliced pineapple cooked on the grill. Note, this can be done on a standard gas grill; key is to use indirect flame.

***Chef's Notes:***
Periodically add beer, to the cook.

## The Colonel's Shashlik

> 320 Teh recipe what sealed the deal. From extensive experimentation adapting my grandmother's recipe.

Posted by: Your Decidedly Devious Uncle Palpatine. Yield: 2 servings. Prep time: one or more days.

---

2 pounds pork shoulder cut into 2-inch cubes
1 cup cheapest gin
4 dashes Angosturo bitters
onions, peeled and cut into quarters
whole garlic cloves

Mix gin and bitters, marinate pork in same. Freeze and then allow to thaw. When meat is at room temperature, thread onto skewers, alternating meat with peeled garlic cloves and onion quarters. Grill over charcoal, preferably. Serve with ajvar and flat bread.

# *Seafood*

## Cedar Plank Grilled Salmon

321 Five-star salmon. I have no idea where this recipe came from; it is just something that we stumbled upon by trial and error after getting crappy cedar plank salmon in chain restaurants and wanting something better.

Posted by: The Great White Scotsman. Yield: 2 – 4 servings. Prep time: 2 hours.

---

8 – 16 ounces salmon fillets, skin on, cut in 4-ounce portions
sea salt to taste
fresh thyme to taste
one cedar plank

Soak the cedar plank in water for 1 – 2 hours before cooking. Light charcoal grill and let burn off for 20 – 30 minutes. If you must you can use a gas grill but you won't get that tasty smoky flavor. Take salmon and liberally sprinkle sea salt on it. Add fresh thyme to taste—caution, this herb goes a long way. Let it sit out for 10 – 15 minutes. You should see a slight film develop from the salt. Place salmon on soaked cedar plank and set over hot coals. Cover grill and move vents to half. Cook about 15 – 20 minutes and check for doneness with fork. You can use a spray bottle of water to douse any flare-ups. Remove from grill and let set for about 5 minutes. Serve and enjoy with any fresh vegetables. Corn on the cob is our favorite.

## Grilled Tilapia Fillets

322 For those pesky pescetarians. From the kitchen of Emmie.

Posted by: Emmie. Yield: 5 servings. Prep time: 20 minutes, not counting marinating time.

---

2 pounds tilapia fillets
1/4 cup (or more to coat fillets) olive oil
1/8 cup tomato paste (such as Amore packaged in a tube)
salt and pepper
dried garlic/spice mix

Thaw and pat dry the tilapia fillets. Season with salt and pepper and set aside.

In a gallon ziplock baggie, mix olive oil, tomato paste, and garlic/spice mix until well-blended. (I massage the bag with my fingers until the tomato paste clumps break up and mix with the oil.) The olive oil should take on an orange color from the tomato paste. Add fillets to the bag. Seal and massage the bag to coat the fish with the marinade. Keep refrigerated until ready to grill (1 hour to 1 day). Turn the bag a time or two to keep the marinade evenly distributed.

Tear aluminum foil into pieces, each large enough to accommodate a single fillet with a bit of a border. Raise the edges of the foil a bit. Place one fillet on each piece of foil. Pour remaining marinade on the fillets if it looks like they need it. Place fillets in their foil boats on the grill over medium heat. Cook until fish begins to flake. If the tomato/olive oil browns a bit at the edges, this is good (and very tasty). Serve in the foil boats so diners can scrape up the browned edges.

### *Chef's Notes:*

I do not really know the correct amounts or ratio of olive oil to tomato paste because I just pour it into the baggie until it looks right. You should have enough tomato paste so that the oil takes on the red color of the paste and the edges brown on the grill.

# *Veggies*

## 'Ettes Grilled Watermelon

323 Hot and sweet (like our 'ettes) grilled watermelon. Adapted over the years from plain grilled watermelon.

Posted by: Duncanthrax. Yield: 6 – 10 servings. Prep time: 25 minutes.

---

1 (about 5 pounds) red seedless watermelon
2 large lemons
3/4 teaspoon kosher salt
1 teaspoon guajillo chili powder (or red chili powder)

Get your grill fire to about 500 degrees F (high). Slice watermelon crosswise into slices 1 1/2 inches thick (approximately 5). Cut each slice into quarters (20 wedges). Grate 2 tablespoons lemon rind from lemons, set aside. Slice lemons into slices 1/2 inch thick. Put watermelon and lemon slices on grill. Grill each side approximately 1 minute each, or until charred nicely. Place watermelon wedges on serving platter. Squeeze the juice from a few lemon slices over the watermelon wedges; place remaining lemon wedges on platter. Sprinkle watermelon evenly with kosher salt, chili powder, and lemon rind. Serve.

## Grilled Cauliflower

324 A side that cooks alongside the steak on the grill. Made it up myself.

Posted by: Vashta Nerada. Yield: 4 – 6 servings. Prep time: 30 minutes.

---

1 head cauliflower
1 thick slice yellow onion, coarsely chopped
1/3 stick butter
a few ounces olive oil
1/3 teaspooon paprika
1/3 teaspoon salt
1/3 teaspoon pepper, or to taste

Technically the cauliflower steams and doesn't grill, but this side is easy to throw on the grill while you cook the main course. Wash the cauliflower and cut apart the fleurettes. Melt the butter in a measuring cup and add olive oil to make up 1/2 cup of liquid. Add the garlic, paprika, salt and pepper to the liquid and stir. Take approximately two feet of aluminum foil and fold one third over to make a double bottom, then fold up the sides to make a box.

Lay the cauliflower in the box and add in the chopped onion, then dribble the butter and oil mixture on top. Fold the top layer of foil over the box and pinch to seal the box. Place the cauliflower in a corner of the grill in indirect heat. The cauliflower should be fully cooked within 30 minutes, and you can transfer it to a serving bowl.

## Grilled Brussel Sprouts with Balsamic Vinaigrette

325 Recipe comes from www.charbroil.com.

Posted by: Tami. Yield: 4 – 6 servings. Prep time: 20 minutes.

---

1 pound brussels sprouts
1 tablespoon olive oil
salt & pepper to taste
1/4 cup balsamic vinegar
1 clove garlic, minced (or more if desired)
1 teaspoon Dijon mustard
1 teaspoon honey
2/3 cup olive oil
grated Parmesan cheese

Preheat grill to medium high. Trim tough ends off the sprouts and remove any discolored outer leaves. Cut in half through the stem. Toss the sprouts with the olive oil and season with salt and pepper. Put the sprouts in a grill basket, cut side down. Grill for 5 – 6 minutes or until they have char marks. Turn over and grill for another 4 – 5 minutes. Remove from grill and place in bowl. Cover with foil and allow them to steam for a few minutes. Combine vinegar, garlic, mustard and honey in a small bowl. Whisk to combine thoroughly. Slowly whisk in the olive oil to create an emulsion. Season with salt and pepper to taste. Drizzle sprouts with the vinaigrette and sprinkle Parmesan cheese on top. This vinaigrette can be used on many vegetables or just as a salad dressing.

## Euro's Secret BBQ Sauce

326 A wee bit in the pot, a wee bit in the chef—some alcohol-fueled creativity on a rare sunny day.

Posted by: Euro. Yield: enough for 2 – 5 pounds meat. Prep time: 5 minutes + drinking.

---

1/2 cup white zinfandel
1/2 cup whisky
1/2 cup ketchup
1/4 cup Heinz 57 sauce
1/4 cup A1 sauce
3 tablespoons brown sugar
squirt mustard
dash celery salt
1 tablespoon garlic powder

Drink shot of whisky, chase with shot of wine. Mix remaining ingredients in bowl. Pour over meat to be grilled—ribs, chicken, chops. Let meat soak for at least one hour, while drinking another shot or three.

## Personal Grilled Pizzas

327 Homemade pizza on everyone's favorite cooking instrument, the grill. Recipe is from my mother.

Posted by: Fishbreath. Yield: 4 servings. Prep time: 20 minutes, plus rising and grilling time.

---

2 teaspoons active dry yeast
1 1/4 cups warm water (110 degrees)
4 1/4 cups flour
2 teaspoons salt
1/4 cup olive oil
shredded mozzarella cheese
pizza sauce
other toppings

Stir the yeast into the water and let sit for 10 – 15 minutes. In a large mixing bowl, combine the flour and salt. Slowly mix in the oil and water in turns. Knead until smooth and slightly sticky. (It shouldn't stick to your hand if your hand is lightly floured. If it sticks, add flour by tablespoons. If it feels gritty, add water by tablespoons.) Lightly coat the inside of another mixing bowl with olive oil. Put the kneaded dough into the bowl, turning it over to evenly coat it with oil. Cover with a damp dish towel and let rise until doubled, about one hour. Punch down the dough and divide into eight equal parts. Press each part into a round pizza crust, first flattening with the heel of your palm, then stretching with your hands.

Heat your grill to medium (or build a medium two-zone fire, if grilling over charcoal). Brush one side of each pizza crust with olive oil and place on the grill over direct heat, oiled side down. Cook for a few minutes, until the bottom of the crust is browned. Oil the other side of the dough, then assemble the pizza on the cooked side. Return to the grill, cooking over direct heat until the bottom of the pizza is browned, then move the pizza to indirect heat until the cheese is melted.

***Chef's Notes:***
If your toppings are thick (mushroom halves or pineapple, say), you may want to pre-cook them to ensure that they're heated through. Makes eight personal-size pizzas.

## Steak Tip Marinade

328 Just what it sounds like. I have no idea who I stole this from. I've been making it for a long time.

Posted by: JackStraw. Yield: 4 servings. Prep time: 20 minutes.

---

1/3 cup soy sauce
3/4 cup salad oil
1/8 cup Worcestershire sauce
1 tablespoon dry mustard
2 teaspoons salt
1 teaspoon chopped parsley
1 1/2 teaspoon pepper
1 crushed garlic clove
1/4 cup lemon juice
Steak tips, cubed

Combine all ingredients and mix vigorously. Refrigerate overnight and stir again. Pour over a bowl of cubed steak tips and allow to marinate about 6 hours. Put steak tips on skewers and pop them on the grill and grill them until they are cooked to your liking. Goes excellent with alcohol.

## Drunken BBQ Sauce

329 Best bourbon BBQ sauce ever. Not sure where the recipe is from; it's in my handwriting on a note card. Years of experimenting I guess?

Posted by: IP. Yield: a large bottle. Prep time: 20 minutes.

---

3/4 cup ketchup
1/2 cup REAL maple syrup
1/4 cup vegetable oil
1/4 to 1/2 cup smooth bourbon
2 tablespoons cider vinegar
2 tablespoons Dijon mustard

Combine all ingredients except bourbon in a sauce pan over medium heat, whisk well to blend. When warm to the touch add bourbon to taste, while drinking any leftover. Heat until it just starts to boil and then remove from heat. Do not cook it. Allow to cool and pour into bottle. Keeping it refrigerated, it will keep a very long time. Great all-around grilling sauce for beef, pork, chicken, fried potatoes, etc.

## Spicy BBQ Sauce

330 Basic BBQ sauce with just a touch of heat. From IPexwife #2.

Posted by: IP. Yield: one large bottle. Prep time: 20 minutes.

---

1 1/2 cups cider vinegar
1/2 cup + 2 tablespoons ketchup
1/2 cup sugar
1 1/2 teaspoons Worcestershire sauce
1 1/2 teaspoons yellow mustard
1 teaspoon favorite hot sauce
3/4 teaspoon black pepper
3/4 teaspoon crushed red pepper
1 1/2 teaspoons salt
1 stick (1/2 cup) butter

Mix all ingredients in a saucepan, whisk and bring to a boil. When cool, bottle and refrigerate.

## Dry BBQ Rub

331 Dry rub marinade for baby back ribs and beef brisket. My recipe says Alton Brown on the bottom.

Posted by: IP Yield: 2 racks worth. Prep time: 20 minutes.

---

8 tablespoons light brown sugar, tightly packed
3 tablespoons kosher salt
1 tablespoon chili powder
1/2 teaspoon black pepper
1/2 teaspoon cayenne pepper
1/2 teaspoon favorite hot sauce
1/2 teaspoon Old Bay seasoning
1/2 teaspoon thyme
1/2 teaspoon onion powder

Mix thoroughly, rub on meat liberally, wrap in plastic wrap, place in fridge. Make sure to allow one hour MINIMUM set time on meat in fridge before baking/grilling/smoking. Leftover rub will keep in sealed container about 30 days in the fridge.

## Awesome Ahi Marinade

322 Super-easy, super-delicious marinade for grilled ahi (tuna). Originally published in "*A Taste of Aloha*" September 1983. Slightly modified by me since then to replace the steak sauce with hoisin sauce.

Posted by: Manny. Yield: 3 servings. Prep time: 5 minutes to assemble.

---

1/3 cup shoyu (soy sauce)
1/3 cup extra-virgin olive oil
2 tablespoons hoisin sauce or steak sauce
2 teaspoons Worcestershire sauce
2 large cloves garlic, minced

Place the 5 ingredients in a jar with a tight-fitting lid and shake well. Marinate thick (1 ½ to 2 inches) ahi steaks in a ziplock bag for 45 minutes to 1 ½ hours in the fridge. Grill fish to your desired doneness, basting it with the marinade while cooking. This tastes best when the fish is cooked medium rare or less. It's so tasty that I usually double the marinade and pour some over the rice I serve with the fish.

## Alex's BBQ Rib Sauce

323 Sauce for BBQ ribs from Alex's BBQ in Shell Beach, California.

Posted by: CaliGirl. Yield: 5 servings. Prep time: 10 minutes.

---

1 cup ketchup
1/2 cube or stick (1/4 cup) butter
1 clove garlic
pinch diced onion
1 – 2 teaspoons liquid smoke
1/2 cup honey
2 tablespoons brown sugar
salt and pepper to taste

Heat to melt butter before using. Stir all ingredients together, mixing well. I season ribs with garlic salt and pepper and grill over red oak coals until ribs are cooked. Then transfer ribs to a baking dish and baste with BBQ sauce. Finish in 350 degree oven for about 30 minutes. Enjoy!

# Main Courses

*For our entree, we have rigatoni*
*On the side, a nice cheese macaroni*
*Can't deny the appeal*
*Of the rest of the meal*
*We'll proceed...but first...abalone!*

## Slow-Cooker Beef Curry

324 Easy and delicious beef curry. I came up with it myself, although "came up with" might be a stretch. It seems like one of those things that you wouldn't think really needs inventing.

Posted by: Moron Robbie. Yield: 4 servings. Prep time: 10 minutes initial, 8 or so hours secondary.

---

1 package (3 ½ ounces) Golden Curry blocks
2 cups water
4 potatoes, peeled
2 cups carrots, peeled and cut into 1" pieces, or you can use baby carrots
1 cut of beef, London broil or similar
1 onion, peeled
2 cups jasmine rice

Heat the water in the microwave for one minute. Separate the curry blocks and dissolve in the water; set aside. Halve the onion; place on the bottom of the slow cooker. Put the beef on top of the halved onion. Cut the potatoes into 1/2" slices and add them to the pot. If you're using whole and not bagged baby carrots, chop them into 1" sections and add them. Stir the curry mixture before pouring it over everything. Cook until fork-tender, 6 – 8 hours or so on low, stirring occasionally. Be sure to go outside and return a few times so you can admire how great your house smells. Twenty minutes before you're ready to eat, prepare the rice. Serve the curry on steaming bed of it.

### *Chef's Notes:*

Like carrots? Add more. Like potatoes? Add more. Like it soupier? Add another cup of water. Like it thicker? Decrease water by 1/2 cup. The onion is mostly to give flavor, but feel free to eat it, too. If you're feeding a group and there won't be any leftovers, then pick a cut of meat with some marbling because the flavor is better. If you'll be refrigerating any then go with the lean London broil type cuts because there won't be as much fat once it cools. Check the foreign-food section of your grocery store for the curry, or just order it online. The prices seem to be similar where I live. Oh, and the carrots are the best part.

## Beef and Noodles

325 Cheap, easy comfort food for real morons. I didn't invent the wheel here. Or the noodle. Or hamburger. But I can't say it came from any one source. Supremely filling, inexpensive and it even re-heats well in the microwave. This is comfort food at its best.

Posted by: Mark Andrew Edwards. Yield: 4 servings. Prep time: 15 minutes.

---

1 pound hamburger
2 cups elbow macaroni or pasta of choice
2 cups Prego Italian tomato sauce
1 teaspoon salt or to taste
tomato sauce (optional)
red wine (optional)

Boil 6 cups of salted water, add pasta to boiling water. Let pasta cook for about 4 minutes and then start cooking the hamburger in a large sauce pan on high heat. Cook pasta and hamburger about five minutes more Add 2 cups Prego tomato sauce to hamburger without draining fat. Strain pasta, add to hamburger and tomato sauce. Stir thoroughly, cover and remove from heat.

***Chef's Notes:***
Leaving the 'beef juice' instead of draining the fat makes the dish more savory. Prego tomato sauce covers a variety of sins. If you prefer, you can add water, tomato paste and spices to taste. But I've found that two cups of the big Costco Prego sauce tastes just as good. Likewise, you can cook the hamburger with a little red wine for extra flavor. But the basics work fine.

## Culturally-Appropriated Lomo Saltado

326 A dish my family appropriated from the Peruvians, who in turn appropriated the techniques from the Chinese. The result is a darned good dish that combines red meat, french fries (that's right!) and a flavorful sauce into something greater than the sum of its parts. I'm not sure where this recipe originated—I learned how to make it from a friend of a friend who served it at a dinner party a few years ago. However, the recipe typically has relied on what I can find at the store or in the refrigerator at any given time.

Posted by: WitchDoktor, AKA VA GOP Sucks. Yield: 4 servings, unless you're hungry. Prep time: varies, up to 25 minutes.

---

1 pound french fries
1 pound steak (whatever you want—strip, tenderloin, etc. I've even used pre-cut stir fry-ready beef)
1/4 cup soy sauce
1 red onion, cut in wedges
6 – 10 cherry tomatoes
3 tablespoons finely chopped ginger
1 tablespoon vinegar

2 tablespoons aji amarillo paste, more or less to taste
oil
rice (optional)

First things first—cook your French fries. I've used both frozen cooked in the oven (good) to freshly deep fried (fantastic!). If you go the oven route, allow yourself plenty of time to finish. If you deep fry, you don't need as much time. Take your beef and slice it up into stir-fry-friendly pieces. Not big chunks, but not super thin either. Fajita-sized is about right. Drizzle it with about half of your soy sauce and set it aside for now. Combine the ginger, aji amarillo, and vinegar. Over medium heat, stir fry the beef until browned in an oiled pan (a wok works great). Remove the cooked beef from the pan and stir fry the onions until softened but not yet translucent. Add ginger, then stir fry for a couple more minutes. Put the beef back in, add the tomatoes, and stir fry the whole shebang until it's nicely melded, just 3-4 minutes. Add the sauce mixture and stir everything up. Mix in the French fries and give it all a toss. To serve, spoon out a serving onto a plate, add some rice on the side (the classic combo) and enjoy!

***Chef's Notes:***
This is a dish that originated from Chinese who emigrated to Peru. They brought the stir-fry technique with them but used local ingredients. One of those ingredients is aji amarillo—a yellow pepper that is as ubiquitous in Peru as ketchup is here in the US. It's not super spicy but there is some heat there. The heat of the dish can be regulated by increasing/decreasing the amount of aji amarillo used. It can be hard to find, though I've had good luck buying it from Amazon. Lastly, don't get concerned about the kind of beef to use. Any steak will work, from strip to flank to whatever. Use whatever you like!

## Dad's Sloppy Joes

327 Turkey sloppy joes. This is a Tonypete original.

Posted by: Tonypete. Yield: 6 – 8 servings. Prep time: 30 minutes.

---

1 pound ground turkey
2 – 3 stalks celery, chopped medium
1 small onion, diced
1 8-ounce can tomato sauce
1/4 cup ketchup
1/4 cup BBQ sauce
1 tablespoon packed brown sugar
1 teaspoon dry mustard powder
1 tablespoon Worcestershire sauce
1 tablespoon vinegar
salt and pepper to taste
cole slaw (optional)

Brown ground turkey, celery and onion. Stir in remaining ingredients and simmer, covered, 20 minutes, stirring occasionally. If too wet, cook uncovered. Cook until consistency is what you like. Great with cole slaw!

## Venison Kabobs

328 What to do with all that deer meat. Pa was a hunter, and let nothing go to waste.

Posted by: Euro. Yield: 6 servings. Prep time: 48 hours.

---

2 pounds venison tenderloin or steak, chunked
3 cups good quality vegetable oil
1/2 cup hearty but cheap burgundy
3 tablespoons vinegar
dash coarse salt
dash pepper
1 teaspoon garlic powder
lots of assorted vegetables and shrooms

Marinade meat in oil, wine, vinegar, and spices for about 36-48 hours in fridge. Reserve marinade. Skewer meat and vegetables, brush on more marinade. Grill until meat reaches desired doneness, basting frequently.

## Best Cheese Steak Sammie

329 'Cause RACISM. I love a good cheese steak, and I have been to a lot of places and had a few that were really good and some not so much. A few years ago, my wife bought me a commercial style Waring griddle that weighs about 40 pounds, and the great cheese steak experiment was on. I've done dozens of iterations between meats, cheeses, and ingredients, and this is the one I like best. If you like something different, great! Hope this will get you started.

Posted by: Greg. Yield: 1 sammie. Prep time: 20 minutes.

---

8 ounces sirloin tip, sliced thin as your butcher can get it
handful sliced portobello mushrooms
handful sliced red peppers
handful sliced green peppers
handful sliced yellow onion
3 slices racist white American cheese
jalapeno peppers, diced, to taste
12-inch hoagie roll
mayonnaise to taste (use real mayo not the light stuff)
real butter
dash salt/pepper
bacon (optional)
Italian salami (optional)

It is easiest to have a flat non-stick pan or griddle on medium heat, but any frying pan you have will work, it just needs to be large enough to brown the hoagie. Preheat griddle. Slice open the hoagie roll but do not cut all the way through. Butter both sides and place face down on your griddle until brown. Once done, apply mayo liberally (this may be the only substance you should not apply conservatively) and set aside. Julienne (slice into long thin strips) veggies. Chop the mushroom and jalapenos. Throw some butter on the griddle and mound all the veggies on top. Make sure you have enough butter under your veggies so everyone is in the pool—add more butter if you need to. As soon as the veggies start to caramelize, spread your sliced steak evenly over top of the veggies. Salt and pepper the steak. Let it set right there until the steak begins to brown. Once the steak is about half done, flip everything over as best you can (don't worry, it won't be neat). Once all the steak is brown, you will need to quickly shred it using two stout spatulas. Once the steak is shredded, mound everything up and smother with the racist white American cheese, because racist white Americans have been known to smother everything for centuries. Once the cheese is completely melted, transfer to the hoagie roll—it should not be a neat process; in fact, the sloppier the better. Enjoy.

***Chef's Notes:***
Recommend a good lager and waffle fries to pair. Two thick slices of bacon is always a bonus! Adding a good Italian salami makes it a steak bomb.

## Cast Iron Dutch Oven Beef Brisket

330 Beef brisket in the Dutch oven over coals. Learned from campouts.

Posted by: Larry Geiger. Yield: 6 servings. Prep time: 3 hours.

---

2 1/2 – 4 pounds brisket
2 to 4 onions
1 Coke, Pepsi, or Dr. Pepper
some seasonings

Heat oven on a pile of coals. Saute onions, remove from oven. Brown brisket. Put brisket on trivet in oven. Rub in seasonings. Cover with onions. Pour in beverage. Place oven on 10 coals. Put 16 coals on top. Replenish coals about every hour. Cook about 45 minutes per pound.

## Rosamond's Beef Stroganoff

331 Great for celebrations or special meals. Rosamond shared this recipe with Mrs. JTB shortly after the latter married JTB. Proof she was now family.

Posted by: JTB and Mrs. JTB. Yield: 8 – 12 servings. Prep time: 30 minutes.

---

3 pounds steak (top, bottom, round or sirloin)
3 or 4 onions, medium or large
1 pound butter

2 (8-ounce) cans mushrooms, bits and pieces
2 (16-ounce) containers sour cream
1/4 cup or less flour
desired amount rice
paprika to taste (optional)
salt and pepper to taste

Depending on the size of your pans, the stroganoff might have to be prepared in two pans. Prepare rice. Set aside and keep warm. Cut steak into bite-sized pieces, dredge in small amount of flour (e.g., put steak in bowl and pour a little amount of flour over pieces and toss until the meat is covered in flour). Dice onions and saute in butter (1/4 pound). Add steak to onions and brown steak (add butter if necessary). When steak is done, add mushrooms including liquid. Stir, then turn heat down or off. Add sour cream and mix thoroughly. After adding sour cream, heat very slowly on low heat. When stroganoff is warm, ladle over rice. Add paprika, salt and pepper to taste. The recipe as shown is as provided to us. Over time, we adjusted it to use significantly less butter and flour. Stroganoff could also be served over noodles. Paprika makes a nice addition.

## Perfect Meatloaf

332 My Dad's favorite meal; simple, straight up comfort food. This was one of my mom's go-to recipes. She was a nurse and worked nights, so this was something she could put together during the day and leave for me or Dad to put in the oven when we got home.

Posted by: antisocialist. Yield: 4 servings. Prep time: 1 hour 20 minutes.

---

1 ½ pounds ground beef
3/4 cup quick cooking oats (not instant)
2 eggs, slightly beaten
1/4 cup chopped onion
2 teaspoons salt
1/4 teaspoon pepper
2 8-ounce cans tomato sauce
cheese (optional)

Mix first six ingredients with one can tomato sauce. Pack into loaf pan and cool one hour in refrigerator. Turn onto a cookie sheet; bake one hour at 350 degrees F. Pour remaining can of sauce over loaf. Bake additional 20 minutes. My oldest daughter puts a layer of cheese inside the loaf before baking. Says it's mmmm good.

## Poor Man's Tacos

> 333 Great for when you are totally broke. I invented this recipe because I was totally broke.

Posted by: Mr_Write. Yield: 2 servings, or 1 for a couple of meals. Prep time: 10 minutes.

---

1 pound hamburger
1 standard can pork and beans
onions (optional)
corn or flour tortilla shells
lettuce, tomatoes, other toppings (optional)

Crumble the hamburger in a pan and brown. Then, empty the can of pork and beans in the pan and heat. That's it, though you can add onions the day after payday. Serve on corn or flour tortilla shells, adding lettuce, tomatoes, or other ingredients as you can afford. Amazingly delicious, and goes a long way for a broke moron. You should really try this!

## Not Yo' Momma's Meatloaf

> 334 Damn good vittles. My wife and I made this up one night when we were trying some creative cooking ideas. While meatloaf is a pretty basic "mom" meal, we think this one is Not Yo' Momma's!

Posted by: Johnny Upton. Yield: 4 moron servings. Prep time: 30 minutes.

---

1 1/2 pounds 80/20 ground beef
1 pound hot breakfast sausage
4 stalks celery, chopped
1 large onion, chopped
2 sleeves crushed Ritz crackers
3/4 cup A-1 steak sauce
1 1/2 cups ketchup
1/2 cup yellow mustard
2 large eggs

Pre-heat your oven to 350 degrees F. Combine all ingredients in a damn big mixing bowl and hammer away at it for about 5 minutes until it looks like Hillary Clinton on election night. Spray a baking dish with non-stick spray and arrange your miasma into a loaf-like shape in the center of the dish, leaving room for grease, oils, and other assorted nasty stuff to exit your masterpiece. Cover with foil and shove into the oven for 50 minutes. Uncover after 50 minutes, add some A-1 and Ketchup spread on top. Broil on high for 5 more minutes to create a delicious shell. I like my meatloaf a little on the spicy side, but you can obviously use any sausage you like. This is also really good if you substitute barbecue sauce for the ketchup.

## Marginally Moroccan Lamb Shanks

335 My own take on lamb shanks with an apricot glaze. The dried apricots disintegrate during cooking to form a glaze. Previously published in The Official Manual for Spice Cadets. Moron labe!

Posted by: Karl Lembke. Yield: 4 servings. Prep time: 3 – 4 hours.

---

4 lamb shanks (about 1 1/2 pounds each)
oil to brown lamb shanks
12 ounces Guinness beer
10 juniper berries (or a shot of gin)
1 head garlic, peeled
1/2 cup apricots halves, dried
rice or couscous

Heat oven to 250 degrees F (unless using slow-cooker). Brown the lamb shanks on all sides in a greased frying pan and transfer to a Dutch oven or slow-cooker. Pour half a cup of the Guinness into the frying pan and scrape with a spatula to get to brown, crispy bits off the bottom of the pan. Pour over the lamb.Sprinkle the garlic and juniper berries (or gin) over the meat, close the pot, and put it in the oven. After 1 hour, open up the pot and scatter the dried apricots over the lamb shanks. Cook an additional 2 – 3 hours, until the lamb is falling off the bones and the apricot halves are quite mushy, if not totally disintegrated. Fish out the bones and as many of the juniper berries as you can find. Serve the lamb with pan drippings over rice or couscous.

***Chef's Notes:***
Other dark beers would probably work about as well. In the Los Angeles area, Lamb shanks can be found in the Middle-Eastern markets.

## Leon's Brown Pudding

336 Blood pudding for the cowardly. My own spin on a traditional Irish blood pudding. Originally published, with commentary, at hostagerecipes.wordpress.com.

Posted by: leoncaruthers. Yield: 4 servings. Prep time: 45 minutes.

---

1 pound calf's liver, de-veined
1 pound unsalted butter
1 cup hulled buckwheat groats
1 cup + 1 tablespoon milk
1 large onion
2 ½ teaspoons salt
1 teaspoon ground allspice
1 ½ teaspoons ground black pepper

Soak buckwheat groats overnight (6 to 24 hours) in clean water, drain. In a blender, grind groats, 1 tablespoon milk, and ½ cup water until oatmeal texture. Ferment groat slurry for

6 – 24 hours (i.e., put it in a jar or bowl with plenty of room and cover with cheesecloth to keep dust out). When fermentation is complete, preheat oven to 325 degrees F. In a food processor, process liver, butter, and onion until smooth. In a big ol' bowl, combine liver mixture, fermented groat slurry, 1 cup milk, salt, allspice, and pepper. Line a 9" x 13" pan with parchment paper. Carefully pour batter into lined pan, tap to level out. Cover pan with foil. Bake for 1 hour, then remove foil and return to oven for 10 minutes. Allow to cool in pan for as long as you like, slide onto cutting board when ready to serve. Can be sliced and eaten as-is, or pan fried. Excellent on toast. I swear this the best way to prepare liver that I've managed thus far. It's a delightful, baked pate.

## Sliders

337 Sliders, you know: small hamburgers. Recipe is from some blog somewhere, trying to copy White Castle sliders.

Posted by: RoyalOil. Yield: 6 – 7 servings. Prep time: 20 minutes.

---

2 pounds ground beef
dehydrated onion flakes
seasoned salt
black pepper
American cheese slices
dill pickle slices
24 potato rolls
crushed red pepper (optional)

In 9x13 glass baking pan, sprinkle onion flakes, salt and black pepper to taste on bottom. Place ground beef in pan and spread out evenly. Sprinkle more onion flakes, salt and black pepper over top of beef. Sprinkle crushed red pepper over beef, optional. Cover with foil and place in 400 degree F oven for about 30 to 40 minutes, or until cooked. Remove from oven and cover top of beef with slices of cheese. Cut into equal sizes squares, around 1.5 to 2 inches each. Place square of beef inside potato roll with 2 – 3 slices of pickles. Serve.

### *Chef's Notes:*

Amount of salt, pepper and onion flakes are to taste—use your judgment. I use 80/20 ground beef. It will shrink 1 – 2 inches from the edges of the pan and will be swimming in grease when done. "Done" is internal temperature of 170 degrees F.

## Pot Roast

338 Basic pot roast recipe, with bonus leftover ideas. This is an idea I got from a friend on a blog. The blog is "Crazy Aunt Purl" but I think it's inactive at this point.

Posted by: Dr Alice. Yield: quite a lot. Prep time: 10 minutes plus cooking time.

---

3 pounds or more chuck roast
oil to sear meat
lemon pepper
garlic powder
black pepper
1 beer OR 1 can beef broth

Take your roast and rub it with the seasonings to taste. Original recipe called for crushed garlic, but I use the powder because lazy. Do use pepper. Lemon pepper also works well. Heat some vegetable oil in a pan till very hot and sear the roast on all sides. Place in Crock Pot. Then take your liquid (beer or broth) and use it to deglaze the pan. Pour the liquid in on top of the roast—it should come about half way up. Set Crock Pot on low and cook 4 – 5 hours, till falling apart. Pour off the liquid and put it in the fridge. It is destined for higher things. Make sure you save out about two cups of meat. Serve the rest with whatever vegetable or starch you want.

***Chef's Notes:***
This is the first of three related recipes.

## Mama's Meatloaf

339 The champagne of meatloaf. This is a recipe my mother says she got off the back of a box of Quaker Oats, but modified as moms are wont to do. I've transcribed it directly from the handwritten recipe she gave me when I went to college, properly concerned over my ability to feed myself at 18. Here's to you ma.

Posted by: Ghost of Kari. Yield: servings for 4 morons. Prep time: 1 hour and 25 minutes.

---

1 – 1 ½ pounds ground beef
3/4 cup oatmeal
8-ounce can tomato sauce or paste
1 white onion (small)
1 egg
1 – 2 tablespoons chopped fresh parsley (or fresh thyme, basil, or other herbs)
1 teaspoon salt
1 teaspoon pepper
1/3 cup wheat germ (honey crunch)
ketchup
grated vegetables, mushrooms, etc. (optional)

Preheat oven to 350 degrees F. Chop onion fine and whisk egg. Mix all ingredients together with a fork (and probably your hands). Place into loaf pan—don't press down too hard! Top with wheat germ, then drizzle ketchup all over top. Bake for one hour. Let cool 5 minutes before slicing.

***Chef's Notes:***

Use 90% lean beef. Thyme, basil, or any herbs can be substituted for parsley provided they are fresh. You can drench the top with ketchup to taste. Grated vegetables, mushrooms, or other leftovers may be added. Serving tip: put potatoes in the oven IMMEDIATELY upon preheating, i.e. before you start mixing ingredients, so they finish along with the meatloaf. Strike back at the marxists wherever you find them.

## Momma's Quick Prep Pot Roast

340 Easiest roast you've ever done. Recipe is from my mother.

Posted by: Holdmyscotch. Yield: 6 – 10 servings. Prep time: 5 minutes.

---

3 – 5 pounds roast of your choice
1 large onion
3 large potatoes
3 carrots
1 package Lipton onion soup mix
1 package dry ranch dressing powder
12 ounces beer of your choice

Place the unseasoned roast in a crockpot. Chop onion, potatoes and carrots and add to crockpot. Add packets of onion soup and ranch dressing, then add beer. Set crockpot to low and cook 8 hours. Roast will literally fall apart in tender bliss. Broth made while cooking will convince you there is a higher power. Easiest roast you have ever made. Have never made in the oven but would suggest cook at 350 degrees F until falling apart.

## Shepherd's Pie

341 This is my version. The basic recipe is pretty common, this is just the version I came up with.

Posted by: harbqll. Yield: a few servings. Prep time: 90 minutes maybe?

---

1 pound ground lamb (or beef), browned and drained
oil to saute vegetables
some thyme, minced garlic (or garlic powder), cayenne

1 cup each chopped onions, sliced mushrooms, grated carrots
some Worcestershire sauce
2 cups beef stock (or lamb if you can find it)
2 tablespoons flour
1 can garlic & onion seasoned diced stewed tomatoes, drained
1/4 cup red wine
1 pie shell, just the bottom
enough mashed potatoes
enough shredded cheddar cheese

Preheat oven to 375 degrees F. Saute onions and mushrooms. Add in carrots and meat. Add in spices to taste, and several good glugs of Worcestershire sauce. Add stock, reserving about 1/2 cup. Whisk flour into reserved stock, and add to pan. Add tomatoes and wine. Reduce until thickened. Pour into pie shell, top with potatoes mixed with cheese. Bake pie 30 – 40 minutes.

***Chef's Notes:***
You can buy carrots already shredded, which is handy. Some people will just dump the meat filling into a pan with no bottom crust, then top with potatoes. These people are known as assholes. Shepherd's pie with no bottom crust is an abomination.

## Natchitoches Meat Pies

342 It's a Louisiana thing, you wouldn't understand. This is a traditional Louisiana dish, reaching back to the before times, handed down from God himself.

Posted by: harbqll. Yield: enough for 1 party. Prep time: about an hour.

---

Filling:
2 tablespoons butter
1/2 pound each coarsely ground beef and pork
1/2 cup each onion and red bell pepper, minced
1/4 cup each celery and green onion, minced
3 tablespoons garlic, minced
2 tablespoons Worcestershire sauce
1 tablespoon Tabasco
1 teaspoon each salt, black pepper, cayenne
1/2 teaspoon white pepper
1/2 cup beef stock
1/8 cup flour

Pastry:
8 cups flour
2 teaspoons salt
1 teaspoon baking powder
1/2 cup lard
2 cups + 1/4 cup milk, if needed
2 eggs, divided

For filling: melt butter in a large skillet. Add meats and brown. Remove from pan and mince as needed. Add onion, bell pepper, celery, and green onion, and wilt. Add garlic, sauces, and spices; cook for 2 minutes more. Whisk flour into stock, add to pot, and bring to the boil.

Reduce for about 5 minutes, then add the meat and remove from heat. Adjust spices as needed.

For pastry: combine dry ingredients. Cut in lard. Whisk 1 egg into 2 cups milk. Add wet to dry in slow stream, while mixing. If needed, add more milk a little at a time, up to ¼ cup additional. Knead until just combined. Roll out pastry to 1/8 inch thickness, and cut into circles - traditionally a coffee can is used.

Beat remaining egg lightly in a small bowl. Add 1 – 2 tablespoons filling (or more, or less, depends on the size of your circles) to each dough circle. Fold over and seal with beaten egg, then glaze pies with beaten egg. To deep fry—heat oil to 360 degrees F, fry in small batches for 3 – 4 minutes and set aside to drain. To bake—heat oven to 350 degrees F, bake for 15 – 20 minutes. Obviously, frying is preferred and is the traditional method. Mere words cannot describe how good these are. I could happily live the rest of life, eating only Natchitoches meat pies. I like to make them so spicy that no one else has the physical strength to eat them, so I can have them all to myself.

## Meat Muffins

343 Stuffed hamburger in a muffin tin! Learned from my mom.

Posted by: Christopher R Taylor. Yield: servings for 3 adults. Prep time: 30-45 minutes.

---

1 pound hamburger
½ cup mustard
½ cup relish
½ of a chopped onion
dash each of salt and pepper
jalepenos, hot sauce, ketchup, cheese (optional)

You will need a muffin tin. Divide your hamburger up as if you were making burgers normally. Instead of frying them, lay each burger on the muffin tin one at a time over one of the muffin "sockets," and mold it to the interior. What you want here is an even, thin layer of burger around all the sides and bottom, leaving a cavity in the middle. Whatever is left over out the top of the depression, cut away and reserve. Do the same to all the muffin sockets until you've got one lined for each burger you prepared. Now, take a spoon and spoon in mustard to each hamburger pocket, leaving about a third of it empty. When you have each one partly filled, fill the rest with relish and onion (and any other add-ins), and salt and pepper each burger. Take the remaining hamburger and create small patties the size of each burger "muffin" and seal them off with the burger. Clean up the spilled mustard and such off the tin.

Stick this whole deal in the oven at 450 degrees F for 10 – 20 minutes depending on your oven and how thin you got the burger. It might even take longer but this cooks a lot faster than meatloaf. Serve individual patties without need for any buns or bread! You can try other variants, but ketchup and barbecue sauce are a bit sweet for my taste. For spice you can add jalepenos or hot sauce, and cheese is always welcome.

## Corned Beef Hash (Stew)

344 Whatever you call it, it's damned good. This is from Mom.

Posted by: Merovign, Dark Lord of the Sith. Yield: enough for some people. Prep time: (holds hands apart).

---

2 pounds cooked corned beef
4 – 6 large potatoes
1 cup Vermouth or other wine
3/4 cup Worcestershire sauce
2 ounces butter
optional plant matter like green onions, bok choy, cauliflower, habaneros, carrots

Cook the corned beef, if it's not already cooked. If you can't corn your own beef, buy some corned beef and follow the instructions. You can even buy cooked corned beef. Sliced corned beef is hard to cube. Cube the corned beef, and trim as necessary. I like to remove veiny and connective tissue. I aim for 3/4" to 1" cubes. Peel (if desired) and cube potatoes—cube size affects how fast they cook and how much flavor seeps in. I go for larger cubes to cook longer and still have some body to the potato chunks. In either a large pan, chef's pan or stock pot, heat the butter and quickly fry the corned beef and potatoes until lightly browned. The goal is not to cook the potatoes, just to get a little more flavor. This is also the point at which one should apply any other plant matter one desires. If not already in a stock pot, transfer the ingredients. Add Vermouth or other wine (I like Merlot or Malbec) and Worcestershire sauce (you can go a little lighter or heavier on that, it's the salt/seasoning component). Add water until everything is covered by at least a half-inch, a little more for larger cubes. Simmer it to death or until you're too hungry to wait any longer. If the potatoes are not done, you didn't wait long enough. If you have burned mashed potatoes, you waited too long. Garnish with green onions, if you like green onions. I use them as straws.

### *Chef's Notes:*

Optional plant matter can include onions, bok choy, cauliflower, habaneros, or, if you're a sick puppy, carrots. Bell peppers are right out. Please consult the UN to see if your ethnic group is allowed to prepare or eat these foods.

## Rosemary Venison

345 Slow-cooked and savory venison. This is modified from a prime rib recipe. I think I got it from *Saveur* magazine.

Posted by: Cocklebur. Yield: servings for 4 fat Morons. Prep time: 1 ½ hours.

---

4 – 5 pounds venison roast
1/2 cup olive oil
1/2 cup garlic cloves
2 – 3 tablespoons salt
2 – 3 tablespoons ground mustard
2 tablespoons black pepper
3 tablespoons chopped fresh rosemary

Clean your venison roast of fat and tendon, cut out any glands. Slice it into pieces 2 – 3 inches thick. Chop up the garlic and rosemary, add all the rest of the dry ingredients in a bowl and mash it all up together. Coat the meat all over with the dry mixture, dump the olive oil on your meat and rub vigorously. Put everything in a large roasting pan with a heavy lid, cook for an hour at 350 degrees F covered, and then uncovered for 20 – 30 minutes more to get a little brown on the meat. Cook this for your girlfriend, then prepare to be raped.

## Cowboy Steak with Red-Eye Gravy

346 Best damn steak in Montana. This is part of a dinner with side recipe. My wife "Giggles," aka the Kitchen Witch, put this together for her "Daring Cooks Challenge." It can be found at her blog, thekitchenwitchblog.com.

Posted by: McGyver. Yield: servings for 2 Morons. Prep time: 30 minutes, not including aging the steaks.

---

2 large rib eye steaks
kosher salt
2 tablespoons instant coffee
1 tablespoon chile powder
1/2 teaspoon smoked paprika
1/2 teaspoon oregano
1/2 teaspoon cumin
1 tablespoon plus 1 teaspoon kosher salt
1/2 teaspoon black pepper
1/2 teaspoon ground coriander
1/4 teaspoon (or more to taste) cayenne pepper
1 tablespoon canola oil
1 tablespoon all-purpose flour
1 cup beef broth
1 tablespoon instant coffee
2 teaspoons tomato powder (or 1 teaspoon of tomato paste)

Up to three days in advance, liberally sprinkle steaks with kosher salt and refrigerate uncovered, turning occasionally. For the rub, in a small bowl mix the spices. Thirty minutes prior to cooking, take steak out of the fridge and liberally cover with chile rub. Heat a cast iron pan over medium high heat, add oil. Cook steaks until desired doneness, set steaks aside and let rest. Drain all but 1 tablespoon of fat from the pan, add flour and stir vigorously, scraping up any stuck-on bits, until flour is hot and bubbly. Dissolve coffee and tomato powder into the beef broth; slowly pour the broth mixture into the pan while continuously stirring. Serve gravy over steaks. If you do not have tomato powder, you can substitute 1 teaspoon of tomato paste.

## Crack Slaw

347 Addictive & low carb. You can find versions of this recipe everywhere, but this one is from Food.com and was submitted by Sooz Cooks.

Posted by: SandyCheeks. Yield: servings for 4 Morons. Prep time: 25 minutes.

---

1 pound ground beef (chicken, turkey or pork)
2 tablespoons toasted sesame oil
2 garlic cloves (minced)
3 green onions, sliced
14 ounces coleslaw mix
2 tablespoons soy sauce
1/2 teaspoon Sriracha sauce (or to taste)
1 or 2 packets Splenda or other non-sugar sweetener
1/2 teaspoon ginger paste, fresh minced ginger or ground ginger
1 teaspoon white vinegar
salt & pepper to taste
Sriracha (to garnish)

Brown meat and season with salt and pepper to taste. Remove from pan and set aside. Heat sesame oil and saute slaw, onions and garlic until cabbage is cooked to desired tenderness. Stir in the soy sauce, Sriracha, Splenda, ginger and vinegar. Add meat back to wok or pan. Mix well and serve. Serve with additional Sriracha on the side for those who like spice.

### *Chef's Notes:*

I go about double or triple on the ginger, vinegar and soy sauce. (Vinegar's great for decreasing appetite.) This is a great recipe for a Sunday night. Double or triple it to have lunch for the week.

## Counterintuitive Burger

348 Burger on a slice of watermelon. Must be tried to be believed. It's the contrasts between sweet and salt, crisp and soft, and the concept of the humble burger as part of a complex pile of food that makes this so surprising. I'm shocked that I had to invent this myself, because it seems like something Bobby Flay would already have come up with.

Posted by: Smallish Bees. Yield: 1 serving. Prep time: 10 minutes.

---

1 pound hamburger
1 watermelon
1 bag mixed greens
olive oil
salt and pepper

Cut a slice of watermelon about a half-inch thick, slightly wider than the width of a hamburger of your design. Cook a burger the way you like. Do avoid overmixing the meat, because it'll become a hard, little hockey puck. Carefully place your hot, delicious, juicy burger on top of the cool, sweet circle of watermelon. Top with greens, pour over some olive oil and salt and pepper. Eat with a fork.

## Yummy Buns

349 Yummy Buns! Recipe is from my mother, who probably got it from a box of Velveeta cheese a long time ago, back in the mid 1970's. This was a favorite staple for growing teenage boys.

Posted by: RB3 & The Wandering Swede, lllooonnnggg time lurkers. Yield: 4 to 6 servings, depending on how hungry they are. Prep time: 30 minutes.

---

6 slices (6 ounces) bacon, cut up
1/2 cup onion, chopped
1 pound hamburger
1 cup (1/2 pound) cubed Velveeta cheese
1 can (10 ounces) Campbell's tomato soup
8 hamburger buns

Fry bacon until almost done, add onion and hamburger, cook until onion is soft and hamburger is no longer pink, and drain off any excess fat. Add cheese and soup, and stir until cheese is melted. Broil buns until golden brown. Spread with filling and broil until tops are well browned, even a little black. Recipe says you can use 6 ounces of Canadian bacon.

## Bachelor Surprise

350 Fast, easy and cheap beef and beans. Developed by me, 45 years ago as a lazy bachelor. Published on my blog Grand Life Cooking, found at grandlifecooking.blogspot.com. A man's ability to cook an edible meal and clean up afterward is an attribute highly valued by women.

Posted by: Grand Life. Yield: 2 servings. Prep time: 15 minutes.

---

1 pound hamburger
1 can pork and beans
handful of cheese
drizzle of molasses (or ketchup)
dash or 2 Worcestershire sauce

Brown the hamburger in a skillet. Pour off the fat. Hold back the hamburger with a spatula while draining the fat. (Try not to lose too much of the meat. Don't use a strainer - it's just something else to wash.) Add one can of beans and some molasses (or ketchup). Stir well then heat over medium low heat until it bubbles. If you are feeling fancy you can add some extras, not necessary to the recipe: a splash of Worcestershire sauce, and/or some cheese on top. Let it melt. I've used grated and sliced cheese. Use what's on hand. It's surprisingly good with a slice of bread or a hot buttered tortilla to push it on the fork. It's dinner for two and maybe some extra. The clean up is a snap.

## Bachelor Chow

351 A tasty meal so stooopid easy even a Moron can make it. When I was a poor, recent college grad, I used to make a lot of Hamburger Helper type meals. Every brand I tried had to be "fixed" to make it taste edible, so eventually I just decided to skip the pre-packaged junk and go it on my own. This recipe has been a staple of the DingusKhan household ever since. The name comes from the show "Futurama" . . . 'Bachelor Chow—now with flavor!'

Posted by: DingusKhan. Yield: 3 – 4 servings. Prep time: 25 minutes.

---

1 pound ground beef
1 pound shredded sharp cheddar
1 pound noodles
2 packets ranch dressing mix
½ pound frozen cut broccoli (if desired)

Because I'm extremely lazy, I cook everything for this recipe in a large noodle pot so that I have only one pot to clean afterwards. Add a small amount of water to the pot and brown your hamburger over a medium-low to medium heat on the stove. Once the meat is cooked, add enough cold water to fill the pot about half way to the top. The excess fat from the hamburger will congeal in the cold water and can be (mostly) skimmed off if done quickly before the water starts to heat up. Add the noodles to the pot. There should be enough water in the pot to more than completely cover the noodles. Add more water if needed. Cook until the noodles are tender, stirring occasionally. If desired, add broccoli. Cook until the broccoli gets hot all the way through. Turn off the stove, then carefully drain out almost all the water from the pot. Add the ranch dressing mix and stir it in. Add the shredded cheddar and stir until it is well mixed and melted. Serve and enjoy.

### *Chef's Notes:*

If you want it creamier, substitute real ranch dressing for the second pack of dressing mix. It doesn't really matter what type of noodles you use, but I've found penne or egg noodles to work the best for me. Be careful not to cook the broccoli too long. If you cook it just until it gets hot, it will have a more crisp, steamed vegetable type texture.

## Uncle John's Cabbage Rolls

352 Meat and rice wrapped in cabbage leaves. Grandfather's recipe.

Posted by: Big V.    Yield: 12 servings.    Prep time: 3 hours.

---

3 pounds ground chuck
3 cups cooked rice
1 teaspoon salt
1/2 teaspoon black pepper
1 pound bacon
2 pounds kielbassi
1 head cabbage
3 16-ounce cans tomato sauce
1 large egg
rye bread

Cook rice, cool. Boil the whole head of cabbage in lightly salted water, then let it cool. Remove core and separate leaves. Remove spine on leaves. Combine cooled rice, ground chuck, salt and pepper. Mix in one egg. Put mixture on cabbage leaf. Roll up and tuck in end. Slice kielbassi on diagonals. Line bottom of big pot, such as a clam/lobster steamer, or a Dutch oven (you may need two), with bacon and kielbassi. Add one can of tomato sauce. Place one layer of cabbage rolls on top of bacon and kielbassi. Add the second can of tomato sauce. Put second layer of cabbage rolls on top of first layer. Add third can of tomato sauce. Put in final layer of cabbage rolls in pot. Cook covered for two hours on the stove on low heat. Check occasionally. Add water as needed. Cook uncovered for 30 minutes. Serve with loaf of good rye bread.

## Rabbit With Leeks and Mustard Sauce

353 Classic French rabbit dish. Adapted from *The Frugal Gourmet Cooks With Wine*, by Jeff Smith.

Posted by: RedMindBlueState. Yield : 4 – 6 Moron servings. Prep time: 15 minutes active, 1 hour total.

---

1 3-pound rabbit, cut into serving pieces (or chicken)
4 tablespoons olive oil
2 garlic cloves, finely minced
2 onions, minced
1/2 teaspoon each dried rosemary, taragon and oregano
1/4 teaspoon dried sage
1 1/2 cups dry white wine
1 large leek, white and green parts only, cut into 2 inch julienne
1 ½ - 2 tablespoons mustard
1/2 cup half-and-half, light cream or evaporated milk
salt and pepper
flat leaf parsley for garnish

In a large 12" skillet or saute pan, brown rabbit pieces in olive oil, about 4 – 5 minutes per side. Remove rabbit to a plate. Add garlic and onions to pan and saute until translucent, about 2 – 3 minutes. Deglaze the pan with the wine, add the rosemary, sage, tarragon and oregano, return the rabbit to the pan along with any accumulated juices, cover and simmer until tender, about 35 minutes. Add more wine if it appears to be evaporating too much. Remove rabbit to a warm serving tray. Add leeks to pan and cook about 5 minutes more. Add the mustard and half-and-half/cream/evaporated milk, bring to a boil, and then simmer for 5 minutes. Add salt and pepper to taste , pour over rabbit, and garnish with chopped parsley. This recipe works very well with chicken, and I find the evaporated milk to be more stable in an acidic, wine-based sauce like this one. Enjoy!

## Texas Taco Soup

354 Best winter soup in South Texas. Recipe is from my grandmother.

Posted by: Holdmyscotch. Yield: 6 – 8 servings. Prep time: 30 minutes.

---

2 pounds lean ground beef
large onion
1 4-ounce can green chilies
2 15-ounce cans of ranch-style beans
1 15-ounce can of Rotel tomatoes
1 15-ounce can of diced tomatoes
2 15-ounce can of sweet corn
1 package (1-ounce) taco seasoning powder
1 package (1-ounce) ranch dressing powder
2 cups water
salt/pepper/garlic powder to taste
grated cheddar cheese and tortilla chips
jalapeno cornbread, picante sauce, jalepenos peppers (optional)

Brown meat, onions and green chilies in large pot. Drain any excess grease and place back in pot. Add all remaining ingredients and bring to a boil. Simmer 45 minutes and enjoy. Once served in a bowl, top with grated cheddar cheese and tortilla chips. Alternate serving: pour over jalapeno corn bread (my favorite way). Add picante sauce and jalapeno peppers for those of us with hair on our backsides. Go easy on the spices when cooking as the taco seasoning has quite a bit of salt and garlic.

## 10 - Minute Teriyaki Stir Fry

355 Fast and yummy! One of my more successful experiments.

Posted by: Armed and Larry. Yield: 4 servings. Prep time: 10 minutes.

---

1 pound hamburger
2 packages Nissin chow mein teriyaki chicken flavor noodles
7-ounce can mushroom stems and pieces
1 1/2 cups water
2 eggs
1/2 tablespoon butter

Brown hamburger in 12 inch non-stick fry pan on medium heat. Take chow mein noodles out of packages, put them in plastic bag and mash them a little to break them up. Add water, mushrooms, noodles, and teriyaki flavoring from chow mein packages. Reduce heat, cover, and simmer till water is almost gone. Push noodles to side, increase heat to medium high, scramble eggs with butter on bare part of pan. Mix it all together and serve. This recipe works with all of the noodle flavors. The spicy hot ones are really good too, if you like that kind of thing.

## French Onion Soup Burger

356 A literal soup sandwich. The recipe is mine—I wanted to combine my two favorite dishes from the local watering hole.

Posted by: josephistan. Yield: 1 serving. Prep time: 25 minutes.

---

8-ounce hamburger patty
1 can French onion soup
1 small sweet onion
1 Kaiser roll
1 slice Gruyere cheese
fries or baked potato

Preheat oven to 375 degrees F. Saute the hamburger patty & onions, while cooking the French onion soup in a small pot. Just before the burger is done to your liking, remove from pan & add it to the French onion soup, along with the sauteed onions. Let it cook for just a little more, until the burger absorbs some of the soup. While that is cooking, slice open the Kaiser roll, and place the 2 halves on a cooking tray. Place the burger, along with the sauteed onions, on one half of the roll (be sure to get some of the soup in there, too). Place the Gruyere cheese on the other half of the roll. Bake in the oven until the cheese gets melted & browned. Remove from oven, and serve with fries or a baked potato, with the rest of the French onion soup ladled over everything. Bring napkins!

## Steak and Gravy

357 Round steak with LOTS of gravy. My mom had access to a lot of cheap cuts of beef as my grandfather was a cattle rancher. We got the cheap cuts like round steak for free.

Posted by: Lester. Yield: 4 – 6 servings. Prep time: 1/2 hour, cook time 2 hours or longer.

---

round steak
1 cup flour
salt and pepper to taste
4 – 5 tablespoons oil for pan
beef bouillon cube or beef stock
5 – 6 cloves fresh minced garlic
mashed potatoes, rice, toast points or grits

Trim round steak of fat and connective tissue. Cut the steak into 2 ½ to 3 inch squares. Season flour with salt and pepper to taste. Dust steak pieces lightly with seasoned flour. Brown in the oil until lightly colored and drain on paper towels. Do this to all pieces of the steak. Return steak to pan and add garlic, and bouillon and water or stock. Add enough to cover the meat. Put on low setting on range and cook for 2 to three hours. Check for enough liquid to continue to cover meat as it cooks. Stir occasionally if it appears to be sticking to pot and turn down heat even lower. The steak should be extremely tender with lots of dense dark gravy. Serve with mashed potatoes, rice, toast points or even grits.

## Traditional Leg of Lamb

358 The smell of lamb on fire evokes primitive urgings.

Posted by: MarkY. Yield: 6 – 8 servings. Prep time: 5 hours with marinating.

---

leg of lamb, deboned, butterflied
parsley
extra virgin olive oil
sage

rosemary
thyme
garlic

Buy the leg de-boned, or have the butcher de-bone it. Butterfly the thicker parts so no one portion is more than 2 inches thick. Rub down with olive oil, and apply the herbs, remembering you are flavoring, not encrusting the roast. Grill the roast until gorgeous, turning to avoid burning. You want the fat side to be crispy, but the thickest part of the roast should not go beyond 140 degrees. I use a covered charcoal grill, but any grill that has a hot side and cooler side will work. Use a meat thermometer. When the thickest part of the roast hits 140, pull it and let it rest under foil for 15 minutes. You'll have medium rare, medium, and well-done roast—something for everyone.

## Baked Cabbage and Meatloaf

359 A kind of cabbage/meatloaf parfait. Swedish recipe from my ex-MiL.

Posted by: Miley, the Duchess. Yield: 4 servings. Prep time: 90 minutes.

---

1/2 pound ground beef
1/2 pound ground pork
2+ pounds cabbage
3+ tablespoons butter
1 1/4 cups bouillon/broth
2 teaspoons salt, divided
1 teaspoon black pepper, divided
1 bay leaf
1/4 teaspoon ground allspice
2 medium boiled potatoes
1 1/4 cups milk

Cut the cabbage into pieces or ribbons. Brown well in butter in a large frying pan. Add bouillon, 1/2 teaspoon salt, 1/4 teaspoon black pepper and bay leaf. Cover and simmer for 10 – 15 minutes. While the cabbage is simmering, prepare the meat loaf: mix together the ground beef and pork with mashed boiled potatoes, 1 1/2 teaspoons salt, 3/4 teaspoon black pepper and allspice. Add the milk a little at a time, mixing well. This will be a very wet meatloaf mixture. Place half of the cabbage in a 9" x 13" baking dish, reserving the broth it's been cooking in (be sure to remove the bay leaf). Spoon the meatloaf mixture over this and spread out evenly. Cover with the rest of the cabbage. Spoon some of the broth over. Bake at 350 degrees F for 40 – 50 minutes, continuing to spoon broth over the top every 10 minutes or so. We served this with boiled potatoes and lingonsylt. You can use whole cranberry sauce in place of the lingon.

## Beef and Snow Peas

360 Adapted from the *Colorado Cache Cookbook*, 7th ed.

Posted by: liz953. Yield: servings for 4 Morons. Prep time: 20 minutes.

---

1/4 cup soy sauce
1 tablespoon dry sherry
1 tablespoon corn starch
1 teaspoon sugar
1 teaspoon minced garlic
1 pound flank steak, trimmed and thinly sliced across the grain
1/2 pound snow peas
2 – 4 tablespoons vegetable oil
1/2 teaspoon salt

Whisk together first five ingredients. Add the steak to the sauce and let sit for only 5 – 10 minutes. This is a sauce, not a marinade, so don't leave the steak in the sauce too long before cooking. Heat oil in wok or large skillet over high heat. Add salt and snow peas and stir-fry 1 minute. Remove to a plate. Add more oil and add steak with sauce. Stir-fry until just cooked through. Return snow peas to pan and heat gently for a minute. Serve over rice.

## Nellie Pauline's Meatloaf

361 No. Green. Peppers. This is my Knoxville grandmother's recipe, developed to suit her finicky husband. No. Green. Peppers.

Posted by: Kerry. Yield: 3 pones. Prep time: 45 minutes to an hour.

---

1 pound 90% lean ground beef
1/2 pound mild sausage
1 onion, chopped
2 – 3 eggs
1/3 cup evaporated milk or half & half
2 cloves garlic, minced
1 tablespoon A1 sauce
2 teaspoons Worcestershire sauce
salt and pepper to taste
15-ounce can whole tomatoes
corn flakes to bind

Combine all ingredients, form 3 pones (loaves) and bake at 350 degrees F for 40 minutes to an hour. Back in the day this would swim in grease; modern pork sausage prevents this. Note that it makes delectable sammiches on light bread.

## Duck with Blackberry Sage Sauce

362 I created this dish myself.

Posted by: Ben Had. Yield: varies. Prep time: depends on how many you make.

---

2 boneless skinless duck breasts per person
fresh sage
1 large container (quart) fresh blackberries
1/2 cup Merlot wine
juice from 1/4 of a fresh lemon
1/4 cup dried sage
blackberry preserves (optional)

Rub the duck breasts with the chopped fresh sage, and grill to medium. Do not overcook. To make the sauce, place blackberries in large pan and simmer on low heat, mashing the berries as they cook. Leave some large pieces. Add the wine (can add more to taste), the lemon juice, and the 1/4 cup of dried sage (can add more to taste). Continue to simmer until flavors are blended. This is not a sweet sauce, but if you would like to sweeten it add 1 tablespoon of blackberry preserves at a time until desired result is reached.

## Healthy Meatloaf

363 A healthier version of the traditional favorite. I blame Mrs. Franpsycho's total ban on beef for this recipe, which I dreamed up based on decades of accumulated cultural culinary appropriation.

Posted by: San Franpsycho. Yield: 4 servings. Prep time: 60 minutes.

---

1 pound ground turkey
1 carrot
1 small yellow onion
1 celery stalk
1 cup breadcrumbs or panko
1/2 cup rolled oats
1 tablespoon salt
1 teaspoon black pepper
1 teaspoon fish sauce or Worcestershire sauce
1 cup ketchup
1/4 cup honey
2 tablespoons olive oil

Put the celery, onion, and carrot into a food processor, and pulse a few times to create a finely shredded mire poix. Saute the mire poix in half the oil, uncovered at low temperature, stirring occasionally, until the mire poix is tender and translucent. Cool. Stir together the glaze: the ketchup, honey, and remaining olive oil. Reserve. Mix the remaining ingredients gently by hand in a big bowl. When Mrs. Franpsycho is not looking, add 1/4 pound lean ground beef. Mix in 1 – 2 tablespoons of the glaze mixture. Form the meat mixture into 1 or

2 loaves of equal and even shape on a shallow baking sheet. Line it first with aluminum foil or silicone. Spread 1/3 of the glaze on all surfaces of the loaf. Cover with tin foil and bake at 325 degrees for approximately 40 minutes, maybe less if 2 loaves. Remove the tin foil, spread the remaining glaze on top, and turn the broiler on low. Broil for an additional 10 minutes or so until the glaze is bubbly and crispy. Remove from oven and let cool a few minutes before slicing and serving.

***Chef's Notes:***

The fish sauce is worth it for the umami, and preferred to Worcestershire. The meatloaf will *not* taste fishy.

## Meatloaf a la Chateau D'Eez

364 Generalized meatloaf algorithm for most tastes and mixtures. My own recipe, originally developed to make a turkey meatloaf to accommodate a "no red meat" house guest, refined over the years to work with other meats, and also to accommodate the gluten-free. Stick to the outline and you will end up with an outstanding meatloaf !

Posted by: sock_rat_eez. Yield: 6 to 8 servings. Prep time: 2 hours, +/-.

---

2 to 3 pounds ground meat
2 to 3 onions
2 to 4 cloves garlic
3 or 4 carrots
3 to 5 stalks celery
1 to 2 cups cooked rice, or breadcrumbs
3 eggs
1/2 cup ketchup
various herbs and spices to taste

Start with your largest mixing bowl, and add the meat, which may be any ground meat: turkey or chicken; the canonical lamb, pork, beef, 1 pound each; pork or other sausage mixture; or any mixture of any of the above totaling between 2 and 3 pounds. Then add 2 or 3 onions, grated or chopped fine, 2 to 6 cloves garlic, to taste, put through the garlic press, 3 or 4 grated carrots, and 3 to 5 stalks celery, chopped fine—I usually slice the stalks lengthwise ¼ - 3/16 inch wide and chop that 1/8 inch or less, then sort of chop up the pile repeatedly. Add rice—from about a cup well parboiled to 2 cups fully cooked—if gluten is not an issue, then 1 to 1 1/2 cups breadcrumbs may substitute. This is needed to soak up the juices generated in cooking. Add 3 whole eggs—rice is not as good a binder as breadcrumbs, so this adds cohesion to the finished product. I usually season with oregano, basil, dill, sage, black pepper, a little rosemary, and sometimes a trace of allspice; or use what you like. Mrs Eez often adds cumin, for instance.

Addressing the pile that has built up in the bowl, get one or both hands in there and start mixing, mostly by grabbing a big handful and squeezing out through your fingers until thoroughly mixed. I suppose you could use a big spoon or spatula, but that's how I do it. I like to have the loaf pans ready on the counter so I can just start loading the result into them.

This will completely fill two standard loaf pans, with possibly some excess. I also like to leave the sink running so I can wash up without touching the valve when done. Apply a heavy coating of ketchup to the top of each loaf. Bake at 325 to 350 degrees F about an hour, more or less—raise the temp to 400ish for last 20 minutes or so if you like it well-browned on top.

This recipe will also make excellent meatballs. Meatballs should be shaped and dropped one at a time into simmering marinara sauce, or whatever you like—I have also used cream of mushroom soup (or a 50/50 mix of cream of mushroom/cream of celery) for this. Go slowly, so as not to stop the boiling. I'm not really a recipe-oriented cook, so this is an approximation from memory of a typical batch; adjust the quantities as required or to your taste.

## Mr. Big Food's Duck Gumbo El Dorado

365 Best gumbo ever. Honest. Mightily adapted from an old Texarkana cookbook. Now a favorite in my husband's "Big Food Manual and Survivalist Flourishing Guide"—a collection of over 29,000 recipes culled from old American (especially Southern) cookbooks.

Posted by: Marica. Yield: 12 generous servings. Prep time: all day and worth every minute.

---

1 5 to 6 pound duck (dressed)
1 cup bacon fat or cooking/olive oil
1 cup flour
2 cups chopped white onion
2 cups chopped celery
1 pound okra, fresh or frozen, sliced
3 cloves garlic, chopped fine
1 6-ounce can tomato paste
15 ounces stewed tomatoes (can use canned, flavored)
2 teaspoons Accent
1 cup chopped bell pepper
1 bunch green onions and tops, sliced
1 bunch parsley, chopped fine
1 teaspoon dried oregano leaves, crushed
1 teaspoon dried thyme leaves, crushed
2 tablespoons salt (or less, to taste)
1 tablespoon black pepper (or to taste)
½ tablespoon cayenne pepper (or to taste)
2 pounds cooked shrimp (cleaned, thawed if frozen)—OR 2 pounds Cajun or Creole sausage, chunked and fried off
box of wild rice, cooked according to package directions (or half wild rice, half rice)
file powder

Boil duck 4 – 5 hours, covered, in slightly salted water to cover. Drain, reserving stock. Melt bacon fat (or heat oil) over medium heat in heavy saucepan and stir in flour until smooth. Cook to make a dark brown roux. The trick is to get the roux as dark as possible without burning. Using a cast iron skillet helps. As roux nears end of cooking time, turn off heat and add onions, celery, and okra. Stir until veggies are slightly browned and roux stops cooking. Stir roux into 2 quarts duck stock. Stir in garlic, tomato paste, tomatoes, Accent, green peppers, green onions and tops, parsley, oregano, thyme, salt, and black and cayenne pepper. Stir in fried-off sausage (if using). Bring to rapid boil, turn down to solid simmer, and simmer uncovered 30 minutes (or more). Cut bite-size pieces of meat from duck carcass, discarding bones and fat, and add meat to gumbo. Add more duck stock to make a rich gumbo. Add cooked shrimp (if using) and simmer until shrimp is heated through. Serve gumbo over piles of wild rice. Sprinkle with file powder. This gumbo freezes well.

## Beer Braised Corned Beef

> 366 My favorite corned beef recipe. It's from allrecipes.com, but I added the beer. It makes a big difference over water.

Posted by: Wiz 427. Yield: servings for 6 Morons. Prep time: 6 ½ hours.

---

5 pounds corned beef brisket
1 tablespoon Kitchen Bouquet browning sauce
12 ounces Yuengling beer or your favorite, as long as it is actual beer, not this froo-froo too-fancy-by-half grapefruit raspberry earwax IPA microbrew crap
1 tablespoon vegetable oil
1 onion
6 cloves garlic

Preheat oven to 275 degrees F. Discard flavor packet and rinse brisket. Pat dry with paper towels. Heat oil in large skillet. Brush brisket with Kitchen Bouquet and sear brisket in skillet, 5 – 8 minutes on each side. Slice onions thick and peel garlic. Pour beer into bottom of roasting pan. Arrange some of onions and garlic on rack in roasting pan. Place seared brisket fat side up on rack on roasting pan and arrange rest of onions and garlic on top of brisket. Cover tightly with foil and roast for 6 hours. Let rest 10 minutes before slicing.

## Cowboy Meat Loaf

> 367 Traditional meat loaf with a twist. This is a take on my Grandma's meat loaf recipe that she probably got out of a ladies' magazine in the 50s. Most measurements are estimates as she adds things until it "looks right."

Posted by: Prince Ludwig the Deplorable. Yield: 4 servings. Prep time: 1 hour 15 minutes.

---

2 pounds ground beef
1 egg
1/2 cup bread crumbs
half of a medium yellow onion, diced
1/2 cup + barbecue sauce
2 – 3 dashes Worcestershire sauce

With your hands, combine meat, onion, egg, ½ cup bbq sauce and Worcestershire sauce in a mixing bowl. Reserve some extra bbq sauce for the glaze. Add bread crumbs until it reaches your desired consistency. Put in a 1 ½-quart loaf pan and place in a preheated 350 degree F oven for 1 hour. Drain the pan, glaze with desired amount of bbq sauce and put back in the oven for 15 minutes. I'd suggest using the 80/20 ground beef for best flavor. You can use ground turkey or chicken if you're into that kind of thing.

## Beef Tips Napoli

368 A little Italian "stew." I don't know where this recipe came from. My mother and grandmother have been making it since I was an ankle-biter.

Posted by: Cheribebe. Yield: servings for 4 hungry morons. Prep time: 20 minutes prep; 1 – 2 hours simmer.

---

3 pounds beef stew meat
1 teaspoon salt
1/4 teaspoon black pepper
1/2 teaspoon sugar
1 1/2 cups water
2 small cans tomato paste
2 tablespoons lemon juice
1 teaspoon oregano
1 clove garlic
1 small carrot thinly sliced
1 pound medium shell pasta
½ cup grated Parmesan cheese
1 tablespoon fresh chopped flat leaf parsley

Cut beef into one-inch cubes. Sprinkle with salt and pepper and brown in batches with 2 tablespoons of olive oil in a Dutch oven . Do not drain out juices. Mix water, tomato paste, chopped garlic, sugar and lemon juice together and pour over meat in Dutch oven. Simmer covered for 30 – 45 minutes, then uncovered for an hour to allow the sauce to thicken. Seasonings may be adjusted to taste; this is not spaghetti sauce but milder. Cook pasta until tender; drain. Return to pot, add 3 tablespoons butter and mix to coat. Then add the Parmesan cheese and the chopped parsley. Mix well. Serve in bowls with beef tips on top. Definitely goes great with bread and with a salad on the side.

### *Chef's Notes:*

This is great for tougher meat and is a very mild-flavored but forgiving recipe. Water can be added if too thick. Decrease water if crockpotting.

## Stir-Fried Beef with Vegetables

369 Mrs. Farmer just made this the other day.

Posted by: Farmer. Yield: 4 – 6 servings. Prep time: 20-25 minutes.

---

1 pound sirloin or strip steak, sliced
1 tablespoon sugar
1 tablespoon corn starch
2 tablespoons red wine or sherry
3 tablespoons soy sauce
1 medium onion, chopped
4 tablespoons canola oil
1 pound veggies—mushrooms, asparagus, pea pods
1 teaspoon salt

Cut beef into 1/8" slices. Add sugar, cornstarch, wine and soy sauce. Cook with onion and oil. Add vegetables after beef is mostly cooked and salt as you desire. Green beans or bamboo shoots may be included or wherever else you like.

## Ragu di Adam

370 Spaghetti Bolognese from the master. My own, (stolen from too many native Italians to attribute.)

Posted by: Adam. Yield: servings for 6 morons. Prep time: 2 – 5 hours depending on your commitment.

---

extra virgin olive oil
2 medium onions
2 medium carrots
3 celery sticks
1 kilo beef and pork mince, half kilo of each (mince = ground meat)
3 tins tomatoes
2 tablespoons tomato paste
750 ml fresh chicken stock
200 ml white wine
1 bay leaf
1 bunch fresh rosemary
2 garlic cloves

Thinly dice the vegetables. Do not use a blender or similar as this leaves the vegetables with no integrity. Leave mince outside the fridge for an hour to come to room temperature, otherwise it will stew when cooked. Splash a good amount of extra virgin olive oil in a large pot and heat. When hot add the onions and reduce heat to low. Simmer for a few minutes and then add the carrot and celery. Simmer on low heat for at least 15 minutes without browning the onions. Add the mince and increase the heat to medium. Move the mince around the pot until it is all broken up. There will be a fair amount of liquid given off by the meat, and you want this to evaporate which will take about 10 or 15 minutes. Keep stirring occasionally and be ready for when the liquid has all evaporated. Turn up the heat to high and 30 seconds later add all the wine so that the alcohol evaporates with a big whoosh. Move around for a minute or so and then add the tinned tomatoes, tomato paste, and bay leaf. After a minute or so add enough stock so that you can leave the pot to comfortably simmer for an hour or so. Leave uncovered and turn down the heat to low. If the sauce gets too dry, add more stock. The longer that you leave this to cook then the better it will be. Typically I will let it cook for at least 3 hours, preferably 5. Once you are happy with the sauce, (it should be firm but still have a good amount of liquid), turn off the heat and let it sit for 10 minutes. In a small pot add the whole peeled garlic and the bunch of whole fresh rosemary. Add enough olive oil so that the herbs and garlic will be just about covered. Heat over a medium-low temperature paying very close attention so that the garlic does not burn. You do not want the taste of burnt garlic through your sauce as it will ruin it. After about 5 minutes or until the garlic is just about to brown, remove from the heat and discard the garlic and herbs. Pour the flavored oil into the sauce and season to taste.

***Chef's Notes:***
I lived in Italy for over 10 years. This sauce is the result of watching various grandmothers, professional chefs, and assorted others cook this sauce, and combining their various techniques. The flavored oil trick at the end is a professional secret amongst high-level Italian chefs. You're welcome. Also, note that the recipe uses white wine instead of red. Italians very rarely use red wine to cook; it is predominantly white.

## Duck Potatoes

371 A melange of shredded duck meat and potatoes fried in duck fat. I've been a big fan of Alton Brown for many years, and long ago he did an episode of his show *Good Eats* that involved duck. I'd never had it and the thought of trying it out intrigued me. After discovering duck is delicious, and that potatoes cooked in duck fat are the best thing ever, I decided to come up with a recipe that just kind of . . . threw them all together. So here it is!

Posted by: Viridian. Yield: 4 – 6 servings. Prep time: 1 1/2 hours.

---

1 duck, frozen
4 red potatoes
1 onion
4 garlic cloves
2 tablespoons parsley flakes
1/2 cup shredded cheese

Thaw the duck until it can be quartered, then quarter it. Slit the skin a few times on each of the pieces but don't cut all the way through to the meat. Steam the four duck quarters in a steamer basket in a large pot, covered, for 45 minutes or until no pink can be seen in the duck meat. Remove the quarters and allow to cool. Separate the duck fat from the water either by boiling the water away, using a gravy separator or putting the water and fat in a container and letting it cool in the freezer. Save the duck fat. Harvest the meat from the duck pieces. I always do this part the night before. Chop about half of the duck meat into ¼" pieces. Dice the onion. Peel, and smash the garlic gloves, then dice them fine. Chop the red potatoes into ¼" pieces.

In a large pan, add 1 tablespoon of the duck fat over medium heat and wait until it shimmers. Add the onion and garlic and a little salt and stir occasionally until the onions turn translucent. Add the potatoes and a little more salt and cook until soft. Add the chopped duck meat and stir, allowing the meat to reheat. Add the parsley flakes, then taste and add any seasoning you desire. Once it tastes the way you like, turn the heat off and sprinkle the shredded cheese on top to form a complete coating. Wait for the cheese to melt and serve. You can make two of these with the meat from one duck.

# *Poultry*

## Poppy Seed Chicken

372 Chicken casserole recipe from church suppers.

Posted by: ALH. Yield: 4 servings. Prep time: 25 minutes.

---

4 cups cooked chicken prepared ahead of time
1 can cream of chicken soup
1 pint sour cream
1 sleeve Ritz Crackers
1 stick (1/2 cup) butter
poppy seeds

Place chicken in bottom of glass baking dish. Mix soup and sour cream, spread evenly over chicken. Crumble Ritz crackers, spread evenly over soup mixture. Cut butter into little pats, place on top of crackers. Sprinkle poppy seeds on top. Bake at 375 degrees F for 40 minutes. I usually serve with Italian- style green beans and brown & serve rolls.

## 40 Clove-Chicken Recipe

373 A delicious new twist on cooking chicken. This recipe was originally from Alton Brown, and is an Eastern European recipe.

Posted by: ziggydog777. Yield: 6 servings. Prep time: 20 minutes.

---

4 pound fryer chicken, cut into 8 pieces
kosher salt & black pepper to taste
2 tablespoons, plus 1/2 cup olive oil
40 cloves of garlic, peeled
thyme
toasted bread (optional)

Heat oven to 350 degrees F. Season the chicken all over with salt and pepper. Coat the chicken pieces on all sides with 2 tablespoons of the oil. In a 12-inch straight-sided oven-safe saute pan over high heat, cook the chicken for 5 to 7 minutes per side, until nicely browned. Remove the pan from the heat; add the remaining 1/2 cup oil, the thyme, and garlic cloves. Cover and bake for 1 hour and 15 minutes. Remove the pan from the oven and set aside for 15 minutes with the lid on. Serve family style with plenty of toasted bread to spread the softened, fragrant garlic on.

## Cajun Chicken Wings

374 An OregonMuse family favorite for 25 years. We really don't know where this came from, maybe the newspaper cooking section, back around 1992 or so. But I notice there's a nearly identical recipe on food.com for "awesome cajun chicken wings." But I swear our recipe did not come from there.

Posted by: OregonMuse. Yield: servings for 4 – 8 morons. Prep time: about 2 hours.

---

24 whole chicken wings
1 tablespoon cayenne pepper
2 tablespoons paprika
2 tablespoons garlic powder
1 tablespoon dried oregano
1 tablespoon thyme
1 tablespoon onion powder
1/2 tablespoon (1 ½ teaspooons) salt
1 teaspoon black pepper
1/4 cup olive oil
Celery stalks, bleu cheese or ranch dressing

Disjoint and separate wings; throw away tip, leaving the other two pieces. Combine all but oil in blender and mix, then slowly add oil to make a paste—add some water if necessary. Put wings and paste in bowl and toss until all wings are coated. Then dump everything into a zip-lock bag and let marinate in refrigerator overnight. Broil in oven about 4 inches from heat for about 10 minutes, then turn and broil other side for 10 minutes. Serve warm with celery stalks, bleu cheese or ranch dressing.

## Chicken in Prison

375 Carbs ahoy! From *Italian Classics In One Pot* by Anna Teresa Callen, King Hill Productions, 1997.

Posted by: Mary Poppins' Practically Perfect Piercing. Yield: servings for 8 morons. Prep time: 40 minutes.

---

3 1/2 pound chicken, cut to serving pieces
1/4 teaspoon salt
1/4 teaspoon pepper
3 tablespoons olive oil
1 onion, chopped
2 cups chicken broth
1 loaf large round bread
2 eggs
2 tablespoons lemon juice
2 tablespoons capers
1 tablespoon chopped parsley

Season the chicken with salt and pepper. In a large skillet, heat the olive oil over medium high heat. Add the chicken and cook, turning until brown all over, 7 minutes. Add the onion, stirring often, until translucent, 3 – 5 minutes. Add 1 cup broth, bring to boil. Reduce heat to low. Cover and simmer, gradually adding 1/2 cup broth, until chicken is no longer pink at the bone, 35 minutes. Remove chicken and reserve liquid. Remove skin and bones from chicken and chop coarsely. Preheat oven to 350 degrees F. Cut off top of bread, scoop out interior and place in a large bowl. Add reserved cooking liquid and remaining 1/2 cup broth. Stir and chop until the mixture is the consistency of thick pudding. Add more broth or water if needed. Add eggs, lemon juice, capers and parsley. Mix well and stir in chopped chicken. Fill bread bowl with the mixture, cover with bread top, place on a baking sheet and bake for 30 minutes.

***Chef's Notes:***
This can also be made with regular deboned chicken breasts instead of bone-in chicken. As well, it can be spread out to 4 small bread bowls if you can't find one big one.

## Chicken Patsy

376 Tasty stuffed chicken breast. This recipe is named for my mother-in-law Patsy. I would make it (or some similar variant) often, and when she would visit she would ask me to make it for her each time. It became the sort of thing that she would tell her friends "what a wonderful cook her son-in-law was" and that I would make it special for her (when in fact I would make it whenever). One day she asked me what the name of the dish was. I just blurted out "Chicken Patsy," and now she asks for it by name. My wife's brother's wife (who has the same mother-in-law) found out and said to me, "You named a recipe after her? How can I compete with that?"

Posted by: chelsea danger. Yield: 4 – 6 Moron servings. Prep time: 1 – 2 glasses of wine or the beer equivalent; cooking time: 1 – 2 glasses of wine or the beer equivalent.

---

6 boneless skinless chicken breasts
1 log/roll spicy breakfast sausage
1 jar roasted red peppers
1 jar pesto
cheese, I leave that up to you—I prefer a sharp cheddar or a strong bleu cheese; more flavor is more better
olive oil
salt/pepper
other spices/herbs as desired

Open wine/beer and take a sip, keep handy but be careful handling raw chicken. Cook the entire roll of spicy breakfast sausage and set aside. Butterfly each chicken breast, being sure not to cut all the way through—this is essentially a stuffed chicken breast recipe. Spread pesto onto the inside of the chicken breast. Onto the pesto spread a layer of cheese, roasted red pepper and cooked sausage. Cut three lengths of butcher's string for each chicken breast. Turn oven to 350 degrees F and have more to drink. On a clean surface place the lengths of string in a position so that each chicken breast can be folded over and then tied. Drizzle olive oil on each stuffed chicken breast. Salt, pepper and add other spices/herbs to satisfaction—it is still raw chicken at this point so don't taste it. Heat the skillet and brown the stuffed chicken breasts, turning so each side is browned. Move skillet with the chicken into the oven; bake until chicken is thoroughly cooked – about 30 minutes. Finish wine/beer. Serve with whatever. Enjoy!!!!!

## Smothered Chicken-Fried Meat

377 Mushroom soup and Velveeta in a crockpot. I consider this mine (I conceived it pre-internet and without a cookbook) but it's so simple, I'm sure it exists in a thousand variations.

Posted by: irright. Yield: variable. Prep time: depends on how drunk you are.

---

chicken-fried meat of some sort, whatever you have
several cans cream of mushroom soup
necessary amount Velveeta
generous splashes of milk (the good stuff, not that 2% crap)
black pepper to taste (I like black pepper)
mashed potatoes (optional)

This isn't an exact recipe. I don't know how much you need of anything. Just take whatever chicken-fried meat you have. Pheasant is awesome and chicken breast is, too. I've never done chicken-fried steak in this, but it should be excellent. Anyway, you just layer mushroom soup, Velveeta, and several good splashes of milk and your chicken-fried meat of choice in a crock-pot and crank it up good for a while so everything melds together. I would practice with it a couple times before using it for an important occasion, but once you get it right, it's damn good. Mashed potatoes are awesome with this. Try not to drool in the pot.

## Grandma's Fried Chicken

378 Easy, old-fashioned fried chicken. I got this recipe from my mom, who got it from her mom. Grandma made this on Sundays when she was a single (deserted) mom.

Posted by: Infidel. Yield: 4 servings. Prep time: 10 minutes.

---

1 whole chicken, cut up
2 cups all-purpose flour
1/8 cup-ish (or more) salt
1 tablespoon pepper
1 tablespoon paprika
3 cups or more Crisco or lard

Put all dry ingredients in paper bag, fold over top of bag and shake to mix. Drop 2 – 3 chicken pieces in bag and shake to coat. Carefully place coated chicken in heated Crisco/lard in a cast iron skillet or Dutch oven on stove top. Turn after about 10 – 15 minutes and cook until done. Continue with remainder of chicken. I drain the chicken on a plate lined with another paper bag. Oil should be hot but not smoking. Not sure what temperature the oil should be. Maybe 300 degrees F? You can adjust as needed. Chicken should sizzle, not splatter much.

## PA Dutch Chicken Pot Pie (Bott Boi)

379 A delicious chicken soup with dumpling noodles. This recipe has been passed down for generations in my PA Dutch family.

Posted by: DangerGirl33 and Her 1.21 Gigawatt SanityProd (tm). Yield: servings for 8 – 10 Morons. Prep time: 2 1/2 hours.

---

4 – 5 pounds chicken (or chicken pieces)
12 cups water
1 tablespoon salt
1/2 tablespoon pepper
1 stalk celery, sliced
4 large carrots, sliced
1 medium onion, chopped
1 tablespoon dried parsley
2 cups all-purpose flour
1 teaspoon salt
2 tablespoons vegetable shortening
3/4 cup hot water
tarragon, saffron or other herbs of choice (optional)

Wash chicken. Place in stock pot with celery, carrot, onion, salt, pepper and parsley (you can also add some other herbs you like, such as tarragon, which is my favorite). Add enough water to just cover chicken. Bring to boil. Turn down heat to a simmer and cook for one hour fifteen minutes. Remove chicken from broth and set aside to cool. Set cooking liquid (broth and veggies) aside in pot, covered. When chicken is cool, remove meat from bones and roughly chop. Combine flour and salt in a large bowl. Cut in shortening until the consistency of cornmeal. Add 3/4 cup hot water, stirring to make a soft, but not sticky, dough. Place dough on floured surface, dust with a lot of flour and roll very thin. Cut into squares (I usually make mine 2"x3", but cut to whatever size you prefer). Bring the cooking liquid back to a rolling boil. Drop dumpling squares into boiling broth and cook for 15 minutes, keeping at a boil and stirring frequently to prevent the dumplings from sticking. Remove from heat, stir chopped chicken back in and let set for five minutes, to let the chicken warm through. Salt and pepper to taste and serve.

### *Chef's Notes:*

This soup is always better on the second day, but darn good on day one too. Don't be afraid to experiment with the herbs/seasonings. This is also good with a pinch of saffron added before boiling the dumplings.

## Northern Chicken

380 Fit for a King, who might live in the north, where Winter is usually on its way. This is taken and *heavily* modified from the website The Inn at the Crossroads, a food blog which recreates dishes from fantasy/medieval literature.

Posted by: harbqll. Yield: depends how much you eat. Prep time: 2 hours, all together, I guess.

---

1 whole chicken, for roasting
2 cups each mushrooms, carrots, potatoes (or turnips), chopped
1 1/2 cups apple cider vinegar, divided
2/3 plus 1/4 cup honey
3 teaspoons ground mint, divided
2/3 plus 1/2 cup dried cherries, halved
1 cup (or so) chicken stock
olive oil or butter, for rubbing on chicken
dash ground cloves, cinnamon, nutmeg, mace, allspice
salt and pepper

Preheat oven to 450 degrees F. Mix 1/2 cup cider vinegar, 1/4 cup honey, 1/2 cup chicken stock, 1/2 cup cherries, and 1 teaspoon mint over low heat to make a sauce. Pour over vegetables in a roasting pan and toss. Add more chicken stock as needed. Rub chicken down with olive oil or butter, then salt and pepper. Place bird over vegetables in roasting pan. Place roasting pan in oven, roast for 30 minutes or so, until done. Meanwhile, make sauce for serving: mix 1 cup apple cider vinegar, 2/3 cup honey, 2 teaspoons mint, and 2/3 cup cherries over low heat. Reduce by about a third. Add in any or all of the following, to your taste - cinnamon, cloves, nutmeg, mace, allspice—anything that makes it a little "Christmasy" to you. When the bird is done, carve and serve with the roast vegetables and the serving sauce. Some may find this meal a little "stark," but add in some bread and a nice stout, and it should keep you plenty warm.

## Mediterranean Chicken

381 Easy dish for a worknight. Made it up one night when I had an empty pantry and limited options. It's easy and tasty. This is so easy even grammie winger could do it!

Posted by: Duke Lowell. Yield: 2 servings. Prep time: 60 minutes.

---

2 large chicken breasts, trimmed
1 16-ounce can stewed tomatoes
1 bunch scallions, sliced
1 teaspoon granulated garlic
1/4 teaspoon cumin
1/4 teaspoon cardamom
salt & pepper
1 tablespoon olive oil
1/4 cup red wine
rice

In a bowl, combine drained tomatoes with the white parts of the scallions, garlic, cumin, cardamom, and salt and pepper to taste. Season both sides of breasts with salt and pepper. Don't be shy here. Seriously, have you ever had oversalted chicken? No, no you have not. Add olive oil to an oven-safe, non-stick skillet and heat over high heat until olive oil is shimmering, almost smoking. Do not use cast iron. Sear breasts on both sides, about 3 – 4 minutes per side. Remove breasts and deglaze with wine, scraping all the tasty bits off the bottom. Replace breasts and cover with tomato mixture. Cover and bake in a 350 degree F oven for 30 minutes or until internal temperature is 160 degrees F. Serve over rice and garnish with green parts of the scallions.

## Fried Chicken

382 I'm too lazy to make "real" fried chicken.

Posted by: Helena Handbasket. Yield: 2 servings. Prep time: 20 minutes.

---

2 boneless, skinless chicken breasts
1 cup extra-virgin olive oil
1 stick (1/2 cup) butter
1/2 cup bacon grease
1 egg
2 teaspoons sage
1 teaspoon freshly ground pepper
1/8 cup milk or half-and-half
1/2 cup Bisquick
1/2 cup panko bread crumbs
2 teaspoons salt

Pour olive oil into frying pan; add butter and bacon grease. Beat egg in a medium bowl with sage, pepper and milk/half-and-half. Mix Bisquick, panko and salt in a small bowl or bread loaf dish. Pound the thicker ends of the chicken breasts with a flat-sided tenderizer so they are more even with the thin ends. Heat oil and fat in the pan. Dip the breasts in the egg mix and then the breading; add to oil when heated. Cover the pan and cook for about 4 minutes; check and turn the chicken when it is browned to taste. Cook for 2 – 4 minutes more after turning. When done, flip once more before removing from pan to coat both sides with the oil mix.

## Chicken Mushroom Parmesan

383 Why I never opened a restaurant. This is from my mom.

Posted by: kbdabear. Yield: enough for 1 or more morons. Prep time: 60 minutes.

---

chicken legs, wings
1 can cream of chicken and mushroom soup
grated Parmesan cheese
1/4 cup butter or margarine, melted
smart phone

Take chicken wings and legs from package; boil for 10 minutes. Pour chicken and mushroom soup into a glass baking dish. It's a good idea to open the can first. Add the melted butter or margarine. Add enough grated Parmesan cheese until the soup and butter mixture is a yellowish color. Add chicken legs and wings. Cook at 325 degrees F for 45 minutes to 1 hour depending on how cooked the chicken was before throwing it into the dish. If the cream crusts up and turns brown, you've spent too long on your smart phone. Let cool for 5 minutes. If it didn't turn out well, use your smart phone to have a chicken entree delivered to your home.

***Chef's Notes:***
*Don't Try This At Home.*

## 273 Easy Chicken and Rice

384 I got this from my mom, but I improved it.

Posted by: GOULD. Yield: 4 – 8 servings. Prep time: 15 minutes.

---

8 chicken thighs, bone-in
3 cups Minute Rice, uncooked
2 cans Campbell's cream of chicken soup (condensed)
2 cans Campbell's cream of mushroom, soup (condensed)
1 box Liptons dry onion soup mix (2 envelopes)

In a 13x9 baking dish, mix rice, all canned soup and one envelope of the onion soup. Spread evenly. Place chicken thighs on top of the rice/soup mixture. Sprinkle the second envelope of onion soup over the top of the chicken & rice. Seal with foil and bake at 350 degrees F for 75 minutes. Uncover and bake for 15 minutes more. Let rest for a few minutes and go to town. If you use chicken leg quarters, I add 15 minutes to base cook time. Chicken breasts can also add to cook time. Just make sure chicken is cooked through. Enjoy! Stores well for a week in the fridge and microwaves well with the addition of a little water for the rice.

## Pecan-Crusted Fried Chicken

385 Fried and finished in the oven. From *Taste of the South* magazine. Sounds time-consuming, but it's easier and less messy than frying chicken old-school. Delish.

Posted by: Jane D'oh. Yield: 4 – 5 servings. Prep time: Depending on number of pieces of chicken you use, 4 minutes/piece, then 25 – 45 minutes in the oven.

---

2 1/4 cups panko bread crumbs
2/3 cup pecan halves
1/2 cup, plus 2 tablespoons flour
2 1/2 teaspoons salt, divided
1 teaspooon fresh ground black pepper, divided
1 1/2 cups whole buttermilk
1 large egg
6 skin-on chicken drumsticks
2 bone-in skin-on chicken thighs
2 bone-in skin-on chicken breasts
vegetable oil for frying
honey to serve

Preheat oven to 350 degrees F. Line a large, rimmed baking sheet with a wire rack; spray with non-stick cooking spray. In a food processor, combine bread crumbs, pecans, 2 tablespoons flour, 2 teaspoons salt, and 1/2 tsp. pepper. Pulse until pecans are coarsely ground and transfer to a large, shallow dish. In a shallow dish, whisk the buttermilk and egg together until combined. In a large, resealable plastic bag, combine half the chicken pieces, remaining 1/2 cup of flour, remaining 1/2 teaspoon salt, and remaining 1/2 teaspoon pepper. Seal bag and shake to coat chicken. Remove chicken pieces, shake off excess coating, and repeat process with remaining chicken. In a large skillet, pour oil to depth of 1/4" and heat over medium heat. While oil heats, dip chicken in buttermilk mixture, draining excess, dredge in pecan mixture, and gently press to coat. Working in batches, cook chicken until golden brown, about 2 minutes per side. Place chicken on prepared rack. Repeat with remaining chicken. Bake until a meat thermometer inserted in thickest portion of chicken pieces registers 165 degrees F, about 25 – 45 minutes. Drizzle cooked chicken with honey, if desired.

## Tia Juanita's Pollo Loco

386 Baked chicken & rice—basic, but good! Adapted from an old church cookbook.

Posted by: rfitz34. Yield: servings for 4 morons. Prep time: 100 minutes.

---

1 chicken, cut up
2 8-ounce boxes Goya rice & beans or similar
2 cans cream of mushroom soup
2 packets Vitarroz sazon or similar
32 ounces chicken broth
1 cup water
red peppers (optional)

Combine all ingredients in a shallow baking dish. Cover with foil and bake at 375 degrees F for 45 minutes. Remove foil and bake for 45 minutes more, or until chicken and rice are tender. A nice addition is some sauteed red peppers, cut into thin slices and added when serving.

## Slow Cooker "Ranch" Chicken

387 Low carb, low fuss, high flavor. This is a recipe I found online and saved years ago. Unfortunately, I don't have the name of the original author.

Posted by: Captain Whitebread. Yield: 8 servings. Prep time: 4 – 8 hours.

---

2 pounds boneless chicken breasts
2 8-ounce blocks cream cheese
2 one-ounce packets dry Ranch seasoning
8 ounces bacon, cooked crispy and crumbled

Place chicken and cream cheese in a slow cooker. Sprinkle Ranch seasoning on top. Cook on "high" for four hours, or on "low" for six to eight hours, until chicken shreds easily. Once the chicken shreds, stir with a large fork or spoon to fully shred chicken and to combine ingredients. Add in crumbled bacon, stir to incorporate. Serve warm. If you want to add extra flavor, substitute 1 block of flavored cream cheese (like bacon or jalapeno) for 1 block of plain cream cheese.

## Slow Cooker Chicken and 40 Cloves

388 Developed flavors, set it and forget it. Originally found scouring the internet when I had half a big pack of Costco chicken breasts and I wanted to cook them all at once. This recipe was found on the website wholeandheavenlyoven.com.

Posted by: Joseph Morand. Yield: 6 servings. Prep time: 30 minutes + 4 – 5 hours cooking.

---

12 chicken thighs
oil to brown meat and saute vegetables
40 garlic cloves, crushed
1 yellow onion, diced
1/4 cup flour
1/2 cup white wine
1 cup chicken broth
1 tablespoon oregano
2 tablespoons parsley
2 tablespoons cooking oil
salt and pepper
rice

Pat chicken thighs dry. Season both sides of all thighs with salt and pepper. Add oil to a saute pan and preheat to medium-high heat. Brown both sides of each thigh and transfer to your slow cooker. Brown the thighs in sets, don't overcrowd the pan. After all the thighs are browned, saute the garlic cloves and the diced onion in the pan for about 5 minutes, stirring often. Add the flour and stir until evenly distributed. Pour in the white wine and chicken broth, stir until thickened and simmering. Pour contents of the pan over the thighs; cook on low for 4 – 5 hours. Serve with rice. The cloves are great to spread over a crusty bread like it's butter.

***Chef's Notes:***
If you're gluten intolerant, cup4cup flour will work fine. I typically use 'Better than Bouillon' instead of broth for convenience. This recipe makes a great base for chicken noodle soup if you thin it out with more chicken broth after it's finished cooking.

## Avocado Chicken Enchiladas

389 This is from the website familyfreshmeals.com.

Posted by: Tami. Yield: 6 – 8 servings. Prep time: 35 minutes.

---

1 tablespoon butter
3 garlic cloves, minced
1 tablespoon flour
1 cup chicken (or vegetable) stock
1 ½ teaspoons cumin
1/4 teaspoon salt
1/4 teaspoon fresh ground pepper
1/4 cup chopped cilantro
1 cup mild or medium salsa verde
1/2 cup sour cream
3 – 4 cups cooked chicken, chopped or shredded
2 cups Mexican blend cheese
3 avocados, peeled and chopped
8 flour tortillas

Preheat oven to 375 degrees F. In medium sauce pan, saute garlic in butter over medium-high heat for about 1 minute. Stir in flour and continue to stir while cooking for 2 more minutes. Next stir in the chicken/veggie broth, cumin, salt and pepper and bring to a simmer. Remove from heat and stir in the sour cream, salsa verde and cilantro. Coat a 9" x 13" baking dish with nonstick spray. Add about 1/2 cup sauce to the bottom of the pan and spread out until bottom of the baking dish is evenly coated. Lay out a tortilla on a flat surface and add chicken, shredded cheese, and avocado to the end of the tortilla and roll. Place each tortilla seam-side down in the dish. Repeat until all tortillas and filling are used up. Pour the remaining sauce over the enchiladas. Cover with leftover cheese and bake for about 20 minutes or until cheese is bubbling.

## Chicken and Broccoli Au Gratin

390 A different chicken dish. I clipped this recipe from a PET milk ad about 20 years ago.

Posted by: WyomingDoglover. Yield: 6 servings. Prep time: about 1 hour.

---

1/4 cup butter
1/4 cup diced onion
1/4 cup plain flour
1 teaspoon salt
1/2 teaspoon curry powder
dash black pepper
4 ounces canned mushrooms
one 13-ounce can PET evaporated milk
10 ounces frozen broccoli, cooked and drained
2 to 3 cups chicken, cooked and diced
1 cup shredded Monterey Jack cheese

Preheat oven to 375 degrees F. Melt butter in skillet. Saute onion until transparent. Remove from heat and stir in flour, salt, curry powder and pepper. Drain mushrooms, reserving liquid. Add water to mushroom liquid to make 1/2 cup liquid. Gradually stir into flour mixture in skillet. Blend in evaporated milk until smooth. Add mushrooms. Cook and stir over medium heat until sauce begins to thicken. Place broccoli and chicken on bottom of ungreased 13 x 9 baking dish. Pour sauce over this and top with cheese. Bake for 20 minutes or until bubbly around edges. Cool 15 minutes before serving. I use broccoli florets. Adjust amount of curry according to how much you like.

## Lettuce Wraps

391 Easy to make and can be eaten one handed, just sayin'. I got this recipe from my cousin Staci, who is an amazing cook.

Posted by: Tammy al-Thor. Yield: Serves 4 dainty eaters, 2 normal people (allowing for some leftovers). Prep time: 10 minutes?

---

16 whole, firm lettuce leaves (Romaine, Boston, bibb or butter ; I prefer Romaine)
1/4 cup hoisin sauce
2 teaspoons minced fresh ginger (I don't care for ginger, so I skip this part and the recipe is still delicious)
2 tablespoons minced garlic (or as much as you dare; I use a lot more)
1 tablespoon rice vinegar
2 teaspoons Asian chili pepper sauce/paste (Sriracha is also fine and may be easier to find, but chili paste is pretty widely available)
1 tablespoon reduced-sodium soy sauce ( regular is fine if you can't find the reduced sodium sort)
1 can (8 ounce size) sliced water chestnuts, drained, finely chopped

1 teaspoon sesame oil (light is probably best, but dark is fine if that's all you can find)
1 pound ground chicken breast
1 bunch green onions, thinly sliced
2/3 cup fresh mushrooms (optional)

Rinse lettuce leaves, keeping them whole. Set aside to drain. Mix together hoisin sauce, ginger, garlic, vinegar, chili paste, and soy sauce; set aside. (I usually make this up a few hours ahead, so the flavors really develop, but you don't need to.) Cook water chestnuts in oil for about 2 minutes. Stir in chicken until well mixed; cook thoroughly. Add sauce, stir until combined and heated through. Add green onions, cook until they begin to wilt, about 2 minutes. Spoon meat mixture in center of lettuce leaves and enjoy!

***Chef's Notes:***
Thor and I are far too refined to eat that which has been scraped off the moldy forest floor, but all y'all hinky fungi eaters can cook 2/3 of a cup of fresh mushrooms in the oil first for 2 minutes, then add the water chestnuts and cook for 2 minutes, then continue as per instructions.

## Dorito Chicken Casserole

392 Easy and good Mexican-style dish. I found this recipe online but I cannot remember where or when . . . that's a song, isn't it?

Posted by: Deplorable Jewells45. Yield: 4 – 5 servings. Prep time: 20 minutes.

---

3 cups shredded cooked chicken
2 cups shredded cheddar cheese
1 can cream of chicken soup
1/2 cup milk
1/2 cup sour cream
1 can Rotel tomatoes
1/2 pack taco seasoning
Dorito chips
diced tomatoes, green onions, lettuce (optional)

Preheat oven to 350 degrees F. In a large bowl mix chicken, 1 cup of the cheese, the soup, milk, sour cream, Rotel and taco seasoning. Layer Dorito chips on bottom of 9" x 13" casserole dish. Top with half the chicken mixture, add another layer of chips and then remaining mixture. Top with the rest of the cheese. Cover and bake 30 minutes. Top with diced tomatoes, green onions, lettuce, etc. I have also used regular tortilla chips and it tasted just as fantastic. I don't use the whole bag of chips as I think that's a little bit much.

## Connie's Lemon Chicken

393 Easy and fast. Like Connie! This is a recipe my mom has been knocking out of the park for four-plus decades. No idea where she got it.

Posted by: Tony Menendez. Yield: 6 servings. Prep time: one hour.

---

1/4 cup canola oil
1/2 cup fresh lemon juice
2 tablespoons finely chopped onion
1/2 teaspoon salt
1 teaspoon pepper
1/2 teaspoon thyme
6 chicken breasts
flour for dusting the chicken

Preheat oven to 350 degrees F. Dust chicken breasts with flour and brown them on the stovetop. Place chicken breasts in baking dish. Drizzle oil over chicken, then sprinkle remainder of ingredients evenly over the chicken. Cover tightly with foil. Bake 45 minutes. Receive accolades. This dish is best when the recipe is followed to the letter. We have tried various modifications, deletions, additions, etc. over the years and this original recipe is the best by far.

## Thanksgiving Turkey, Dressing, and Gravy

394 Thanksgiving turkey, dressing, and gravy. My favorite meal is my father's Thanksgiving. The recipe is an amalgam of various twists and turns that he has added over the years. Several years back, I spent a Thanksgiving watching and writing down everything he did. I think this is a recipe that even aficionados can appreciate but is truly meant for the moron who wants to host their first Thanksgiving, but feels overwhelmed by the notion of doing so.

Posted by: JT in KC. Yield: servings for 15 morons. Prep time: 3 hours.

---

10 pounds frozen whole turkey or turkey breast
3 tablespoons salt
1 tablespoon dried rosemary
3 heads of garlic
3 large onions
2 lemons
1 apple
2 heads of celery
baby carrots
fresh thyme
fresh bay leaves
fresh rosemary
ground poultry seasoning
olive oil
1 stick (8 ounces) + 2 tablespoons butter
2 packages of stuffing (the 14-ounce Pepperidge Farm will do)
dried rosemary
cinnamon sticks
large turkey stock (chicken stock if they don't have it)

1 – 2 eggs
1 cup half and half
2 tablespoons flour
fresh ginger (one piece of ginger root)
package of bacon
Worcestershire sauce
fresh sage
2 – 3 packs of frozen pork sausage (with sage)

Defrost the turkey in the refrigerator on a platter starting a few days ahead. Two days before cooking, mix salt with dried rosemary. Rub the turkey cavity and outside with the mixture. Then wrap turkey in plastic wrap. One day before cooking, unwrap the turkey. On the day of cooking, place garlic bulbs (don't need to peel), onion slices, lemon slices, celery stalks, ¼ of the apple, a few carrots, fresh thyme, fresh rosemary, bay leaves, and 2 cinnamon sticks in both end of the turkey cavity, then sprinkle poultry season in cavities. Use cheese cloth and pins to seal both ends of cavity. Rub olive oil on top of turkey, squeeze lemons over turkey, and sprinkle turkey with salt, pepper and poultry seasoning.

Have oven at 450 degrees F and roast turkey for 45 minutes. Take out of oven and pour a melted stick of butter over the turkey. Place 5 slices of bacon on top of the turkey. In the bottom of the roasting pan, place some celery stalks, unpeeled garlic, onion quarters, ginger (cut into pieces), bay leaves, rosemary, thyme, sage, cinnamon sticks, the rest of the apple, and about 8 – 10 baby carrots. This is in addition to what you already put in the cavities of the turkey. Lower the oven temperature to 325 degrees F and put turkey back in. Take the turkey out every 20 minutes, baste, and take the temperature. Once the internal temperature of the turkey is 150 degrees, put foil loosely over turkey. Continue cooking the turkey breast to 165 degrees F (if you are doing a whole turkey then the thighs need to be 185 degrees). Once the turkey is done, transfer turkey to aluminum pan, place foil over, use an old blanket to cover it and keep it warm.

For the dressing: chop one large onion and brown onion in frying pan with ¼ stick (2 tablespoons) of butter. Peel the backsides of 5 celery stalks (like a carrot) and chop up. Then add celery to frying pan until soft. Add 4 sage leaves, 4 sprigs of thyme and crush in 4 garlic cloves towards the end. Remove this mixture from frying pan and put on a plate. Cook the (thawed) pork sausage in frying pan (use a paper towel to soak up excess fat). Once pork is cooked, mix the pork and vegetable mix in a large aluminum pan. If using the 14 ounce Pepperidge Farms stuffing, add about 1 to 1 1/2 packages (to your desired consistency) to the pork and vegetables. Combine 1 to 2 beaten eggs, 1 teaspoon of salt, 1/2 teaspoon pepper, 2 teaspoons poultry seasoning, 1 tablespoon Worcestershire sauce and 1 cup of stock. Pour this mixture over the stuffing and mix well. Bake in oven at 325 degrees F while the turkey is cooking. Cover at the start but uncover towards the end to crisp the top. Add some additional stock if it looks like it is drying out. You can add 2 tablespoons of honey and 1/2 cup of white wine to mixture while cooking (optional). Cover with foil and wrap in an old blanket to keep warm when done.

For the gravy: take the pan juices from the turkey roast and put in a bowl after pouring through a strainer. After it cools, skim off the top layer of fat. Take 2 tablespoons of flour and 2 tablespoons of butter; heat together in pan to make a roux under low/medium heat. Add the strained (and skimmed) pan juices to the roux. Mix in 1 cup half and half; add more if necessary. Whisk gravy in the heated pan until thick.

# Champagne Chicken

395 Two burner meal that looks classy, but isn't. My father taught me this to impress a woman with my culinary skills. It worked. She never cooked anything . . . .

Posted by: MrScience. Yield: 4 servings. Prep time: 30 minutes.

---

- 4 bonesless, skinless chicken boobs
- 1 bottle (750 ml) cheap champagne (see Note 1)
- 1 bag (8 ounces) washed spinach (see Note 2)
- 1 pound pasta (see Note 3)
- 1/4 cup flour
- 1/2 teaspoon fresh ground pepper
- 1 tablespoon olive oil

Put water on stove in a large pot to boil the noodles. (Covering pot makes water boil faster because water molecules are sneaky that way.) Heat oil over medium-high in frying pan large enough for all four chicken hooters. Mix pepper and flour together as well as possible and then put on a dinner plate in thin layer. One at a time, coat both sides of chicken bazongas in flour-pepper mixture and then place into hot oil. Move often to avoid sticking to pan, flip after four minutes or so. Chicken is done when internal temperature reaches 165 degrees F (or 75 degrees C for people with funny-colored money) which should be at 8 – 10 minutes. Water should be boiling by now; if not stop looking at it. (A watched pot never, etc.) When it boils add noodles and cook according to directions. Lower heat in frying pan to simmer. Immediately pop champagne and add whole bottle to pan. If whole bottle doesn't fit, either chug what's left or pour in pan after minute or two passes, when the alcohol boils off. Let this simmer for at least 10 minutes. It will thicken with time to a consistency of light cream. Stir occasionally to bring up flavorful bits from bottom of frying pan. Drain pasta and toss bag of spinach in with hot noodles. It will wilt very quickly. Toss noodles to mix with pasta. Put pasta in four portions on plates. Serve chicken chi-chis over pasta and spoon pan sauce over each portion.

ote 1: This really is best with very cheap champagne. Having made it with an expensive bottle, it turned out no better than with cheap bubbly.

Note 2: You can use unwashed spinach bunches, you hippy, you, in which case you need to stem the bigger leaves. Wash well to remove sand. There is a LOT of sand in unwashed spinach.

Note 3: This works best with flat noodles: fettuccine, farfalle, campanelle, even wide egg noodles.

Final Note: I don't add salt because I was always told to let the consumer add it to taste.

## Keyser's Healthier Chulent

396 A healthier version of a traditional Ashkenazi Jewish Sabbath dish. This dish traditionally is prepared on Friday afternoon and allowed to slow cook until Saturday lunch since cooking itself, including turning on appliances, adjusting temperatues, and even mixing food that is cooking on a fire, is prohibited on the Jewish Sabbath for those who keep Jewish law. Chulent is a traditional Ashkenazi Jewish staple. I have a general knowledge of what it is composed of without referencing a specific recipe. I modified the traditional ingredients used and made up my own spice blend to make a healthier version.

Posted by: Keyser. Yield: 4 servings. Prep time: 25 minutes.

---

8 ounces dry black beans
8 ounces pearled barley
1 1/4 pounds chicken breast fillet
15 ounces tomato sauce
1 – 2 ounces Frank's Red Hot sauce
garlic powder to taste
onion powder to taste
chili powder to taste
black pepper to taste
paprika to taste
turmeric to taste
enough water to cover food

You will need a crockpot. For lunch: Soak black beans in water overnight. After overnight soak, the next afternoon/evening, place beans and barley in crockpot. Chop chicken breast into cubes and add to crockpot. Sprinkle liberal amounts of garlic powder, onion powder, chili powder, black pepper, paprika, and turmeric into crockpot. Add tomato sauce to crockpot (generic canned tomato sauce, not pasta sauce from a jar). Add Franks Red Hot sauce (or equivalent such as Tabasco sauce) to taste (more = spicier). Mix ingredients together. Add water to cover ingredients with about 1 centimeter extra water over top of ingredients (this is not an exact science and trial and error will yield the proper amount). Turn crockpot on to high setting. Serve for lunch next day. I use the 6 quart Crockpot brand crockpot without any bells or whistles (no electronic display, just a switch between off, warm, high, and low).

## Chicken Baked with Beans and Tomatoes

397 Original recipe was from *Gourmet* in December 2004.

Posted by: Ann Fitzgerald. Yield: 6 to 8 servings. Prep time: 35 minutes.

---

6 to 8 bacon slices, cut up
3 pounds chicken thighs, bone in or boneless
2 to 3 onions, chopped
2 large cans tomatoes, chopped

2 to 3 cans white beans, rinsed and drained
salt and pepper
2 or more jalapenos, chopped

Preheat oven to 350 degrees F. Have husband brown seasoned chicken on grill. Cook bacon in cast iron Dutch oven or skillet. Pour off some of grease. Brown onions, stir in chopped tomatoes and jalapenos. Add salt and pepper to taste. Stir in beans and chicken. Bake uncovered until chicken is done.

***Chef's Notes:***
Chicken can be browned in skillet. You can use legs, wings, etc. also. Add pintos with or in place of white beans.

## Chicken a la King

398 It's an absolute favorite of ours that comes from my wife's family.

Posted by: BCochran1981. Yield: 4 – 6 servings. Prep time: 30 minutes.

---

8 mushrooms
1 green pepper
4-ounce jar of chopped pimientos
16 ounces heavy whipping cream
1 1/2 pounds cooked chicken
2 cups chicken broth
1/2 cup flour
1/2 cup butter
black pepper
garlic salt
cooked white rice

Dice mushrooms and green pepper. Melt butter in pan, cook mushrooms for 3 to 4 minutes. Add green pepper, black pepper, garlic salt. Increase heat to medium high, cook for 1 to 2 minutes. Sprinkle in the flour. Stir in broth, then stir in half of the cream. Let stand 1 to 2 minutes and let heat through. Add other half of cream and continue stirring. Add chicken; let cook until mixture begins to boil. At boiling, remove from heat, add pimento. Serve over rice.

## Javanese Chicken

399 From my mother.

Posted by: aelf. Yield: 4 servings. Prep time: 1 hour.

---

- 1 chicken, cut in pieces
- 1 cup cornstarch
- 2 teaspoons salt
- 1 teaspoon ground black pepper (optional)
- olive oil (for browning chicken)
- 1 medium onion, chopped
- 1 large bell pepper, cut in large pieces
- 1 teaspoon minced garlic (optional)
- 1 ounce soy sauce
- ¼ cup chunky peanut butter
- 1 ½ teaspoons ground ginger (optional)
- 1 15-ounce can pineapple chunks in heavy syrup
- 2 cups water

Mix cornstarch, salt, and black pepper (if using). Coat chicken in cornstarch mixture. In a large pot, brown chicken in oil, then set aside. Add onion, bell pepper, and garlic and cook lightly (until the onion has yellowed). Add chunky peanut butter; when softened, blend in soy sauce, ginger, and water until you have a light to medium sauce. Add pineapple chunks and syrup; when mixed, return browned chicken to pot and cover. Simmer until chicken is tender, 30 to 45 minutes. Serve over rice. If preferred, 4 chicken breasts can be substituted for the chicken pieces.

## Chicken Scarpariello "Publius"

400 Classsic Italian baked chicken and sausages—*Abbondanza*! A standby recipe in the Redux house is a recipe for chicken and sausage (sometimes called chicken scarpariello) which is based upon the recipes from the Italian side of the Redux family. This is a dish that feeds a bunch of people and feeds them well. It is also flavorful and makes the whole house smell fantastic AND is made with simple ingredients. It also lends itself to personalization. So feel free to make your own version—there are as many versions of this dish as there are Italian households. Enjoy.

Posted by: Publius Redux. Yield: 6 to 8 servings. Prep time: 2 to 3 hours.

---

- 4 chicken thighs (with bones/skin)
- 1 split chicken breast (with bones/skin) cut in half
- 6 sweet Italian pork sausages
- 1 tablespoon olive oil
- 1/4 cup dry white wine
- 1 tablespoon apple cider vinegar
- juice of 1/2 lemon
- 1 medium-sized onion, peeled, halved and cut into 1/4 inch wide slivers
- 2 large cloves of garlic, peeled and sliced
- 1 small to medium sweet red bell pepper, cored and sliced into strips
- 1 green apple, cored, peeled and sliced
- 1 teaspoon brown sugar
- 1 tablespoon of pignoli nuts (or substitute walnuts or pecans)
- 3 – 4 cremini mushrooms, sliced (or one portobello mushroom)
- 2 bay leaves
- 1 tablespoon chopped fresh parsley
- ½ tablespoon chopped oregano
- 1 tablespoon chopped rosemary
- ½ teaspoon thyme (whole leaves)
- 1 ½ teaspoons salt
- ½ teaspoon cracked pepper

½ teaspoon paprika

Preheat oven to 350 degrees F. In a large cast iron Dutch oven (or any other cast iron fryer or pan that can be placed in the oven covered and baked) place the olive oil to coat the pan. On medium to high heat on the stove brown the sausages. Remove from heat and place on side. Next, brown the chicken well. When the chicken is brown, return the sausages to the pan and put the heat up to high. When everything starts to sizzle add the white wine and cook until the wine is about ¾ reduced. Reduce the heat to low and add the vinegar and the lemon. Then add the rest of the ingredients and the herbs and spices in the order given above. You can toss them on randomly but most of the vegetables should be between the meats on the pan bottom. The meats themselves should all be on the pan bottom as well, with no overlapping. Cover the pot and place in the hot oven, reducing the temperature immediately to 300 degrees F. Bake for one hour and 20 minutes, basting only one time. Then uncover and increase heat to 325 degrees F. Bake for 30 minutes, making sure to add liquid and baste frequently (do not let this dish dry out—it is meant to be juicy! But also the meats should not be submerged, they should be surrounded by liquid with the top of the meat well exposed so the chicken skin and sausages get browned). This is also a good time to taste the liquid, as well, and add salt and pepper as required and to your taste. When the chicken is brown and crispy on top (again it should take about ½ an hour or so but your time may vary) remove and serve with separately prepared white (Raaaacist!) rice (or you may add 3 to 4 large, cubed white-skinned (Raaaacist!) potatoes to the dish after all the other ingredients and before placing in the oven).

***Chef's Notes:***

The meat should fall off the bone and be juicy and the sauce loaded with vegetables and richness. You may skim the fat of the top of the juice before serving if looking to lower your fat intake. I also sometimes add broccoli di rape (rape culture!) to this dish as well for a lovely splash of green (so you get red, green, and white for an Italian Tricolore). Or you can throw in 2 cups of baby spinach before you put the pot into the oven. Please always try to use fresh herbs and spices if you can. Serve with a dry Italian white such as a Gavi for true Italian experience. *Cent Anni!*

## Artichoke Chicken

401 My mom got this recipe from her late friend, Missy Uhlich, back in the early '70's. I've adapted it somewhat.

Posted by: California Girl. Yield: about 4 servings. Prep time: an hour or so.

---

1 chicken fryer, cut up OR 4 pounds chicken pieces
1/2 cup vegetable oil
flour
1/2 teaspoon dried thyme
1/2 teaspoon rosemary
seasoning salt
pepper

1/2 pound sliced mushrooms
1 small jar marinated artichoke hearts
1/2 cup dry white wine
1 can black olives

Preheat oven to 350 degrees F. Clean chicken and pat dry. Heat oil in large frying pan until shimmering. Flour chicken and fry until golden brown. While browning, season chicken with the herbs and salt and pepper to taste. Remove chicken from pan and place in roaster. Sprinkle with mushrooms. Cut artichoke hearts in half and add them with their liquid to the chicken. Pour wine over all. (Water can be substituted for the wine, if preferred.) Cover and bake for about 45 minutes or until chicken is tender. Baste every 15 minutes. Add drained olives the last 15 minutes.

## Tired Bachelor Chicken 'n Peppers

402 Minimalistic baked chicken and peppers, and some onions. Made it up myself in a flash of laziness. This makes quite a bit of meat with a small amount of veggies, so it would go well with a side dish of some kind. You could also cut up the meat into chunks before cooking and add it to noodles or rice.

Posted by: Grey Fox. Yield: 1 serving. Prep time: 25 minutes.

---

1 chicken breast
3 sweet peppers
dried onion to taste
garlic to taste
Supreme poutry seasoning to taset
1 jalapeno pepper (optional)

Cook the chicken breast in a covered dish—I tend to put it in frozen with a bit of water at the bottom and cook it on "medium" until it is thawed and then turn up the heat and cook the chicken, still covered, until it is cooked through as measured with a meat thermometer. As it cooks it will periodically run low on water, at which point you can add water or let it go dry and sear a bit before adding more. In any case you end up with a bit of broth at the bottom of the pan by the time the chicken is cooked. Clean and cut up the sweet peppers (I use small ones, but larger ones would be fine, I'm sure), and when the chicken is done throw the peppers, onion, and garlic (I never measure, so use your discretion) into the pan and let them saute until done. I add the poultry seasoning at this point, too—I don't really know what is in it but it adds just a bit of sweetness. When everything has cooked for awhile, long enough to blend the flavors a bit, spoon everything onto a plate and eat in front of your computer while reading AoS.

## Chicken Banana Curry

403 A tasty one-dish meal. It's original! I thought it up!

Posted by: Oaktownette. Yield: 2 or 3 servings. Prep time: 20 – 25 minutes.

---

4 boneless, skinless chicken thighs
2 bananas
6 ounces coconut milk (canned)
2 tablespoons curry powder (use the best masala/mix you can get)
1/2 cup chopped onions
2 tablespoons cooking oil
cooked rice for serving

Start your rice cooking. Chop the onion. Peel the bananas and split each of them lengthwise, then cut them into half moons. Cut the chicken thighs into bite-size pieces. Saute the onion in the cooking oil until nearly translucent. Add the chicken thighs and spices and saute till the chicken is nearly cooked, stirring to coat it with the spices. Add the banana, stir, and cook till they start to soften. Add the coconut milk, stir, and saute till the spices blend with it and make a sauce. Serve over cooked rice.

***Chef's Notes:***
If you can, get a spice mix from an Indian/Pakistani food store, or online. If you must use supermarket "curry powder," choose Madras or something else specialty. Basmati rice is best.

## Chicken and Grits Dinner

404 Quick and tasty casserole. Basic grits recipe from back of Bob's Red Mill grits. Rest is from personal trials.

Posted by: PicklePete. Yield: 6 servings. Prep time: 20 minutes.

---

1 1/2 cups grits (Bob's Red Mill)
4 1/2 cups water
1/4 teaspoon salt
1 1/2 cups cooked chopped chicken
1/2 cup BBQ sauce
3/4 cup cheddar cheese
4 tablespoons butter

Preheat oven to 350 degrees F. Bring all of the water to a boil in a saucepan. Add the salt and grits. Drop the heat to low. After 5 minutes, remove from the heat. Add the butter and stir until mixed in. Bring out an 8 x 8 casserole dish. Spread two-thirds of the cooked grits on the bottom of the dish. Next, add all of the chicken on top, then add the BBQ sauce. Make sure the chicken and BBQ sauce are evenly distributed. Sprinkle with 1/2 cup of cheese. Top with the remaining grits. If you have a little leftover grits, it is ok. Stop adding grits once it is covered. Top with the remaining cheese. Place in the oven on the top rack until the cheese is brown. It will take 5 – 8 minutes.

***Chef's Notes:***
If you prefer rubs to BBQ sauce, great, just go light on the seasoning. Any leftover meat works well; we use rotisserie chicken leftovers. Chop meat into small pieces.

## JCP's Famous Greek Hobo Dumpling

405 I did this.

Posted by: Gentlemen, This is democracy manifest. Yield: servings for 5 Morons. Prep time: 25 minutes.

---

1 pound ricotta cheese
8 ounces frozen peas
5/8 pound chicken breast (huh huh huh . . .)
1 pack filo dough
2 egg
1 onion
1 teaspoon cinnamon
1 teaspoon basil flakes
2 tablespoons parsley flakes
salt and pepper to taste
8 ounces (1 stick) butter

Mince the onion. Slice up the chicken to bite-sized pieces. Stick every thing in a bowl and mix. Use your own judgment on salt, pepper, and other flavorings, but don't overdo it—we are going for a subtle savory with nothing overpowering. Lay out three sheets of filo and brush with butter (keep rest of pack covered to prevent drying). Cut filo into four strips longways. Place dollop of mix on end of each strip and roll up like a paper football. Now you know your dollop was too big, so adjust for next one. Place on cookie sheet, and brush with butter. When all done, brush with more butter and cook at 350 degrees F for 30 minutes, or until nicely browned.

## Bluebell's Chicken

406 I have yet to meet the person that doesn't like this. My mom used to make this, and she never measured a thing. So I don't measure anything, and none of you better either because if you do, it won't taste right and then you'll all come crying to me. All right, I feel bad, so I've given you some approximate measurements. *Approximate.*

Posted by: bluebell. Yield: 4 – 6 servings. Prep time: 5 minutes, tops.

---

8 chicken thighs, with bones and skin still on
8 teaspoons olive oil
½ cup lemon juice
1 – 2 teaspoons dried oregano
1 teaspoon garlic powder
salt and pepper to taste

Put the chicken pieces in a 13 x 9 baking pan, drizzle with the olive oil, and pour a fair amount of lemon juice over top, about a tablespoon per piece, but DON'T MEASURE! The lemon juice can either be fresh-squeezed, or from a bottle; it will be good either way. It's impossible to mess up this recipe. Sprinkle with oregano, garlic powder, and salt and pepper. Don't skimp on any of those, and if you please, use only garlic powder, not fresh garlic, or you'll ruin it. Bake at 375 degrees F for about 45 minutes or so, until the skin is nice and brown and it looks like something you'd like to eat. Serve with rice to soak up the juices, or if you're feeling decadent, with mashed potatoes. And eat every bit of that skin.

## One Pot Moron Ghetto Dinner

407 Made at all the finest SRO's. I created this.

Posted by: Gentlemen, This is democracy manifest. Yield: 1 serving. Prep time: 25 minutes.

---

2 potatoes
2 – 4 chicken legs
1 apple
1 ear of corn
1/2 cup flour
1/2 cup light brown sugar
1 tablespoon cinnamon
1/2 teaspoon nutmeg
1 teaspoon vanilla
3/4 stick (6 tablespoons) butter

Go to Walmart and buy one of those $20 electric skillets with the glass lid. Yes, I have all the expensive Williams-Sonoma crap too, but nothing works as good for a slow, even cook as these electric aluminum non stick skillets. Put pat of butter under chicken skin, and sprinkle both sides of each leg with salt and pepper. Place in one corner of skillet. Chop up potatoes. I prefer 1/4" batonnet cut (sticks). Place in skillet as a berm or dam around the chicken. Slice up apple and put in corner opposite the chicken. This is dessert and we do not want it contaminated. Put corn wherever it fits. You can substitute any vegetable you like, if you like any vegetables. Baby carrots work well. Stick some butter on veggies and apple. Salt and pepper the potato. Cook in skillet at low setting (225 to 250 degrees F or so, lower than you would think) with glass cover on at all times. While cooking, prepare the apple crumb mix: combine flour, brown sugar, 1/2 stick (4 tablespoons) butter, cinnamon, nutmeg, vanilla, salt to taste.) This will be enough for several apples, but make it all and you can use it again tomorrow. After 10 minutes, rotate the chicken and corn, and flip the veggies. Add crumb mix to apple. After 10 more minutes, flip everything again and check how everything is cooking. Should be all done in about 30 minutes. The skin should pull away from the bone on the chicken. The potato should be cooked through with some browning on bottom. Apple should be soft with the topping hard and crunchy.

These skillets are not too accurate, but they are consistent so you may have to adjust temperature to get it where you want. This has to be a slow cook to give the moisture a chance to boil out through that little hole in the lid, and to give everything time to cook. If it cooks too quick it will not brown due to water in the pan. This works because the chicken fat and butter flavor the potato. You can substitute pork chops for the chicken, but the potato will not taste as good. And when you eat it, use a dish, dammit! If you try to eat from the skillet you will scratch the non stick surface.

## Sour Cream & Mushroom Chicken

408 Chicken with mushrooms and sour cream My mama made this for me, and it is good. Every time I made this for teh ladies, we ended up knockin' the boots. Wash your freakin' mitts before making this. This is my Mama's recipe and it deserves better than your Cheetoh dust encased paws ruining it.

Posted by: Ashley Judd's Puffy Scamper. Yield: 4 servings. Prep time: 60 minutes.

---

4 boneless chicken breasts
1 can cream of mushroom soup
8 ounces chicken broth
8 ounces sour cream
1 package dried beef
4 – 6 cups prepared rice

Preheat oven to 325 American degrees. Mix soup, broth and sour cream in a mixing bowl. Line an 8 x 8 glass dish with the dried beef. Place boneless chicken breasts on top of dried beef, and then pour the soup/broth/sour cream mix over the chicken. Place in oven and bake for 45 to 60 minutes. Remove and serve over the rice. You can substitute egg noodles for the rice if you choose to do so.

# *Pork*

## Italian-Style Slow-Roasted Pork Roast

409 Cook as roast; use leftovers for sandwiches, with rice, etc. Recipe from Wegmans grocery store (*Menu* magazine and at wegmans.com).

Posted by: JTB and Mrs. JTB   Yield: 8 servings.   Prep time: active time: 30 minutes; marinate time: 8 to 10 hours; total time: 15 – 18 hours.

---

3 small onions, peeled, halved, and sliced
2 navel oranges, unpeeled, sliced
7 – 10 pounds pork shoulder
6 cloves peeled garlic, minced
1 tablespoon fennel seeds
Salt and cracked black pepper to taste

Day before: combine onion and orange slices in roasting pan. Diagonally score fat-side (top) of pork about ¾-inch deep in a diamond pattern. Rub garlic, then fennel seeds into top of pork. Season well with salt and pepper. Place pork on top of onion and orange slices. Cover with plastic wrap; refrigerate overnight.

Day of meal: preheat oven to 275 degrees F. Remove plastic wrap. Bake uncovered, 7 – 8 hours. (Note: we cook the roast for an extra hour or two to make the top extra crispy. Watch carefully so it doesn't burn or get charred.) Remove from oven; carefully place roast on clean platter and allow to rest. As roast rests, ladle hot juices into gravy separator. Reserve de-fatted juices (au jus); keep warm. Reserve onions if desired. Serve au jus with pork. This roast can be served as sliced meat, chopped, or shredded with forks.

## Pork Chops and Taters

410 Damn fine easy dinner. This one is mine, but I've seen similar elsewhere.

Posted by: tcn.   Yield: 6 servings.   Prep time: 20 minutes.

---

6 pork chops, any cut
oil to brown chops
1 mess potatoes, as many as you like
1 large onion, chopped
1/2 pound bacon, cooked and chopped
1/2 pound shredded cheese, I like cheddar
1/2 cup milk
garlic salt
salt and pepper to taste

2 tablespoons flour
bread crumbs (optional)

Use a mandoline to finely slice the potatoes. Leave the skins on. Then layer the pototoes in a casserole with the onion, bacon and cheese. I use a very large glass roaster for this one, but any casserole with a lid will do. Sprinkle the chops with garlic salt to taste. Brown the chops in a hot pan with a little oil, but just until they are brown. Put the chops on top of the casserole. Whisk the milk with the flour, salt and pepper (adjust seasoning to the amount of potatoes), and pour it over the top of everything. You can sprinkle this with bread crumbs but I find that dries out the pork chops. Put on the cover and bake this in a 375 degree F oven for about 2 1/2 hours, until the potatoes are nice and tender.

***Chef's Notes:***

If you have a beagle, do not leave this on the bottom shelf of the refrigerator for left overs. Let's just say she didn't need another meal for about a week, and I miss the big glass roaster pan.

# Carnitas

411 Pulled pork, done Mexican-style. This is the family recipe for pork carnitas, modified a bit by yours truly. Just the thing for soft tacos or sliders. Previously published in The Official Manual for Spice Cadets.

Posted by: Karl Lembke. Yield: 10 servings. Prep time: 3½ hours.

---

5 pounds pork shoulder
oil to brown pork
2 teaspoons coriander seed, ground
1 onion, large, cut into quarters
12 – 20 ounces beer, canned, mass-market
2 heads garlic
1 teaspoon salt
lime (optional)

Heat your oven to 275 degrees F. (Alternatively, you can use a slow-cooker on "high".) Oil a large frying pan and brown the pork on all surfaces. Once nicely seared, move the meat to a Dutch oven or similar cast-iron pot. Pour half a cup or so of beer into the frying pan and use a spatula to scrape the browned bits and juices from the bottom of the pan. Pour this over the meat, and pour in the rest of the can of beer. Sprinkle the salt and coriander powder over the meat and drop the pieces of onion into the pot. Cover and cook until meat can be shaken off of the bones, some 2 to 3 hours. Transfer the meat to a casserole dish, remove the bones, and shred the meat into small pieces. Chop the garlic very finely. (Real morons should remember to separate the garlic cloves from the heads and peel them first!) Sprinkle over the top of the shredded pork and place under a hot broiler until the top layer is slightly crispy, about 5 minutes. If extra crispness is desired, stir and repeat. It is now ready to devour . . . er . . . serve. It may need additional salt, or a squeeze of lime.

***Chef's Notes:***
Use a mass-market "chugging" beer such as Bud or Coors. A craft beer would either overpower the dish or be wasted.

## Garlic Eggplant and Pork

412 It's garlic, eggplant, and pork. What more do you want? A form of this recipe for Pajama Boy can be found in *Best of Food & Wine 1997*, page 321. It lacks pork and uses an Asian wine instead of English gin.

Posted by: Stephen Price Blair. Yield: 4 servings. Prep time: 40 minutes.

---

1 tablespoon soy sauce
2 teaspoons oyster sauce
2 teaspoons sugar
1 teaspoon cornstarch
2 ½ tablespoons water
1 teaspoon white vinegar
½ teaspoon Bombay Sapphire (gin)
2 teaspoons chopped jalapeno
¼ teaspoon salt
1 pound eggplant
1½ teaspoons peanut oil
½ pound ground pork (or ground chicken, beef, or whatever meat you choose)
3 teaspoons minced garlic

Dissolve the cornstarch into one tablespoon of the water. Combine soy sauce, oyster sauce, sugar, dissolved corn starch, vinegar, gin, jalapeno, and salt in a small bowl, mixing well. Slice the eggplants lengthwise, about half-an-inch thick, and then cut the slices into about half-inch-wide strips. Steam the eggplant until tender, about 25 minutes. Heat the peanut oil in a large pan. Stir-fry ground pork until done. Add the garlic and stir-fry a few seconds, until golden. Add the eggplant and remaining water; cook until the eggplant begins to fall apart, which will only take about three to five minutes. Stir the sauce into the eggplant and cook until bubbling and thick, about two to four minutes. You may substitute ground chicken, beef, or whatever meat you wish for the ground pork.

## Big V's Pork Loin and Zucchini

413 Low-salt pork loin that still packs in the yum. My own recipe made up due to low-salt diet and a huge crop of zucchini.

Posted by: Big V. Yield: variable. Prep time: about an hour.

---

pork loin, 4 ounces per person
olive oil, 1 tablespoon per person
fresh peeled zucchini, 4 ounces per person
apple cider vinegar, 1 ounce per person
cumin, 1/8 teaspoon per person
coriander, 1/8 teaspoon per person
mustard seed, 1/8 teaspoon per person
Vidalia onion, 1 ounce per person
coconut oil (or bacon fat)
Mrs. Dash Garlic & Herb Seasoning
1 slice apple per person

Peel and cut the zucchini and the onion into disks and place in a ziplock bag with the olive oil, apple cider vinegar, cumin, coriander and mustard seed. Put in the fridge for at least 30 minutes. Put enough coconut oil in your cast iron pan to coat the bottom and bring to a medium high heat. Brush the pork loin with olive oil and dust with the Mrs Dash. Using tongs, get a good sear on all 4 sides of the pork then move to a cutting board for 1 minute. Remove the pan from heat and put the veggie cider mix in it. Note this will make a good deal of smoke and a strong cider smell so either do this on a outdoor grill or have a good kitchen fan. Watch the onions, stirring them as needed for about 10 minutes, then cover the veggies. Slice the apple and set it aside. Slice the pork loin into disks and place on top of the veggie mix, then put the apple on top of the pork. Bring the heat back up to low, cover and cook for 30 minutes. To plate the dish, put the zucchini disks on the bottom, then a pork loin disk, then a bit of onion and an apple slice on top of the pork. Serve 3 or 4 disks per person depending on how thick you made your slices. If salt is not an issue for you, use bacon fat instead of coconut oil.

## Pork Pie (Tourtiere)

414 This recipe is mine.

Posted by: Artisanal ette. Yield: 4 – 6 servings. Prep time: 2 hours total.

---

2 pounds of ground pork (at least one pound of ground pork and the other half ground beef, or ground veal and ground beef)
1 - 2 teaspoons salt
½ teaspoon ground black pepper
¼ - ½ teaspoon nutmeg
1/8 – ¼ teaspoon mace (use this sparingly and to taste)
pinch of dry sage (optional)
small pinch dry thyme, ground or leaves (optional)
pinch dry mustard (optional)
small pinch of allspice (optional)
1 – 2 tablespoons cornstarch (you need to adjust depending on the juiciness of meat if very fatty ground beef used, for example)
1 ½ - 2 cups water (or broth)
1 medium to large onion
2 – 3 garlic cloves
2 tablespoons or so of vegetable oil (I use canola for this)
Pastry for a 2-crust pie (adjust recipe for deep dish pie if making 2 pounds meat mixture)

Add the pork/meats, seasonings, cornstarch and water or broth to a large saucepan or stock pot. Cover and simmer for about 30 minutes. Uncover and cook for about 10 20 minutes more (this depends on how much moisture is left. You do not want it too soupy and some will bake out, but you want your pie to be sturdy to cut after it bakes). Meanwhile, preheat oven to 425 degrees F. Divide pastry dough; roll out half and line pie dish. Roll out second half of dough in preparation of sealing pie. Saute the onion and garlic in a separate pan or small skillet until softened, but not browned. Add to meat mixture when it is done cooking on the stove-top. Pour the meat mixture into pie dish. Top with the second rolled out pastry dough; pinch the edges to seal, and prick top to allow steam to release. You can make small, fancy cut-outs if you like, in the center, and prick with a fork around the outer circle. Have fun with it. Bake the pie about 10 minutes at 425 degrees F, and then reduce the oven temperature to 350 degrees F for about 30 minutes longer. Serve hot with homemade sweet tomato relish or ketchup.

***Chef's Notes:***

These amounts are for one deep dish pie. For a regular 9" pie dish, cut recipe in half to 1 pound of meat; adjust seasonings to taste. This is a forgiving dish and there are many variations of spices and meat mixtures. Pork is key, and should be used for the full 1 pound or 2 pounds on your first try, to taste it. Many variations exist with the meat choices (shredded pork shoulder, or mixed with veal or ground beef, or other game meats, etc.), and also with the spice choices (nutmeg and mace are key in my opinion). Some will add potato, grated or mashed. I like it in its purest form of pork only, or at least 3/4 of the total meat mixture and 1/4 beef or veal. This recipe is the one I use the most and is the most simple to make, but it depends on what I have on hand. I do use all of the spices I list as optional. But you can use just the nutmeg and mace to simplify the flavor. For the piecrust, I use half lard and half butter with flour salt, and water. And, I do refrigerate until use.

## Spam Casserole

415 An artery clogging wonder! Original recipe came from my mother-in-law. I modified it over the years. This dish is extremely flexible, so play around with it. It's really great on a freezing winter night.

Posted by: Deplorable lady with a deplorable basket of deplorable cats. Yield: servings for 2 Morons, or 4 mini-Morons. Prep time: 1 1/2 hours.

---

2 tablespoons butter
onion to your taste
1 can Spam (or browned ground beef or diced ham)
1 jar Ragu Double Cheddar sauce
1 – 2 cups half and half
8 ounces (or more) rotini
salt and pepper to taste
French fried onions, to taste
1 can golden mushroom soup

Melt butter in skillet. Mince as much onion as you like (I like lots), and saute in melted butter. Dice Spam and toss into skillet with onions. Saute until onions are light brown and some of the Spam has browned. Meanwhile, combine Double Cheddar sauce, half and half, undiluted golden mushroom soup and uncooked rotini in round casserole dish. (You can vary the amount of half and half and rotini to accommodate the number of diners, which is why some of the amounts listed are so vague.) Season to taste with salt and pepper. When onions and Spam are browned to your liking, stir them into the rotini mixture. Place in 350 degree F oven on middle shelf—do not cover the casserole. Set timer for 30 minutes. At that point, slide casserole out of the oven long enough to give it a good stir and judge how much longer the rotini need to cook. I usually cook it about another 20 to 25 minutes. When you are satisfied with the doneness of the rotini, pull it out again and top with the French fried onions, again to your liking. (I sometimes use the whole package, and at other times just around half that amount.) Stick it back in the oven until the French onions are nice and toasted. Remove from oven and dig in. Variations: My mother-in-law used browned ground beef instead of Spam. I sometimes use diced ham instead of Spam.

## Easy Baked Pork Chops

416 Cajun seasoning-based chops. By sheer luck I found this in an Internet search and have used it for some time. It is easy and as far as I can tell impossible to screw up if you have a loud enough timer! I just wish I could actually get some of their meats! The recipe can be found on the Zweber Farms website—look for simple oven-baked pork chops.

Posted by: Hrothgar. Yield: variable. Prep time: about 30 minutes.

---

As many inch-thick pork chops as required
2 ½ tablespoons kosher salt
1 tablespoon dried oregano
1 tablespoon paprika
1/4 teaspoon onion powder
1/2 teaspoon dried sweet basil
1 tablespoon cayenne pepper
1 tablespoon fresh cracked black pepper
bacon grease

Preheat oven to 350 degrees F. Pat chops dry with paper towel, discard paper towel in an appropriate green recycling container. Mix dry ingredients to create the Cajun Seasoning. Note that this makes a lot of seasoning so have a storage jar handy for the extra as it keeps well. Personally I think this is too salty a mix so I cut back a bit on the salt to about 1 ½ tablespoons. I view this recipe as guidelines, matey, and I've experimented with seasoning salt, lemon pepper, cilantro, less cayenne pepper, etc. Line a baking pan with aluminum foil and swab down with bacon grease. I dust the chops fairly lightly with the seasoning and roll the edges in the excess before putting in baking pan. Put in oven, open a beer, turn chops once at 15 minutes, and remove at 20 – 30 minutes total (145 degrees on meat thermometer). I've found 28 minutes in my oven is about perfect! Let the chops rest for a few minutes before serving. Done. I always use boneless chops, but Zweber Farms recommends the bone-in (ribeye) cut which I really need to try.

## Tuscan Baby Back Ribs

417 Totally different and worth the effort. Found in a *Food & Wine* magazine years ago.

Posted by: Jane D'oh. Yield: 6 servings. Prep time: 3 hours, plus overnight brining.

---

2 cups water
¼ cup plus 3 tablespoons kosher salt
1/3 cup sugar
2 tablespoons cracked black peppercorns
2 tablespoons ground fennel seeds
1 tablespoon coriander seeds
2 teaspoons crushed juniper berries
2 teaspoons crumbled dried marjoram
4 bay leaves
1 head of garlic, halved horizontally
2 2-pound racks baby back ribs
6 cups cold water
4 large anchovy fillets, mashed
2 teaspoons minced garlic
6 tablespoons fresh lemon juice
1/2 cup olive oil, plus more for brushing
2 tablespoons chopped Italian parsley

Combine first ten ingredients (water through head of garlic) in a medium saucepan to make brine. Bring brine to a simmer, stirring, until the sugar dissolves. Arrange the racks in a single layer in a roasting pan just large enough to hold them. Add the brine and 6 cups of cold water. Cover and refrigerate overnight. (You can also use a jumbo Zip-lock bag instead of the roasting pan to marinate.) Preheat the oven to 325 degrees F. Drain and rinse the ribs and pat dry. Set the racks on a large, rimmed baking sheet in a single layer and cover with foil. Roast for about two hours, or until very tender. To make the dressing, in a large bowl, mash the anchovies with the minced garlic, then stir in the lemon juice. Add the ½ cup olive oil and parsley, reserve dressing. Light a grill, and brush the grate with olive oil. Grill the racks over medium hot fire for 5 minutes, turning occasionally, until crisp and browned. Transfer the racks to a cutting board and cut in between the ribs. Toss the ribs in the dressing and pile on a platter. Serve hot, warm, or at room temperature. Don't freak over the anchovies, and don't tell anyone they're in the dressing. No one will know and they'll devour the ribs like the mainstream media falling for an epic Trump trolling.

## Pork Chops with Apples, Onions & Cider

418 Great fall/winter dinner. This recipe came from the box of a Calphalon pan I bought—I've changed it slightly. Hope you enjoy it as much as we do!

Posted by: Toni. Yield: 4 servings Prep time: 10 minutes prep, 1 – 1 ½ hours cooking time.

---

6 pork chops (thick cut) (or chicken breasts)
1 1/2 teaspoons Bell's poultry seasoning
1/2 cup flour

3 tablespoons olive oil
5 Granny Smith apples, cored and sliced into 6 pieces
1 large Spanish onion sliced
2 cups apple cider
noodles (optional)

Preheat oven to 375 degrees F. Coat the pork chops with flour. Preheat oven-proof pan on medium heat. When the edges are hot to the touch, add olive oil, then place chops in pan and brown on both sides. When they're brown, turn off heat under pan and add the apples and onions. Sprinkle the poultry seasoning over the chops, apples and onions. Add the apple cider to the pan. Cover pan and place in oven. Bake for 30 minutes. Remove the cover and bake for an additional 30 – 45 minutes, until cider/apple mixture is thickened. During the final minutes of baking, I usually stir a couple of times to make sure all the apple pieces are moist. Serve with noodles, if you like. The original recipe called for chicken breasts. The instructions are the same, but I prefer pork chops in this recipe.

## Slow Cooker Pork Loin

419 Super simple, tender pork with gravy. My mom made this forever. I'm sure she got the idea from some crockpot cookbook back in the 70's when crockpots were all the new big thing and they even held classes at the department stores to teach you how to use one.

Posted by: cfo mom. Yield: 8 servings. Prep time: 15 minutes to prep, 8 hours in crockpot.

---

4 pound boneless pork loin
2 medium onions, diced or sliced
2 cans mushrooms, drained, liquid reserved, OR 8 ounces fresh mushrooms, sliced
2 cans condensed cream of whatever soup (mushroom, onion, celery - whatever you like and have on hand.)
2 envelopes gravy mix (I use 1 chicken and one beef because it is hard to find pork gravy mix)
1 teaspoon or as needed for color (optional) GravyMaster
potatoes (optional)

Put the pork loin, fat side up, in an oval crockpot (so it completely fits). If you've only got a small round crockpot, cut the loin in half and cut the recipe quantities in half and put the other 2 pounds of pork loin away for another time. Put the onions and mushrooms on top of the pork loin. Put the condensed soup on top of that. Do not reconstitute the soup—use right from the can. Sprinkle the 2 envelopes of gravy mix evenly over everything. Add 1/2 cup of the reserved liquid from the mushrooms (or water). Add GravyMaster if you think the sauce looks like it will be too pale to be appetizing. Cover and turn crockpot on low for 8 hours or put on high for the first couple hours and then turn to low for another 4. Remove loin from crockpot, slice, scoop gravy over and enjoy.

***Chef's Notes:***
Halve the recipe for a 2 pound roast. Throw in some potatoes if you like after all the other ingredients. If you use pork tenderloins instead of pork loin add a bit more water as they are very lean and need a bit extra moisture.

## Stuffed ham

420 A very old recipe from nineteenth century Louisiana. Recipe is from my wife's family, many of whom are still sugarcane farmers.

Posted by: Lester. Yield: a lot. Prep time: several hours.

---

12 pound ham or thereabouts
1/4 cup vinegar
1/4 cup brown sugar
1 – 2 cups ham fat
16 ounces crackers
3 tablespoons sugar
1 teaspoon mustard seed
1 teaspoon French mustard
1 stalk celery, finely chopped
2 finely chopped medium onions
1/2 cup sweet pickle relish
4 beaten eggs
1 cup sherry
hot sauce to taste
additional vinegar
biscuits, sweet pickles, mustard

Cut off the hock with a meat saw and save for future use. Add vinegar and brown sugar to a pot of water big enough to hold the ham. Boil it until the bone feels loose. Remove from water and cool enough to touch. Remove the bone (you will have to use a knife on some parts) and as much of the fat as possible. Save 1 cup fat and grind it or pulverize in food processor. Mix with finely crushed crackers, sugar, mustards, celery, onions, pickle, eggs, sherry, hot sauce and enough vinegar to make a paste. Put the stuffing into the ham and on the exterior. Wrap in cheesecloth and bake at 300 degrees for an hour. Chill overnight in the fridge. Remove cheesecloth and slice very thinly to serve. Excellent for holiday or church buffets. Serve with small biscuits and sweet tiny pickles and good mustard.

## Sunk New Dawn Stuffed Porky Pigchops

421 Panty-droppingest pork chops west of the Pecos! Origin, self.

Posted by: Jim, Sunk New Dawn, Galveston, TX. Yield: 2 servings. Prep time: 1 hour.

---

2 pork loin chops, 1 inch thick
2 strips thick-cut hickory-smoked bacon
4 tablespoons Philly whipped cream cheese

2 tablespoons mayonnaise
½ teaspoon black pepper
1 teaspoon McCormack "Perfect Pinch" series, Caribbean Jerk Seasoning
1 teaspoon garlic powder
scant ¼ teaspoon cayenne pepper
4 tablespoons Parmesan or Romano Cheese, grated

Get a pair of chops cut from the thickest section of the largest pork loin you can get your hands on. Have them cut to be one inch thick. Get two or three slices of thick cut, hickory smoked bacon. Fry 'em up just short of "crispy," but they must be cooked well enough to get that salty tang, vs. the fatty softness of undercooked bacon. Once cooled, tear the bacon into bits no more than 3/4" in any dimension; set aside. With the chop laid flat on a cutting board, use a RAZOR SHARP knife, and cut a pocket, laterally, through the length and breadth of the chop, taking care to not cut all the way through the other side. You want a pocket, not two slices of a meat sandwich. Scoop out about a quarter cup of Philly whipped cream cheese, into a small dish (don't do this step directly from the cream cheese container, or you'll contaminate the contents with uncooked pork pathogens). Using an ordinary butter knife, trowel a generous amount of the cream cheese into the pockets of each chop. Next, divide those bacon bits into two piles, and evenly stuff said bits into the cream cheese filled pockets. Use three toothpicks per chop, and "stitch" the pockets closed. This is a MUST, or the chops will "burst open" when cooking! Grab that wee bowl of mayo now (don't do this step directly from the mayonnaise jar, or you'll contaminate the contents with uncooked pork pathogens). Using a spatula or just your fingers, smear a generous film of mayo atop each chop, also with a layer covering the exposed sides. Now, you're ready for seasoning.

A light to medium sprinkling of black pepper. A medium coating of the McCormick "Perfect Pinch" series "Caribbean Jerk" seasoning. Careful with this stuff—it cango from "interesting" to "too damn hot" in just a couple of shakes. A medium coating of garlic powder. More, if you wish, but not to excess. A very light dusting (optional) of cayenne pepper. This will add a unique "sweetness" to the mix. Too much cayenne though, and you just get heat. Tread lightly here! Finally, a generous topping of grated Parmesan or Romano cheese. Place chops onto an ungreased, foil-covered cookie sheet, and into a 325 degrees F oven for 20 minutes. Then, bump the oven to 400 degrees F, for a final 10 minute run. This is a very visual dish, so pull 'em from the oven when you get that perfect, slightly burnt around the edges toasty "done" look to the cheese. Spatula 'em off of the foil, and serve at once. Goes well with all kinds of sides and all kinds of drink.

### *Chef's Notes:*

When learning the dish, it's actually better if you slightly undercook. You can always nuke 'em for 30 seconds if needed. But overcooked pork is a tough, shoe-leathery disaster. Done right, these will have a very, VERY light bit of "barely" pink remaining, and will be very juicy and succulent. And yet, safe. Commercial pork has a nearly zero rate of trichinosis, proven over the past forty years or so. Bon Appetit!

## Jack's World Famous Filipino Pork and Chicken Adobo

422 Braised pork and chicken stew. A traditional Filipino dish that is highly representative of their cuisine.

Posted by: My High Tech Security. Yield: 8 servings. Prep time: 90 minutes.

---

1 pound one-inch cubed pork shoulder
1 pound chicken thighs
1 cup cider vinegar
1 cup high-quality soy sauce
5 – 15 garlic cloves
20 black peppercorns
1 – 2 whole bay leaves

Place the pork and chicken into a five-quart pot. Add the peppercorns, garlic and bay leaf, and then pour the wet ingredients over the meat. Bring to a boil for about five minutes, and then lower the heat to a low simmer. Cover pot. Stir every 15 minutes or so for 90 minutes, or until the meat is falling apart tender. Serve with rice. This is a very addictive meal and will have people begging for more. Leftovers are even better the next day.

## Chile Verde

423 Green chili. This is my dad's recipe. He was in a labor union, and they were given lunch for walking the picket line. The food provided sucked. He asked if he could cook the next lunch. After word spread they had to double the budget for all the people showing up to walk the line. Side note, he told me if I ever joined the union he would break every bone in my body.

Posted by: Paladin. Yield: 10 servings, with left overs. Prep time: 2 hours.

---

1 pork roast (traditional) or beef, large roast or shoulder
10 – 15 fresh anaheim green chilis
large can whole tomatoes
3 – 5 jalapeno peppers
2 – 4 cloves garlic
3 – 4 onions
2 – 3 tablespoons salt

Cook the roast in a very large pot with the garlic. Dad used a pressure cooker to cut down on time. Cover with water, which will make the broth, and cook until fork tender. Pull the roast and garlic from the broth, and let cool. Thinly slice the onions and add to the broth with a puño of salt. (Cup your hand and fill with salt. I am guessing 2 – 3 tablespoons?) Puree the can of tomatoes, and add to the broth. Roast the chilis on the grill until the outer skin bubbles and burns, turning constantly. This makes it easy to peal the outer tough skin of the chilis, leaving the soften inner meat of the chili. Shred the chilis with a fork and remove the tails. I leave in the seed of both the green chilis and the jalapenos. That is where the "hot" comes from, so don't be a wuss. Add the shredded chilis to the slowly simmering broth. Now shred the roast the same way, and add to the pot. Let it blend for a half hour or so. Serve with Spanish rice and refried beans with flour tortillas. Use more jalapenos if you want it spicy; the anaheim chilis are not hot at all.

***Chef's Notes:***
Search the web for "Cooking with Chavo" for Mexican rice (he points out the "Spanish" don't have the rice that we Mexicans make as a staple). He also has a recipe for refried beans from scratch. It takes a while. This is why my grandmother spent all day in the kitchen. Tortillas are a "special kind of magic." All they are is flour, salt, and lard, but I can't get the proportions right. I do not cook with precise measurements, but I do cook with a bottle of Dos Exquis in hand.

## Red Beans and Sausage

424 Really easy, really good, really tasty! It's a copy of a copy of a copy, so yellowed over time with various folds and splashes that its origin is unknown. I'll give credit to someone's Aunt Millie . . . somewhere.

Posted by: Lady in Black—Death to the Man Bun. Yield: servings for 8 morons. Prep time: 15 – 20 minutes.

---

1 package (the horseshoe thing) smoked sausage or andouille, sliced
1 large onion
1 medium red bell pepper
1 medium green bell pepper
5 cloves (Chez Black uses much more) garlic, minced—fresh, not the jarred stuff!
3 16-ounce cans red or pink beans, drained
1 14.5-ounce can stewed tomatoes, undrained
1 6-ounce can tomato paste
1 1/2 cups water
1 teaspoon EACH dried oregano, thyme
1 bay leaf
several shakes hot sauce (I use Frank's)

In Dutch oven, over medium-high heat, brown sliced smoked sausage for 3 – 5 minutes in a little olive oil. Then add onions and peppers. (Add additional olive oil, if needed.) Continue to saute until onions start to become translucent. Add garlic and saute until garlic is fragrant, about 1 minute. Add drained beans, stewed tomatoes, tomato paste, water, oregano, thyme and bay leaf. Add shakes of hot sauce, as desired. Bring to boil and reduce heat. Simmer for about 20 minutes. Discard bay leaf and serve over white rice.

***Chef's Notes:***
During simmer time, I usually tilt a lid on top. It will keep the mixture simmering, but not allow condensation to collect and water down your dish. I also use Frank's hot sauce because it adds a good, smoky flavor, but doesn't burn the daylights out of your mouth either.

# Polpettine

425 Tiny Italian meatballs. From the culinary adventure we have enjoyed in Italy.

Posted by: westminsterdogshow. Yield: 6 – 8 servings. Prep time: 1 hour.

---

1 pound ground pork
1 pound ground veal
2 eggs
1 cup grated Parmigiano cheese
1 cup bread crumbs
1 clove garlic
1/2 teaspoon pepper
2 teaspoons salt

Combine all ingredients until mixed well. Form dime-sized meat balls and place them on a foil lined cookie sheet. Place them in a 400 degree F oven for 15 minutes until cooked through. Alternatively, you can fry them in olive oil until cooked through, 10 – 12 minutes. We use these for homemade lasagna. They are excellent with tomato sauce and spaghetti. Also, they freeze very well.

# Golden Pork Chops

426 Pan fried Asian inspired chops. I was inspired by Fat Rice's pork chop recipe to add baking soda to the brine.

Posted by: None (lurker). Yield: 2 servings. Prep time: 25 minutes cooking time, 4 – 8 hours wait time.

---

2 bone-in pork rib chops (at least 1 inch thick)
at least ¼ cups peanut oil (or another neutral high temperature oil)
1 cup cold water
2 tablespoons sugar
2 tablespoons soy sauce
1/2 teaspoon baking soda
1 teaspoon fresh grated ginger
1 teaspoon rice wine vinegar
2 cloves fresh garlic

Whisk together marinade ingredients. Double for more chops. Brine chops in a ziplock for 4 – 8 hours. Remove from fridge, toss brine and pat dry 30 minutes before frying. Heat oil in a large pan or skillet over medium-high heat. Use at least ¼ cup per chop. When hot, fry chops until golden brown on each side. A food thermometer is helpful for thicker chops—fry until 135 degrees F. Let chops rest 5 minutes. Temperature should rise another 5 – 10 degrees while resting. Salt and pepper to taste. Serve on a soft roll, or over sticky rice.

## Tinfoilbaby's Wet Burrito

427 Excellent. A good wet burrito should weigh about 3 pounds, and will be the only thing that you eat that day.

Posted by: Tinfoilbaby. Yield: enough for 5 Morons. Prep time: 25 minutes.

---

a very large flour tortilla
meat of your choice
rice and beans
shredded lettuce
fresh pico de gallo
sour cream
red or green sauce
cheese

Lay out giant flour tortilla, and I mean giant, 16" at least, and never use a Mission tortilla, they suck. Place leftover meat of choice in the middle along with the rice and beans, roll up into a giant package of goodness. Put on plate and then smother in red or green sauce, pile cheese on top; pepper jack is my choice. Put in 450 degree F oven for 5 – 7 minutes. To serve, on the side put pico, sour cream and guacamole on a bed of lettuce.

## Low Tide

428 A variation on Portuguese pork and clams. This recipe is adapted from my Aunt Maria's pork & clams.

Posted by: lauraw. Yield: 8 – 12 servings. Prep time: 1 to 1 1/2 hours.

---

2 pounds pork loin, cubed
1 pound linguica or chourico Portuguese sausage
1 medium Spanish onion, chopped
1 cup white wine
4 cups cubed white or red potatoes
1 teaspoon dried marjoram
30 – 50 littleneck clams, scrubbed and purged in saltwater
1 or 2 large bunches kale, cleaned, stems removed

In a large heavy stock pot over medium-high heat, quickly brown the pork loin cubes in a little oil. Add the Portuguese sausage and sliced onions to the pot and saute until the onions are softened. Add the white wine, marjoram, and potatoes. Stir, then cover the pot tightly. Bring to a low simmer and cook until the potatoes are not quite halfway cooked. The centers should still be a little hard. If the pot starts to get dry, add some more wine or water. Remove clams from the salt water, rinse in fresh water, and press them each into the stew, hinges down, in the liquid. Fill the whole top of the stew pot with your kale leaves and replace the lid. Quickly bring back to a simmer, then drop the heat. Every few minutes, lift the lid and turn the kale so that it steams evenly. When it is all wilted, start pressing it into the broth between the clams. When the first clams start to open, stir up the stew, cover it, and give it a shake to settle the contents. Continue to simmer slowly. After all the clams are open, remove from heat. Ladle the stew into big bowls, and serve with crusty bread to soak up the broth. Discard any clams that did not open.

***Chef's Notes:***
This is beach party food and it goes great with beer and margaritas. Have a big pot or bowl handy for people to chuck their clamshells into. Google up how to purge clams properly, it makes a difference. Nobody wants to bite into a big sharp piece of grit. If you're near the ocean, you can cut corners by using fresh ocean water from a clean source.

## Braised Short Ribs

429 Ribs with beer! *hic*. Adapted from *The Williams-Sonoma Cookbook.*

Posted by: atomicplaygirl. Yield: 6 servings. Prep time: 3 hours.

---

5 pounds beef short ribs
salt and pepper to taste
3 tablespoons vegetable oil (I use peanut), divided
3 peeled and sliced medium onions (into thick half rings)
6 peeled carrots, cut into 1/2" chunks
4 pressed cloves garlic
1 28-ounce can pureed tomatoes
1 bottle beer (ale or amber, preferably)
2 tablespoons country Dijon mustard
2 tablespoons light brown sugar

Season ribs with salt and pepper. Heat 2 tablespoons oil in large Dutch oven (big enough to hold all ingredients) over medium heat. Working in batches to avoid overcrowding, brown the ribs nicely on all sides. Add a little oil at any time if you need it during the browning process but be careful to not make it too oily! Briefly drain on paper towels before placing them in a large bowl to collect juices. Turn heat up to medium-high and add 1 tablespoon oil to Dutch oven. Saute onions until browned (be careful to richly brown, not burn). Add carrots and saute for approximately 3 – 4 minutes, then add the garlic and cook for one minute longer. Add the remaining ingredients (except for the meat), season with a little more salt and pepper, and simmer for 2 – 3 minutes to allow the flavours to start to combine. Add the ribs back in, tucking them into the sauce. Bake for approximately 2 ½ - 3 hours at 325 degrees F, stirring and turning the ribs periodically. Taste to adjust the seasoning, then serve. I serve this with mashed potatoes or bread (or both, if I'm feeling bad!). Great re-heated. You can chill it after cooking; remove the bits of fat when they coagulate and then heat it up.

## Slow Cooker Kalua Pork with Teriyaki Sauce

430 My imitation version of Mo' Bettah's pork and sauce. Cooks perfect every time and I always get asked for the recipe! Pork is modified from a recipe by Mei at AllRecipes.com and sauce is modified from ILoveHawaiianFoodRecipes.com.

Posted by: LizLem. Yield: 10 servings. Prep time: 10 hours, 45 minutes.

---

- 1 5-pound bone-in pork shoulder roast, uncooked
- 2 teaspoons ground black pepper
- 1 1/2 teaspoons + 1 teaspoon grated fresh ginger
- 2 tablespoons kosher salt
- 1 tablespoon + 1 cup soy sauce
- 2 teaspoons Worcestershire sauce
- 3/4 cup water
- 1 ¼ cup brown sugar
- 1/4 cup rice vinegar
- 1/4 cup honey
- 1 teaspoon grated or minced garlic
- 1 small head cabbage

Mix together salt, the 1 ½ teaspoons of ginger and the pepper in a bowl, then rub evenly onto surface of the uncooked pork roast. (More ginger can be used if desired.) Place roast into slow cooker and turn cooker on to the low setting. Stir a tablespoon of the soy sauce and the Worcestershire sauce together and pour over pork roast. Place lid on cooker and let roast cook for 10 ½ hours on low. (If speeding up the process is necessary, pork can also be cooked for 5 hours on high setting of the cooker.) Shred pork. To make the sauce, combine the cup of soy sauce, water, brown sugar, rice vinegar, honey, garlic, and the teaspoon of grated ginger in a saucepan and bring to a boil. Let simmer; either keep it warm for the meal or cool and store it in the fridge (makes 2 ½ cups). Serve pork over a bed of sticky rice, or sandwich style in buns. Chop up the small head of cabbage into thin strips and serve on the side. Generously ladle sauce on top of meat. Eat!

### *Chef's Notes:*

The ginger I usually store in my freezer, then take out and grate however much I need. Feel free to be generous with ginger in this recipe. I tend to make a double batch of sauce so there is more than enough and save the extra for other meals. Sauce is also good over chicken and salmon and in veggie stir-fry.

# *Seafood*

## Judy's Best Seafood Gumbo Evah!

431 Tbe best thing you'll put in your mouth all day—I guarantee! Adapted from an original recipe from Judy Hebert (she married a real coon-ass Cajun).

Posted by: thefritz. Yield: 15 servings. Prep time: 9 hours.

---

1 pound okra
¼ cup flour
½ cup olive oil
1 medium onion, chopped
2 ½ stalks of celery, chopped
½ tablespoon cayenne pepper
1 – 3 tablespoons hot sauce (your choice)
3 cloves of garlic, minced or chopped
3 bay leaves
4 tablespoons Worcestershire sauce
salt and pepper to taste
1 quart reduced-sodium chicken stock
1 ½ quarts water
2 diced tomatoes (large pieces)
2 halved blue crabs or 8 ounces canned lump crab meat
½ pound shrimp
1 pint oysters
1 pound boudin sausage (smoked of course), sliced and quartered
Rice and French bread (optional)

Wash okra, cut into ¼ inch rounds, set aside. In large pot heat olive oil over medium/low heat, stir in flour. Reduce heat to low and whisk frequently until it turns a nice mocha color (about 15 – 20 minutes). Add okra, chopped onions, celery, chopped garlic, salt to taste and cayenne. Make sure heat is very low and put on the lid. Pour yourself a nice glass of red wine and pop in a Neville Brothers CD. After every other song, lift the lid, stir quickly and return lid. When the Brothers have finished singing, you should have yourself a nice gumbo roux (about an hour). Now you should at least be on the better side of your second glass of wine. If not, pour another immediately. Add the chicken stock and water, stir in the hot sauce of your choice, the Worcestershire, the black pepper to taste, the bay leaves, sliced tomatoes and halved blue crabs. Simmer lidless for 3 hours.

Now depending on whether you had two or three glasses of red wine, it's ok to take a 3-hour nap. Just be sure to wake up after three hours cuz now it's time to add the sausage. Then simmer lidless for one more hour. Remove from heat, cover and let stand to room temperature (or close) then put into the refrigerator for at least 24 hours, 48 is better. When it's time to eat, reheat over medium until gumbo just starts to simmer. Stir well and add shrimp and oysters. Cook for 10 minutes more then serve up that simmerin' slice of Cajun heaven over a mess of white rice or on a thick slice of fresh French bread. It'll be the best thing you put in your mouth all day, I guarantee!

## Primeaux Creole

432 Shrimp or seafood creole. An old lady in New Iberia named Mrs. Gagne gave it to my dad. He used to occasionally consult on oilfield workovers there.

Posted by: Dave at Buffalo Roam. Yield: enough for 6 – 8 hungry folks. Prep time: 40 minutes.

---

1 pound butter
1 cup chopped onions
1/2 cup chopped bell peppers
3 tablespoons flour
3 tablespoons tomato sauce
3 cups water
3 pounds cleaned shrimp
1 pound crab meat
Cajun hot sauce to taste
rice

Cook the onion and bell pepper in ¾ pound of butter until almost brown. Add 3 cups of water, the tomato sauce and seafood. You can add more seafood if you like; put another 1/4 pound butter for each pound additional seafood. Bring to a boil while you make your roux. In a separate skillet cook a light golden roux with 1/4 pound of butter and 3 tablespoons of flour. Do not burn your roux! (That's Cajun for Pay Attention!). Carefully pour it in the boiling pot. Simmer for 30 minutes. Add Cajun hot sauce to taste, usually a tablespoon for a start and let people spice it up to their own taste. Serve over rice. If I catch you using Minute Rice you're in trouble. Some good baguettes sop up a nice taste! Champagne!

## Shrimp Scampi

433 My wife doesn't order this at restaurants anymore. I have worked this out over the years but I am sure that it is very similar to other recipes.

Posted by: RKinRoanoke. Yield: 2 servings. Prep time: less than 30 minutes.

---

1 pound shrimp
3 – 4 medium to large cloves garlic
2 large shallots
1 medium sweet onion
1 stick (1/2 cup) butter
1/2 cup white wine
2 tablespoons olive oil
salt and pepper to taste
angel hair pasta
red pepper flakes (optional)

Peel and devein the shrimp. I like to buy larger shrimp, 16 – 20 per pound. Run cold water over them and set aside. Mince the garlic; the smaller the cut, the more garlic flavor. Chop the shallot and the onion, not too small. Heat a large frying pan over medium heat. When hot, add olive oil. Saute the garlic, onion and shallot until the onion begins to get translucent. Add the butter to melt. When the butter is melted, add the shrimp in one layer.

Salt and pepper to your taste. If your pan is not big enough don't put all the shrimp in. They need some room. Cook the shrimp until pink on one side (2 minutes max). Flip the shrimp, add the wine and cook another 1 – 2 minutes. While the onion and shallots cook, boil your favorite pasta. We like angel hair, which cooks in 2 – 3 minutes. Drain the angel hair, put the shrimp and all its juices into the pan with the angel hair. Toss and serve. A nice Pinot Grigio or Sauvignon Blanc will go well. Don't over-cook shrimp, they get tough. If you like some kick, add some red pepper flakes when you add the salt and pepper.

## Shrimp and Cognac Cream

434 A favorite—it needs to be made at the last minute before serving or the sauce will start to separate. Try it with scallops! A family recipe from the mists of time.

Posted by: WitchDoktor, AKA VA GOP Sucks. Yield: 4 servings. Prep time: 10 – 15 minutes-ish.

---

1/4 cup butter
1 1/2 pounds shrimp, peeled
salt and pepper to taste
6 tablespoons chopped shallots
6 tablespoons warm cognac
3/4 cup tomato paste
3/4 cup heavy cream
1 1/2 teaspoons basil
1 1/2 teaspoons chives
3 tablespoons heavy cream
3 egg yolks
1 pound pasta (capellini)
1/4 cup butter
fresh chopped parsley, for garnish

Heat butter in skillet. Add shrimp, sprinkle with salt and pepper and cook for 4 minutes, turning once. When shrimp are bright pink, sprinkle with shallots and cook for 1 minute more. Add cognac and ignite it to burn off the alcohol (yeah, baby!). Cook for 1 minute. Add tomato paste and cover over high heat for 1 minute. Remove from heat and add ¾ cup cream, basil, and chives. Beat the egg yolks and 3 tablespoons heavy cream together, then add to sauce. Cook pasta to al dente and drain well. Add back into pan with sauce and 1/4 cup butter. Toss everything well and serve, sprinkled with parsley.

## Pre-Med Catfish Burritos

435 Fast, nutritious, cheap! When I was a poor pre-med student I became a vegan. In my 3rd year (I graduated in 3 1/2) I decided I would die without more protein and made up this recipe from things around the apartment and a nearby lake.

Posted by: Daybrother. Yield: servings for 2 Morons. Prep time: 20 minutes.

---

1 pound catfish filet
1 cup jasmine rice
2 cups water
1/2 can cream of mushroom soup
4 ounces blanco melting type cheese
quarter head iceberg lettuce
1 red tomato
salt and freshly cracked black pepper to taste
hot habenero salsa to taste
8 flour or corn tortillas
quarter stick (2 tablespoons) butter

Add half the amount of butter to a large saucepan on medium-high heat. As butter melts add rice and stir until you hear the rice applaud (pop and crackle). Pour in two cups water and increase heat until it begins to boil, stirring occasionally. Cover and reduce heat to simmer. Cut catfish into half inch chunks, feeling for bones (remove them, you chucklehead). Dice tomato and queso (any kind of good melting cheese will do) and shred lettuce. After 20 minutes quickly uncover rice and add half a can of mushroom soup, catfish, remaining butter and diced queso. Stir well and quickly! Recover. Heat tortillas directly on gas burners or hot skillet, turning so both sides are barely browned and wrap in paper towels or tortilla warmer. Put lettuce and tomato on plates. Remove saucepan from heat after 10 more minutes. Assemble burritos with tomato, lettuce, salt, pepper and salsa. Serve hot with cold beer.

***Chef's Notes:***
Mrs. Renfro's hot habanero or any good salsa is preferred. When removing saucepan from heat, open cover and remove one chunk of catfish. Check that it is cooked through and give to cat who has been bugging you the whole time. He won't eat it but will lick it and drag it around the kitchen floor.

## Baked Orange-Ginger Mahi-Mahi

436 Delicious way to cook mahi-mahi or snapper. Recipe was obtained from my server at Keoki's Restaurant in Poipu, Kauai, where it is no longer available. It has only been published in my family's cookbook, submitted by me.

Posted by: Manny. Yield: servings for 3 – 4 morons. Prep time: 50 minutes?

---

~1 cup mayonnaise (NOT salad dressing)
4 – 5 tablespoons orange marmalade
1 clove garlic (optional)
2 thumb-sized pieces ginger root
1 ½ pounds fresh fillets of white fish (mahi-mahi, wahoo, snapper, etc.)

Combine mayo and marmalade in a bowl. [Press the juice out of the garlic clove into the bowl if using it. Go easy on the garlic lest it overwhelm.] Peel and very finely grate as much of the ginger as you have the patience for into the bowl and press the juice out of the rest in there too. Discard the fibrous remainder. Blend the ingredients well with a fork or whisk. The consistency should resemble pancake batter—adjust the ratio of marmalade to mayo accordingly. Spread a small amount in the bottom of a greased oven-proof container large enough to hold the fish in a single layer. Place fish on top and cover with the rest of the mixture. [Make more if you don't have enough.] Bake for 30 – 40 minutes in a pre-heated 350 degrees F oven, depending on the thickness of your fillets and how you well you like your fish done. Any marmalade will work, but I prefer the kind with the peel. I've also used Trader Joe's lemon-lime-ginger marmalade with great results.

## Potato Chip Fish

437 Easy and family-friendly. I improvised!

Posted by: Otto Zilch. Yield: 4 or 5 servings. Prep time: 20 minutes.

---

1 pound (about 5 or 6) flounder fillets
1 medium bag (4 – 5 ounces) potato chips
(salt and pepper variety works best)
1/4 cup panko bread crumbs
1 teaspoon fines herbes (optional)
1 egg (beaten)

Preheat oven to 400 degrees F. Line a large baking sheet with aluminum foil. If you have an oil sprayer, spray the foil generously for easy transfer and a little more browning. If the potato chips came in a larger bag, transfer 4 or 5 ounces to a separate bag. Crush the potato chips, first with your hand and then with a rolling pin, until they are medium-fine crumbs (this is a good kid job). Mix in the panko, and the fines herbes (if using), then pour the mixture onto a large plate. Beat the egg and pour onto a separate plate. Using one hand, draw each fillet through the egg and pat it onto the crumbs. Flip the fillet and coat the other side. Using your other hand, transfer the fillet to the baking sheet. After all the fillets are coated, use the remaining crumbs to coat any areas you missed. Bake for about 10 minutes or until done. Serve with a crisp white wine like sauvignon blanc or a white Rhone (such as Roussanne or Marsanne or Grenache blanc).

## Bonecrusher's Fillets

438 Sauteed fillet of fish. From the spooky crags of my brain. Difficulty level: dumbass easy.

Posted by: Bonecrusher. Yield: depends on how much fish you have. Prep time: 3 – 5 minutes.

---

4 parts flour
1 part garlic salt
½ part cayenne pepper
speckled trout fillets (or any damn fish you can get)

Mix flour, garlic salt and cayenne pepper in a shallow dish. Get a skillet hot (almost smoking) with equal parts olive oil and butter. Dredge fillets in flour mixture and knock off most of it. Fry about 60 – 90 seconds per side and pull out. Cover with fresh cut green onions. Eat. Don't burn the fish or overcook it. Quick and hot!

## New Baby Crabcakes

439 Good make-ahead dish. Adapted from Myra Waldo's *Beer and Good Food* (Doubleday, 1958).

Posted by: Otto Zilch. Yield: 4 – 6 servings. Prep time: 30 minutes.

---

1 pound crabmeat
1/4 cup finely chopped onion
1/4 cup finely chopped red bell pepper
2 tablespoons thinly chopped green scallions
2 eggs (separated)
1/4 cup olive oil
1 drop Tabasco sauce
3/4 cup panko bread crumbs
2 tablespoons Old Bay seasoning
1/2 teaspoon pepper
2 pinches salt
2 tablespoons butter for sauteeing

Saute the onions gently in 1 teaspoon butter until they start to become translucent; add the peppers and scallion about halfway through. Meanwhile, separate the eggs. Add olive oil, Worcestershire, and Tabasco to the yolks and beat gently In a large mixing bowl, combine the dry ingredients: panko, Old Bay, salt, and pepper. When onions and peppers are done, let cool a minute or three while you beat the egg whites until foamy. Fold the egg yolk mixture and the vegetables into the panko mixture, and mix together with your hand until well blended. Add the crabmeat and mix gently until binder is evenly distributed through the crab. There should be a lot more crab than binder—be faithful! Add the egg white, keep mixing with your hand and it will all start holding together. Allow to stand about 15 minutes and it will hold together better. Form into 12 spheres about 1 to 2 inches in diameter. Melt remaining butter over medium-high heat. Saute cakes about four minutes or until brown and firm on bottom. Turn over, smash down a little bit, and saute until done. For appetizers, make about 24 spheres and cook an accordingly shorter time. Serve with a moderately hoppy ale, or with a white Rhine-type wine like Marsanne, Rousanne, or Viognier.

### *Chef's Notes:*

If you can find it, the "Crab Cake Combo" from Handy is excellent—it mixes nice big crabby lumps with the backfin and claw meat that helps hold the cakes together. The recipe got its name because once I made it the day a work colleague of mine and his wife had their first child. Since the recipe serves four, I wrapped up the extra cakes in wax paper and brought them to my colleague so he and his wife could have a nice dinner without too much work. Since then, crabcakes have been a traditional gift for our friends who are welcoming a new baby.

## Javems Spaghetti With Meat Sauce

440 New Orleans style, kind of. The basic method was one I learned from an Italian guy while in Lagos, Nigeria. His name, to us, was Spaghetti. His wife, a ditz from Dallas, was Meatball. The rest is mine.

Posted by: Javems. Yield: 6 – 8 servings. Prep time: 90 minutes.

---

1 pound ground chuck
8 ounces sliced mushrooms
2 cups chopped sweet onion
1 cup chopped red bell pepper
1 cup chopped celery
2 tablespoons dried parsley
24 ounces tomato sauce
salt and pepper to taste
1 tablespoon dried oregano
2 tablespoons olive oil, plus more if necessary
1 pound dry spaghetti
3 chopped garlic cloves

In a big pot, 4 - 6 quart, cook the ground meat through. Set aside. Remove excess grease; add olive oil and cook onions and mushrooms till starting to get tender. Add salt and pepper, parsley, oregano, celery and bell pepper and cook till tender. Add garlic and cook a minute or two more. Add ground meat and tomato sauce. Bring to a boil and simmer, stirring often, for 45 minutes to an hour. Add salt and pepper as needed. When sauce is about done, cook spaghetti in salted water till al dente. Strain into a serving bowl. Pour the sauce over the pasta and stir till mixed. I like the sauce mixed with the pasta, but not everyone does. You might reserve some to serve individually.

## Linguine Ai Funghi

441 Amazing mushroom pasta. This dish is served during mushroom season at Tre Colonne (The Three Columns) in Turin. Piemonte is where the best wild mushrooms and truffles are found and every restaurant has a special mushroom dish. We loved the dish so much that I had to re-create it. Linguine ai funghi makes a wonderful starter, especially if you plan to serve roast chicken as the main course.

Posted by: Shanks for the memory. Yield: 4 main course servings, or 6 – 8 starter servings. Prep time: 25 – 30 minutes.

---

1 ½ pounds medium-sized cremini mushrooms, sliced medium thick
1/4 cup thinly sliced yellow onion (sliced pole-to-pole, not into rings please!)
8 ounces good quality chicken stock
2 cloves coarsely diced garlic
1/4 cup olive oil
pinch of red pepper flakes
3 – 4 coarse grinds black pepper
1/2 cup red wine
2 tablespoons butter
¼ cup coarsely chopped Italian parsley
freshly grated Parmigiano cheese
1 pound (16 ounces) fresh or dried linguini

Heat olive oil over medium heat in a large frying pan or heavy saute pan. Add onions, garlic, red pepper, and black pepper and saute for 2 – 3 minutes until onions are translucent, then add mushrooms. Toss and stir mushrooms to coat. Saute for about five minutes until the juices begin to flow from the mushrooms. Add the wine and saute for 3 – 4 minutes over high heat to burn off the alcohol. Add chicken stock to barely cover the mushrooms and the parsley. Cover the pan & simmer over medium-low heat for 20 minutes. Cook the linguine as per directions, or your usual way (any long pasta may be used, we like thin spaghetti and fettucine too). When you are about to put the pasta in the boiling water to cook; uncover and turn up the heat under the mushrooms to medium-high; reducing the liquid about a third. Add the butter and the sauce will thicken. At this point the sauce can hold covered on low heat for 5 – 10 minutes if need be.

You may toss the cooked linguine with the sauce in a serving bowl and lightly mix, then garnish with cheese, a bit more parsley & black pepper, or serve as we prefer: fork a serving of linguine into a heated wide rimmed pasta bowl or dinner plate, sprinkle with a scant dusting of cheese, and spoon the mushroom sauce into the middle, garnish with more cheese, parsley, and lots of black pepper! That's it! Very simple and a perfect quick meal. It is also an inexpensive dish *for a crowd. All you need is a salad and crusty bread for a satisfying meal. It's a good comfort dish for a cold winter night too!

*To increase the servings for a big bowl to feed a crowd: increase the amount of pasta to 2 pounds and don't reduce the sauce after adding butter. At the last minute before draining the pasta add 1/2 cup ladle of the pasta cooking water and stir; the sauce will thicken without reducing the volume. Toss the sauce and pasta together, garnish with grated Parm and parsley. Serve while hot as the dish will thicken as the bowl cools. Buon Appetito!

### *Chef's Notes:*

A tip or two:
1. Any time a pasta sauce isn't thick enough: just before you drain the pasta add a ladle of the pasta water, it will be milky or white in color. It is full of starch and will act as a thickening agent, plus the flavor enhances the sauce (as long as you don't over-salt the water!).
2. If you use dried pasta add 2 – 3 sprigs of fresh parsley to the cooking water and the pasta will taste as good as fresh—the "tooth" will be the same as dried pasta but the flavor is much enhanced and the cooked parsley is an extra treat.

## Talley Family Spaghetti

442 Spaghetti sauce for the ages. My maternal grandmother made this sauce for every family gathering. She called it Hawaiian spaghetti sauce, but I have searched online to see if it was previously printed as such and Hawaiian spaghetti sauce is very different. It goes really well with cornbread and strawberry and banana jello salad.

Posted by: Ramblingmother. Yield: 4 moron servings. Prep time: 25 minutes.

---

1 tablespoon olive oil
1 pound ground beef
1 tablespoon chili powder
1/2 teaspoon salt
1 teaspoon cinnamon
1 tablespoon sugar
1/4 teaspoon pepper
2 cloves garlic, or 1 medium chopped onion
1 can tomato soup
1 can tomato sauce
2 tomato sauce cans water
8-ounce box of spaghetti noodles

Heat oil in sauce pan. Add beef, chili powder, salt, pepper, sugar, cinnamon, and garlic or onion. Cook over low heat stirring until meat is brown. Add tomato soup, sauce and water. Mix well. Simmer 45 minutes. Serve over 8 ounce box or package of spaghetti noodles cooked according to package directions. If you want to drain the meat, cook it before adding the seasoning or you will lose the flavors.

## Shell-a-roni

443 For when stroganoff is just too hard. My mom made this as far back as I can remember. It was the first thing I learned how to make, and the first recipe I taught my 12 year-old son.

Posted by: Weirddave. Yield: 6 – 8 servings. Prep time: 15 minutes.

---

1 pound ground beef
2 cans cream of mushroom soup
1 can sliced mushrooms
1 medium onion, diced
1 tablespoon olive oil
1 box (16 ounces) medium pasta shells
salt and pepper to taste

Prepare the noodles according to package directions, drain. While the noodles are boiling, brown the ground beef, drain. Saute mushrooms and onions in olive oil until the onions are soft and light brown.
Combine all ingredients in a large bowl, salt and pepper liberally, and mix well. QED.

# Teresa's Spaghetti and Meatballs

444 Make copies to hand out - everyone will ask for one! Originally found in the *Houston Chronicle*'s food section, circa 1980, right after we were married. This is one of the "early" recipes that didn't kill Mr. TiFW....

Posted by: Teresa in Fort Worth, Texas. Yield: 4 – 6 servings. Prep time: 2 hours.

---

32-ounce can crushed tomatoes (Hunt's)
3 cloves garlic, crushed
1/2 small yellow onion, diced
1 tablespoon oregano
salt and pepper to taste
1 pound ground meat (at least 15% fat)
1 egg
1/2 cup WHOLE milk
3/4 cup bread crumbs
1 tablespoon chopped parsley
2 cloves garlic, crushed
1 teaspoon rosemary, minced
salt and pepper to taste
3/4 cup olive oil (Pompeiian)
12-ounce can tomato paste (Hunt's)
spaghetti noodles

For the sauce: combine the tomatoes, garlic, onion, oregano, salt, and pepper in a large pot. Rinse out tomato can with 1/2 cup of water and add to the pot. Bring to a boil, then reduce heat to a low boil/simmer. Let cook for about an hour, stirring every 10 – 15 minutes. Add more water if necessary. For the meatballs: while sauce is cooking, combine meat, egg, milk, bread crumbs, parsley, garlic, rosemary, salt, and pepper and shape into meatballs. Brown the meatballs on both sides in olive oil, adding more oil if necessary. After sauce has cooked for an hour, add all of the meatballs and half of the oil that remains in the pan, along with the drippings, to the sauce. (If you do not make meatballs, add 1/2 of the olive oil.) Spoon half of the tomato paste on top of the sauce, partially cover, and simmer for 30 minutes, stirring every 5 – 10 minutes to prevent burning. Sauce will thicken considerably. After 30 minutes, add remaining tomato paste. Keep pot partially covered and continue to simmer for another 30 minutes, stirring every 5 – 10 minutes to prevent burning. The sauce will be thick and delicious. Serve over cooked spaghetti noodles.

### *Chef's Notes:*

The secret to the delicious sauce is the olive oil, and the secret to delicious meatballs is the whole milk. It is important to use meat that has at least 15% fat, as the fat acts as a binder for the meatballs. This recipe can be made gluten-free by using GF breadcrumbs (put a few pieces of GF bread in a food processor) and GF spaghetti noodles. Because my family likes this recipe so much, I usually quadruple the recipe and can the remaining sauce for later use.

## Beef Mushroom Spaghetti

445 This is what to do with leftover pot roast! I got this from a blog called "Not Just Leftovers," and it is attributed to *Taste of Home* originally (though the blogger states she modified it).

Posted by: Dr Alice. Yield: a lot Prep time: 20 minutes.

---

8 – 10 ounces spaghetti
8-ounce can tomato sauce
small or medium can sliced mushrooms, drained
1/2 to 1 cup leftover pot roast, chopped
1 cup juice from roast
1 cup shredded mozzarella or other mild cheese
1/4 teaspoon salt, or more to taste

This is stunningly easy and tastes much better than it has any right to. Mix all of the above except for the cheese (drain the mushrooms first) and place in a greased 8-inch square pan. Place mozzarella (or jack, or Parmesan, or a combination) on top. Bake at 350 degrees F for 30 minutes. Give it about 10 minutes to cool before you try to cut into it. Assuming you let the pot roast juice sit overnight, it will be very easy to get the fat off the top. Also, you can make this ahead to freeze. If you do, don't put the cheese on it before you freeze it, just wait till it is thawing.

***Chef's Notes:***
This is second of three recipes. If you use these, you can stretch a pot roast like a rubber band.

## Tonypete's Friday Pasta

446 Shrimp, tomato, cheese pasta with basil. A Tonypete family recipe.

Posted by: Tonypete. Yield: 6 servings. Prep time: 30 minutes.

---

1/4 cup olive oil
1 pound shrimp (big ones)
1 pint small tomatoes
4 cloves garlic, chopped
2 tablespoons chopped basil
1/2 pound pasta—cooked per directions
1/2 cup shredded Manchego cheese

Heat olive oil in skillet and fry garlic over medium heat. Cook for 45 seconds to 1 minute. Add shrimp and stir. Cook for 1 – 2 minutes or until just turning pink. Add basil and tomatoes. Cover skillet and cook for 5 – 6 minutes until tomatoes have cooked down a bit. Cook 1 minute uncovered. Toss shrimp with cooked pasta. Stir in cheese and serve.

## Seduction Spaghetti Sauce

447 Whenever my college roommate got a new honey he would cook this for her first time over, and it always worked for him. It worked for him, for me . . . not so much, but still tasty!

Posted by: Vlad the Impaler, whittling away like mad. Yield: 4 servings Prep time: couple hours.

---

3 cans stewed tomatoes
3 cans tomato paste
1 can tomato sauce
3 cloves garlic
1 large yellow onion, chopped
1 pound hot Italian sausage
1 pound ground beef
1 package Lawry's spaghetti sauce spices and seasonings mix
a few glugs red wine
oregano to taste
1 bay leaf
1/2 teaspoon cinnamon
1 teaspoon sugar

In large pot squish up stewed tomatoes. Add tomato paste and tomato sauce. Begin heating on medium-low. In skillet brown whole sausage, then cut up in pan and add ground beef; cook until browned. Add the meat to the tomatoes, reserving fat in the skillet. Pour off half of grease, then brown onion. Add garlic to mostly browned onion for ~ 45 seconds, then add both to tomato/meat mixture. Add package of spaghetti sauce mix, raise heat to medium and cook for 30 minutes. Lower heat to simmer and add oregano, bay leaf, cinnamon, sugar and wine (some in the dish, some in the cook). The longer you let it simmer, the better. Very thick and meaty. You can cut back the meats by half for a more liquid-like sauce.

## White Lasagna

448 No red sauce, just the most delicious (albeit rich) cheese sauce ever devised! Recipe is from Peggy Card (aka Cricketmom).

Posted by: Cricket. Yield: 8 – 10 servings. Prep time: 45 minutes.

---

8 ounces lasagna noodles
1 pound ground beef
3/4 cup chopped onion
1 clove garlic
2 teaspoons dried basil, crushed
1 teaspoon dried oregano
3/4 teaspoon salt
½ teaspoon pepper
1/2 teaspoon Italian herb seasoning
1 cup light (table) cream
3 ounces cream cheese, cubed
1/2 cup dry white wine
2 cups shredded cheddar cheese
1 1/2 cups shredded Gouda cheese
1 1/2 cups cream-style cottage cheese
1 egg, slightly beaten

12 ounces sliced mozzarella cheese

Preheat oven to 375 degrees F. Cook lasagna noodles according to package directions. Drain and set aside. Cook ground beef, onion, and garlic until meat is browned. Drain fat. Stir in basil, oregano, salt, pepper, and Italian seasoning. Add cream and cream cheese. Cook and stir over low heat until cheese melts. Stir in wine. Add cheddar and Gouda cheese. Stir and heat until cheese melts. In separate bowl, stir together cottage cheese and egg. Layer half of the noodles in a greased 13x9x2 inch baking pan. Top with half of the meat sauce, half of the cottage cheese mixture and half of the mozzarella cheese. Repeat. Bake, uncovered, for 30-35 minutes. Let stand 10 minutes before serving.

## Puttanesca

449 Pasta with a tuna red sauce. The recipe came from Bruno, an Italian exchange student many years ago. He called it Tunafish Pasta. I didn't know its real name for years—understandable, perhaps, because it translates as Whore's Pasta and we were all about 14 at the time. All ingredients are approximate--I could have easily said a slosh of olive oil.

Posted by: Wenda (sic). Yield: enough for 6 piggy people. Prep time: perhaps 1/2 hour, scattered through the afternoon.

---

1/4 cup olive oil
1/2 teaspoon red pepper flakes
3 – 5 cloves garlic, minced
2 jars good commercial tomato sauce (or if you must, your own)
2 tablespoons capers, well rinsed
1 teaspoon dried oregano
2/3 cup black olives, preferably Calamata, halved
2 cans tuna, drained
handful fresh basil, cut in slivers
1 pound spaghetti

Heat the oil with the pepper flakes in a nonreactive saucepan on medium. When warm, remove from heat, add the garlic, and let it turn pale gold—5 to 10 minutes. Stir in the tomato sauce, capers, and oregano. Bring to a boil and simmer for as long as you have. Two hours? Two days? Either will work. A half-hour before serving, stir in the olives and tuna. (Too much cooking time and they seem to take over the sauce and flatten it.) This is also the time to bring (ample) water to boil and cook the pasta. Dump the cooked pasta in a large bowl, pour the sauce over it, and sprinkle with the slivered basil. *Mangia.*

## Wednesday Pasta

450 Pasta dish we make every Wednesday. We made up this one all on our own.

Posted by: RB3 & The Wandering Swede, lllooonnnggg time lurkers. Yield: 2 servings. Prep time: 30 minutes.

---

5 – 6 ounces spaghetti, uncooked
1 tablespoon olive oil
2 – 3 ounces sausage links (pork, breakfast style)
1/4 cup chopped onion
2 – 3 garlic cloves, minced
1 medium jalapeno, seeded and chopped
1/4 cup chopped bell pepper
1 small tomato, chopped
6 ounces canned clams, partially drained
1 tablespoon vodka
1/4 teaspoon anchovy paste
1/3 cup heavy cream
salt, pepper, paprika, cayenne, parsley
grated parmesan cheese

Start a large pot of water heating while making the sauce. and add salt and spaghetti when the water boils. In a large frying pan, cook sausage in oil until mostly done, then add onion, garlic, peppers, tomato, anchovy paste and vodka, and cook until soft. Add clams with some of the liquid and cook a few minutes. Add cream and seasonings (salt, pepper, paprika, cayenne and parsley) to taste, and let simmer until spaghetti is done, about 8 minutes. When spaghetti is cooked, use tongs to remove it from the boiling water and add it to the hot sauce. Mix lightly and serve topped with a little grated parmesan cheese. Sauce should be fairly tight (thick) so don't use too much of the clam juice, and do use plenty of seasonings.

## Pepperonaghetti

451 Cured meat sauce. Came up with this one summer when I had a ton of tomatoes and no fresh meats for a sauce. Noticing that there was a stick of pepperoni in the fridge, I thought, "this could be a different taste". It was and still is. The pepperoni spices the flavor and adds a depth that you do not get from simple sauces, regardless of how meaty you make them. Using the oils of the cured meat as a method of cooking the supporting flavors of onion and garlic is a great change to boring olive oil. We have explored using other cured meats as well and it has not ceased to amaze.

Posted by: Jdubya_AZ. Yield: 4 servings. Prep time: 45 minutes.

---

1 cup pepperoni cut into 1/4 inch (or smaller) cubes
1 – 2 pounds garden fresh tomatoes (heirloom is always better) (or 1 28-ounce can of whole tomatoes)
1/2 cup garden fresh basil

1 yellow onion, finely diced
4 or more garlic cloves, finely crushed
salt and pepper to taste
1 pound spaghetti or bucatini or any pasta you desire
1 tablespoon butter
2 cups whole milk (or lighter fat, if you want)
1 – 2 cups Parmesan or Romano cheese, finely grated

Prepare a simmering, sub-boiling pot of water. If using garden fresh tomatoes, cut out/off any ugly scars, blemishes, any core. Blanch tomatoes and remove skins. If not using fresh tomatoes, you can replace with a can (28 ounces) of whole tomatoes (Italian is better). Place tomatoes and basil in a blender or immersion blender and puree. Set aside. In a slightly hot (not very hot) sauce or saute pan, pour in pepperonni and allow to heat up. You will see oil coming out of the meat. You want that. You want that bad, don't you. Er. When meat has slowly cooked (about 5 – 7 minutes) remove meat and place into a bowel. Leave oil in pan. Bring heat in sauce or saute pan up a bit and add the onion. Cook until translucent. Onion will take on a red hue from the oil. That is perfect. Add garlic. Cook another 1 – 2 minutes. Add tomato/basil puree. Bring to a boil then turn down to simmer. Add pepperoni and allow to simmer slow.

Fill a big pot with water, but add the 2 cups of whole milk. Bring to an almost boil, do not boil as the milk will scald and you will get a mess. Add pasta to water/milk and stir. The pasta will take a little longer but it will cook thoroughly. When the pasta is ready, reserve one cup of the water/milk and set aside. Drain pasta, then place back into pot. Add the one cup reserved water/milk, butter, and begin stirring. Stir vigorously and don't be a sissy about it. This is the important part. Begin adding the Parmesian cheese in small amounts to mix into the pasta. Place pasta into bowls and cover with the sauce. Eat. There are several variation that can add value to this meal. It really is a different twist to use cured meats as opposed to standard fare. Try soppressata or capicola as well. Also, this really is not a bad snack served cold.

## Blue Pasta on the Trail

452 A simple spaghetti dish featuring blue cheese. Inspired by a dish served in the long-extinct Borsodi's Coffeehouse in Isla Vista.

Posted by: Corndog. Yield: servings for 4 Morons. Prep time: 30 minutes.

---

4 green onions
4 cloves garlic
4 tablespoons olive oil
1 pound spaghetti
6 ounces crumbled blue cheese (Gorgonzola, Bleu and/or Stilton)
red chili flakes to taste
coarse ground black pepper to taste

In a small pan, under low/medium heat, cook minced garlic cloves and chopped *white* part of the green onions in half the olive oil until soft. Keep warm 'til spaghetti is done.

Meanwhile, cook the spaghetti, just like it says on the box! Drain well. Immediately toss everything together, while the pasta is still nice and hot. Use Gorgonzola for a milder dish, standard Bleu for stronger flavor. I like the flavor best when using Stilton, the King of Cheeses.

## Macaroni and Cheese

453 This is mine, all mine . . . I think.

Posted by: Grannysaurus Rex. Yield: 4 – 6 servings. Prep time: 50 minutes.

---

4 tablespoons butter, divided usage
3 tablespoons flour
1/4 cup finely minced onions
1/2 teaspoon dry mustard
1/2 teaspoon salt
1/2 teaspoon freshly ground coarse black pepper
¼ - ½ teaspoon Tabasco sauce, plus more for serving
8 ounces elbow or cavatappi pasta
2 1/2 cups milk, heated in the microwave about 3 minutes
8 ounces extra sharp cheddar, shredded
1/2 cup panko breadcrumbs

Heat the oven to 350 degrees F and grease an 8" baking dish. Prepare the pasta according to package directions, using salted water. Drain and very briefly rinse with cool water to remove excess starch on the pasta. I find it makes a smoother finished product. Meanwhile, melt 2 tablespoons butter in a large saucepan over medium heat. Saute the onion for 5 minutes until translucent. Add the dry mustard, salt, pepper, and flour. Cook, stirring constantly, for 2 minutes. Slowly add the hot milk, stirring constantly with a whisk to blend. Once blended, stir frequently until the sauce comes to a boil. Reduce the heat to low and whisk in the Tabasco and cheese. Add the cheese in 3 – 4 batches, whisking to completely melt the cheese before adding more. Taste and correct for salt. Stir the pasta into the sauce. Pour the contents in the prepared pan. Melt the remaining 2 tablespoons of butter on medium-low heat in the pasta cooking pan (why dirty another dish?). Add the panko breadcrumbs and stir to combine. Sprinkle the breadcrumbs over the casserole. Bake for 20 – 30 minutes, or until bubbling. Let cool 5 minutes before serving with extra Tabasco at the table.

***Chef's Notes:***

Use chunk cheese you have shredded yourself for a smooth sauce. If you have some aged reserve cheddar like Cabot Farmhouse Reserve, Cracker Barrel Reserve, Kerrygold Reserve, or Heluva Special Reserve you might want to reduce the cheese to 6 ounces in the sauce with the remaining 2 ounces sprinkled on top before the bread crumbs. The Reserve cheeses are great but some might find the sauce too rich. This recipe doubles easily. Feel free to stir in cooked broccoli, cubed ham, crab meat, or whatever you have on hand.

# Pasta with Sausage and Pumpkin Sauce

454 It's orange. Really orange. Really, really orange. I got this from my sister. She probably got it from one of the fancy cooking magazines but the evidence is lost in the mists of time.

Posted by: Tonestaple. Yield: 6 – 8 servings. Prep time: a while.

---

4 tablespoons olive oil
1 pound spicy Italian sausage
1 cup chopped onion
10 cloves garlic
3 tablespoons chopped fresh sage
1/4 teaspoon hot red pepper flakes
1 ¼ cup white wine
1 ¼ cup canned pumpkin
1/4 teaspoon ground cinnamon
2 cups chicken stock
1 pound pasta (I use penne)
lots of grated Parmigiano Reggiano

Heat 1 tablespoon olive oil in saucepan over high heat. Add sausage and cook about 3 minutes or until brown, breaking up the pieces with a spoon. Remove from the heat and transfer meat to a bowl. Reserve 1 tablespoon of fat from the sausage in the pot, and discard the rest. Add the remaining 3 tablespoons olive oil to the pot, heat over medium heat, and add the onion, garlic and sage. Cook about 10 minutes until the onion and garlic start to brown. Add the red pepper flakes and sausage and cook for 2 minutes, stirring well. Deglaze the pan with the wine and cook for about 8 minutes, stirring well to dislodge the brown bits on the bottom of the pan. Add the pumpkin puree and cook for 2 minutes, stirring well. Add the chicken stock and cinnamon. Bring to a boil, then reduce heat and simmer for about 30 minutes. Add salt and pepper to taste. Cook the pasta in salted boiling water for time indicated on package. Drain well. Add to sauce and cook over medium heat for about 3 minutes. Remove from heat. Add Parmesan and serve.

This freezes well and reheats well in the microwave and is also delicious cold, if you're feeling really unmotivated. (True about the freezing and microwaving, but my sister is the one who says it's good cold (I've never tried that.) If you are feeling really ambitious and want to make this with fresh pumpkin, DO NOT use sugar pumpkins (suitable for pie) as it just doesn't taste right. This is a very forgiving recipe so feel free to mess with ingredients in whatever fashion you please. I never count garlic cloves, nor do I measure the sage, and I always use one big can of Libby's pumpkin puree (and for heaven's sake, don't use the pumpkin pie filling!).

# Pasta Aglio e Olio

455 Classic Italian pasta course. I first saw this recipe demonstrated by Lidia Bastianich and it is a variation on her theme.

Posted by: J.J. Sefton. Yield: 2 – 4 servings. Prep time: no more than half hour start to finish.

---

½ to 1 pound spaghetti or linguine (I use DeCecco)
1/2 cup kosher salt for water
at least 10 to as many as you can handle sliced garlic cloves
1/2 teaspoon or more dried red pepper flakes, to taste
3/4 cup or more fresh chopped Italian parsley
2 – 3 tablespoons good quality olive oil
as much as you like grated Parmigiano Reggiano
Optional: no more than 1/2 teaspoon sea salt for the pan (see instructions)

Pasta aglio e olio, that is pasta with garlic and oil, is one of the truly classic Italian dishes. As with much of the cuisine of this country, especially the further south you travel down the boot, it relies on just a few basic ingredients and a fairly simple and quick preparation, but the ingredients have to be absolutely fresh and of the best quality --especially the cheese. If you use Kraft Parmesan in a can I will personally hunt you down and pelt you with an unpleasant unguent, so get real Parmigiano Reggiano. It really is worth the price. And all things considered, it's incredibly delicious and satisfying. What's strange about this dish is that it seemingly ignores the one inviolable rule of cooking pasta and that is never to mix oil into the water. Technically, we are mixing both but not by pouring the oil into the pasta pot, which is the fatal mistake most people make.

You'll notice that there's a lot of leeway in the measurements so you can easily cook this for two with half a box or it's a great meal for four with a full pound and a touch more. You'll just need a pan that can accommodate larger quantities. Cooking this dish is not difficult, but that said, it really does rely on timing to get it perfect. Basta cosi, so andiamo a cucina!

Place a large pot of water on a burner and turn it on high. As the water is coming to a boil, peel and slice the garlic cloves. You don't have to slice it gossamer thin with a razor blade so it liquifies in the pan a la Goodfellas. Peeling garlic can be a big pain in the ass. You can buy whole peeled garlic cloves at the market but it's expensive. Here's a trick; press a head of unpeeled garlic down on your cutting board just to loosen the cloves, then put the entire head into a metal mixing bowl, cover with another metal mixing bowl so you have a sphere, then shake it vigorously for about 20 seconds and voila! An entire head of peeled garlic cloves, dead easy. Also, to get the garlic smell off your hands, rinse with soap while rubbing a stainless steel utensil. I love garlic and I use minimally 15 large cloves or even more. As the garlic cooks, it mellows quite a bit but the flavor is still there. Place the sliced garlic cloves into a large, wide saucepan or skillet with high sides. I use one from AllClad that is essentially a wok. Then, add enough olive oil to just coat the pan and the garlic slices. Optional step: Add no more than half a teaspoon of sea salt to the garlic and oil. I do this as a precaution in case I under salt the cooking water, but it's all too easy to ruin the dish this way. Don't ask me how I know. When the water is at a rolling boil, add the half cup or so of kosher salt. The rule of thumb is that your pasta water should taste about as salty as the sea, so carefully try a little without napalming your mouth. If it is salty enough, omit the previous optional step.

When it comes back to the boil, add your pasta and gently settle it into the water as it softens without breaking the pieces. Set your timer to about 6 1/2 minutes and start it. Turn the fire on the garlic and oil to a low setting. Don't worry; it will get hot pretty quickly but the low setting prevents browning too quickly. Shake the pan a bit every now and again to keep the garlic from sticking to the bottom. Wash the parsley thoroughly and roughly chop a good handful of the leaves as the pasta and the garlic are cooking away, and set aside. When the timer is down to about 2:00 minutes, throw the red pepper flakes in with the garlic and oil and turn the heat up to high for no more than 30 seconds to a minute, just to release the oils. With the heat still on high, take a cup or so of the boiling pasta water and pour it into the pan with the garlic and oil. Sizzle!!!

Check the pasta. It should be at a stage called duro which means hard; not yet al dente. Using a pair of tongs in one hand, and holding the lid of the pasta pot in the other, transfer the undercooked pasta to the pan with the garlic, oil, water and pepper flakes. The pot lid helps catch the water and saves on clean up. By the way, you may be ahead of the timer, so if it goes off no big deal. This kind of a dish is done mostly by "feel" and the timer is more of a guidepost. Turn the pasta in with the boiling liquid. This is where the magic happens; the pasta is going to absorb the garlic-infused oil along with the salted water. Keep turning, trying to mix the cloves in with the mass of noodles. If you see the liquid has evaporated, just add a little more of the pasta water. Not too much. Taste to see if it's done. It should just be al dente. If so, turn off the fire, throw in the parsley and combine. Plate up a nice mound and make sure to serve a generous amount of garlic slices. Grate Parmigiano Reggiano on top, serve and enjoy!

***Chef's Notes:***
A fresh garden salad or perhaps a Greek salad with arugula, red onions, sliced olives and feta goes great with this dish. For wine, try a fruitier, full-bodied white to balance the strong flavors and spiciness, or a chianti, Barolo or barbaresco if you prefer a red.

## Roasted Cherry Tomato and Kalamata Summer Pasta

456 Tangy tasty pasta using fresh cherry/grape tomatoes—perfect summer pasta dish. From *Bon Appetit*, March 2002.

Posted by: Rhomboid. Yield: 6 servings. Prep time: 1 hour—mostly cooking, not prep time.

---

2 1/2 pounds cherry tomatoes
1/3 cup olive oil
1 tablespoon balsamic vinegar
5 cloves garlic
1/4 teaspoon crushed red pepper
3 tablespoons fresh oregano
1 pound farfalle or other short pasta
1/2 cup pitted kalamata olives
1/4 cup capers
6 ounces crumbled feta cheese
1/4 cup toasted pine nuts

Preheat oven or grill to 375 degrees F. Mince garlic. Halve tomatoes. Add to baking dish, along with olive oil, balsamic vinegar, and crushed red pepper. Roast for 45 minutes, stirring half-way through. Remove from heat, add oregano. Meanwhile, cook pasta to taste, drain, and return to pot. Add olives, capers, and tomato mixture. Stir over low heat for a few minutes. Add feta and stir until cheese begins to melt. Serve pasta with pine nuts sprinkled on top.

***Chef's Notes:***
If possible, use fresh cherry or grape tomatoes—I "discovered" this recipe while looking for a way to use a bumper crop of tomatoes from my yard. This is one of my favorite recipes, period—with fresh tomatoes it is simply fantastic. I add more balsamic vinegar than the recipe calls for, and usually more red pepper. Fantastic with a nice chilled rose wine on a warm summer evening.

## Meaty Ziti

457 With sausage and bacon, maybe it should be "Infidel Ziti." A combination of at least 3 recipes, one from *Cook's Country*, and two from pasta boxes, plus an idea or two of my own.

Posted by: Katja. Yield: 12 servings. Prep time: 25 minutes.

---

1/2 pound uncased sausage (Italian is good, but even breakfast sausage will work)
2 tablespoons olive oil
2 cloves minced garlic
1 28-ounce can crushed tomatoes
1 teaspoon basil leaves
1 teaspoon salt
1/4 teaspoon pepper
1 one-pound box ziti
1 pound thin to medium-sliced bacon
2 cups (8 ounces) shredded mozzarella cheese
2 cups (8 ounces, or about 18 slices) shredded or sliced Swiss cheese
½ cup grated Parmesan cheese

Preheat oven to 375 degrees F. Gently brown uncased sausage, stirring to remove any larger chunks. Drain grease and set aside. Heat olive oil and garlic in a skillet until the garlic is fragrant but not brown. Stir in tomatoes and let mixture simmer until it has thickened slightly (about 10 minutes). Take skillet off heat, then stir in basil, salt, and pepper. Cook ziti noodles to al dente. In a pan or in the oven, begin cooking bacon so that it is partially cooked, but not crispy. (This is in order to release some of the grease.) Mix together sauce, ziti, sausage, and mozzarella cheese, then add about 1/4 cup water. Pour half of this mixture into a 9 x 13 baking dish. Layer 2/3 of the Swiss cheese (12 slices) over this, then pour the other half of the noodle mixture over the cheese. Lay partially-cooked bacon crosswise over the top, then the Parmesan cheese, then the remainder of the Swiss cheese. Bake for approximately 30 minutes. Dish is done when cheese on top is browning (and any visible bacon ends are getting crispy).

## Mom's Homemade Spaghetti Sauce

458 Meat gravy for your spaghetti. My mom's version of my Italian grandmother's spaghetti sauce.

Posted by: FarkinClownshoes. Yield: servings for 4 to 6 Morons. Prep time: 4 hours.

---

2 green peppers
2 or 3 cloves of garlic
1 pound hamburger (85 to 90% lean)
1 16-ounce can chopped tomatoes
8 ounces tomato sauce
4 ounces tomato paste
1 tablespoon white sugar
3 tablespoons olive oil or butter
2 or 3 tablespoons of parsley
1 teaspoon sage
1 teaspoon rosemary
1/2 teaspoon thyme
1 tablespoon oregano
1 tablespoon basil
1 bay leaf (be sure to take it after cooking is complete)
salt and pepper to taste (not more than a teaspoon of salt)

Chop the peppers, onions, and garlic. Put tomato paste in a bowl with equal amount of water, stir until dissolved. Put a big ol' pot on medium to medium-high heat, and heat oil or melt butter. Saute onions and peppers until they are soft (about 5 minutes). Throw in garlic, saute everything for a few more minutes. Crumble in burger, saute until brown. Pour in dissolved tomato paste. Make sure the liquid level covers the burger. Add more water until this is so. Add in cans of tomato sauce and chopped tomatoes. Add spices, salt, pepper and sugar. Let simmer with cover on for about 2 or 3 hours. Then simmer with cover off until sauce reaches the appropriate thickness. Stir early, stir often: when adding new ingredients and every 20 or 30 minutes.

***Chef's Notes:***

This is a good base sauce for other Italian dishes, like lasagna. You can drop in Italian sausages (hot or sweet) or meatballs after an hour or so of simmering if this is going to be pasta sauce. If multiplying ingredients to make a bigger batch, do not add more sage or bay leaves. The other spices can be adjusted as needed. You can replace the white sugar with a couple of splashes of a sweet red wine. The sugar cuts the acidity in the tomato.

## Aiko's Noodles

459 Quick dinner for one or more. Aiko was a college student from Japan who lived down the block back in the 70's.

Posted by: sock_rat_eez. Yield: 1 serving. Prep time: 20 minutes.

---

1/2 cup ground beef
1 cup chopped cabbage
1 or 2 green onions
1 clove garlic
1 or 2 cups soba or other noodles, cooked

Start the ground beef frying in a good sized pan. When well browned there is enough fat to start cooking the rest of the ingredients. I like this with the cabbage still a bit al dente, so do not overcook. If the noodles are still nice and hot you can dump this on top of them in a big bowl. You can also add the noodles to the pan and stir a bit to warm them up. Add soy sauce to taste. Originally this was made with those fat buckwheat soba noodles, but it will work with anything. Thai rice thread noodles are good too; I have even used the brick of noodles from a ramen pack with good results. I added the garlic because I like garlic. Most Japanese people don't.

## EZ (Lazy?) Hamburger Stroganoff

460 Quick and painless, like your sex life. Recipe is from my ma.

Posted by: Boardpusher. Yield: 3 servings. Prep time: 15 minutes.

---

1 pound ground sirloin
1 package Skinner egg noodles
1 pack Lipton's onion soup mix
1 can Campbell's cream of mushroom soup
8 ounces Daisy sour cream
1/2 tablespoon dill
salt to taste

Boil egg noodles 10 – 12 minutes (or however long you want, they're your noodles). Meanwhile (after about 5 minutes), in a separate pan, brown the sirloin. Add the mushroom soup and Lipton's (keep all those sweet hamburger juices, draining is for liberals). Cover and simmer for 5 minutes. At the last moment, add sour cream and dill. Stir, then serve over (cooked hopefully) egg noodles.

## Spiced Cold Noodles

461 Cold Oriental noodle dish with peanut and hot sauces. This was a favorite dish for gatherings of my graduate school research colleagues at UC Berkeley. So far as I know, it originated from a family restaurant that one of our research assistant's families once owned and operated.

Posted by: Krebs v Carnot: Epic Battle of the Cycling Stars (TM). Yield: dunno -- lots?
Prep time: 120 minutes.

-----------------------------------------------------------------------------------------------------------

1/2 pound lo mein noodles
2 to 3 quarts water at a rolling boil
small amount cooking oil
1 pound chicken
12 ounces bean sprouts
3 or 4 carrots
1 large cucumber
1 bunch green onions

*For peanut sauce:*
1 cup chicken broth
1/2 head garlic, peeled and chopped
1/8 cup fresh ginger, peeled and chopped
1/4 cup brown sugar, loosely packed
1/2 teaspoon white pepper
1/2 cup dry sherry
1/2 cup vinegar
1 to 1 1/2 cups soy sauce
1 teaspoon salt (optional)
1/2 cup cooking oil
1 pound chunky peanut butter

*For hot sauce:*
1 ounce crushed red peppers
1/2 cup chopped garlic
1/2 cup chopped ginger
10 black mushrooms
3 tablespoons fermented black bean sauce
sesame oil to saute
sugar to taste
ground pepper to taste

Drop noodles into boiling water in a large pot. When water starts to reboil, pour in 1 cup of cold water. Cook until noodles are soft, then drain, reserving water. Pour a small amount of oil over noodles, mix and then refrigerate. Place chicken pieces in reserved boiling water. Cook for 20 minutes at a boil, then remove pot from heat. Cover pot and let stand for 1 hour. Remove pieces from pot, drain, and shred meat from bones and skin, then refrigerate. Drain sprouts and wash, then refrigerate. Wash and peel carrots and cucumber, then shred them and refrigerate separately. Wash and dice green onions, including as much of the green portion as desired.

To make the peanut sauce: finely chop garlic and ginger. Combine and blend all remaining peanut sauce ingredients in pot over low heat, stirring until all is blended. Refrigerate, covered, when complete. Stir to mix when using. (To freeze, mix all ingredients except oil and peanut butter. Add proportionate amount of oil and peanut butter to defrosted mixture when ready to use.)

To make the hot sauce: soak mushrooms and chop to medium size. Heat oil in wok. Add ginger, garlic, black bean sauce, and mushrooms. Saute briefly. Remove from heat and add peppers (don't brown them). Add sugar and pepper to taste. Refrigerate.

When you are ready to eat, serve smorgasbord style. Dish out individual servings of noodles. Place chicken and other ingredients on top, then add peanut sauce and hot sauce to taste. Mix and eat.

## Sausage, Pasta, and Broccoli Rabe

462 Inspired by similar dishes we had at various Italian restaurants, this particular variation is our own creation.

Posted by: boomstick. Yield: 8 servings. Prep time: 30 minutes.

---

1 pound Italian sausage
1 pound cavatelli
1 pound broccoli rabe
5 cloves garlic
1/2 cup trated Parmigiano Reggiano cheese
1/4 cup olive oil

Boil water for the pasta, according to the instructions on the package. While the water is heating, chop the broccoli rabe (I prefer half-inch-wide strips) and mince the garlic. Remove sausage casings, if applicable. Once the cavatelli goes into the water, brown the sausage filling in a Dutch oven or a skillet with high sides, breaking up the sausage into small chunks (the smaller the better). When the sausage is cooked, add some olive oil and the minced garlic, and saute for 30 seconds. Add the broccoli rabe to the sausage, mix, and cover for a minute. The cavatelli should be close to done. Drain, and add to the sausage/rabe mixture. Mix well, cooking for an additional minute or so. Transfer to a big serving dish, top with cheese, and it's done, just like Hillary's political career!

***Chef's Notes:***

We prefer cavatelli to the more common use of orecchiette. Sausage may be hot or mild, according to your preference. We usually go light on the cheese and let people add more at the table. We sometimes double the rabe. Use less garlic if you prefer. It's okay not to mince the garlic, rough chopping or a quick smash will do (Morons aren't particular).

# Shrimp with Feta Cheese Over Vermicelli (or Linguine)

463 Simple yet rich pasta dish. (Great "get lucky" meal for single guys.) This probably came from a recipe somewhere and there are similar variant on the intertubes. I've been making it for 20 years and modified after observing it made for me.

Posted by: Coop. Yield: 6 – 8 servings. Prep time: 40 minutes.

---

1 ½ + pounds shrimp, peeled, deveined, tails removed
4 cloves garlic, thinly slivered
1 teaspoon red pepper flakes
salt to taste
2 14-ounce cans diced or chunky tomatoes (flavored, like basil and garlic)
enough olive oil to coat pan
8-ounce block feta cheese (plain or flavored)
favorite Italian herbs to taste
some wine—Chardonnay (1st choice) or red (2nd choice)
2 8-ounce packages fresh pasta (vermicelli, linguine)

In a nonstick large skillet, add enough olive oil to coat the pan. Add slivered garlic and red pepper flakes and bring to medium heat. After about a minute or as the garlic softens but does not brown, add in the shrimp. Make a very light sprinkling of your favorite herbs and salt to taste. Stir/toss/turn over medium heat for a few minutes until the shrimp is starting to turn pink. Remove shrimp with slotted spoon to large casserole dish. Crumble and sprinkle some of the feta cheese over the shrimp, generously or not depending on how much you like feta. Preheat oven to 350 degrees F. Pour the canned tomatoes into the pan and increase heat to medium-high. Bring to a faster simmer and begin reducing the tomatoes down to a thick, chunky consistency. Add a little wine to help cut the oil and sprinkle some more herbs and salt to taste. Cook for around 10 minutes. Spoon the tomato chunks over the shrimp (it won't completely cover) and sprinkle some more feta cheese on top of the tomatoes. Place in oven and bake for about 20 minutes or until the exposed feta starts to brown a little. Start the pasta water when the shrimp go in the oven. Cook pasta according to directions. Serve with the shrimp and tomatoes over the pasta, using a spoon to dip into the casserole to get get some of the liquids that settle.

### *Chef's Notes:*

This is very rich so be conservative on the initial servings. I like to serve it with buttered garlic bread for sopping and a very simple salad. It makes awesome leftovers that will not last very long, and it's also a surprisingly good breakfast!

## Steve's Insanity Chili

464 This is a chili recipe I've used to win the chili cookoff at church a couple times. I took a few chili recipes from the web, combined them, and tweaked the result to arrive at a pleasing balance. I make it for family reunions and parties. I also like to make extra to freeze leftovers in lunch-sized portions. This dish handles freezing and reheating very well.

Posted by: StevePoling. Yield: 8 servings. Prep time: 60 mins.

---

30 ounces Philly Cheesesteak "pucks" (or stew meat)
3 ½ onions, chopped
2 stalks celery, chopped
½ bell pepper, chopped
5 jalapeno peppers, minced
5 habanero peppers, minced
1 ghost pepper, minced
42 ounces canned tomatoes
12 ounces chili sauce
2 ounces chili powder
Garlic to taste
1 teapoon cumin
1 ½ teaspoons fresh ginger, minced
3 teaspoons Dave's Insanity Sauce
red kidney beans, black beans, garbanzos, corn (optional)

Drain canned tomatoes, retaining the liquid. Brown cheesesteak and deglaze pan with liquid from the canned tomatoes. In your soup pot sweat the onions, peppers, and celery until translucent. Add tomatoes, chili sauce, garlic, ginger, jalapenos, habaneros, chili pepper, and cumin. Simmer for 20 minutes or MUCH longer. Add Dave's Insanity Sauce (or any other 1 million Scoville sauce) near the end of the simmer (or omit to spare yourself some delicious pain). If you're inclined toward beans in your chili, toss in cans of red kidney, black beans, and garbanzos during the simmer. My son likes to toss in a can of corn. Your mileage may vary. You can substitute stew meat, but I prefer the flavor and texture of cheesesteak hoagie meat that I get from a local restaurant supply store (Gordon Food Service: www.gfs.com). Look for SKU #1230-200 "Sliced and shaped beef sirloin steak.")

## Lentil-Hot Sausage Soup

465 Hot soup for a cold night. I created this recipe myself.

Posted by: Pat*. Yield: 2 servings. Prep time: 30 – 40 minutes.

---

4 cups water
1 cup dry lentils
4 beef bouillon cubes
½ cup frozen corn (or dried)
1/3 cup chopped carrots (or dried)
1 bay leaf (optional)
4 ounces or more hot Italian sausage (or cooked bacon)
¼ of an onion, chopped
2 cloves garlic, minced
½ teaspoon cumin (optional)
olive oil (optional)
salt and pepper

Bring the water to a boil in your soup pot. Add lentils, bouillon cubes, corn, and carrots (plus the bay leaf, if you use one). Turn down heat to simmer. Cover and cook for 20 – 25 minutes or until lentils are soft. At the same time, fry the hot Italian sausage—use a pinch of olive oil if desired. (If it's a single sausage and not bulk meat, slice it or break it up when it's cooked.) When it's nearly cooked, saute the onion and garlic in with it. (Don't burn the garlic!) When the lentils are soft, and the meat is cooked, add the meat mixture to the soup pot and stir. Add salt, pepper and cumin to taste. (Remove the bay leaf if you used one.) I tried making it with cooked bacon, omitting the cumin, but I prefer the sausage version. You can vary the amounts of the ingredients to taste.

## 38 Ricochet Richard's Rootin' Tootin' 4th Place Chili

466 This started out as the chili from Alton Brown's show Good Eats. But I have changed the cooking method, time, and at least 5 ingredients. It's really only vaguely associated with that recipe now but that is where it originated.

Posted by: Rihar. Yield: 5 servings. Prep time: 1 – 2 hours.

---

1 pound ground beef (80% lean preferred)
1 pound breakfast sausage
25+ tortilla chips (crushed)
16 ounce bottle of salsa
12 ounces Dr. Pepper
1 jalapeno (chopped, seeded)
1 tablespoon chili powder
1 teaspoon cumin
cornbread or saltines (optional)

In a 3 ½-quart pot, brown ground beef over medium heat and drain, set aside. Brown breakfast sausage (hot/sage/or regular), drain. Reduce heat and return ground beef to pot. Add salsa, Dr. Pepper, tortilla chips, chopped jalapeno, chili powder, and cumin. Heat at medium flame til boiling, then reduce heat to low. Cover and simmer for 30 minutes or to taste. Add liquid as needed. Serve with cornbread or saltines. NO BEANS! Heat (spiciness) can be modified by the type of salsa used, number of jalapenos, or use of hot breakfast sausage.

## Euro's Gumbo

467 It's gumbo—nuff said. Whipped up by my pa in self-defense against fund-raising Brunswick stew.

Posted by: Euro. Yield: 10 servings. Prep time: 60 minutes.

---

8 tablespons (1/2 cup) real butter
8 tablespoons all-purpose flour
2 – 3 pounds okra (frozen easier)
4 medium onions, diced
4 bell peppers, chopped
5 stalks celery, chopped
palmful of mixed thyme, basil, garlic, cayenne pepper
1 tablespoon Worcestershire sauce
2 15-ounce cans tomato sauce
2 15-ounce cans diced tomatoes
3 pounds peeled shrimp
2 quarts water
Old Bay, tabasco, cooked chicken, rice (optional)

Get a really big pot and a skillet. Saute vegetables in some butter in skillet, set aside. Make brown roux with butter and flour in pot. Slowly stir in water; once smooth, add okra. Stir in vegetables and seasonings. Simmer about 45 minutes. Add shrimp and simmer until they're pink.Check seasoning. Old Bay and tabasco are good additions here. Shredded cooked chicken can also be added. Usually served over rice.

## Grandma Ruby's Chicken & Dumplings

468 The real deal homemade kind. Recipe is from Grandma and likely her mother, Big Granny.

Posted by: Dave at Buffalo Roam. Yield: 10 or so servings. Prep time: 45 minutes.

---

1 whole fryer
3 – 4 cups flour
1 cup sweet milk
2 quarts water
salt and pepper to taste

Start the chicken boiling and cook until it is completely tender and easy to debone. Save all the broth and shred the chicken meat into it. While the chicken boils, start your dumplings by packing the flour into a medium bowl and leave a depression in the middle. Pour in the cup of room temp sweet milk. Here is the critical part: gently rub the moistened flour on the bottom and sides with your fingertips and very slowly keep doing it until a sticky paste forms. When you can handle that goopy mix, knead in enough flour to roll it out without sticking to everything. Dust it with flour, roll, flop it over, dust it etc. Roll the dough very thin. It will try to spring back but keep at it until it's thin. Cut in strips; a pizza cutter works well. Get your chicken boiling hard and pinch off bits of the dumplings to drop right in the middle of the hardest boiling place. Reduce to simmer for 30 minutes. Salt and pepper to taste.

### *Chef's Notes:*

Works well with squirrels too but they need some extra fat.

## Vegetable Beef Soup

469 A staple in my family for decades. I have been eating this soup ever since I can remember. My grandmother did a lot of canning and used to put up quart jars of "soup mix" (tomatoes and corn mixed together). This plus leftover pot roast made a meal. I have modified it somewhat

Posted by: Dr Alice. Yield: a lot. Prep time: 20 minutes plus cooking.

---

1 cup leftover pot roast
28-ounce can crushed or chopped tomatoes
leftover roast juice
1 can beef broth (optional)
1 – 2 carrots, chopped
1 large onion, chopped
2 stalks celery, chopped
1 – 2 cups green beans, chopped
1 bag frozen corn
1 bag frozen peas

Take a soup pot. Put in the tomatoes and any roast juice you have left. Rinse the can(s) with water and add that. Chop and add the vegetables—most of what I have listed is not mandatory. It's soup; use whatever you have. I do think the tomatoes and corn are necessary, they really make the soup. Bring to boil, turn down heat and simmer about an hour. Then toss in the beef and frozen vegetables. Cook about another hour or till done. Very good with corn muffins and deviled eggs. I serve the soup with these as a traditional Super Bowl meal every year.

### *Chef's Notes:*

Third of three recipes. I told you to get a big roast!

## Oyster Stew

470 We had this every Christmas Eve until my mother's unexpected death in 1985. She never wrote down the recipe. Where hers came from I don't know as she had a Masters in "Foods and Nutrition" and could have come across it anywhere. We lived in Michigan and fresh seafood was not available when I was a kid and so most times this was made from canned oysters. I came across the *Saveur* one due to my wife subscribing and it tastes and looks just like my mom's one. The adaptation is mine to use the refrigerated packaged oysters that are available here and easier to get than fresh in the shell.

Posted by: geoffb5. Yield: 4 servings. Prep time: 20 minutes.

---

1 pint oysters
6 tablespoons butter, divided
2 teaspoons Worcestershire sauce
1 teaspoon paprika
1/2 teaspoon celery salt
1 cup milk
1 cup half & half
salt to taste
oyster crackers (optional)

Pour oysters in strainer over a medium bowl to catch oyster liquor, put oysters into another bowl and if large cut into bite size pieces. Melt 4 tablespoons of the butter in a saucepan over medium-high heat. Stir in Worcestershire, paprika, and celery salt, then add oysters and bring to a simmer. Add the reserved oyster liquor to pan and bring to a boil. Add milk and half-and-half to pan and heat, stirring occasionally until just about to boil (do not boil, or it will curdle), 3 to 6 minutes. Season to taste with salt. Place 1/2 tablespoon butter in each of 4 warm soup bowls just before ladling in stew. Serve with oyster crackers.

## Scarborough Chicken Stew

471 It's better than fasting! My children were complaining about steak, steak, steak every night. And then I heard this song on the radio . . . .

Posted by: GolfBoy. Yield: 4 servings, or 2 for Morons. Prep time: 55 minutes.

---

butter (or bacon fat) to saute vegetables
2 teaspoons dried parsley
1/4 teaspoon rubbed sage
1/4 teaspoon dried rosemary
1/2 teaspoon dried thyme
salt and pepper to taste
4 cooked chicken breasts, diced
3 carrots, diced
3 celery stalks, diced
1 onion, diced
3/4 cup frozen peas
4 cups chicken broth
4 tablespoons corn starch
noodles or rice

In a large pot, cook the onion, carrot and celery in the butter over medium heat until the onions are translucent. Bacon fat could be used in place of butter. Add the sage, rosemary and thyme, and stir briefly until fragrant. Add the broth, bring to a simmer, and cook uncovered until the carrots are tender, approximately 25 minutes. Just to be clear, "uncovered" refers to the pot. Add frozen peas, and continue simmering until they are cooked through. In a small bowl, add water to the corn starch and whisk to make a slurry. If you don't own a whisk, four fingers will suffice. Drizzle the mixture into the pot, stirring rapidly, until desired thickness. Add salt and pepper to taste. Add the diced chicken and parsley, and stir until just heated through. Serve over rice or noodles. Follow up with Twinkies and Old Milwaukee.

***Chef's Notes***

If you don't have 4 cooked chicken breasts lying around, you can do the following: Coat 4 chicken breasts (approximately 3 pounds, uncooked) lightly with olive oil, then season with salt and pepper and arrange on a baking pan. Bake at 375 degrees F for approximately 30 minutes, or until internal temperature of 161 degrees F is reached. Let rest at room temperature for 20 minutes before dicing.

## Texas Twista Asparagus Soup

472 The twist is the black pepper, which gives the soup bite. IDK where I got this. Maybe it started from a recipe.com thing, but I couldn't say for sure. In any case, this recipe has been customized a lot.

Posted by: Deafdog. Yield: 5 servings as a meal; 10-12 as a starter. Prep time: 45 minutes.

---

About 16 ounces fresh asparagus (I usually get 2 of the rubberband bundles at the supermarket)
1 onion
2 – 3 shallots
2 garlic cloves
1/2 green bell pepper
2 teaspoons black pepper, divided
oregano, bay leaf, basil, thyme, rosemary to taste (optional)
4 cups vegetable stock
6 ounces frozen peas
a very large handful fresh spinach
4 ounces butter
2 teaspoons black pepper
some olive oil and goat cheese
1 loaf rustic bread (sourdough or French)

Chop the onion, shallots, garlic and bell pepper. In a large saucepan, saute them in butter for about 3 minutes. Trim an inch from the asparagus spear tips (trim the tasty side of the asparagus; don't be a moron and use the woody side). Boil the spear tips till cooked (about 10 minutes), drain and dry the tips on a paper towel and set them aside. Chop the remaining asparagus (i.e., the stalks without the tips) and stir the chopped asparagus into the chopped onions/shallots mix. Add 1 teaspoon of black pepper. Saute for 5 more minutes until asparagus is a little soft and bright. Stir regularly. Stir the fresh spinach into the mixture.

Continue sauteing an additional 5 minutes. Stir regularly. Add in the vegetable stock, 1 teaspoon of black pepper and other spices (oregano, bay leaf, basil, thyme, and rosemary) to taste. Cover and let it slow bubble for 10 minutes. Uncover, stir in the peas, and slow bubble for 2 minutes more. Liquefy the mixture in a blender until smooth. Then, return to the pan. Add the asparagus tips and a dollop of goat cheese and simmer. Be sure to stir so that the goat cheese dissolves equally in the soup. When you're ready to serve, warm the soup. Add a splash more water if the soup is too thick. Sprinkle olive oil on the bread and toast it. Ladle the soup into bowls. Be sure that each bowl includes asparagus tips. Serve toast, with the remaining goat cheese, on the side. You can add more or less black pepper to taste. Also, the woody end of the asparagus is white and hard and less tasty. I will buy extra asparagus and discard about an inch from the woody end of the asparagus.

## Bean Soup

473 Black-eye peas & ham hocks. I came up with this on my own, many years ago.

Posted by: Peaches. Yield: How hungry are you? Prep time: I was told there would be no math.

---

2 regular size bags black-eyed peas
2 smoked pork shank (better than hocks)—get the meaty ones
1 large onion, chopped
1 – 6 garlic cloves, up to you
2 – 3 celery ribs, chopped
10 or so whole peppercorns
3 – 4 bay leaves
10 or so whole cloves
1 huge carrot, or two smaller, diced
salt to taste
sour cream (optional)
crusty bread (optional)

Rinse beans well, put in Dutch oven with 9 cups water, bring to boil. Boil 2 minutes, remove from heat, cover, and let stand 1 hour. Add hambones, onion, celery, garlic, bay leaves, peppercorns, cloves, carrot, and more boiling water, enough to get the consistency you like. Cook slowly for 3 hours. Remove hambones, and take the meat off. At this point you can blend the soup until smooth, if desired. Chop the meat in edible pieces and put it back in the soup. Correct seasoning. Serve with crusty bread and, if you want to be fancy, a little dollop of sour cream is nice.

## Rotisserie Chicken Soup

474 Fantastic chicken soup, especially for colds. I have no idea where I originally came across this recipe, which in any case I've modified over the years to my own tastes. If someone else wishes to claim credit, that's totally fine with me. All I know is it makes an awesome soup.

Posted by: Law of Self Defense. Yield: 4 – 6 servings. Prep time: 30 – 60 minutes (stages).

---

1 rotisserie chicken
1 medium yellow onion
2 – 3 cloves garlic, pressed
2 carrots, peeled, sliced chunky
2 stalks celery, sliced chunky
1 teaspoon to 1 tablespoon dried Italian seasoning (or a mix of basil, parsley, and oregano)
salt to taste
olive oil for sauteeing
1 can petite diced tomatoes
1 can stewed tomatoes
2 large cans or boxes chicken broth
4 – 8 ounces noodles (e.g. fideo, pastene)
couple of boxes or large cans of chicken broth
grated cheese to taste

Get a rotisserie chicken from the store. Take the chicken apart, separating the skin and bones into one container (may as well be the soup pot, I use a large 6-quart enameled cast-iron pot), and setting aside the meat. Add a couple of boxes or large cans of chicken broth to the pot with the skin and bones, bring to a boil, then lower heat and simmer for a while. I generally do an hour. (Make a mental note of about how high the liquid level is.) The longer, the more flavor you'll get out of the skin and bones. If you boil too long or too hard you'll boil away all the broth, however, so keep an eye on that. While that's happening, take a couple of forks and shred up the chicken breasts, tearing it up with the forks, and also any of the dark meat that's too large to fit in a tablespoon when being eaten with the soup later. Set that aside (in the fridge is a good idea).

Next roughly chop up a medium-sized onion, and saute in some olive oil in a largish pan (you'll be adding the garlic, carrots, and celery to the same pan). Keep the temp relatively low; you want to soften the onion until it's translucent, you don't want to brown or blacken it. (If it starts to blacken it's not ruined, just lower the heat.) After you've been cooking the onions a couple of minutes, add the garlic. The garlic is very sticky so you need to move it around. It is very important to not burn the garlic, as it gets very bitter. If you don't cook it at least a couple of minutes, however, you'll end up with a very sharp garlic taste in the soup, so it does have to be cooked a couple of minutes with the onions. Give the onions and garlic a stir every minute or so while they are cooking. While that's happening, chop up a couple of carrots (peeled) and a couple of celery (clean the celery well first, or you'll get dirt in the soup), and toss them in with the onion and garlic.

At this point add some salt and pepper, and also some Italian seasoning—a teaspoon of the seasoning should be plenty (or a teaspoon combination of other herbs like basil and parsley and oregano if you don't have the mixed Italian seasoning). I'm usually pretty generous with the salt. Cook at a reasonably low temperature until the carrots begin to soften a bit. You can accelerate this by place a lid on the pan, but patience is a virtue here. Then take the whole mix off heat and set aside. Now it's time to separate the simmering broth from the skin and bones. To do this you need some cheesecloth. Use the cheesecloth to line a strainer. Then place the strainer over a second soup pot. That second pot will capture the broth you're about to pour into the strainer. Pour the broth into the strainer, and the strainer and cheesecloth will catch the skin and bones. These can be discarded. The broth in the second pot is your final broth. Chances are much of the broth will have boiled off, but most of what boiled off was just water; just add in enough water to bring the level back to where it was before boiling—or even a higher level, it's fine. Just be sure to leave a good 3 inches from the top of the pot for the stuff you'll be adding in now.

Pour the broth back into the original soup pot, and place back on the stove, and raise the heat to bring broth to a boil. Add the petite diced tomatoes (I prefer the Italian-style) into the broth. Open the can of stewed tomatoes (again, I prefer the Italian-style), but don't add these directly to the soup as they're too large to eat conveniently. I use a wand blender to blend these up. Alternatively, you could use a potato masher or something similar to smash them up. Whichever way you do it, afterwards dump them into the soup. Once you've brought the broth back to a boil, add the carrot/celery/onion/garlic mix. Doing so will cool the broth, so wait until it's back at a boil. Add the noodles and boil, stirring occasionally so they don't stick to the pot, for whatever time the package says (this process will also finish softening the carrots & celery). THEN TURN OFF THE HEAT. (If the soup looks too thick, more like a stew, it's just as tasty, but if you'd like it less thick just add more water and bring back to a boil momentarily, THEN TURN OFF THE HEAT. Adding the water changes the flavor of the soup remarkably little.)

Add the shredded chicken you set aside earlier to the hot broth. Do NOT boil the chicken, you'll make it tough—just add it to the hot soup after the noodles are done and the heat turned off. Even if you've been storing the chicken in the fridge, the hot soup will warm it right up if you give the soup a few stirs. That's it, it's ready to eat. :-) Some grated cheese on the soup after it's been ladled into bowls is usually tasty. This is also awesome over the next day or two as leftovers.

## Uncle Bert's Best Chili

475 An excellent chili recipe, invented by me.

Posted by: Spaceman. Yield: enough for 10 morons/moronettes. Prep time: 25 minutes.

---

1 1/4 pounds ground beef
1 package chili mix (McCormick or French's)
3 medium onions, chopped
1 green pepper, chopped
two 8-ounce cans tomato sauce

1 can stewed tomatoes
1 can chili hot beans (or kidney beans)
2 tablespoons chili powder
5 teaspoons sugar
1/2 tablespoon cumin powder
1/4 teaspoon garlic powder
1/8 teaspoon cayenne pepper
1 teaspoon black pepper
1 can Rotel brand tomatoes
1 sliced jalepeno
1 teaspoon Louisiana hot sauce

Brown hamburger beef and pour off excess grease. Add in the rest of ingredients. Add water to medium consistency. Cook at low boil for 1 1/2 hours, stirring occasionally. This recipe is mildly hot and will suit most people. If you want it hotter, add 1/2 teaspoon Louisiana hot sauce, another sliced jalapeno, and 1/8 teaspoon cayenne pepper (in whatever multiples suit you for hotness). Maybe add a little more sugar to kill off the acid taste from the peppers if you like (to taste).

## Tongue Lash Chili

476 Giving you a spicy mouthful of what you need. I dedicate the recipe to my wife and dogs who have suffered through countless batches of deadly and dull chili to achieve perfection.

Posted by: yankeefifth. Yield: 10 servings. Prep time: 2 hours.

---

2 pounds ground beef
two heads garlic, minced
2 large Spanish onions, diced
3 habanero peppers, minced
3 jalapeno peppers, minced
3 serrano peppers, minced
2 28-ounce cans petite diced tomatoes
2 15.5-ounce cans pinto beans
2 15.5-ounce cans kidney beans
2 tablespoons salt
1 tablespoon brown sugar
1 tablespoon coriander
1 tablespoon cumin
1 tablespoon granulated onion
1 tablespoon granulated garlic
1 tablespoon oregano
NO CARROTS
grated cheese, sour cream, saltine crackers
bacon (optional)

Brown the ground beef in a large stockpot on medium heat for approximately 10 minutes. Be careful to stir the meat gently so you do not reduce it to granular level. You want the ground beef to be in pieces that are approximately the size of 12 gauge shotgun slugs. When the beef is browned, cooked to medium so there is barely a touch of pink in the middle of the pieces, add the spice mixture. Pour the spice mixture into the ground beef and stir gently until the spice mixture is evenly distributed throughout the ground beef. Cover, wait five minutes. Add the diced onions into the chili and stir gently until they are evenly mixed into chili. Cover, wait 10 minutes, stir gently at the midpoint. Reduce to medium low heat. At five minute intervals, add the following ingredients in this order: garlic, peppers, tomatoes, and beans. Make sure that each ingredient is gently and thoroughly mixed into the chili as it is added. Cover, reduce to low heat. Simmer for one hour, stirring gently every five to ten minutes.Serve with grated cheese, sour cream, and saltine crackers. When chili is complete, police up any carrots in your house and discard.

### *Chef's Notes:*

This is a very good basic chili recipe which is fine on its own but is easily adapted to personal taste. On a heat level it scores a 5. One very well-received variation is to begin by rough chopping and frying one half pound of bacon before browning the ground beef. Feel free to exclude any or all of the following:

Garlic: pull the heads of garlic apart into individual cloves. Peel the cloves. Toss into food processor, process until minced. I usually use the Sabatier S-shaped blade. Be careful not to over process them, you do not want to reduce them to liquid, only to very tiny pieces. Usually, pulsing the processor 10 times and then running it for two or three seconds is sufficient. If you do not have a food processor you can use a grater. Peppers: rinse the peppers under cool water. Cut the top one-quarter of an inch off the top of each pepper and discard. Put the entirety of the remaining peppers, with the seeds in them, into the food processor and process; use the same Sabatier S-shaped blade you used for the garlic. Be careful not to over process them, you do not want to reduce them to liquid only to very tiny pieces. Usually, pulsing the processor 10 times and the running it for two or three seconds is sufficient. Immediately add the peppers into the chili. Rinse the food processor with a quarter cup of water to get out any remaining garlic and pepper and pour it into the chili. If you do not have a food processor you can also use a grater for this step, however, do not do this unless you have vegetable oil in your kitchen and be sure to rinse your hands with the vegetable oil immediately after grating the peppers. If you have not worked extensively with peppers, be advised, the combination of minced peppers is weapons-grade, do not touch or inhale.

## Curried Turkey (or Chicken) Soup

477 Wonderful recipe for leftover turkey or for ready-made roasted chicken. From the *Washington Post* Food Section, Thanksgiving issue, from AT LEAST 20 years ago.

Posted by: Cricket. Yield: 4 servings (I always double or triple it). Prep time: 30 minutes or so.

---

1 tablespoon butter
1/4 cup chopped onion
1 tablespoon curry powder, or to taste
1 tablespoon flour
1 cup coconut milk
1 teaspoon salt (optional)
1/4 teaspoon white pepper
1 cup diced cooked turkey or chicken
1 tablespoon fresh lime juice
2 cups turkey or chicken stock
optional (not optional at all if you ask me!) garnishes: crumbled crisp bacon, chopped scallions, shredded coconut,

crushed roasted peanuts, mango chutney, chopped candied ginger

basmati rice (optional)

In large saucepan or stockpot over medium heat, heat 2 tablespoons water and the butter until butter melts. Add onion and cook, stirring occasionally, until transparent but not brown. Reduce heat to low, sprinkle curry powder and flour over onions and cook, stirring constantly, for 2 minutes. Stirring constantly, slowly add coconut milk and cook until smooth, about 3 minutes. Still stirring, slowly add 1 cup of stock, salt, white pepper and turkey/chicken. Increase heat to medium and cook, stirring occasionally, until warmed through—about 10 minutes. Stir in lime juice. Serve immediately with garnishes on the side. Many times I serve this with a scoop of basmati rice in the bowl. This recipe is very flexible in terms of how thick or thin you want the soup to be. Add more stock to thin it or add more chicken to thicken it, but do yourself a favor and at least double the recipe because it's even tastier the second day.

## 6-Quart Lazy Man's Stew

478 Easy, delicious, low effort stew. I wanted to see what would happen if I layered the food when I cooked it.

Posted by: lonetown. Yield: 8 – 10 servings. Prep time: 10 – 15 minutes.

---

2 cups water
2 tablespoons salt
2 medium onions
2 pounds red potatoes
2 pounds California carrots
10 ounces sliced mushrooms
2 pounds stew beef cubed
1 head celery
1 package frozen peas

Brown beef over medium heat. Meanwhile, in a 6-quart pot begin boiling water with salt. Cut onion in quarters, and cut potato into medium to large dice. Add to pot. Peel carrots and cut into bite-sized pieces; add carrots, sliced mushrooms, and beef (including juices) to pot. Remove outer stalks and bottom of celery. Slice the whole head into slivers, pack on top. By now the 6-quart pot is filled to the top, and the water is boiling away. Tamp it down and add peas on top. Cover and put on simmer for an hour. Stir and let sit for 10 minutes. Enjoy. This is great for a single type guy who wants to cook infrequently but have plenty on hand.

## Waterfront Cheese Soup

479 A twist to chicken soup. Adapted from a recipe in *Midwest Living*, June 1991.

Posted by: Cicero Kaboom! Kid. Yield: 11 cups Prep time: 40 minutes.

---

2 cups water
2 – 3 cups fresh broccoli florets
1 cup chopped celery
1 cup chopped onions
oil to saute vegetables
1 cup chicken stock
1 1/2 teaspoons oregano
1 1/2 cups whole milk
1 10-ounce can cream of chicken soup
1 cup mashed or very well cooked potato dices
1 cup evaporated milk
1/2 cup all-purpose flour
4 ounces shredded smoked Cheddar cheese
salt and pepper to taste
sourdough bread

In a large kettle or Dutch oven, saute onions and celery in a little oil until they turn translucent. Add water, chicken stock, and oregano. Bring to a boil, reduce heat to simmer and cover for 7 minutes. Stir in the milk, canned soup and potatoes. Combine evaporated milk and flour, stir into the pot. Cook and stir until slightly thickened and bubbly. Add the cheese and broccoli and heat 1 – 2 minutes more. Season with salt and pepper to taste. Serve with sourdough bread. Don't overcook the broccoli!

## Lin-duh's Unknown Black Bean Soup

480 One of the easiest "homemade" soups evah!!! I pulled this one out of my ass one night. This really is a super simple homemade soup that really tastes great. Any Moron can make it. It's pretty hard to screw this up.

Posted by: lin-duh fell. Yield: 3 – 4 servings. Prep time: 25 – 30 minutes, maybe.

---

1 can (1 pound 13 ounces) Goya brand black beans
1 small onion, diced fine
2 cloves garlic, minced
2 – 3 cups chicken stock or broth
1 tablespoon dried oregano
1 tablespoon dried parsley
salt and pepper
dollop sour cream (optional)
dash or more hot sauce or Sriracha (optional)
1 – 2 cups cooked rice (optional)
1 tablespoon olive oil

Saute the onions in the oil until translucent. Add garlic and the can of beans with liquid. Cook for a minute or two until garlic is fragrant. You can mash the beans a little bit here or not. Add the chicken stock/broth to the consistency you like your soup, I usually do closer to the 2 cups. Add the oregano, parsley, salt, and pepper. Simmer for 10 – 15 minutes. Taste, and adjust seasonings, if necessary. Serve alone or over a little rice for a heartier meal. Garnish with a dollop of sour cream and hot sauce, if desired. Enjoy. I always use the Goya brand of beans because I think they have the best flavor and consistency but you can use whatever you have handy.

## Kurulounge Chili

481 Thick, hearty, medium heat chili. I just messed around until I found something I liked.

Posted by: chad. Yield: 10 bowls. Prep time: 25 – 40 minutes prep, 4+ hours slow cooker.

---

1/4 pound hickory smoked bacon
1 ¼ to 1 ½ pound steak (usually round)
1/2 to 1 onion (to taste)
2 cloves garlic (minced or chopped)
1 8-ounce can tomato paste
2 16-ounce cans tomato sauce
1 16-ounce can red beans
1 16-ounce can black beans
2 pinches cayene pepper
2 tablespoons paprika
2 teaspoons oregano
2 tablespoons chili powder
4 teaspoons cumin
1 tablespoon chipotle powder
1/2 can Ortega diced jalapenos
2 caps liquid smoke
1 can beer (Miller or Budweiser)
Salt and pepper to taste

Cut the bacon into small pieces and fry until crisp. While the bacon is frying, cube the steak and season with salt and pepper. Place the bacon in the crockpot but save the grease. Brown the steak in the bacon grease. While steak is browning, chop the onion. Place the steak in the crockpot, but again save the grease. Sweat the onions in the grease until they are translucent (if the pan is dry add a little butter). While the onion is cooking, chop the garlic. Add the garlic and the half can of jalapenos to the onion. When the onion, garlic and jalapeno is soft, transfer it to the crockpot, then add the cayene, paprika, oregano, chili powder, chipotle powder, cumin, and liquid smoke to the crock pot. If you are going to use the beer, add as much as you want and drink the rest. If not add the first can of tomato sauce and stir all the meat and spices together. Add the beans, the rest of the tomato sauce (add both cans now if you used beer earlier) and tomato paste. Cook 8 hours on low in the crockpot, or until the meat is tender enough for you and the sauce is hot. If the sauce is too thick, add some water, beer, beef broth, or red wine—whatever works for you.

## Hungarian Goulash

482 Fulfills your need for beef. Adapted from a recipe found in the *Women's Day Encyclopedia of Cooking*.

Posted by: Miley, the Duchess. Yield: 6 – 8 servings. Prep time: 2 1/2 hours.

---

2 1/2 pounds stew beef
4 tablespoons butter
1 1/2 pounds sliced onions
2 tablespoons Hungarian paprika (I use hot)
1 tablespoon all-purpose flour
water or white wine to cover
2 cups sour cream
1 package egg noodles
salt and pepper to taste

Cut beef into chunks, then sprinkle with salt and pepper. Using a stew pot, brown in butter at medium-high heat (do this in 3 batches, placing the already browned meat in a bowl while you continue to brown the rest). Return all of the meat into the pot and lower the temperature to medium. Place the onions over, then sprinkle with paprika. When excess liquid has evaporated, sprinkle the flour over and stir for a minute. Add the water or wine to almost cover the meat. Simmer under cover until the beef is tender, about 90 minutes. Stir in the sour cream and heat (but do not bring to a boil again or the sour cream will break). Serve over egg noodles.

## Chicken Corn Chowdah

483 Like clam chowdah, but with chicken. I made it up!

Posted by: ChrisP. Yield: 4 servings Prep time: 35 minutes.

---

1 ½ pounds chicken breast or thighs, cut in chunks
½ cup chopped onion (sweet)
4 cloves garlic (diced)
3 tablespoons butter
1 15-ounce can chicken broth
1 medium russet potato, diced
¾ teaspoon ground cumin
2 cups half & half or cream
2 cups shredded Monterey Jack or Mex-blend cheese
1 can creamed corn
1 can cut corn (or equivalent in frozen corn)
2 cans green chilies
1 can Rotel tomato & green chili
hot pepper sauce to taste
cilantro for garnish

In a Dutch oven, brown chicken, onion, and garlic in butter until chicken is no longer pink. Pour the chicken broth into the Dutch oven, and season with cumin. Bring to a boil. Reduce heat to low, cover, and simmer for 5 minutes. Stir in corn, chilies, potato, chopped Rotel tomatos and hot pepper sauce. Cook, stirring frequently, until the potato is cooked through. Stir in half & half and cheese. Heat until cheese is melted. Garnish with cilantro. It's RGS(Really Good Shit) and will keep (make) you regular.

## Chicken Chili Soup

| 484 It's like a party for your mouth! It's mine. |
|---|

Posted by: Cicero Kaboom! Kid. Yield: servings for one teenaged-girl and two adults. Prep time: 45 minutes or so.

---

4 big, fat, chicken thighs
2 tablespoons oil
1 cup chopped onion
2 garlic cloves, minced or pressed
24 ounces chicken stock
10 ounces or so green tomatillo salsa
1 16-ounce can diced tomatoes
1 7-ounce can diced green chiles
1 1/2 teaspoons each oregano, ground cumin, ground coriander seed
1 15-ounce can white beans
1 can Summer Crisp corn

Remove skin and debone chicken thighs, and cube meat into small pieces. Heat oil in Dutch oven or deep pan. Salt and pepper the meat and bones and cook in the hot oil until no longer pink. Remove from pot. Saute onions until tender. Add garlic and spices and saute a couple of minutes. Add chiles and heat a minute. Add green salsa and heat until bubbly. Add tomatoes and again heat until bubbly. Add chicken and chicken stock and bring to a boil. Reduce heat and simmer 10 minutes with a lid on the pot. Add beans and corn. Bring back to a boil, reduce heat and simmer another 5 minutes or so.

***Chef's Notes:***
You can replace the canned tomatoes with fresh tomatoes blanched in boiling water to remove skins, then chopped and drained. You can replace the corn with two ears of fresh corn cut from the cob. Eat with good quality corn tortillas or corn cakes.

## Slow-cooker Beef or Venison Stew

| 485 Sleep while cooking. Brilliant! Recipe is from Emeril Lagasse, Food Network, to which I have made some 'corrections'. |
|---|

Posted by: Cicero Kaboom! Kid. Yield: 4 – 6 servings. Prep time: 20 minutes.

---

2 tablespoons oil
2 pounds any cubed stew beef or venison
1 1/2 teaspoons salt
1 teaspoon Cajun seasoning
1 cup each frozen pearl onions, sliced carrots, and frozen peas
2 tablespoons butter
1/2 pound white button mushrooms, thinly sliced
3 tablespoons all-purpose flour
2 tablespoons tomato paste
3 cups stock
1 teaspoon Italian seasoning
1/8 teaspoon ground allspice
1 pound potatoes, peeled and cubed into 1-inch pieces

Salt and pepper beef or venison. Toss with Cajun seasoning. Saute in pan with a little oil until brown. Remove from pan and put in crock pot. Deglaze the pan with the stock and scrape up the goody bits. Pour over the beef. Add butter, mushrooms, flour, herbs, spices, and tomato paste. Cover the slow-cooker, set to high and cook one hour. Add potatoes and carrots, cover and cook for 7 hours. During the last hour, add the pearl onions and peas.

***Chef's Notes:***
For the stock, use one cup chicken stock and two cups beef stock. A can of drained peas works fine instead of frozen.

## Beef Stew "of Doom"

486 Standard beef stew. My own recipe—developed when Mrs. Eez caught me using Dinty Moore in a shepherd's pie.

Posted by: sock_rat_eez. Yield: 6 to 8 servings. Prep time: 1 ½ hours.

---

3 pounds stew beef
2 pounds carrots
3 pounds onions
4 pounds red potatoes
1 whole head of celery
1 ½ cups peas—fresh or frozen
1 ½ cups whole kernel corn - fresh or frozen
6 cloves garlic

I find it helpful to chop up all the vegetables first, to whatever fineness you prefer—I like it fairly chunky: onions cut in eighths, then cut 2 or 3 times lengthwise, carrot cut into coins 3/8 to 1/2 inch thick, potatoes quartered if small or cut up to less-than-golf-ball size chunks if large, celery chopped about 1/2 inch. In a 12-quart soup pot, start browning the beef in a few tablespoons of olive or other oil, stirring as required. When browned, add the chopped onions and continue sauteing. Stir intermittently as required, throughout this and the following steps. When the onions start getting translucent, add the carrots, wait a few minutes, add the celery, wait 5 or 10 minutes, then add the potatoes. Let it all cook another 5 or 10 minutes, then add water to cover everything plus an inch or so (about 1/2 gallon, in my experience). When it all comes back to a boil, add the peas (cut-up green beans can substitute, or use both!), corn, and add the garlic via a garlic press. Simmer until well-cooked and of proper consistency (45 minutes? 1 hour?).

***Chef's Notes:***
One of the few written recipes I have—I winged this the first time and wrote it down because it worked out so well. Other herbs and spices may be added, to taste, but I like it as-is. Garlic may be increased, decreased, or omitted altogether to suit your preference.

## Mrs. Dall's Pork Pumpkin Stew

487 Simple fall stew. This family favorite was inspired by a South American recipe, but Mrs. Dall replaced beef with pork, and about 6 out of 8 other ingredients. She did not replace the salt and pepper. This was created because Mrs. Dall loves to grow pumpkins and winter squashes.

Posted by: Hal Dall. Yield: 6 – 8 servings. Prep time: 1 hour prep, 1 ½ hours cooking.

---

3 pounds boneless pork shoulder
1 medium pumpkin or winter squash
2 large onions
1 head garlic
bacon grease to brown pork
3 14.5-ounce cans stewed tomatoes
1 tablespoon or more ground coriander
1 tablespoon or more ground cumin
1 tablespoon salt
1 – 2 teaspoons fresh ground black pepper
1 cup flour
1/2 to 1 cup water

Mix spices, salt and pepper with flour in medium bowl. Cube pork, toss with flour to coat. Peel and chunk onions; peel and crush garlic. Peel and de-seed pumpkin, cut into 1 inch cubes. Using a large cast iron Dutch oven, melt some bacon grease and toss in pork pieces to brown. Do in batches so they get brown and not ucky. When all of the meat is browned, place it back in the Dutch oven, then add pumpkin, onions, garlic and tomatoes, and water as needed. (Don't overdo the water, or the stew will be too runny.) Cover Dutch oven, and simmer until meat and pumpkin are tender, about 1 to 1 ½ hours. Stir occasionally to prevent meat from sticking. Adjust seasoning to taste. Serve with rustic bread or cornbread. If you use winter squash, the stew can be sweet, depending on variety used. Other additions can include tart apples, parsnips, corn.

## My Chili Recipe

488 The best hot dog chili in the world! While I found the base recipe on a website years ago, I've pretty much changed every ingredient and added quite a few, so at this point, this is really my baby. And this is 100% pork + beer chili, so perfect for pissing off jihadi @$$holes!

Posted by: Wiz 427. Yield: servings for 10+ Morons. Prep time: 3 hours.

---

2 pounds bulk hot Italian sausage (I use Kroger brand)
2 pounds ground pork
8 cloves garlic, minced
1 cup minced white onion
1 cup water
24 ounces Genesee beer or similar American macrobrew. If you are feeling saucy, use a 25 ounce Bud Light Michelada
8 ounces tomato sauce
1 teaspoon Frank's Red Hot sauce
3 tablespoons chili powder
2 tablespoons roasted ground cumin
2 teaspoons smoked paprika
2 teaspoons oregano
1 teaspoon unsweetened cocoa
1/2 teaspoon ground coriander
1/2 teaspoon star anise powder
3 cubes beef bouillon
2 cubes sugar

In a large stockpot, brown half the meat. Remove the meat and drain the fat. Brown the rest of the meat. Remove the meat and drain, saving 2 – 3 tablespoons of the fat. Return the reserved fat to the stockpot and use it to cook the onions and garlic until tender. Add more fat as needed, you don't want the onions and garlic to burn. Add meat back to stockpot. Add tomato sauce, water, beer, chili powder, bouillon, cumin, paprika, oregano, sugar, coriander, cocoa, star anise and hot sauce. Mix well. Bring to boil, then reduce heat and simmer, covered, for two hours. Use a stick blender to achieve the proper consistency for hot dog chili. Leave the chunks larger if you just want to eat it with a spoon. Serve on hot dogs or over pasta, Cincinnati style. Also good for Frito pies. Or on just about anything—I've eaten it with rice, over hash browns, on burgers, fries, etc. It's freakin' awesome.

## Night Owl (or Early Bird) Hobo Stew

489 What is best in life? To crush your enemies, cook them into a savory slurry, and hear the rejoicing of the women when you serve it. My standard M.O. is to start throwing things into a crockpot when I get home from a gig at 3 or 4 AM. I can usually find a hobo near the venue, but beef is great too, and the women actually prefer it for some reason. If you are one of those insufferable early bird types, you'll have to get up even earlier to go into town for hobo meat, but you know it makes your innards tickle with desire and satisfaction to get up at 3 AM, and tell everyone how good and virtuous you are for dragging yourself out of bed while they were still up having fun, you humorless, soulless scold. You're probably Scandinavian. Anyhoo, for dinner, start between 3 & 6 AM. For lunch, start before midnight, possibly as early as 9 PM.

Posted by: Mephistefales. Yield: 1 – 16 servings, depending on gluttony/temperance. Prep time: 30 minutes prep, 12+ hours cook time.

---

6 – 8 cups high quality H2O (No, really. RO or similar)
1 pat butter
¼ - 1/3 jar Better Than Bouillon Brand beef stock
generous handful carrot chips
2 heaping teaspoons diced pimentos (optional)
short pour soy sauce
short pour dark beer
2 pounds hobo (or stew beef), cut in chunks
2 garlic cloves, pressed
1/2 teaspoon salt
1/2 teaspoon pepper
1/2 teaspoon onion powder (or between 1/2 and 2 chopped green onions, depending on size/preference)
2 tablespoons sweet paprika
1 dash of thyme
1/2 teaspoon ground rosemary
2 bay leaves
1/2 teaspoon ground coriander
1 large pinch dried basil
5 – 8 red potatoes, skins on, random chop size
a good amount of parsley
1 or 2 handfuls of barley, optional
flour to thicken, if necessary

Brown the meat, either in butter or oil, or flour coated. Don't overdo it. If you are a master of meat prep, disregard previous and just sear the flesh your way, baby. Put the water in the crockpot. Turn it on. Toss in the butter. Dissolve the stock. Work your way down the ingredients, stirring each addition in. When chopping the potatoes, vary the size between 1 1/2" cubes, and paper-thin slivers, so that everyone can dig out the potato size they like, and the small slivers disintegrate, thickening the slurry. Shoot for a median size of 1" to 1 1/4". Cook it for at least 12 hours. I usually keep it on low while I sleep, then crank it up while I'm available to keep it stirred. Yes, mess with it all day. Stir a lot. Opening the lid periodically will help it thicken. You don't want it to be too watery (though you also don't want it to become gravy). Six to eight hours in, if it is still too soupy, sift in a little flour. No more than 6 hours total on high, though. Four hours on high is usually plenty. Optional: 15-20 minutes before you serve it, you can stir a generous handful or two of barley in there, but you'll need to plan to have the consistency a little on the thin side to compensate. The progeny loves this, the wife doesn't, so this step depends on who's been nicer lately.

Do not skimp on the following ingredients! Water—this is stew. I shouldn't have to mention this, but I know I do. If your tap water tastes like rust, so will the stew. Meat—hobos aren't everyone's style, but they have a pungent, gamey flavor, with notes of Valu-Rite. Like I said though, the women prefer beef, so get it at an actual meat market, you freakin' barbarian. Paprika—believe it or not, the quality of paprika is third in importance only to the meat and water. High quality sweet paprika makes or breaks this stew. Beer—the bigger, the better. I prefer to sacrifice a tithe of the Old Rasputin, Narwhal, or Unidragon I'm enjoying at the time.

## Shrimp and Sausage Gumbo

490 A versatile gumbo from a WASP who's never been to Louisiana. This recipe just comes from the various times I've watched Emeril do it over the years. BAM!

Posted by: Prince Ludwig the Deplorable. Yield: 8 servings. Prep time: 2 hours.

---

2 – 3 quarts chicken broth
1 1/2 cups rice
1 24-ounce package smoked sausage, cut into bite-sized pieces
1 pound raw, peeled and deveined shrimp
3 – 4 tablespoons rendered bacon fat
3 – 4 tablespoons flour
1 medium yellow onion, diced
1 green bell pepper, diced
4 – 5 ribs celery, diced
1 tablespoon cayenne pepper
2 – 3 teaspoons hot sauce
salt, pepper and file powder to taste

In an 8-quart pot, melt bacon fat over medium heat. Add equal amount of flour and stir continually until roux gets a little darker than Skippy Super Chunk peanut butter. Stir in onion, celery and bell pepper and cook until onion is translucent. Add 2 quarts of chicken broth and rice. (If you're adding raw rice, you'll need the third quart for later to keep the gumbo consistency. With raw rice and 2 quarts, you'll have more of a jambalaya.) When the rice is done, add the shrimp and sausage and simmer, covered, until shrimp curls and turns pink. Season to taste with the salt, cayenne, hot sauce and file powder.

***Chef's Notes:***
As with all gumbo recipes, you can change it up with various meat combinations. Other oils can be substituted for bacon fat, but trust me, use bacon fat. I prefer to leave the file powder out of the pot and stir it into the bowl right before serving.

## Reuben Casserole

491 Goes great with beer. While having a drunken argument with the old lady about the origin of the reuben sandwich, we took to the internet to answer the question and stumbled on this recipe. Somewhere. Beats me.

Posted by: harbqll. Yield: enough for 4 morons, or 8 humans. Prep time: 45 minutes. Maybe an hour.

---

6 slices dark rye bread, cubed
1 (16 oz can) sauerkraut, well drained
1 pount deli-sliced corned beef, cut into strips
3/4 cup russian salad dressing
2 cups shredded swiss cheese

Preheat oven to 400 degrees F. Spread bread cubes over the bottom of a greased 9x13 baking dish. Spread sauerkraut evenly over the bread, then layer beef strips over sauerkraut. Pour dressing over all. Spray aluminum foil with cooking spray and use to cover baking dish, sprayed side down you morons. Bake at 400 degrees F for 20 minutes. Remove foil cover, sprinkle the cheese over top, and bake uncovered another 10 minutes, or until cheese is melted and bubbly. I like a stout with this. But I like a stout with pretty much everything. My 8 year old likes milk with this.

## Potato and Sausage Casserole

492 A casserole a bit of my own making.

Posted by: BCochran1981. Yield: varies Prep time: depends.

---

kielbasa
red and gold potatoes
onion
olive oil
garlic salt
black pepper
red pepper
2 tablespoons cornstarch
cheddar cheese
four-cheese blend

Dice kielbasa, and potatoes. Chop onion. Put kielbasa, potatoes, and onions in large bowl, dust with garlic salt, black pepper, and red pepper, and drizzle generously with olive oil. Toss until evenly coated. Cook in large pan on medium-high until potatoes have softened, about 10 minutes. Combine 2 tablespoons corn starch in 2 cups cold water until fully blended, pour into pan. Increase heat until simmering, leave simmering until sauce has thickened to "creamy." Pour all into 13 x 9 pan and top with cheddar cheese. Put in oven, broil until cheese has fully melted. Remove and sprinkle with four-cheese blend.

## THE Tuna Casserole I Finally Liked

493 Tuna-noodle casserole made with sour cream. Jo, my neighbor in Chesterfield County, VA, introduced me to this recipe in the early '90s. Prior to tasting this, I had hated any and all tuna-noodle casseroles from birth. This is similar to a recipe on cooks.com, but I know that wasn't the source for this. I'm convinced what makes this so good is the sour cream and the topping, plus it is a relatively dry casserole dish.

Posted by: Krebs v Carnot: Epic Battle of the Cycling Stars (TM). Yield: 8 servings (6 if really hungry). Prep time: 45 minutes.

---

4 1/2 cups flat egg noodles, cooked to slightly firm
13 ounces tuna, water-packed, drained
4 ounces mushrooms, sliced
2 ounces pimento, sliced into strips
1 1/2 cups sour cream
2/3 cup milk, whole or 2%
1/2 teaspoon salt
1/4 teaspoon pepper
1/4 cup bread crumbs
1/4 cup Parmesan cheese, grated
2 tablespoons butter, melted

Cook egg noodles per instructions to required firmness. Combine noodles, tuna, sliced mushrooms, pimento strips, sour cream, milk, salt and pepper in an appropriately-sized dish that can be covered and used in a microwave oven. Stir well and microwave at 50% level for 10 minutes, covered. Remove cover and stir again at completion of this heating. In a small bowl, stir together bread crumbs, Parmesan cheese and butter. Spread mixture evenly over top of tuna-noodle mixture. Return dish to microwave oven, uncovered, and heat for 4 to 7 minutes until mixture is hot and bubbly. Remove dish from microwave and allow it to cool for a minute or two before serving.

## Body Builder Spaghetti Casserole

494 A simple casserole for feeding those sick Gainz. Just something I threw together based on a spaghetti casserole my mom used to make.

Posted by: Prince Ludwig the Deplorable. Yield: 5 – 6 servings. Prep time: 1 hour.

---

2 chicken breasts, cooked
1 1/2 cups brown rice
1 jar pasta sauce
1 can black olives (optional)
salt to taste
2 – 3 pinches oregano
1 cup mozzarella cheese
1 package pepperoni

Cut cooked chicken breast into bite-sized pieces and cook 1 1/2 cups brown rice in your rice cooker or on stove top. Combine chicken, sauce, rice and black olives in mixing bowl and season to taste with salt, oregano and/or an "Italian seasoning" of your choice. Spread evenly in a 9 x 13 baking dish and place in a preheated 375 degree F oven for 45 minutes. Top with cheese and pepperoni and put back in the oven for an additional 15 minutes. Keeps well so you can make ahead of time and refrigerate.

# *Other*

## Gyouza

495 Third generation take on a familiar Japanese bar food. Recipe handed down from my Japanese grandmother, with some modifications from my mother and myself. The recipe is well-suited for personal taste.

Posted by: Where's my prezzy? Yield: 10 servings. Prep time: 30 minutes.

---

1 small head of cabbage
2 – 4 carrots
5 bunches green onions
5 – 10 garlic cloves (crushed)
1 ½ pounds ground meat (beef/pork/chicken)
16 ounces pork sausage/ground pork
at least 1/2 tablespoon grated ginger root
2 – 3 teaspoons salt
2 – 3 tablespoons sesame oil
1 – 3 teaspoons black/red pepper
2 – 3 packages gyouza/wonton wrappers
vegetable oil
rice vinegar and soy sauce (optional dipping sauce)

Place meat in large mixing bowl—must be large enough to hold meat and vegetables (or split between two or more bowls). In stages, chop all vegetables (cabbage, carrots, green onions, garlic) fine—it's best to use a food processor—and add to mixing bowl. Add grated ginger, salt, sesame oil, and pepper to meat and vegetables, then mix by hand or with large spoon. Mixing by hand is recommended, as this will ensure an even distribution of ingredients—use a kneading motion until all ingredients are incorporated.

Ensure there is enough counter space for mixing bowl, gyouza/wonton skin package, other materials, and units of labor (deployment of latter should emphasize access to the mixing bowl). Place a single gyouza skin in palm of hand. Use tablespoon to place a ¾-to-full spoon's worth of mix in center of skin. Using the tip of your free hand's index finger, brush the upper three-quarters (8-'clock-to-4-o'clock) of the gyouza skin with water. Fold the skin in half, bottom of dry half up to top of wet half (6-o'clock-to-12-o'clock), and press firmly. Seal the rest of the skin by folding the small parts of the wet skin over each other, then pressing firmly against the dry skin. If there are any gaps in the folds, use a SMALL amount of water to seal them, and place the folded gyouza on a waxed-paper lined cookie sheet. Repeat steps 4 through 8 until either all the skins or the mix are used.

Place a frying pan at least 9" in diameter on the stove and turn heat to mid-high heat. Pour 2 – 4 tablespoons of oil into the pan (depending on the size of the pan—enough to coat the bottom). Quickly and carefully place the wrapped gyouza into the pan, ensuring each gyouza is coated with oil on the bottom. Place until the pan is full of gyouza which have full bottom contact with pan. Fry the gyouza until the bottom of the last gyouza placed turn a slight caramel-brown (check by either lifting with one's hand or with a pair of chopsticks). Have frying pan lid on hand. Carefully pour 1/4 - 1/2 cup water into the pan (watch for splatter!), and cover with lid. Allow water to come to boil, turn heat down to medium, and boil for 5 minutes. The skin of the gyouza should become semi-translucent and wrinkled) If there is still water in the pan after the gyouza have cooked, remove the lid and allow it to boil off, loosening gyouza by shaking pan or with a spatula. Turn the heat down and transfer the gyouza to a platter. The easiest way is to simply flip the pan over the platter, but more cautious chefs can use a spatula to transfer multiple gyouza to a platter. Repeat steps 10 – 15 until all of the gyouza have been cooked. You can keep batches of gyouza in a warm (210 degrees F) oven until all are cooked, but not for more than an hour. Serve warm with dipping sauce (1 part rice vinegar, 2 parts soy sauce).

***Chef's Notes:***
Optional first step: Cook meat, and allow to cool. This step is for anyone uncomfortable with raw meat, or if you want to freeze the mix for use later. If freezing for later use, DO NOT add spices and oil. There are several decent "wrapping gyouza" tutorials on YouTube! Suggested sides include rice, daikon pickles, tsukemono, miso soup, ramen, and beer!

## Cheese in Bread

496 Cheese in bread. Recipe developed from day-to-day life.

Posted by: Alcoholic Asshole Shut In. Yield: 1 serving. Prep time: Depends how far along the recipe you are. First phase: 5 minutes. Terminal phases: 1 – 3 hours.

---

About an ounce, could be 2 or 3, of cheese (cheddar is good)
1 slice bread, whatever you have around
A handful of lettuce—Romaine, iceberg, whatever you last bought, preferably washed
Whatever whisky your budget affords you, to taste

Take the piece of cheese. Put it on a slice of bread and fold the bread around the cheese. Eat this over the sink. If it is too dry, have some scotch. Or just have some anyways. Eat the lettuce, preferably also over the sink. Have some scotch. It's OK. Find the laptop. (Have some scotch)---->repeat part in brackets as necessary.

## Swedish Smorgasbord

497 Scandinavian spread. A twist on an old world recipe, from family members who actually knew how to cook. I don't cook so this is the best I can come up with. Recipe works best if you are in the Upper Midwest.

Posted by: grammie winger. Yield: varies according to how many people will eat with you. Prep time: about 5 minutes, not counting the drive.

---

Swedish pancakes
lingonberries
Svenska kottbullar (meatballs)
korv (sausage)
lutefisk (cod, lye)
pickled herring
rice pudding
julskinka (ham)
pickled beets
boiled potatoes
limpa (bread)
Havarti or Herrgardsost cheese

Find a Swedish restaurant in your area. Call in November and make reservations for December 13th. Drive to the restaurant. After you are seated at your table, take a plate and choose from the large expanse of beige food. The pickled beets will add a dash of color. There are no desserts because Swedes cannot seem to create any edible sweets. You will be served coffee and perhaps lingonberry juice. There may or may not be alcohol. If they serve glogg, you will have to take a cab home. Skal!

## Nana Riley's Belgium Waffles

498 Real, homemade waffles. From my great, Irish grandmother.

Posted by: BacktoGA. Yield: 4 servings. Prep time: 5 minutes.

---

2 cups flour
1 tablespoon baking powder
3 tablespoons sugar
3/4 teaspoon salt
2 egg yolks
1 2/3 cups milk
1/2 cup oil
2 egg whites

Sift dry ingredients in small bowl. In large mixing bowl, mix yolks, milk and oil. Add dry ingredients. Beat egg whites with electric mixer for approximately 1 minute until peaks form when mixer is lifted up. Fold in egg whites by hand. Don't overmix. Cook batter on high in waffle maker until done. Makes approximately 4 – 6 waffles depending on size of waffle maker. Your kids will love you.

## Low-Carb Farmer's Breakfast

499 Low-carb breakfast. Recipe is self-made.

Posted by: Anon Y. Mous. Yield: 1 serving. Prep time: 15 minutes.

---

1 – 2 tablespoons chopped onion
1/4 pound ground beef
1 – 2 tablespoons cream cheese
2 beaten eggs
1/4 teaspoon salt
1/8 teaspoon pepper
1/2 teaspoon butter

Beat eggs in bowl with salt and pepper and 1 tablespoon water. Melt butter in skillet. Brown onions until caramelized. Add hamburger and brown. Drain fat if necessary—use lower-fat hamburger to avoid having to drain. Add cream cheese and melt. Add beaten eggs and cook to desired consistency (similar to scrambled eggs). Serve. Keeping chopped onions in the freezer makes it easy to grab a tablespoon or two when needed.

## Breakfast Smoothie

500 Filling flavorful fruit smoothie.

Posted by: Big V. Yield: 5 –10 servings. Prep time: Overnight + 5 minutes.

---

8 ounces frozen fruit
32 ounces whole milk yogurt
1/4 cup lactose-free whole milk
1 tablespoon clover or Florida citrus honey
2 teaspoons vanilla extract

The night before, place the frozen fruit in your blender and put it in the fridge to thaw. In the morning add the milk, honey, and vanilla and give the blender two good pulses. Then add the yogurt and give 5 to 10 pulses using a rubber spatula to clear any unblended yogurt between pulses. Makes five 8-ounce servings, so good for a work week, or ten 4-ounce servings for a quick meal before heading out on the weekend with family. I prefer to use mangos with this and forego the honey personally but to get teenagers to eat it, use honey and mixed berries.

## Shakshouka

501 Eggs poached in tomatoes with garlic and peppers. Recipe inspired by AoS, various online recipes and working it up for the way I cook.

Posted by: Kindltot. Yield: 1 serving. Prep time: 15 minutes.

---

1 tablespoon olive oil
1 medium onion, diced fine
3 garlic cloves, peeled and crushed
4 ripe, cored and chopped tomatoes
salt
1 seeded jalapeno pepper, or anaheim, or other fresh or dried pepper to taste, finely chopped
2 eggs
2 slices toast

Heat oil in a skillet to medium-hot, just about to where it starts to smoke. Add the chopped onions and crushed garlic and stir until the onions are translucent—it is OK if the onions stick a bit, that gives them more flavor. Add the salt, tomatoes and the peppers to the skillet and cook them down to thicken a little bit while crushing them and stirring them. You mostly want the tomatoes to be cooked through, and uniformly hot. The point is you will be poaching eggs in this, so it needs to be hot. Crack the two eggs on top of the thickening tomato sauce. Let them cook a minute or so, then turn off the heat and cover to let them continue to cook. When the eggs are poached to your satisfaction, spoon them and the tomato sauce onto the toast on a plate.

***Chef's Notes:***
First, use a wooden spoon or one of those wooden spatulas to prepare; that works better than a fork or a broader metal spatula. Second, this is a summer recipe, when I have lots of dead-ripe tomatoes and fresh peppers. In the winter I have to use dried peppers and tomatoes that I froze, usually in a panic when the first rain starts splitting all the remaining fruit on the vine. But, either way it is a good use of tomatoes, and is amenable to variations in spices, servings, and proportions.

## Joe's Famous Eggs

502 Scrambled eggs. I developed this after watching my dad cook some 50 years ago. My daughter and her friends named them Joe's Famous Eggs. My grandchildren call them Poppy's Cheezy Eggs.

Posted by: Real Joe. Yield: 2 – 3 servings. Prep time: 15 minutes.

---

butter
diced ham
4 eggs
salt and pepper

splash of milk or shredded cheese
dash of Worcestershire sauce
dash of Tabasco or other pepper sauce, to taste. I like Sriracha.
splash of water
shredded cheese (optional)

Heat butter to medium and saute the diced ham. Scramble eggs with salt, pepper, milk, pepper sauce, Worcestershire sauce and water. Scramble thoroughly and add immediately to hot pan with butter and ham—do not let the scrambled eggs sit. Add shredded cheese if wanted. Cook at medium high temperature. Do not overcook and they will come out light, fluffy and delicious.

## Tater Cakes

503 Potato pancakes, the quick and easy way. My personal invention.

Posted by: Christopher R Taylor. Yield: 1 serving. Prep time: 20 minutes.

---

butter or bacon grease
1 egg
1 medium potato
1/4 chopped onion
dash each of salt and pepper
bacon (optional)
sour cream, plain yogurt, salsa (optional)
diced green onions, jalapenos, garlic (optional)

Grate the potato on a cheese grater to hash brown consistency. You don't even need to peel it, just wash it. Start a frying pan heating on the stove, with some butter—or (better) fry a few strips of bacon for the grease, and to eat. Mix the potato and the egg with the diced onion, salt and pepper in a bowl. Take half of the mixture and form a patty in the frying pan about a quarter inch thick. It will take a few minutes to fry on one side before it is solid enough to turn; the very edges will start to brown slightly when it is ready. Flip and cook a minute or so—this side won't take long as the inside will be mostly cooked already and all you want to do is brown the outside. Repeat with the rest of the mixture for a second patty. Top both with sour cream (or, if lactose intolerant, use plain yogurt), and salsa if you wish. Other toppings can include crumbled bacon, diced green onions, jalepenos, garlic, and so on—anything you'd put on a baked potato.

## Denver Sandwich

504 A classic west of the Mississippi river. Old recipe of unknown origin, one my mom used to make for us.

Posted by: Christopher R Taylor. Yield: 1 serving. Prep time: 15 minutes.

---

2 slices bread, toasted with butter/mayonnaise
1/4 of an onion, diced
1/4 of a green pepper, diced
1 large egg
butter, margarine or shortening
dash each of salt and pepper
jalepenos, cheese, bacon, chopped ham, tomatoes (optional)

Toss the onions and green peppers in a skillet with some butter, margarine or shortening on medium high. While that melts and sautes slightly, mix up the egg, salt, and pepper in a bowl, whisking it until it gets at least a little frothy. You don't want a super light, fluffy omelet for this, it needs to be fairly solid so don't go nuts. Toss bread into the toaster and toast it. Untoasted bread will get soggy and not work at all here: you must use toast. Butter the toast. By this time the onions and peppers should be at least starting to cook, so drain them and add the veggies to the egg in the bowl and blend them in. Melt butter, margarine or bacon grease in the pan, then pour in the egg, and cook on both sides like an ordinary omelet. Spread mayonnaise on the toast, then fold and place the omelet on the toast for a sandwich. Optional additions include jalepenos, cheese, bacon, chopped ham, and tomatoes.

## Stuffed Artichokes

505 Recipe is from my dearly departed father.

Posted by: Tami. Yield: 6 servings. Prep time: 30 minutes + or -.

---

6 artichokes
Parmesan cheese, cut into small pieces
6 green onions, chopped
1 1/2 cups seasoned bread crumbs
1/4 – 1/2 cup olive oil
1 tablespoon minced garlic
1 tablespoon parsley
some grated Parmesan cheese
salt and pepper to taste

Cut off stem and about 1 1/2" off the top of the artichoke. With scissors, cut the spine off the top of each leaf. Open leaves and rinse. Drain upside down. Cut many, many pieces of Parmesan cheese. They shouldn't be chunks, but thin pieces that will fit down into the leaves of the artichoke. Chop green onions. Begin by stuffing a piece of cheese down each leaf, or every other one if that's too tedious. When finished with the cheese, drop the pieces of green onions down the leaves too. In a bowl, mix together breadcrumbs, garlic, parsley, salt/pepper and olive oil until mixture is wet but not soaking wet. It's optional to add grated Parmesan cheese to this mixture. (DO IT!) Fill large Dutch oven type pot (or a roasting pan) with about 1 – 2 inches of water. Place artichokes in and gently spoon breadcrumb mixture on top. Drizzle some more olive oil on them and into the water. Bring to a boil then reduce to simmer. Simmer for about 1 – 1 ½ hours. Test doneness by pulling out a leaf. They should come out easily when done.

## Two-Minute Hate-To-Cook Breakfast

506 Because the Mickey D drive through takes too long. Recipe developed through desperation.

Posted by: JEM. Yield: 1 serving. Prep time: 2 minutes.

---

3 slices bacon, turkey bacon, Frozen Tundra bacon, etc.
2 ounces liquid egg or egg-white
spritz cooking oil
1 English muffin or tortilla
butter
salt, pepper, dried onion flakes, etc. to taste
shredded cheese to taste

Split English muffin and drop in toaster. Spray or coat small Corelle or equivalent bowl with oil. Fold three slices of something meat-like (I use turkey bacon usually, real stuff will work too) into the bowl. Microwave for 1 minute (hey, I don't know how to use anything but full power anyway). Remove one slice from bowl and eat. Pour 3/8 inch (10 mm) of liquid egg type stuff into bowl, add seasoning to suit (for me it's a few good shakes—the 'shake' is in fact an engineering unit—of Costco dried-onion flakes and some pepper.) Return to microwave and radiate for another 45 seconds. Remove English muffin from toaster and apply one of the not-yet-rancid butter pats you brought home from your last fast-food foray (you DID bring them home, didn't you?). Spread a little shredded cheese on the egg and return to the microwave for another 15 seconds. Remove egg-and-bacon patty from bowl, apply to muffin, eat.

## Abruzzo Pizza Sauce

507 From the land of Meremortal.

Posted by: westminsterdogshow. Yield: 3 cups. Prep time: 30 minutes.

---

1 28-ounce can tomatoes (San Marzano)
1 to 2 garlic cloves
1 teaspoon dried oregano
1 tablespoon fresh basil
1 bay leaf
1 teaspoon crushed red pepper
salt and pepper to taste

Place all ingredients in a saucepan. Cover and bring to a boil. Uncover and let simmer, stirring occasionally, 30 minutes. Use to make pizza!

## Eggs Goldenrod

508 The ultimate comfort food. This recipe is a staple at our house, and my mommy always made it for me on bad days. It was published in our family cookbook called *Grammy's Cookbook 2007*. Obviously good for breakfast but we usually have it for dinner.

Posted by: shinypie. Yield: 3 servings. Prep time: 20 minutes.

---

1 stick butter
2 tablespoons whole wheat flour
2 cups milk
6 hardboiled eggs, peeled
6 slices whole wheat toast
1 bag frozen peas, cooked (optional)

Cut eggs in half lengthwise, and separate yolks from whites. Chop egg whites. Press yolks through a sieve, or crumble finely by mashing with a fork. Melt butter and make a paste with the flour. Add milk, a little at a time. Cook over medium heat until thick, whisking constantly. Remove from heat but keep hot. Add egg whites to the hot sauce. Pour sauce mixture over toast. Sprinkle the yolks on top. In our family, we always sprinkle the peas on top too, but that's optional if you don't like peas. Barbarian.

## Grit Cake Base

509 Grit cakes make a wonderful base to add Etouffee or shrimp and grits. Basic recipe is from Quaker Old Fashioned Grits.

Posted by: rdohd. Yield: 8 servings. Prep time: 40 minutes combined.

---

8 cups water
1 teaspoon salt
2 cups long cook grits
3 cups sharp cheddar
1/2 cup fresh Parmesan
1 fresh green jalapeno pepper

3 eggs 2 cups panko bread crumbs

Heat water and salt to a boil, add grits, cover and simmer over low heat for 15 minutes. Evenly slice halved and seeded jalapeno pepper into strips 1/8 inch wide, and dice into match head pieces. Fold cheddar and Parmesan into grits until evenly incorporated, and remove from heat. Add jalapeno pieces and stir until evenly distributed. The goal is to allow the floral note to remain so don't add too early, cooking the freshness out of the flesh. Move grits into a parchment lined 9 x 12 baking dish and spread evenly. Cool overnight to completely rehydrate the grits. Cut grits using a spatula or biscuit cutter. Heat pan over medium to medium low adding oil right before the pan fry. Dip grit cakes into the beaten eggs, lightly coat with panko and add to heated pan. The grit cake will warm quickly and the panko will brown. Flip and cook sides of cake, rotating until all golden brown. Traditionally I make this as an event dish and use as a base for Etouffee, but it works well under any sauced seafood. The grits are incredibly smooth and warm, complementing the rest of the dish.

# Nood!

*Roses are red*
*Violets are blue*
*Willow's recipe is last*
*It's chicken zucchini stew*

## Chicken Zucchini Stew

999 I'm pretty sure my mother got this from somewhere, she wasn't a cook so it's probably a Betty Crocker dealio.

Posted by: willow.  Yield: varies.  Prep time: 30 minutes.

---

3 ounces diced chicken
1 small green pepper, chopped
1 cup zucchini cubed
½ teaspoon oregano
8 ounces tomato juice
1 small onion, chopped
croutons

Simmer tomato juice, green pepper, onion, and zucchini until tender, add pre-cooked chicken and simmer for 20 minutes. Add croutons.

*Hello?*

*Hello?*

*Hello?*

# Index

*Index of contributors.*

## 7



## A



## B



## C

## D



## E



## F



## G



## H



## I

## J



## K



## L



## M



## N

## O



## P



## Q



## R



## S



## T



## V

## W



## X



## Y



## Z